A STUDY IN
THE THEORY OF
INFLATION AND UNEMPLOYMENT

Studies in Monetary Economics

Editors

Volume 4

NORTH-HOLLAND PUBLISHING COMPANY
AMSTERDAM • NEW YORK • OXFORD

A Study in the Theory of Inflation and Unemployment

CLAES-HENRIC SIVEN
Department of Economics
University of Uppsala

1979

NORTH-HOLLAND PUBLISHING COMPANY
AMSTERDAM • NEW YORK • OXFORD

ISBN: 0 444 85252 2

Publishers:
NORTH-HOLLAND PUBLISHING COMPANY
AMSTERDAM • NEW YORK • OXFORD

Sole distributors for the U.S.A. and Canada:
ELSEVIER NORTH-HOLLAND, INC.
52 VANDERBILT AVENUE
NEW YORK, N.Y. 10017

Library of Congress Cataloging in Publication Data

Siven, Claes-Henric, 1940-
A study in the theory of inflation and unemployment.

(Studies in monetary economics ; v. 4)
Originally presented as the author's thesis, Stockholm, 1975.
Bibliography: p.
1. Inflation (Finance) and Unemployment--Mathematical models. 2. Microeconomics. I. Title.
HD5707.S53 1978 332.4'1'01 78-24271
ISBN 0-444-85252-2

PRINTED IN THE NETHERLANDS

INTRODUCTION TO THE SERIES

This series publishes books of interest to students and researchers working in the fields of macro-economics, monetary theory and policy, banking and the operation of financial markets. It is intended that works of empirical emphasis will be included in the series along with theoretical contributions. Publications will include research monographs and the proceedings of significant conferences. The editors welcome submissions of manuscripts for inclusion in the series.

PREFACE

This book is an outgrow of my interest in short run macroeconomics and the impulses I got from the Workshop of the International Economic Association in Bergen in 1971. Prototypes for chapters II and III were presented at that occasion and much of the work since then has been refinements and extensions of those prototypes.

Various versions of the chapters have been discussed in seminars at the Institute of Economics at Stockholm University. Foremost I want to thank my teacher, Lars Werin, for his interest in my work, encouragement and constructive advice. I am also very grateful to Tõnu Puu, Ragnar Bentzel and Harald Dickson, who have given many valuable suggestions for improving the mathematical analysis. Chapter III (as well as the rest of the book) has benefited a great deal from the criticism by Bo Axell. Chapter IV might never have been written were it not for constructive advice from Karl-Göran Mäler. Hans Söderström and Jan Herin have given me many good ideas for chapter V. Chapter VI has greatly improved from the advice by Nils-Henrik Schager. I also want to thank the other members of the seminar for their criticism and constructive advice: Kerstin Lövgren, Irma Rosenberg, Thomas Franzén, Bengt-Christer Ysander, Lewis Taylor, Richard Murray, Lars Nyberg, and Staffan Viotti.

William Melton has translated Chapter II and corrected the English of the other chapters. Kerstin Edwardsson, Kerstin Grundberg, and Ulla Blomqvist have typed various preliminary versions of the chapters. Kerstin Lindskog has done the typing of the final version. By a kind generosity by The Industrial Institute for Economic and Social Research, the figures were drawn by Berit Lindberg. Financial support has been given by Svenska Handelsbanken Foundation for Social Science Research and by The Swedish Council for Social Science Research.

With the exception of a few corrections, the book was completed in October 1975.

Uppsala, September 1978

Claes-Henric Siven

CONTENTS

CHAPTER I. INTRODUCTION

1. Starting Points, Problems, and Purpose of the Analysis

Two important objections could be made to the "traditional" inflation and unemployment theory.[1] The first of these objections is that, despite the simultaneity of inflation and unemployment in reality, there is no common, integrated theory for these two phenomena. To the extent that the mechanisms generating inflation and unemployment are independent, this of course is not much of a problem. But since that is probably not generally the case, the bifurcation of short-run macroeconomics constitutes a problem both from a scientific and an economic policy point of view.

The second objection is that neither inflation nor unemployment theory builds on relevant microeconomics. This is a drawback, since it is difficult to determine the exact assumptions about household and firm behavior which the postulated macro dynamic process builds on. The basic reason for the deficiency of the microeconomic foundations of inflation and unemployment theory was the fact that microeconomics - *i.e.*, general equilibrium theory - in deducing the macroeconomic relationships started from an analysis of the behavior of individual economic agents in perfect competition. The abstraction from adjustment costs caused by, *e.g.*, incomplete information concerning the market situation and transactions possibilities implied that microeconomics was not very suitable for describing phenomena, the driving forces of which to a great extent probably depend on these frictions.

Presently rather extensive work is being done to develop short-run macroeconomics on the basis of studies of the behavior of "rational" economic agents in a generalized neoclassical milieu.[2] This research is being done in two directions. The first

---

1) Here is meant the theory of demand and cost inflation developed during the forties and fifties and keynesian employment theory, respectively.

2) Chapter II contains a rather detailed survey of this work.

of these is associated with the names of Clower, Patinkin, Leijonhufvud, Barro, and Grossman. It implies an investigation of the fundamentals of the multiplier mechanism: What effects will restrictions on the transaction possibilities generated by disequilibrium in some markets have on the course of events on the other markets of the economy? To what extent do feed-back mechanisms tend to amplify or modify the effects of various disturbances?

The general starting point for this analysis has been an exogenously given and fixed price system. Given this price system, excess supply or excess demand on different markets will imply rationing restrictions of different kinds. This will influence the behavior of the firms and households on other markets through the spill-over effects induced by the extra restrictions. The advantage of this analysis is that the restrictions on the choice possibilities of the economic agents (e.g., involuntary unemployment) caused by disequilibrium are the focus of interest. The main disadvantage is the assumption of an exogenously given price system. For the analysis of the behavior of rational economic agents to be carried through satisfactorily, price and wage determination must also be studied. The abstraction from this important aspect of the problem has also implied that the process of inflation, and the interaction between inflation and unemployment, have been out of reach of the analysis.

The second direction of research is represented inter alia by contributions of Stigler, Alchian, Phelps, Holt, and Mortensen. The common starting point has been a study of markets in which information concerning transaction possibilities is imperfect and in which the absence of a common market price not only induces search activities, but also constitutes one possible explanation for unutilized resources, e.g., unemployment. The thought here is that it is not profitable for persons who have newly entered the labor market to accept all employment offers since they could get better offers by further search.

The strategy of the unemployed could therefore be described by minimum requirements on the employment offers which they accept. These minimum requirements should neither be too low, nor too high. If they are too high, the expected length of the unemployment period will be unduly long. The minimum requirements should further be coupled to present market conditions. The higher the demand for labor, the higher the minimum requirements should be.

The fact that both firms and household have an incomplete overview of the market however means that various sorts of mistakes are possible. As to the firms, their attempts during a boom to attract employees from other firms by increasing their wage offers in relation to the offers of the other firms may result in an increase in the actual rate of wage inflation in comparison to the expected rate. For the unemployed, the rate of unexpected wage inflation implies that a greater fraction of the employment offers will be accepted, since the minimum requirements relate to expected market conditions. This implies that the number of new hirings will increase on the same time as the rate of unemployment falls.

The above reasoning also implies a connection between the rate of inflation (more strictly the rate of wage inflation) and the rate of unemployment. This means that it has been possible, starting from an analysis of the behavior of "rational" economic agents on markets with imperfect information, analytically to derive the connection between unemployment and wage increases which has been empirically observed (the Phillips curve).

If this direction of research thus represents the first attempt to construct an integrated theory of inflation and unemployment on a microeconomic basis, the limitations of the analysis must nevertheless be stressed.

a. Unemployment is mainly voluntary. Variations in the rate of unemployment are due to faulty expectations about market conditions which cause the unemployed sometimes to refrain from accepting "good" employment offers, sometimes to accept "bad" employment offers.

b. The analysis is restricted to developments in the labor market. Events in the goods market are exogenously determined. This implies that it is impossible to study the interactions between the processes of wage and price inflation -- an interaction which is of central importance for modern inflation theory.

c. Furthermore, it is not clear to what extent events in the goods market will influence the development of unemployment. Is it possible, for example, to speak about a unique connection between "the rate of inflation" and the development of unemployment?

d. If it is clear that the "new" multiplier theory essentially does not build on equilibrium assumptions, the answer to the same question is less determinate as regards the "new" theory of inflation and unemployment. On the one hand, the emphasis of the latter theory on the significance of different imperfections on the labor market implies assumptions which are not consistent with the assumptions of perfect information concerning the transactions possibilities underlying traditional equilibrium concepts. On the other hand, the high degree of (price and) wage flexibility assumed by this direction of research implies possibilities of market clearing via the price system. The problem thus is whether the analysis is based on equilibrium assumptions or not.

The list above touches on problems concerning the properties of the different macroeconomic models. However, the underlying microeconomic analysis also leaves open several questions.

e. What role does the coordination of the price and wage setting of firms play for their planning in markets with imperfect information? What implications will this coordination have for the process of price and wage increases?

f. When discussing markets with imperfect information, not only variations of prices and wage rates, but also of the supply of information, should be important for the individual firms when trying to attract new customers and recruit new employees. The question then is what role the coordination between the price, wage and information policy plays in the planning of the firm. It should be stressed that the possibility that the firms may attract new employees by other means than by increasing their wage offers implies <u>one</u> possible mechanism generating involuntary variations in the rate of unemployment. If the firms plan to decrease the number of their employees, this could be done by diminishing the supply of information implied by the number of vacancies. This means - irrespective of the wage level and the minimum requirements of the unemployed - increased difficulties of getting a job.

g. Just as firms may vary their supply of information, households may vary their search activity on the goods and labor markets.

In the micro analyses which have formed the basis for analytical derivations of the Phillips curve, no precise analysis has been made of what conditions govern the search activity of households. Instead the basis of the analysis has been a rather vague notion that there is some sort of indivisibility which implies that the unemployed have a comparative advantage for searching. This indivisibility is also a possible explanation for the minimum requirements for accepting a job offer. An unemployed who accepts an employment offer will according to this discussion thereby gain an immediate increase of the income but on the other hand loose much of the possibilities of further search.

h. Not only an endogenous explanation of the intensity of search is needed, however. Various other aspects of search are of great interest and should be analyzed. One example is simultaneous search on several markets. Another is repetitive search. The acceptance decision of the unemployed can not be regarded as a one-time event, as has usually been the analytical assumption. The first employment constitutes but a link in a chain of future employments. The value of an employment offer could thus not be calculated without consideration of future on-the-job search. Search thus has to be analyzed within an intertemporal context.

The problems outlined above constitute some of the most important starting points for the present study. The main goal is to further develop the new inflation and unemployment theory so as to take into consideration the interaction between the processes of price increases and wage increases. To this end, it has been considered important to base the macro model on a microeconomic analysis of the behavior of rational firms and households acting in a world where information about transaction possibilities is imperfect and where contacts between trading partners are costly to achieve. Thus constructed, a microeconomic foundation of the macro analysis creates the possibility of studying the actual macroeconomic implications of various assumptions about the milieu in which the economic agents live, plan and act.

But the microeconomic studies also have an intrinsic value. The development of the neoclassical theory has to a considerable extent been held back by the assumptions of complete market information and the absence of transactions costs which constitute such an important explanation for many of the institutional conditions which characterize the economies of "reality". It may suffice to point out that, in spite of many important recent results, we still lack a convincing theory of the role which money plays in the economic process.

The microeconomic studies of the behavior of households and firms in the following chapters have a rather limited scope, however. As to the behavior of households, the simultaneous choice of consumption, supply of labor and search on an aggregated goods market and an aggregated labor market is investigated. An important innovation in comparison to earlier research is that repetitive search activities are stressed. This implies inter alia that search must be analyzed from an intertemporal point of view and that search has many similarities to saving.

All search contains a certain stochastic element. This implies that households' attitudes towards risk will influence their search behavior. This is a neglected question in search theory. I have therefore considered it important to investigate the conditions, under which it is legitimate to abstract from the element of risk and to restrict the analysis of the planning of households to the mathematical expectations of stochastic variables.

In analyzing the planning of firms, the starting point has been to investigate their behavior under the assumption that households are imperfectly informed about their transaction possibilities, but to a certain extent are able to dissipate these uncertainties by search activities in the goods and labor markets. An important problem has thus been in what way the stochastic milieu constituted by the searching customers and employees of the firm and of other firms affects the behavior of the firm. What role does its price and wage setting play in attracting imperfectly informed customers and employees? Will the imperfect market information imply monopolistic tendencies in price setting and monopsonistic tendencies in wage setting? What role does the coordination between the price, wage and information policies of the firm play? Are there, similarly to the case of the households, elements of capital theory in the planning problem of the firm?

The macroeconomic analysis which then follows from the micro analysis via aggregation of firm and household behavior equations implies a generalization of the "new" theory of inflation and unemployment to cover also the interaction between the processes of price and wage increases. A main question has been what implications this direction of research has if one replaces the partial analysis of the labor market with a multimarket analysis.

For example, are the analytical derivations of the Phillips curve left intact? To what extent will the inflation process be amplified by interactions between price and wage increases? Does the macro model contain positive or negative feedback mechanisms which modify the sensitivity of inflation and unemployment to various disturbances? Could one, similarly to the case of Bent Hansen's theory of open inflation, speak of quasi-equilibrium in connection with the new type of theory? If there exists a quasi-equilibrium in some sence, what then is its relation to inflation in the long run, i.e., inflation which is fully expected? Does there exist, even for the extended inflation and unemployment model, a "natural" rate of unemployment, i.e., a rate of unemployment which is independent of the actual rate of inflation if this is completely expected? In addition, are there any other "natural" rates which are independent of the level of a fully expected rate of inflation?

Already from the above enumeration of problems it should appear that the intention with the inflation-unemployment model is of a theoretical nature, not to give a "realistic" description of the fundamental driving forces behind real macro-dynamic processes. The emphasis has instead been put on a clarification of the implications for inflation and unemployment theory of the new line of development. Thus, it has been found to be important to investigate what the fundamental differences are between the "new" multiplier theory and the "new" theory of inflation and unemployment.

To explain the connection between the two lines of research, chapter II contains a rather detailed account of the assumptions and results of the various contributions together with an attempt to discuss systematically the similarities and differences between the two modes of approach.

A conclusion of this discussion is that neither of the two macroeconomic lines of research could separately be said to represent a good basis for revising short-run macroeconomics. On the other hand, I am convinced that they together contain very promising development possibilities. Thus, the choice made here of developing further only one of the two lines of research should not be taken to reflect an attitude that there are greater realism, development possibilities, and explanatory power in the "new" theory of inflation and unemployment.

2. Summary of the Plan, Method, and Results of the Analysis

The contents of the following chapters may be divided into a survey of the literature (chapter II), a microeconomic analysis of the behavior of households and firms in markets with imperfect information (chapters III-V), and a macroeconomic analysis of the interaction between the inflation process and the development of unemployment over time (chapter VI).

2.1. Survey of the literature (chapter II)

The survey of the literature is intended to give an introduction to and a survey of the type of economic theory which in the following chapters will be given a more careful, but also more restricted, treatment. The survey starts with a discussion of the neoclassical adjustment mechanisms, the *tâtonnement* and *non-tâtonnement* processes. An important question discussed in this connection is why it has not been possible to base short-run dynamic macroeconomics on these adjustment mechanisms.

A problem with the *tâtonnement* mechanism is that it presupposes that transactions are only carried through under equilibrium conditions. Since the adjustment process may be of a very long duration, this implicitly means that the economic agents do not attach importance to *when* they are able to carry through their selling and buying plans. If convergence towards the equilibrium price set is not finished in finite time, then transactions will *never* be carried through.

Non-tâtonnement processes allow transactions to take place outside equilibrium conditions. This of course implies a greater realism in comparison to *tâtonnement* mechanisms. But the point of departure is still a unique price in each market in each point of time. This price is not explained as the result of the behavior of optimizing firms and households. Changes in the price system are instead mechanically determined as a function of the (quantitative) excess demands on the various markets. There does not exist any neoclassical <u>economic</u> theory of adjustment movements outside equilibrium.

Arrow's classic article "Towards a Theory of Price Adjustment" may be seen as both a critique of the neoclassical adjustment mechanisms and an introduction to the microeconomic theory of disequilibrium price formation.

Arrow's first observation was that perfect competition with a common market price is only concievable in equilibrium. Outside equilibrium situations buyers and sellers have a certain monopolistic and monopsonistic power, respectively, which means that the price under these conditions is not given by the market but is a result of the optimal planning of the economic agents under disequilibrium. Arrow's point that firms generally have incomplete information about their marketing possibilities implies that one cannot presuppose that the partial market between the firm and its customers is constantly cleared by the price. This is one microeconomic explanation for the rationing restrictions which are the basis of the "new" multiplier theory. Arrow's observation that there generally will not be any common market price at disequilibrium and that therefore not only firms but also households are engaged in search processes constitutes a key to the basic postulate of the "new" theory of inflation and unemployment of imperfectly informed but searching households.

In the following survey of search theory and market organization when information is imperfect, the extensive[1] and intensive[2] search activities of households in the goods markets are treated first. It is pointed out that the prevalence of costs for evaluating the offers of different sellers is one example of extensive search costs (it is thus not necessary to assume that different sellers are located at different geographical points). In addition

---

1) Attempts to get into contact with different sellers.

2) Attempts to evaluate the characteristics of the offer, given a contact with a certain seller.

to contacts with different sellers who can offer a low price and a good quality, extensive search activity has revenues in the form of giving the household better information about market conditions. Differences and similarities between household search activities in the goods and labor markets are then discussed. Firm policy in markets with imperfect information is also treated.

A summary is also presented of the discussion about the characteristics of the market solution. An important unresolved problem is what the necessary and sufficient conditions are for the existence of equilibrium solutions with price and quality distributions with a positive variance.

Starting from the previous survey of the microeconomics of markets with imperfect information about the transaction possibilities, the most important contributions to the "new" theory of inflation and unemployment are discussed. The emphasis is on what the fundamental assumptions are and where the decisive problems are to be found.

The survey of the literature is concluded with a summary of the most important results of the "new" multiplier theory. An attempt is also made, starting from Arrow's analysis of price formation in disequilibrium, to examine what the fundamental differences are between the two modern, macro-dynamic lines of research.

2.2. The microeconomic analysis (chapters III-V)

The economy is assumed to consist of one homogeneous goods market and one homogeneous labor market. In the two markets, a very large number of firms trade with a still larger number of households. There is moreover a public authority which taxes the firms and the employed households and pays unemployment compensation to the unemployed. There is no public investment or consumption, however. Households are not assumed to be engaged in financial saving, but firm profits imply a loan market between firms with profits and losses, respectively, and the government which lends and borrows at a constant (real) rate of interest.

Both prices and wage rates vary between firms. This *inter alia* has to do with the fact that it is costly for households to get into contact with low-price firms and high-wage rate firms.

The price and wage levels are expected by the economic agents to rise with the expected rate of inflation. Inflationary expectations are held with subjective certainty and are the same for all households and firms. Moreover, price inflation is expected to be equal to wage inflation. There are thus no expectations of a changing (average) real wage rate. The actual rates of price and wage inflation may differ from the expected rates, however. The price and wage distributions will continually shift outwards as inflation proceeds. However, the distributions over relative prices (the prices of the individual firms in comparison to the average price in the market) and relative wage rates (the wage rates of the individual firms in comparison to the average wage rate on the market) will remain constant.

Households and firms get information about the actual wage level with a constant time lag of length h_W. The current expected wage level is then projected via the expected rate of wage inflation. If the actual rate of wage inflation is higher than that expected, this means that the actual wage level will be higher than that expected and that the relative wage rate which the firm pays and the household recieves is expected to be higher than is actually the case. The corresponding argument holds for prices.

In order that there be turnover in the labor force, households (or individuals) are assumed to be subject to a certain "death-risk". This implies that the expected remaining lifetime (or time in the labor force) is finite and that the horizon is stochastically determined. However, firms are assumed to have an unlimited lifetime.

2.2.1. Household behavior (chapters III-IV)

The life-trajectory of the households may be separated into two parts. During the first period, when one has newly entered the labor force, one searches for a job while unemployed. During the second period, the household is employed. Both unemployed and employed households are assumed to behave as if they maximized the mathematical expectation of the discounted sum of all future instantaneous utilities. Consumption is the only argument of the instantaneous utility function, and this means that the problem is to choose the best trajectory of consumption over time.

In its planning the household has to take two stochastic elements into consideration. The first has to do with the stochastic time horizon, the second with the uncertainty as to which firm the household will get into contact with in the labor market and the goods market when searching for firms with higher wage rates and lower prices.

If the death-risk is independent of the age and the behavior of the household, the first stochastic element may be taken into consideration in the following way. Assume that the household behaves as if it maximizes the mathematical expectation of the discounted sum of all future utilities, the exact point of time of the horizon being a stochastic variable. If the rate of discount, the subjective rate of time preference, is constant, and if time varies continually (which is a common assumption), then it is possible to show that this problem may be converted into a deterministic problem of maximizing all discounted future instantaneous utilities up to an infinite time horizon, the rate of discount now being the <u>sum</u> of the "pure" rate of subjective time preference and the death risk. This means that under certain conditions, it is possible to convert a problem with a finite but stochastic time horizon into a more easily handled problem with a determinate but infinite time horizon.

The second stochastic element of the household's planning problem is stochastically independent of the first and may therefore be treated independently. The problem is to what extent risk-averse behavior is implied by the uncertainty as to which firms the household will get into contact with when searching for firms with a higher wage rate than that of the present employer and lower prices than those of the present supplier, if the (instantaneous) utility function is strictly concave. In an appendix to chapter III it is shown that it is not the form of the instantaneous utility function but the form of the utility functional (the discounted sum of all future instantaneous utilities) which determines the answer to this question. If the utility functional, given optimal behavior, is linear in the initial values of the relative price which the household pays and the relative wage rate which it recieves, then the planning problem of the household may be discussed as if it were the problem of maximizing the utility functional under conditions in which the relative wage rate and the relative price develop according to their mathematical expectations.

2.2.1.a. The behavior of the employed household (chapter III)

The planning problem of the employed household may be described in the following way. Since there only exists one good, and since leisure is not included as an argument of the utility function, the planning problem of the household may be reduced to that of finding the best trajectory for consumption over time. However, it is assumed that the households do not engage in financial saving or borrowing. Thus, although intertemporal reallocations of consumption may not be made via saving in the traditional sense, it is assumed instead that the household is free to vary its labor time. Less labor time implies, via the budget equation, that instantaneous consumption must fall. Since leisure is exogenously given (and not included in the analysis) the time remaining may, via the time budget equation, be used for search on the goods and labor markets. The increased search activity will increase the probability of getting into contact with firms offering a lower price and a higher wage rate, respectively. This is likely to increase the future real wage rate of the household and thus to imply a higher future level of consumption. Thus, there is a possibility of intertemporal reallocation of consumption through search activity.

The optimization problem of the household - to maximize the discounted sum of all future utilities subject to the budget and time-budget constraints and subject to the differential equations of the relative price and the relative wage rate (expressed as functions of inter alia household search activity) - is then solved with the help of Arrow's version of Pontryagin's maximum principle. This involves both definition of the relevant Hamiltonian and finding the maximum of the Hamiltonian.

By totally differentiating the first-order maximum conditions of the Hamiltonian, it is possible to derive the incomplete behavior equations of the household. These equations describe how the choice of values of the control variables is affected by changes in the exogenous variables or some of the phase variables (the relative price which the household pays or the relative wage rate which it recieves), the same time as the two adjoint variables (the shadow prices on changes in the relative price and the relative wage rate) are assumed to be constant. Generally, the values of the adjoint variables must be determined as a result of the optimization analysis. Changes in the exogenous or phase variables will also imply that the adjoint variables will be affected. Consequently, the changed values of the adjoint variables must be taken into account when deriving the optimal response of the control variables to various disturbances.

The development of the adjoint variables is described by differential equations and terminal conditions. The latter are derived as transversality conditions concerning the relative price and the relative wage rate which must apply when time tends to infinity. The values of the adjoint variables at a certain point of time may then be determined in such a way that their initial conditions, when inserted into the differential equations, imply fulfillment of the terminal conditions. If this is the case, and if at the same time the phase variables converge to finite stationary values, the maximization of the Hamiltonian will also imply maximization of the utility functional.

Different disturbances will generally imply new conditions for this stability analysis, so that the initial values of the adjoint variables will change. By taking this into consideration, the complete behavior equations of the household may be derived. These equations describe the behavior of the household at each point of time, given the values of the exogenous and phase variables.

2.2.1.b. The behavior of the unemployed (chapter IV)

The chapters on the behavior of the employed and the unemployed do not follow chronological order because it is necessary to know the behavior of the employed to be able to derive the behavior of the unemployed. This is a consequence of the fact that the unemployed worker must know what he will do after his first employment, since the choice between employment and further search while unemployed is dependent on a comparison between the values of the utility functionals at optimal behavior, given employment or unemployment.

The situation of the unemployed worker differs from that of the employed in that his work time is identically equal to zero, his wages consequently are equal to zero, and he recieves unemployment compensation.

Since the income of the unemployed household is fixed, consumption is given as soon as the relative price is given. The planning problem of the unemployed then consists of choosing how much time to allocate to search in the goods and on the labor markets and of determination of the minimum requirement for accepting a job offer. The more time used for search on the goods market, the faster the relative price will fall on the average. This will ameliorate the situation of the household, both if it continues searching while unemployed or accepts a job offer. But this time must be taken from search in the labor market, which diminishes the frequency of contacts with employers and therefore increases the mathematical expectation of the length of the remaining unemployment period.

The expectation of the remaining unemployment period also depends on the acceptance wage rate. The higher this is, the smaller the probability that a recieved wage offer will exceed the minimum requirements, and the longer the expected remaining unemployment period. But a higher acceptance wage rate will also imply a higher mathematical expectation of the wage rate the day one actually recieves a job.

In analyzing the behavior of the unemployed, it has not been possible directly to start from Pontryagin's maximum principle, due to the fact that the optimization problem of the unemployed has to be analyzed explicitly as a stochastic problem, since the probability of receiving during a short time period, an employment offer exceeding the aspiration level is of central significance for the choice problem. The optimization problem has therefore been formulated as a stochastic dynamic programming problem. It appears that it is possible from this starting point to derive a generalized Pontryagin expression with an interesting economic interpretation.

2.2.2. The behavior of the firm (chapter V)

The firm is assumed to behave as if it maximized the discounted sum of all future profits, using the real rate of interest as the rate of discount.

In spite of the fact that the firm does not own any real capital, labor being the only factor of production, there is still an intertemporal optimization problem. This is due to the fact that it is possible for the firm to increase its stock of customers by decreasing its price relative to its competitors' or by advertising more, and to increase its stock of employees by increasing its wage rate relative to the average wage rate in the market or recruiting more intensively. These actions will decrease momentary present profits but will increase future profits. The number of customers (the "good-will" capital) and the number of employees may be regarded as two stocks of immaterial capital.

The firm is involved in three types of production processes. These are (1) production in the usual sense, (2) supply of information on the goods market ("advertising"), and (3) supply of information on the labor market ("recruiting"). The firm may thus be said to be divided into three divisions, the production division, the market division, and the personnel division.

The optimization problem may be formulated so that the firm maximizes the discounted sum of all future profits subject to the constraints that the total amount of available labor hours be exactly allocated among the three "production divisions" (the labor force balance of the firm), that the goods production be exactly sold (the goods balance), and two intertemporal restrictions which are the differential equations determining the net flows of customers and employees.

The firm has the following control variables at its disposal: the relative price, the relative wage rate, and the number of labor hours allocated to goods production and information production in the goods and the labor market, respectively. A higher relative price implies that the customers' demand will fall, at the same time as the net flow of customers will decrease. A higher relative wage rate will increase the supply of labor of the firm's employees and increase the net flow of employees. The latter effect has to do with the fact that a greater fraction of the unemployed which the firm gets into contact with will have a lower reservation wage rate than the wage rate which the firm can now offer, that a greater number of employees in other firms with whom the firm gets into contact will have a lower wage rate than offered by the firm, and finally, that a greater number of the employees which get into contact with <u>other</u> firms will now find that their present employer offers a higher wage rate than that of the other firms.

If the number of labor hours allocated to recruiting is increased, the probability of getting into contact with an arbitrary job seeker will increase. This will increase the net flow of employees, and thus also future profits. On the other hand, these labor hours could instead be used for current goods production which would mean higher current profits.

The firm is assumed to vary its relative price and relative wage rate continuously, so as to fulfill at all times the labor force and goods balance constraints. This implies an equilibrium assumption -- there is a permanent equilibrium in the partial labor and goods markets of the individual firms.

Similarly to the analysis of household behavior, the firm's optimal behavior is then solved for with the help of Arrow's version of Pontryagin's maximum principle.

2.3. <u>The macroeconomic analysis (chapter VI)</u>

The preceding analysis of firm behavior constitutes a step towards the macroeconomic model since it contains a certain amount of aggregation. Each firm has a comparatively large number of customers and employees, and the firm varies its relative price and relative wage rate as to attain constantly equilibrium in the "own" goods market and the labor market.

In the discussion of inflation and unemployment, the aggregation is carried to completion.[1)] The first step is to take the weighted sums of the expected relative prices and expected relative wage rates of the individual firms. These two arithmetic

---

1) The macro analysis builds on a simplified model of the firm in which no labor hours are allocated to information production in the goods and labor markets.

averages are equal to unity only when the expected rate of price inflation equals the actual rate of price inflation and the expected rate of wage inflation equals the actual rate of wage inflation.

If all firms try to increase their relative prices (e.g., in response to an increased demand for goods by their customers), this will be possible for some individual firms but not for the firms as a whole. Attempts to increase relative prices will instead cause the actual rate of price inflation to increase in comparison to the expected rate.

The actual rate of price inflation may be divided into two components. The first of these is the expected rate of price inflation. If this is 5%, all firms must increase their prices by 5% in order to maintain relative prices unchanged. If each of the firms then tries to increase its relative price by, say, 2%, the actual rate of price inflation will be 5% + 2% = 7%. This implies that aggregation of the (subjectively certain) expected relative prices of the individual firms gives information about the gap between the actual and the expected rates of price inflation. An analogous line of argument holds with respect to the rate of wage inflation.

This implies in turn that the comparative statics of the relative prices and relative wage rates of individual firms in chapter V may be used for investigating how the unexpected rates of price and wage inflation are affected by various disturbances. However, there exists a certain interdependence between the price and wage determination of individual firms on the one hand, and the search activity, consumption demand, and supply of labor of the households on the other. This means that the unexpected rates of price and wage inflation must be simultaneously determined.

It is true that the attempt of an individual firm to increase its relative price will leave the supply of labor by its employees unaffected, since these are customers of other firms. But if the firms as a group try to increase their relative prices, the labor market conditions will be influenced and each firm will be confronted with a lower supply of labor than before. To increase the available number or labor hours (and to try to attract employees from other firms) the firms will then try to increase their relative wage rates, and the unexpected rate of wage inflation will consequently increase. This in turn will affect positively consumer demand and thus also the unexpected rate of price inflation.

In principle, the mechanism outlined above is the same as the price-wage spiral of "traditional" inflation models. But contrary to these models, the present analysis is based on an equilibrium model in the sense that there is equilibrium at all times in all the individual firm's "own" goods markets and labor markets. The actual rate of price inflation and the actual rate of wage inflation are obtained as equilibrium solutions. The disequilibrium which exists in this case has to do with expectations.

In the instantaneous equilibrium model, the unexpected rates of price and wage inflation are obtained as equilibrium solutions. The same is the case for total goods production, search activity on the labor market by the unemployed and the aspiration wages. The latter two variables are important to know since they influence the development of unemployment.

The solution of the instantaneous equilibrium model will at each point of time influence the development of the real wage rate, the rate of unemployment, and the expected rate of inflation (note that the expected rates of price and wage inflation for simplicity are assumed to be equal). These three variables change according to differential equations. Since these variables moreover are exogeneous with respect to the instantaneous equilibrium model, their changes will imply a continuous change in the equilibrium solution of this model.

The real wage rate in the market is given at each point of time. But its development depends on the difference between the actual rate of wage inflation and the actual rate of price inflation.

In the quasi-equilibrium analysis, the time derivatives of the real wage rate and of the rate of unemployment are by definition constant at the same time as inflationary expectations are assumed to be exogeniously given. Quasi-equilibrium presupposes instantaneous equilibrium, but the contrary is not true. At quasi-equilibrium, the actual rate of price inflation may very well differ from the expected rate. The same holds for the rate of wage inflation. What is important is that the actual rates of price and wage inflation are equal.

Starting from an analysis of the stability properties of the quasi-equilibrium, it is possible to show that intermittent wage increases (by collective agreement) will produce oscilations in the real wage rate and the rate of unemployment, and thus in the unexpected rates of price and wage inflation. Continuous collective wage increases will produce a kind of cost inflation which results in a higher real wage rate, a higher rate of unemployment, and a higher rate of price and wage inflation than would otherwise be the case.

In a section of the chapter concerning the Phillips surface, it is stressed that the Phillips curve - according to the analytical derivations of Holt, Phelps, and Mortensen - should be interpreted as one of the structural equations of the economic model. This means that statistically observed scatters describing the connection between unemployment and wage inflation should only have the postulated form if the structural equation does not shift. Thus, identification of the Phillips curve - i.e., observation of a negative relation between unemployment and inflation - depends on the nature of the disturbances in the empirical observations. Given the assumptions indicated above, it is possible to predict a positive relationship between unemployment and price inflation.

The Phillips curve may therefore be looked upon as the projection onto the unemployment - wage inflation plane of a multidimensional surface. The exact appearance of the Phillips curve will then depend on the point at which this projection has been made. Another argument against the stability of the Phillips curve is that changed expectations of inflation will shift it. This argument is wellknown, and it is shown that it also holds for the more general Phillips surface.

In long-run equilibrium the rates of price and wage inflation are equal at the same time as inflation is completely expected. Since the expected rate of inflation does not significantly influence household and firm behavior, the long run equilibrium is neutral with respect to the level of the expected rate of inflation. This may be illustrated in the following way.

Assume that the economy is in a long run equilibrium to start with. The rate of unemployment, the real wage rate, the rates of price and wage inflation, and inflation expectations are constant over time. Inflation is completely expected. In this situation the government might use fiscal and monetary policy to decrease temporarily (at a possible cost of a transient increase of the rate of unemployment) the actual rates of price and wage inflation. Since inflationary expectations successively adjust to the lower rate of actual price and wage inflation, the expected rate of inflation will fall after a certain time to the desired level. When this level is attained, fiscal and monetary parameters should return to their original values. In this case, exactly the same long-run equilibrium as before will be attained. The only difference is that the actual and expected rates of price and wage inflation will be lower than before.

The comparative statics analysis of the long-run equilibrium model gives the following results. First, the "natural" rate of unemployment will increase if the income tax rate or unemployment compensation are increased. The former conclusion is compatible with "ordinary" analysis, the second not. This phenomenon has to do with the way in which the model is constructed. More concretely, the result is due to the fact that the aspiration wage rates of the unemployed will increase when unemployment compensation increases.

The "natural" rate of unemployment also depends on the strength of the information flows in the labor market. If for example a public labor exchange is instituted, or the resources of an already existing one are increased, the "natural" rate of unemployment will decrease. The result is however only certain if the behavior of households and firms is unaffected by the change.

The effect on the "natural" real wage rate is only of unique sign in one case: if both the average and marginal productivity of labor increase, the real wage rate will increase.

If the subjective rate of time preference of households increases the "natural" real rate of interest will also increase. This is an interesting result since there is no direct connection between what happens on the loan market and the behavior of the households (according to the model, households are not engaged in financial saving and do not own any financial assets). Disturbances which make it more difficult for firms to keep their "capital" in the form of many customers and many employees also imply an increased "natural" real rate of interest. For example, this will be the case if the parameter of the "death" probability of households increases. With a given population, this will mean a higher rate of turnover of the labor force and of the stock of customers in the economy.

CHAPTER II. THE MICROECONOMIC FOUNDATIONS OF THE NEW THEORY OF INFLATION AND UNEMPLOYMENT: A SURVEY

1. Introduction

Important progress has been made in the last decade in macroeconomic theory. Both a microeconomic explanation of the multiplier mechanism and analytical derivations of the relation between unemployment and inflation have been developed. These innovations in macroeconomic theory have been made possible by a generalization of neoclassical microeconomic theory. Through consideration of the rational behavior of households and firms in an environment more general than that of the neoclassical theory, macro relations have been successfully derived which were formerly based only on *ad hoc* reasoning.

In this chapter is presented first the "new" microeconomic theory. As a point of departure for this discussion, I have chosen to present the basic features of neoclassical stability analysis together with its weaknesses. A conclusion of the discussion is that there never existed in any real meaning an *economic* theory for the adjustment process from one equilibrium situation to another. The neoclassical theory was exclusively an equilibrium theory. Taking as a point of departure the assumption of rational economic behavior on the part of individuals and firms, the theory had its strength in its logically rigorous derivation of macro relationships. But these macro relationships were only defined for equilibrium, since the behavior of firms and individuals was derived under the assumption that the price system constituted an equilibrium solution.

The problem with the neoclassical microeconomic theory was naturally the assumptions which it employed. The new development of micro theory which was begun about a decade ago can be characterized by saying that it retained the advances of neoclassical preference theory, but broadened the analysis so as to take note of economic friction as well. In other words the assumption that it is not costly to maintain markets was dispensed with.

The fact that neoclassical micro theory was an equilibrium theory implied not only disadvantages in itself, but also had negative consequences for the development of short-run dynamic macro theory. Since the object of the latter was precisely to describe situations out of equilibrium (*e.g.*, inflation processes), it could not take advantage of an established microeconomic foundation. To the extent that work on a generalization of microeconomic theory leads to a satisfactory description of individuals' economic behavior out of equilibrium, an important step has been taken toward creating just such a microeconomic foundation for macroeconomic theory.

This chapter surveys both the work which has attempted to generalize micro theory and the work which has attempted to utilize the generalized micro theory as a foundation for macro theory. It has not been my ambition to give a complete history of the development of the subject in the last decade.[1] On the other hand, I hope that the most important problems and their interrelations have been presented. However, one important limitation in this respect is that I have not discussed the interesting normative implications of the new micro and macro theories. Another is that the discussion concerns only theoretical developments; accordingly I do not consider the closely related empirical research (*e.g.*, that concerning the stability of the Phillips curve).

The following chapters contain an integrated model of inflation and unemployment which is built on the generalized microeconomic theory. The neoclassical element of the model consists of preference theory, but the rest of the analysis in these chapters is built on a number of highly restrictive assumptions which are a consequence of the fact that it is costly to come in contact with "trading partners". This is an important line of thought in the generalized micro theory which will be presented below. The objective of this chapter is therefore not only to

---

[1] Since a large part of the important contributions to the new theory have circulated as manuscripts between various American universities, in certain cases for several years before being published, it is very difficult from a European perspective to assign priority to individuals for any particular new idea.

give a survey of the "neo-neoclassical" micro theory and its macroeconomic implications, but also to give an introduction to the kinds of questions which later in the book will receive a more rigorous but also more restrictive treatment.

The chapter is organized as follows. In section two are discussed the problems which arose as a result of the neoclassical theory's abstraction from the fact that the process of exchange is costly. In this context the most important problem was the impossibility for the neoclassical assumptions to provide a satisfactory explanation of what happens in an economy out of equilibrium and thus to analyze the stability problem. The neoclassical discussion of various adjustment mechanisms is presented and criticized. The section is completed by a relatively thorough treatment of Arrow's seminal article of 1959, "Toward a Theory of Price Adjustment", which in many ways anticipated later developments.

Section three contains a survey of the theory of costly market processes when no market administrator exists. What information channels exist in the different markets, and how do individuals behave in order to contact one another? How does the individual search for different alternatives in order to achieve advantageous terms of exchange, and how do firms and households balance the costs and revenues of searching? What role is played by price and quality differences in this search behavior? What are the implications of this search phenomenon for the operation of the commodity and labor markets? These are several of the questions which are taken up in the section. They have in common the assumption that individuals do not have perfect information about possibilities of exchange but that they can allocate resources so as to increase their information through search. An important conclusion to which this theory leads is that it is possible to explain through reference to rational economic behavior the occurrence of unutilized resources in general and of unemployment in particular, even in equilibrium. The choice variables and the restrictions to which they are subject, which individuals take as given from the outside, are however different from those of the usual neoclassical analysis.

Section four contains a survey of work which has attempted to base a macro analysis on the more general micro theory. The center of attention is occupied by those contributions which have succeeded in deriving analytically the Phillips curve. These results are important not only in that they succeed in deriving macroeconomic relationships from an analysis of individual behavior, but also because the derivation means that the theory of inflation and unemployment has been integrated successfully.

The discussion up to and including section four has concerned essentially events in one market. In section five is found a presentation of a number of microeconomic studies of how disequilibrium in one market affects other markets. Thus the problem is, what are the effects of a lack of coordination of individuals' plans in one market on events in other markets? How are the economy's structural equations affected by the fact that rationing occurs in one or several markets?

In this connection the principal emphasis of the section is on the attempts of Patinkin, Clower, Leijonhufvud, and Barro and Grossman to explain the Keynesian multiplier mechanism through individuals' optimizing behavior under more general conditions than those permitted by the neoclassical equilibrium theory. However, a problem with the "new" multiplier theory is that it does not give scope for rational behavior with respect to price determination. At the same time the macro theory which was presented in section three suffers from the weakness that it takes no notice of involuntary unemployment and that it does not generate the quantitative interrelations between different markets which are exemplified in the multiplier mechanism. These problems are taken up in the conclusion of this section. There the question is also raised as to the possibilities of building on a microeconomic basis a general macroeconomic theory which integrates both the modern theory of the Phillips curve, and the "new" multiplier theory.

2. The Market Process as a Costly Coordination Mechanism: A Critique of Neoclassical Stability Analysis[1]

2.1. Introduction

A principal result of neoclassical microeconomic theory is how little information is needed in order to coordinate individuals' economic plans. The theorems on the existence, uniqueness and optimal properties of general equilibrium are quite concerned with the question of whether it is possible to combine a multiplicity of disparate plans in an efficient, consistent plan without this requiring centralization of all information.[2] The significance of this result can scarcely be understated; it is in fact one of the truly great scientific achievements. But it is important to be clear as to precisely how far this result goes. We know that under certain conditions there exists a solution to the coordination problem. On the other hand, neoclassical general equilibrium theory says nothing about how this solution is reached.[3] There

---

1) By the term "neoclassical stability analysis" (both tâtonnement and non-tâtonnement models) is meant investigations of whether and how an equilibrium (or equilibria) in a perfectly competitive general equilibrium model is reached. A characteristic feature (which does not, however, constitute a definition) of this type of investigation is that even out of equilibrium there occurs one price for every good in every instant of time. Jevons' "law of indifference" thus applies even out of equilibrium. This requires in turn that individuals in all situations have perfect information about their possibilities of exchange. Prices are determined in general by a market administrator whose behavior is described by the "law of markets" -- i.e., the rate of increase of a price depends positively on the size of the commodity's excess demand. One can also imagine that the price change in disequilibrium is determined by the activities of buyers and sellers in the market. However, it is very difficult to justify adjustment processes of this type.

2) The natural reference here is to Debreu (1959). For a modern survey cf. Arrow and Hahn (1971).

3) This view is scarcely new. "In this way ... prices are determined mathematically. Now there remains only to show -- and this is the essential point -- that the problem of exchange for which we have just given a theoretical solution, is the selfsame problem that is solved empirically on the market by the mechanism of free competition." (Walras (1954), pp. 162-63), cited in Patinkin (1965), p. 532.) The observation recurs from time to time in the economic literature; cf., e.g., Haavelmo (1958), Samuelson (1961), p. 9, and Hahn (1970), p. 1.

exist ad hoc solutions to the stability problem, but there does not exist any economic theory of how the "system of equations" is solved or of what happens if one does not succeed in solving for the equilibrium set of prices.

If the problem of finding an equilibrium solution is to be taken seriously, it must be shown how it comes about. If one takes neoclassical microeconomic theory as a point of departure, it is natural to see this procedure as a production process. This can take place either collectively (via a market administrator) or through the interrelation of different individuals' behavior. Existing institutional arrangements should of course be explained endogenously. Furthermore, the explanation should build on an economic argument. If then the production process is costly, where do the resources come from? What costs and revenues does this imply for the individuals involved? Is it possible that corner solutions occur in which the costs are so high that no "production" at all is profitable?[1] What role is played by the time horizon?

Even if these questions are formulated a bit unusually, it is easy to recognize them in the general economic discussion. The questions of the advantages and disadvantages of various economic systems, the stability properties of equilibrium situations, the fundamental reason for the occurrence of "external effects",[2] and the role of money in an exchange economy[3] -- all of these are

---

1) This consideration is important in the discussion of the number of markets which are comprised in the equilibrium solution. For example, what is the basis of temporary and intertemporal equilibrium? Why does there not exist a full complement of futures markets?

2) Demsetz (1964) contains a discussion of why there do not exist markets for certain goods and "bads". He suggests that this has to do with the existence of costs for maintaining markets. The occurrence of transactions costs (exchange costs) and costs of maintaining and controlling property rights (police costs, among others) can lead to situations in which it is not consistent with individuals' economic interests to maintain certain markets. We speak then of market imperfections in the form of external effects. But external effects must be explained endogenously. In Arrow (1974) there is an analogous discussion of the reasons why there exist so few futures markets.

3) Cf. Brunner and Meltzer (1971).

germane to the basic problem.

The comparison of different economic systems may serve as an example. If we restrict ourselves to that aspect of the comparison which has to do with the advantages and disadvantages of decentralized and centralized decision making in order to find an equilibrium solution (we disregard the occurrence of market imperfections which would imply another dimension of the comparison), the question is: in what way does the process of information collection and decision making to find an equilibrium solution proceed most effectively? In this discussion the question of how much information is needed in both types of system is of course important. Hayek has argued in his classic article of 1945 that the market mechanism (i.e., decentralized decision making) is efficient since it economizes on information. His argument can be summarized in the following way. The economy is continually subject to disturbances. The majority of these are of quite local nature; e.g., small changes in the conditions of production of individual plants. Decentralization is necessary because these small disturbances continually arise in different places and at different times. Local problems are solved best by those who are affected and who are acquainted with the situation. But reaction and adjustment must at the same time take place with reference to the effects on the whole economic system. If demand for a certain commodity or service is changed, other individuals do not need to know why it took place. The important thing for them is to know how urgent a certain need has become in comparison with others. In the presence of decentralized decision making, the price system constitutes a way to economize on information. Only that information which is relevant is procured. Hayek writes further: "The problem is thus in no way solved if we can show that all the facts if they were known to a single mind ... would uniquely determine the solution; instead we must show how a solution is produced by the interactions of people each of whom possesses only partial knowledge." It is easy to concur. In order to be able to compare different decision-making processes, one must investigate how the processes actually operate (this might best be done when each process has been optimized). What resources are used up in both cases? How much time is required? To what extent does a tradeoff take place between consumption of resources and desires for the final product?

2.2. Adjustment processes of the tâtonnement type

The question of how a decentralized market economy actually finds an equilibrium solution is of fundamental significance. For practical reasons it is not enough that there exists a solution to the problem of coordination -- the solution must also be found. The modern discussion in this area started from two points: Samuelson's stabiliby analysis in his Foundations of 1947 and Patinkin's rediscovery of Walras' tâtonnement theory in 1956.

Samuelson's contribution consisted in his analytical formulation of the "law of markets" in a system of differential equations in which the rate of price increase in a certain market was a monotonically increasing function of the excess demand in that market and perhaps as well a function of the excess demand in the economy's other markets.[1] Samuelson's formulation of the stability problem took place partly in a polemic against Hicks' attempt[2] to discuss the conditions of stability in context of a static model.[3] The significance of Samuelson's contribution lay partly in that he paved the way for an investigation of the stability problem with analytical methods and partly in that he demonstrated the relation (but not the identity) between static and dynamic models. This relation can be exemplified by the correspondence principle,[4] while the lack of an identity between static and dynamic models[5] is most vividly emphasized by the fact that the same static model can constitute the stationary solution to several dynamic models. Thus one cannot speak of the stability of an equilibrium situation, only of the stability of the corresponding dynamic model.

---

1) Samuelson (1961), pp. 269-76.

2) Hicks (1962) Chapter VIII and Appendix, §§21-22.

3) By the term "static" model is meant here an equilibrium model. It can very well be "dynamic" in the sense that it spans several time periods and has explicitly time-indexed, endogenously determined variables. The essential point is that the price system is such that in every period there exists an equilibrium (temporary equilibrium) in all markets. There can also -- but not necessarily -- be a dynamic equilibrium. In this latter case the conditions for temporary equilibrium are fulfilled, and there is consistency between plans and expectations for several periods into the future (in general to the horizon). This consistency can be achieved, for example, through futures markets (perhaps contingent markets) so that all contracts are made in the first period, after which the process automatically develops according to the original decisions.

4) If a certain corresponding dynamic model converges to the equilibrium of a static model, this result can be utilized to provide information about the static model's comparative-static properties. For an excellent survey of the discussion concerning the correspondence principle, cf. Thalberg (1968).

5) By the term "dynamic model" (or "corresponding dynamic model") is meant in this context a model the price system of which is not determined by an equilibrium condition. More generally expressed, the endogenous variables are not determined by equilibrium conditions.

The relationship between static and dynamic models can be interpreted in different ways. For example, one can argue that equilibrium is fundamentally a dynamic phenomenon, since the solution of a static model constitutes the stationary solution of a dynamic model.[1] Equilibrium is thus the result of a balance of forces. But on the other hand, static models can "produce" a multiplicity of corresponding dynamic models. This implies that one cannot regard the equilibrium solution as the stationary solution of a single dynamic model.

The problem is made more difficult in that the economic content of the static model and its corresponding dynamic models is different. Static models of a general equilibrium character are derived through aggregation of behavior equations for households and firms which are assumed to behave as if they are maximizing their preference functions, given certain side conditions. These side constraints are defined for equilibrium. But what happens outside of that situation? "If, for instance, the net rate of increase in price is assumed to be proportional to the excess of demand over supply, whose behavior is thereby expressed? And how is that behavior motivated?"[2] We must give an economic explanation of the process which generates the equilibrium solution. In the first place we wish as economists to give an explanation in which all "economic" phenomena are endogenous. This is not simply a matter of increasing the body of economic knowledge; it is also important to base the equilibrium and disequilibrium theories on the same type of theoretical considerations. An extension of the microeconomic theory which is based on preference theory (in its broad meaning) so that it also covers situations outside of equilibrium is moreover important for the reason that in this way we have a possibility of restrict-

---

[1] Cf., e.g., Hansen (1966), p. 2, and Hicks (1965), p. 15.

[2] Koopmans (1957), p. 179.

ing the number of conceivable corresponding dynamic models.[1)]

Patinkin's note on Walras' tâtonnement theory implied that two principal types of adjustment mechanisms began to be distinguished.[2)] In the first, tâtonnement,[3)] trading takes place only when an equilibrium situation has be reached. The other principal type of adjustment mechanism, non-tàtonnement,[4)] implies that trading takes place before the final equilibrium has been reached. The discussion of stability which was conducted prior to 1960 concerned only the former type of model.[5)]

---

1) The following quotation from Frank Hahn may serve to emphasize the importance of the question, without necessarily indicating agreement with its pessimistic tone: "We all know the endless variety of adjustment models, not uncongenial to common sense, one is capable of constructing. No unifying principle, such as maximization, seems available; no elegant separation theorems reduce the mass of ugly differential or difference equations to the splendid order of a chapter in Debreu. To discuss and analyze how the economy works it may be necessary to go and look.

The achievements of economic theory in the last two decades are both impressive and in many ways beautiful. But it cannot be denied that there is something scandalous in the spectacle of so many people refining the analyses of economic states which they give no reason to suppose will ever, or have ever, come about." Hahn (1970), p. 1.

2) Patinkin (1965), Note B, pp. 531-40.

3) Tâtonnement means literally "groping" and suggests that one approaches equilibrium experimentally. This can take place, for example, through individuals making preliminary contracts (recontracting in Edgeworth´s terminology) which are all annulled if they do not constitute an equilibrium; only when an equilibrium set of prices is reached do the contracts become binding.

4) As a linguistic expression this term is admittedly not particularly successful. If both terms are to be retained, it would be reasonable to redefine them; cf. Jaffé (1967), p. 13. However, the usage seems to have become so conventional (perhaps primarily as a result of Negishi´s survey article from 1962) that there is no reason to depart from it.

5) I mean here formal analytical contributions. As an example of an early contribution in the debate about non-tâtonnement models, may be noted Hicks (1962), pp. 127-129.

For an excellent survey of the discussion prior to 1962, reference may be made to Negishi (1962). The important contributions were made before then. What has happened since is foremost that one has attempted to take into consideration the existence of money; cf., e.g., Hahn (1965) and Arrow and Hahn (1971).

The greatest problem with adjustment processes of the *tâtonnement* type is that it can take a very long time to reach equilibrium. If the process takes place in real time, it is difficult to imagine that producers and consumers will completely abstain from any form of trade before equilibrium has been reached. In this context it is not sufficient to emphasize as Negishi does that, "convergence of the process to some neighborhood of the equilibrium must be rapid enough for practical purposes."[1) As soon as the subjective rate of time preference is finite, there will always exist a set of prices, different from the equilibrium price set, which will make trading advantageous for at least some individuals.[2) The *tâtonnement* models become still more problematical if they are instable *or* if they fail to converge in finite time. In this latter case one can maintain that trading never takes place.[3) A conceivable, but scarcely satisfactory, possibility of "saving" the *tâtonnement* models from this criticism would be to assume that the adjustment process takes place in a system of time different from that of the process of exchange and that the time dimension of the adjustment process is zero when expressed in the time measure of the exchange process.[4)

---

1) Negishi (1962), p. 640, fn. 8.

2) Assume for example that all relative prices (we abstract from the existence of money) except for one have achieved their equilibrium values. If this price is higher than its equilibrium value, it is clear that those individuals who in equilibrium are sellers of the commodity in question always would gain by trading before equilibrium is reached. But this can also hold for buyers, since they can value consumption now at a relatively high price, more than the corresponding consumption in the next period if the price differential is sufficiently small. This argument can be made significantly more rigorous, but I believe that this short observation is sufficient to illuminate the matter.

3) Arrow and Hahn (1971), p. 324.

4) In this case "entropy time" corresponds to the time system of the exchange process, while the adjustment process proceeds in "clock time". For a discussion of these concepts, *cf.* Murphy (1965), pp. 14-15, 127.

2.3. Adjustment processes of the non-tâtonnement type

The criticism of the tâtonnement models imply that an adjustment process can scarcely be regarded as economically meaningful if it is not of the non-tâtonnement type. However, there are also problems with this type of adjustment mechanism, a number of which are removed in tâtonnement mechanisms.

The problems in connection with non-tâtonnement models consist for the most part of analytical complications which arise because of the fact that transactions are made even outside of equilibrium. These transactions take place at prices which depart from the equilibrium price set, and this fact affects, among other things, the division of incomes (in a pure exchange economy, the division of wealth), which in turn affects the final equilibrium. The adjustment process is thus not neutral with respect to the equilibrium solution. Therefore, given the initial conditions, there is associated with every adjustment process a final equilibrium. In other words, the static model's parameters, and thus the equilibrium solution, are affected by those transactions which take place in disequilibrium.

Hicks takes up this problem in Value and Capital. Income effects introduce a certain indeterminateness in the comparative statics analysis. However,

> All that happens as a result of false trading is that this indeterminateness is somewhat intensified. How much intensified depends, of course, upon the extent of false trading; if very extensive transactions take place at prices very different from equilibrium prices, the disturbance will be serious. But I think we may reasonably suppose that the transactions which take place at "very false" prices are limited in volume. If any intelligence is shown in price-fixing, they will be.[1]

One can naturally mock Hicks' truism: if transactions only to an insignificant extent take place at prices which are "much" different from equilibrium prices, the problem posed by such

---

1) Hicks (1962), p. 129.

transactions is insignificant.[1] Hicks was in any case the first to raise the problem explicitly; it seems likely, however, that Walras was aware of the problem.[2]

Apart from effects on the distribution of income and wealth, trading at "false prices" can also have intertemporal effects on production. In a pure exchange economy the individual's possession of physical assets is affected. In an economy with production, consumers' incomes are affected, thus indirectly affecting their possession of financial assets. Moreover, firms' inventories will be affected directly, and their other physical assets indirectly. Thus, the system's movement through time is also affected through the effect on the firms' real capital: "If we were further to allow for the embodiment of production decisions in some durable concrete objects, the path of the system will at any time be strewn with the remnants of past mistakes."[3]

Adjustment mechanisms of the tâtonnement type exclude all transactions out of equilibrium. In a non-tâtonnement process certain transactions are excluded, since disequilibrium in a certain market implies that some individuals' buying and selling plans in the market cannot be realized. Unsatisfied demand would thus cause spill-over effects, implying that the demand for substitutes increases, while the demand for complements to the rationed commodities falls.[4] This implies, among other

---

1) Clower (1965), p. 113.

2) Jaffé maintains that Walras' "theorem of equivalent redistributions of commodity holdings" implies this. Cf. Jaffé (1967), p. 3.

3) Hahn (1970), p. 3.
According to Jaffé, Walras was aware of the complication involved by production decisions made on the basis of false prices. Cf. Jaffé (1967), p. 9.

4) Cf., e.g., Hicks (1965), p. 81. Negishi (1965) argues on page 160 that spill-overs can only be conceived of in connection with non-tâtonnement models. In a tâtonnement process no transactions occur before the equilibrium solution has been found. Hence there is no motive for the individual to attempt to replace unsatisfied demands for certain commodities with substitutes.

things, that the excess demand functions for the other markets are affected.[1] Hence we cannot employ directly the structural equations of the static model in order to analyze the course of adjustment for a process in which transactions are permitted even out of equilibrium. Moreover, if the behavioral equations are affected by the presence of disequilibrium, the use of the correspondence principle is made more difficult. The convergence properties of the "corresponding" dynamic model can no longer give certain information about the comparative-static properties of the static model. The correspondence principle should therefore be classified with corresponding dynamic models of the *tâtonnement* type.[2]

2.4. Arrow's analysis of a decentralized adjustment process

A common feature of adjustment processes of both the *tâtonnement* and *non-tâtonnement* types is that at every instant of time there is but one price in each market. The individual is

---

[1] The microeconomic theory of spill-over effects and their macroeconomic implications are discussed in more detail in section five, below.

[2] This was probably also Samuelson's intention. It should however be emphasized that, to the extent that one explains the rate of price increase in a particular market not only by reference to the excess demand in that market but also by reference to excess demand in other markets through the means of spill-over effects, the adjustment process must be assumed to be of the *non-tâtonnement* type. Samuelson writes in his *Foundations* (p. 274) that, "We have no choice but to admit that the rate of adjustment in one market may depend on the excess demand in *other* markets." Patinkin and Friedman have criticized Samuelson's correspondence principle on the basis of this point, since the occurrence of spill-over effects means that one cannot draw comparative-static conclusions from the stability of the corresponding dynamic model. *Cf.* Patinkin (1965), pp. 247, 296-298. It should however be pointed out that Samuelson did not justify the more general rule for the change of the price set through time by reference to spill-over effects, but rather through the view that different coefficients of price adjustment in different markets are not sufficiently general "unless a particular commodity classification is to be favored, and if our formulation is to be invariant under linear transformations of commodities and prices". Samuelson (1961), p. 274.

thus always a quantity adjuster. One way to justify this assumption is to assume the existence of a market administrator.[1] The market administrator's function is both to announce the price (or price set) at every instant of time and to change it so as to reach equilibrium.[2] However, this construction is problematical; we must be able to justify economically the existence of the market administrator. Even if his activities are not costly, one must still show that it is consistent with the interests of all individuals to behave according to the rules of the adjustment process. If we assume that transactions are conducted out of equilibrium, this will in general not be the case. Assume, for example, that certain individuals cannot, given the proclaimed price set, carry out their desired transactions. They would then be able to alter the queue or rationing order by offering a better price than the market price in order to buy or sell more. Such behavior is not permitted in the model. Hence one can make the same type of objection to both non-tâtonnement and tâtonnement models: it is not consistent with the interests of private individuals to follow the rules which the adjustment mechanisms stipulate.

On the other hand, if we do not assume the existence of a market administrator, individuals will behave in different ways in equilibrium and disequilibrium. In the first case they will be quantity adjusters, while in the latter case at least some of them will be price adjusters. Those individuals who in equilibrium would take prices as exogenously given must, in a disequilibrium situation, actively attempt to determine prices if a price change is to occur at all. An important question in this context is whether individuals have an incentive to undertake price changes, and if so, how the adjustment process takes place.

---

[1] Arrow and Hahn (1971), p. 324.

[2] To explain the existence of a market administrator, one could probably maintain that transactions costs would then be less than they would be if the contracts were not mediated centrally. In this case the existence of the market administrator as an institution can be justified analogously to the discussion of brokers in Alchian (1969).

This question was raised for the first time in 1959 in an article by Kenneth Arrow.[1] The first important observation which Arrow makes is that even if the demand curve for an individual firm is infinitely elastic in equilibrium, this is not necessarily the case in disequilibrium. In the presence of excess demand, competing firms cannot satisfy consumers' demand at the prevailing market price. It is thus possible for an individual firm to raise its price without thereby losing all of its customers. If instead there is an excess supply, the firm cannot sell all of its product at the prevailing market price. If the firm lowers its price while the other firms maintain theirs, it can possibly sell more. This line of reasoning in turn implies that the assumptions of perfect competition are only fulfilled in equilibrium. In the presence of disequilibrium, an individual firm's demand curve will have a negative slope, in which case it can be regarded (at least temporarily) as a monopolist. <u>If</u> the individual firm knows its demand curve and attempts to maximize profit in disequilibrium, then the quantity sold and the price are determined at the point where the marginal revenue curve cuts the marginal cost curve. But if <u>all</u> firms apply the same decision rule, they will all change their prices. This shifts the first firm's demand curve, and it will choose a new quantity and price. In the presence of excess demand the prices of individual firms will "zig-zag" upward as they move up their demand curves while these are shifted outward due to other firms' price increases.

Arrow further maintains that, since price determination in disequilibrium is decentralized to individual firms, there is no longer any reason to assume that only one price prevails on the market. Even if a market <u>in equilibrium</u> can be described as perfectly competitive, in that market <u>in disequilibrium</u> Jevons' "law of indifference" is not satisfied, since individual

---

1) Arrow (1959).

sellers can themselves determine their prices.[1] Since different firms can have different cost relationships and different demand curves, the prices which maximize profit will vary from firm to firm.

In addition Arrow emphasizes that, "the amount of uncertainty during this process is apt to be very considerable. Any estimate of the demand curve to a single entrepreneur involves a guess as to both the supply conditions and the prices of other sellers, as well as some idea of the demand curve to the industry as a whole."[2] One can add, perhaps, that the occurrence of price differentials and the potential uncertainty (in presence of excess demand) as to whether a certain seller can deliver the desired quantity implies uncertainty on the part of buyers. Considering how intensively this latter has been discussed, it may be worthwhile to comment in more detail on Arrow's discussion of the point.

The occurrence of price differentials requires either that it is costly for consumers to come in contact with other sellers and/or a consumer who trades with a high price firm cannot expect to have his demand satisfied in other firms.[3] If the former assumption holds in disequilibrium,[4] it should also hold in equilibrium. This implies in turn that an incomplete comprehension of the market on the part of consumers in disequilibrium is difficult to reconcile with an assumption that in equilibrium the market would satisfy the requirements of perfect competition.[5] If the latter assumption holds, one

---

1) Arrow assumes that the sellers side is more "concentrated" than the buyers´ side. He adds however that, "The most general picture is that of a shifting set of bilateral monopolies. The range of indeterminacy in each bargaining situation is limited but not completely eliminated by the possibilities of other bargains." Arrow (1959), p. 47.

2) Arrow (1959), p. 46.

3) Otherwise a firm with a higher price than the other firms would not be able to keep its customers, so that the "law of indifference" would apply even out of equilibrium.

4) This is Leijonhufvud´s view. Cf. Leijonhufvud (1968), p. 76.

5) Cf., e.g., Iwai (1974), pp. 275-276, and Rothchild (1973a), pp. 1291-1292.

must conclude that Arrow's adjustment process with price determination decentralized to individual firms is not an alternative to rationing and formation of queues in a non-tâtonnement model with a market administrator and a uniform price even out of equilibrium.[1)] The fact that individual sellers (in presence of excess demand) ration, despite the inconsistency of this behavior with profit maximation, must depend on their incomplete information about the shape of their demand curves and their movement through time together with their incapability for various reason to vary their prices continuously.

One of the interesting features in Arrow's article is that he even discusses the cost which the adjustment process involves in the form of occasional monopolistic and monopsonistic elements in price determination. Traditional welfare theory may justly be criticized for only treating the welfare aspects of an economy or economic system in equilibrium, while neglecting the costs which are required under various circumstances to reach equilibrium.[2)]

The temporary increase in monopolistic elements in price determination which occurs during the adjustment process is naturally only one example of the costs which the process involves. The monopolistic elements cause a poorer efficiency of allocation (in comparison with that obtained if the new equilibrium is immediately reached) which can be seen as an indirect cost of the adjustment process. The process also involves direct costs in the form of information collection on the part of both

---

1) Gogerty and Winston (1964) have however interpreted Arrow in such a way that there does not occur any unsatisfied demand or supply during the adjustment process. For further discussion see section five.

2) "Any method of resource allocation requires a process for equating supply and demand (or some equivalent), and such a process may be in itself costly, though such costs are not considered in the usual formal analysis of welfare economics. Thus, a completely centralized system will incur high computational and information costs. The monopolistic and monopsonistic misallocations implied by the model of the present paper may be thought of as costs alternative to those associated with centralization." Arrow (1959), p. 50.

firms and households. Firms expend resources to acquire information about competitors' prices and about its customers' demand functions. Households seek to come into contact with firms which maintain a low price in relation to the average price in the market.[1] In the presence of excess demand with elements of rationing, they also attempt to make contact with sellers who can make deliveries.

3. The Market Process as a Costly Coordination Mechanism: Search Theory and Market Organization with Imperfect Information

3.1. Introduction

An important element in the criticism of the neoclassical adjustment mechanisms is that they assume that individuals do not always behave in the way most advantageous for themselves. This problem is closely connected with the resource input which the adjustment process requires.[2] In general, however, not only is the process by which equilibrium is "sought out"

---

[1] Observe however that if the adjustment mechanism converges to a perfectly competitive equilibrium, it is reasonable to assume that individuals also have perfect information about their transaction possibilities out of equilibrium. But this does not imply that firms necessarily know the market demand curve or their customers´ demand relations; see the discussion above.

[2] In non-tâtonnement models it is assumed that individuals accept that all transactions take place at a unique market price, despite the fact that it can be in their interest to offer a higher price (buyers in presence of excess demand) or a lower price (sellers in presence of excess supply) in order that the transactions volume be increased, even at the cost of a worsed exchange relation. If instead individuals behave rationally, this will in general lead to price differentials and also to the expenditure of resources to be able to carry out more advantageous transactions.

costly, but also the maintenance of the equilibrium.[1] Regardless of the form of social organization which brings together sellers and buyers, whether there exists a market administrator, brokers, or direct search by buyers and sellers, this activity will not in general be costless.[2] The present section containes a survey of the theory of the behavior of households and firms in markets with many buyers and sellers in which it is costly to make contact with trading partners.[3] The commodity or service which is sold on the market is not necessarily assumed to be homogeneous, and this implies in turn that there can be uncertainty about its properties. This uncertainty can be removed completely or partly through collection of information, but this involves a certain cost.[4]

---

1) Discussions of adjustment mechanisms can easily acquire a teleological lopsidedness. Particularly in cases in which a market administrator does not exist, it is important to note that the individual in his trading cannot be assumed to strive consciously after the establishment of the equilibrium solution. To the extent that it is costly to maintain an equilibrium, its properties will be affected. In that case there is an "equilibrium" which is dependent on, *e.g.*, transactions costs.

2) In a general analysis the market organization must be determined within the frame of the economic model. One of the most important determinants of market organization is precisely the *differential* costs for maintenance of markets.

3) At the present time research has gone quite far toward describing the actions of households and firms *given* the market solution. On the other hand there remains a great deal of work to be done to realize a satisfactory theory of how, under these more general circumstances, the market solution arises.

4) Both of these types of incomplete information -- *i.e.*, concerning price and quality -- are in practice related to the costs of reducing uncertainty. The cost of search for a consumer is often exemplified by the spatial distribution of firms which implies that it costs time and money to gather information about, *e.g.*, the different prices which sellers cite for a certain commodity. But these costs can also depend of the fact that the commodity's properties differ from seller to seller. The cost of contact is thus not necessarily a cost of communication; it can also take the form of costs of inspection and evaluation. It may also be added that other types of costs of making contacts are conceivable, *e.g.*, costs of negotiation when the price and/or the quality specification are not already determined by the seller.

3.2. The search activity of households in commodity markets

Let us begin with a very simple case. Assume that there exists a commodity market in which a very large number of firms sell a homogenous commodity. The firms are price setters, and the price varies from firm to firm. A household which knows the probability distribution of prices, but which does not know the prices posted by individual firms, has the possibility of searching over the price distribution to try to come into contact with a firm which is maintaining a low price. Even if it makes no difference when the purchase takes place, it is not profitable to search for an unlimited amount of time, since search activity has an opportunity cost. The household must therefore determine the number of inquiries so that the difference between profit in the form of a low (expected) price and the cost of searching is maximized. Alternatively, we can say that the problem is to minimize both the sum of search costs, which depend on the number of firms contacted, and the (expected) price, which also depends on the number of inquiries. This problem, which can serve as a point of departure for the theory of search, was formulated for the first time in an article by George Stigler, "The Economics of Information".[1)]

Stigler's formulation of the problem has been criticized from various points of view. Stigler calculated the number of search steps before the search begins; in actual fact this can lead to one searching altogether too long. It can certainly happen that already at the first contact one gets a price so low that it does not pay to search further. Accordingly, the optimization problem should instead be formulated recursively so that one calculates the highest price which the consumer can accept at each step of the search without searching further.[2)] If the sample price exceeds the reservation price, the search continues, but if the sample price is less than or equal to the reservation price, one buys the commodity from

---

1) Stigler (1961).

2) Cf. McCall (1965), pp. 310-311, Nelson (1970), p. 313, and Rothschild (1973a), p. 1287.

the sampled firm.[1)]

Stigler assumed further that the quantity demanded of the commodity was determined before the search activity began. In a more general analysis the quantity should be determined simultaneously with the aspiration price as a function of the number of search steps. This is because every step of the search incurs costs which, among other things, affect the position of the budget surface. The resulting income effect affects the balance in consumption between the commodity for which one is searching after a low price and other commodities. Furthermore, the price at which the search is actually terminated will also affect the quantity consumed of both the commodity searched for and of other commodities through the income and substitution effects.[2)]

In order that the optimization problem be properly formulated, the objective function must also be specified correctly. The search activity implies that the consumer is sampling prices from a probability distribution. Thus the problem is one of behavior under uncertainty and maximization of the mathematical expectation of utility.[3)]

In actual fact search theory can be seen as a generalization of the theory of behavior under uncertainty. In the latter, price uncertainty implies that the household, so to speak, draws a price from a population with a known probability distribution; the number of draws is exogenously determined to be one. According to the search theory, the consumer can take a new sample if the previously sampled price is too high. Thus one can choose the number of drawings, but every new step of the search involves costs. Also, the drawings can take place with "no recall" or with "recall". In the latter case, earlier

---

1) In what follows the terms "reservation price", "acceptance price", and "aspiration price" are used synonomously.

2) Among others, this has been discussed by Gould (1972) and Herin (1974).

3) Cf. Gould (1972). To my knowledge there is still no systematic investigation of the relation between the theory of search and the theory of behavior under uncertainty. Here in all likelihood a great number of interesting questions are waiting to be formulated and treated.

offers which one has obtained continue to hold, and this tends to reduce the aspiration price.

Search activity can also be regarded as a stochastic production process. Inputs consist of the individual's search time plus factors of production which are purchased from the outside, e.g., transport and other communication services. The occurrence of different factors of production leads, among other things, to a cost minimization problem.[1] However, the problem cannot be formulated so as to minimize costs, given the level of production (in the form of a low price). This is due to both the fact that the price is exogenously determined and the fact that one does not know the exact point of time when the search activity will cease. In search strategies of the aspiration type, not only is the final price stochastic, but also the number of steps of the search.

The parallel with production theory is further emphasized in that one can speak of external effects in production. A household which comes into contact with a firm which maintains a low price can certainly inform its friends about it.[2] Another example of an external factor of production in the stochastic production function of a household consists of firms' price announcements.

If the household does not have complete (subjective) knowledge about the parameters of the distribution of prices, then its drawings give not only the possibility of a low price, but also information about the shape of the distribution. One way to formulate the decision problem in this case is searching for the maximum mathematical expectation for the utility function given that the consolidated frequency function[3] over prices is changed according to Bayes' law.[4] The household

---

1) Cf. Gronau (1971), pp. 296-297.

2) Information can thus be transmitted directly or indirectly.

3) The consolidated frequency function defines the probability for a certain price as the sum of the probabilities of that price at different parameter constellations, weighed by the probabilities of the respective parameter constellations.

4) Cf., e.g., Hadley (1967), pp. 296-298.

does not know the parameters of the distribution of prices, but its expectations of these are described by a frequency function.[1] Thus the probability of a certain price objective differs depending on which parameter constellation applies to the price distribution. Or, to put it the other way around, the frequency function of the parameters of the price distribution is affected every time the household receives information about a price. With expectations which are constantly revised according to Bayes' law, one can imagine two types of optimization procedures. First, the household can plan at every instant of time as if it had complete information about the shape of the price distribution but make revisions as new information flows in.[2] In planning search activity one must, in order to optimize the process, take notice of the new information about the shape of the price distribution which will be received at every step of the search, and this must be done before the new information has been procured.[3]

---

1) Otherwise expressed, one is uncertain as to the shape of the distribution of prices. Different distributions are conceivable, and how believable they are is described by a probability which is applied to the distributions themselves.

2) This is a rather common assumption, and the analysis in the following chapter builds on it. Also, cf. Mortensen (1970) and Axell (1974).

3) An excellent discussion of this type of dynamic optimization is to be found in Aoki (1967), chapter II. For the first analysis within the theory of search with this point of departure, cf. McCall (1965) and McCall (1970), pp. 125-126.

Bayesian analysis is not, however, free of problems.[1] It can happen that the expectations with respect to the parameters of the price distribution are so vague that they cannot be described by a probability distribution.[2] For this case Lester Telser has proposed the following search strategy: a certain number of price samples are collected initially only in order to acquire information about the price distribution; after that, the search proceeds in the usual way.[3] However, it is not clear that this strategy (which is surely a good description of how people in many cases behave) conflicts with Bayesian decision rules. If at the outset a very large number of different price distributions are possible, and the mass of probability is relatively evenly distributed over them, the optimal search strategy can imply that the aspiration price is so low that in practice the price samples in the first steps of the search are only used to give information about the shape of the price distribution.

The discussion above raises the question of whether a

---

1) Optimization in general and Bayesian strategy in particular require a very extensive capacity to handle data. Even if we restrict ourselves to the assumption that the household behaves as if it were solving an optimization problem, it is doubtful whether that is sufficient. A red thread which runs through this chapter is that the market mechanism should be seen as a costly production process. Analogously, one should study the decision process as a costly activity which also can be explained as balancing of costs and revenues. The more information collected and the more intensive its analysis, the "better" the decision will be. But the revenues of a "good" decision must be weighed against the costs of achieving it. Some decision processes can probably be described as search processes in which several alternatives of action are studied and their consequences evaluated. The more alternatives considered, the higher are the search costs, but the higher also is the probability of finding a relatively good decision alternative. To the extent that the optimization rule for this search process can be described with an aspiration level, this implies that a bridge has been established between (generalized) optimization theory and the satisficing theories. Cf. Winter (1971) and Radner (1973).

2) However, if an individual's preference ordering over alternatives of action is consistent, his expectations can be described by a probability distribution. Cf. Savage (1954) and Borch (1968), pp. 84-87.

3) Telser (1973).

Bayesian search strategy always gives rise to a solution with the reservation-price property. In other words, is it always the case that the optimal search strategy, even when the price distribution is not known, contains at every instant of time a highest price at which an offer will be accepted, while offers which exceed the price will lead to continued search? This question is important for the reason, among others, that a price increase otherwise can lead to an increased quantity demanded.

It is easy to give examples of situations in which there does not exist any reservation price when searching over an unknown price distribution. Assume for example that the uncertainty concerning the properties of the price distribution can be described by two nonoverlapping distributions which are equally likely -- i.e., each has been assigned an a priori probability equal to one half. (See figure 1.) In this case there will not exist a reservation price at the time of the first

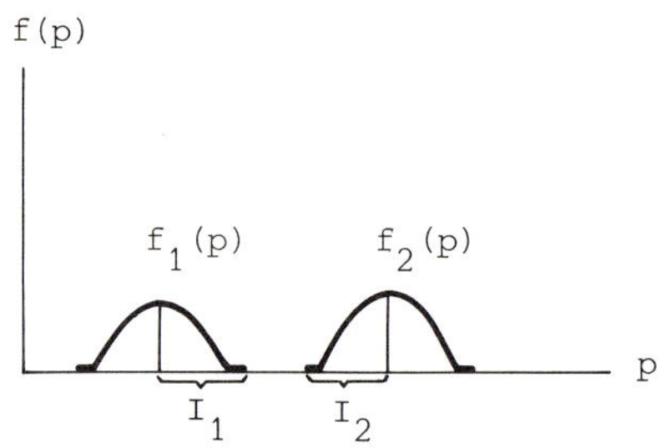

Fig. II:1. Searching under uncertainty about the true price distribution. The two nonoverlapping distributions imply the nonexistence of a reservation price at the time of the first drawing.

drawing, although there will thereafter. In this case the first sample price completely determines the price distribution, since one then knows with certainty whether $f_1(p)$ or $f_2(p)$ applies. In the first search step there is an interval I_1 of price offers which are rejected and which are lower than another interval, I_2, the price offers of which imply acceptance and termination of the search. The question of the reservation price property of an optimal Bayesian search strategy is connected with the properties of the prior probability distribution over the parameters of the price distribution. In the example above a price sample gives a great deal of information as to which price distribution applies. However, if instead f_1 and f_2 had almost all of the probability mass in common -- i.e., if the distributions had been almost totally overlapping -- then the optimal search rule would have the reservation price property.[1)]

Perhaps the economically most important aspect of the fact that the households do not know with certainty the price distribution does not, however, have to do with the reservation-price property and thus with the existence of a well behaved demand function. As soon as expectations with respect to the shape of the price distribution are incorrect, the reservation price (if it exists) is either set too low or too high.[2)] This implies search times which are considerably longer or shorter than those which would take place if one possessed correct information. This matter is discussed in more detail in the next section.

The time dimension of search activity is also important from other viewpoints. Among other things, the time aspect is connected with the type of commodity involved. An analytically simple assumption is that the consumer plans to buy a durable good, e.g., an automobile or a house. The purchase is a one-time event[3)], and one continues to search until coming

---

1) Cf. Rothchild (1973b). In this paper Rothchild has also shown that if the price distribution is discrete and bounded and if the prior distribution is a Dirichlet distribution, then the optimal search rule has the reservation price property. (A Dirichlet distribution is the conjugate prior distribution for the multinominal distribution. The assumption that the prior distribution is a Dirichlet distribution implies that while a price sample gives a posterior distribution which differs from the prior distribution, the posterior is still a Dirichlet distribution.)

2) This can imply either that one is subjectively certain with respect to the parameters of the price distribution but that their expected values differ from the true values, or that the prior distribution over the parameters of the price distribution has a probability mass the center of which is far from the true values. The former assumption is perhaps the most common, and it is also the point of departure for the argument in the following chapters.

3) Naturally this is very seldom true in practice. The existence of second-hand markets makes it possible for individuals to buy and sell capital goods. Reasonably this is going to affect the search behavior.

in contact with a seller whose price does not exceed the aspiration price. In this case both the search costs and the utility of consumption of the commodity in question can be affected by the duration of search. The search costs and the price paid afterwards for the commodity are discounted back to the original planning period. Furthermore, a long search time can cause inconvenience through the consumption periods being pushed further off into time.[1] Thus search activity can be formulated as an investment problem: costs in the form of resources devoted to searching and in the form of delay of consumption are weighed against the lower price which one can succeed in obtaining later. The higher the rate of discount, the higher the aspiration price and the shorter the expected length of the search period.

Instead of a purchase of a one-time character, one can imagine that the consumer is searching in a market for a daily commodity or in a market for leasing capital goods. If there then do not exist any costs connected with switching from one seller to another, the aspiration price will be equal to the price of the present supplier.[2] Even in this case the time factor can come into the analysis in an interesting way. The possibility of making contact in the future with a firm which holds a lower price affects the balance between present and future consumption of the commodity. Furthermore, expectations with respect to the development through time of the prices of individual firms also affects the search strategy.[3] If a low price is only temporary, search is less rewarding than if there exists a high positive correlation in time for the prices of the individual firms.[4]

The discussion has heretofore concerned the search pro-

---

1) More precisely, the starting point for the stream of services from the capital good is pushed forward in time.

2) This is the point of departure for the analysis of the next chapter.

3) Cf. Stigler (1961).

4) This is also the case when one searches for a one-time purchase with recall. The longer earlier offers remain valid, the lower the aspiration price can be set.

cess in a market for a homogenous commodity. In actuality a very large part of all search activities depend on quality differences of different kinds. In this case the consumer does not search over a price distribution but instead over a valuation distribution in which the valuation function contains the commodity's price and a vector of its properties as arguments.[1] The value of the valuation function varies then over different sellers according to a probability distribution.

Quality differences involve a whole line of new problems in describing search processes. First, different sellers' offers must be able to be compared through a valuation function. Here it is not simply a question of investigating what direct utility the purchase of the commodity from a certain seller would imply for the consumer. To the extent that the commodity is a capital good, a judgment must also be made as to the possibilities of resale in the future, which involves among other things the individual's expectations with respect to the preferences of the other consumers.

Second, quality differences raise the question of whether it is costly to estimate them. We thus have two types of search activity: extensive search[2], in which one attempts to come into contact with different sellers, and intensive search, in which one attempts to estimate the content of a given offer. Intensive search can take place before or after the purchase. The former case, inspection, is naturally the only possibility in connection with a one-time purchase. On the other hand, in the case of repeated purchases of a commodity, knowledge with respect to its properties is acquired through experience; if one is not satisfied, he can switch to another seller.[3]

Intensive search, like extensive search, can formally be regarded as a stochastic production process. The experience

---

1) Instead of regarding quality differences as constituting different commodities, we define a certain commodity as a point in the property space. Cf. Lancaster (1971).

2) Cf. Rees (1966). Rees used these terms to describe search activity in the labor market, but of course they are just as applicable to the commodity market.

3) Cf. Phillip Nelson's discussion of "inspection goods" and "experience goods" in Nelson (1970).

one can acquire indirectly (among other ways, through advice) together with the commodity's directly observable properties give a first expected conception of the commodity's properties. The expectations can be described through a probability distribution over the property space. At a certain cost one can make experiments of different types (different forms of more careful inspection). A certain result (which can be regarded as a stochastic output of the production process) is more or less likely in different property constellations. The probability distribution over the property space is thereby revised via Bayes' Law as a consequence of the result of the experiment. The more discriminatingly the experiment is designed, the more knowledge it gives about the properties of the commodity.

On the other hand, the costs for the experiment increase as well. How much information one collects is of course determined as a result of a balancing of costs and revenues of the information collection. In this connection it should be emphasized that since the result of the experiment (or the sequence of results in a series of planned experiments) is stochastically determined, the planning process takes place under risk. That policy alternative is chosen which maximizes the mathematical expectation of the preference function.[1)] The problem of increasing the information about a certain commodity's properties is analytical identical to the problem of getting more information, for example, about the parameters of the price distribution. In both cases Bayesian decision theory can be applied.[2)]

---

1) Strictly speaking one should also make reference to those costs which the decision process itself requires. It is not only a matter of striking a balance between costs and revenues so as to improve the basis of the decision; even the question of processing of information must in a more general analysis become a matter for discussion. Cf. footnote 1, p. 47.

2) The natural reference here is Raiffa and Schlaifer (1961). For a simple introduction, cf. Hadley (1967), chapter 8. The subject is also treated in McCall (1965). Experiments as the basis of the decisions of groups is discussed in Raiffa (1968), chapter 8; this book also contains an interesting discussion of how in practice one can apply statistical (Bayesian) decision theory.

3.3. The search activity of households in the labor market

Search processes in the labor market have received a very extensive treatment in the literature in the last ten years. However, the presentation here will be kept relatively brief since the problems resemble to a great extent those which have been treated above. In what way does the problem of search in the labor market differ from that in the commodity market?

A first observation is that an individual searches over an income distribution in order to get the highest possible income.[1] In contrast to the aspiration price, the aspiration income is defined as a minimum level. Apart from the fact that the individuals now sell a service, this observation is rather trivial. However, it raises the question of whether it is the sellers or the buyers (or both) who search.[2]

In the second place, in the commodity market it is in general only the buyer who is interested in the quality properties which the opposite party can offer.[3] In the labor market the firm desires information about the properties of job applicants (education, practical experience, ability to cooperate with others, etc.), while the unemployed wishes to get information about the properties of the job (job environment, qualifications, future prospects, etc.).[4] This implies

---

1) In the case of the labor market, Stigler was also the first to discuss search processes; cf. Stigler (1962).

2) This problem is closely connected with the question of whether the seller or the buyer sets the price (the income). Who searches, or who searches most, depends on who conducts the search most efficiently. Cf. Stigler (1962), p. 102.

3) This is not generally true. If a store also extends credit, the seller (if it is he who extends the credit) is obviously interested in the buyer's creditworthiness. (Note however that selling on credit can be characterized as a firm's simultaneous selling of a commodity and purchase of a debt instrument.) The properties of the buyer are similarly an important question for the seller in a rental market.

4) In a very interesting analysis of frictional unemployment, Reder has assumed that the properties of the unemployed are identical, but that they have stochastically independent preferences for different jobs (the properties of which differ). He assumes further that incomes are equal in all firms. Thus that which causes search activity on the part of the unemployed is differences in the job environment between different firms with job openings. Cf. Reder (1969).

that the individual searches over a distribution of incomes and properties. Both sellers and buyers thus search intensively, while sellers (and in certain cases buyers) search extensively.

A third difference in the conditions of search activity in the commodity and labor markets is that the income effect of a given percentage income increase is often greater than the corresponding price reduction in a commodity market. A significant part of the household's total search activity should therefore take place in the labor market. This view is particularly important if one compares the return to searching in the labor market with the corresponding return to searching in a market for a non-capital good. For certain more expensive capital goods (e.g., housing) the opposite is surely true, though one should then compare the capitalized value of a given percentage income increase with the corresponding price reduction for the capital good.

Fourth, the job searcher's activity must be assumed to be a systematic part of an intertemporal plan for his remaining professional career. The strong intertemporal connection has several causes. A job almost always implies new practical experience which -- among other things -- can be of use in future employment. This implies that the content of a job offer must be evaluated against the background of the possibilities it gives for future employment and related job search.[1] Furthermore, the switch from one job to another involves certain costs, which are partly connected with environmental factors the value of which is positively correlated with the length of employment.[2] The costs of a change of employers also depend indirectly on the costs to employers

---

1) In an interesting article Yoram Weiss has treated the employment decision as an investment in future professional experience; cf. Weiss (1971). The effect of this on search behavior is discussed in Whipple (1973).

2) As examples may be mentioned friendships formed in a job locale, knowledge about its surroundings, and specific practical experience which is tied to the locale.

of employee turnover.[1] Firms have a clear incentive to shape the wage system and other conditions of employment so that it is advantageous for employees to remain employed with their firms for relatively long periods.[2]

The costs involved in switching from one job to another are one of the reasons why an unemployed worker does not accept his first job offer, but instead searches for another,

---

1) In general a certain training period is required in order that an employee function efficiently in a new job. Among other things, this has to do with the length of time it takes for an employee to become incorporated in the job organization; cf. Söderström (1974). Another important point is that the employer has better knowledge about the qualities of the existing employees than of the job searcher -- see the discussion above about the need for intensive search also on the part of the firm. High employee turnover thus involves not only training costs, but also costs of choosing those one wishes to employee.

2) Another way for firms to hold employee turnover down is to stipulate certain minimum demands for those one wishes to employ. In general these minimum demands can be formulated as the minimum value of the firm's valuation function, in which the qualities of job applicants are arguments. In certain cases the valuation function (or valuation correspondence) can be specified through acceptable intervals for the different arguments. It is evidently not only a question of minimum demands; e.g., a job applicant can be "over qualified" and thus not expected to remain very long in the job. The firm's aspiration level for those it wishes to hire (i.e., the minimum value of its valuation function for job applicants) is fundamentally important because it limits the population in which a job searcher samples offers of employment; cf. Mortensen (1970b) and Whipple (1973). Moreover, from an analytical viewpoint firings may be said to take place when the employee does not fulfill the minimum demands on the valuation function. One possible reason for this is that the firm, despite its intensive search activity, does not in general have perfect information about the qualities of new employees. As these are successively revealed during the course of employment, it becomes apparent that some relatively newly employees have a lower "marginal product" than that which their observed characteristics gave reason to expect at the time of hiring.

better offer.[1] Thus in order to reduce the number of jobs or job switches, the job searcher has an aspiration wage which is higher, the higher the costs of switching.[2] The higher the aspiration or reservation income, the longer is the expected length of unemployment. But the offers of employment which are later accepted are also better, which also increases the likelihood of a long period of employment.[3]

3.4. The behavior of firms in markets with imperfect information

Up to this point the discussion has concerned the behavior of an individual in a market in which it is costly to get information about prices and/or quantities. It has been assumed that there are significantly fewer firms than households. Prices and quantities are thus instruments for the subject in the concentrated part of the market, *i.e.*, the firms, while price and quantity variations give an incentive for households to

---

1) Other assumptions which lead to the same results are connected with the fact that employment in itself involves certain opportunity costs for the search process. This indivisibility can be caused by a fixed working time which makes it difficult to search for a new job or that the unemployed must receive a relatively good job offer if it is to be better than unemployment compensation. The analysis in Chapter IV builds on the latter assumption. For a discussion of the significance of switching costs for the aspiration wage, *cf*. Parsons (1973).

2) More generally one can tie a valuation function to the employment offers. The arguments of the valuation function consist of, among others, wage offers (possibly the wage development of the job), environmental factors, and how the employment affects the job applicant's qualities, *i.e*. the professional experience it gives. Through the valuation function every employment offer is then assigned a certain value. The individual searches over a distribution of these values, and the aspiration level is constituted by the minimum value of the valuation function which is required in order that an offer of employment shall be accepted.

3) Most investigators who have analyzed search behavior in the labor market have concentrated on the situation of the unemployed. *Cf., e.g*. the excellent contributions of McCall (1970), Mortensen (1970b), and Gronau (1971). The next chapter contains a discussion of the search behavior of the *employed* in the labor market.

search.[1] Naturally this setup is not self-evident. In the first place one must be able to motivate economically this division of functions.[2] In the second place it is necessary to show that the interaction between households and firms really leads to price and quality differences in certain markets. This last question is just as difficult as it is general: as a special case it contains the problem of under what conditions there exists a unique price and quantity in a market. This problem is taken up below.

Let us start from the assumption that it is the individual firm which determines the prices in a market for a homogenous commodity or service. What restrictions must the firm then observe in the more general milieu which has been sketched in the previous pages? If the number of firms is large, the individual firm does not have any monopoly power in the traditional sense over price. Nor can one say that it is in monopolistic competition, since the commodity in question is homogeneous.[3] On the other hand, the consumers' deficient comprehen-

---

1) Note, however, that both sellers and buyers are interested in the qualities of the opposite party in certain cases, e.g., in the labor market, and that the quality decision can then be made by both sides of the market. This is discussed below.

2) A reasonable motivation for the price and quality decisions being made in the concentrated part of the market is the occurrence of "economies of scale" in price setting and quality determination. For example, the firms ought to negotiate individually with each of their customers concerning price and quality. But if the number of customers per firm is very large, if each customer accounts only for a small part of sales, and if it is costly for the firm to get information about the preferences of the individual customers, then the solution of the more general optimization problem for the firm can be precisely a uniform price and quantity. This can be regarded as one extreme case on a scale which contains price and quality differentiation as the middle ground and individual negotiations with each customer as the other extreme case.

3) In the case where the search cost is motivated by the fact that the firms are located in different geographic points, this can imply in certain cases that the consumer is not indifferent as to where he trades, even if the price marked is the same for all firms. However, the fact that firms are located in different places does not automatically lead to monopolistic competition. As a rather unrealistic counterexample in which there exist search costs in the form of communication costs but in which, given the price, customers are indifferent as to where they trade, one can conceive of a case in which all customers are located at a certain point, while the firms are evenly spread out on a circle around this point.

sion of the market implies that a firm in the relevant interval can raise its price without losing all of its customers.[1)]

A firm which sells a commodity of nondurable nature can be conceived to receive a certain stochastically determined flow of price inquiries each period. Those consumers who come into contact with the firm and who have a reservation price higher than the price which the firm has set for the commodity will buy the firm's product. If the firm raises the price, potential customers are thereby excluded who have reservation prices which lie between the original and new prices. However, the firm has in this case not only the possibility of affecting sales through the price, which determines the share of inquiries which lead to purchases. It can also affect the flow of customers through advertising. If we abstract from the fact that a firm can make itself known for a low price (i.e., advertising has only a temporary effect, receivers of price information have no memory, and price information is not spread indirectly), the problem becomes relatively simple. If instead the firm through its pricing and information policy not only affects current demand, but also that in the future, then there arises a capital-theoretical problem. The firm must now take note of the fact that its current decision making has consequences for the development of demand in the future. The problem is thus not only to choose a price and information offer so that current profit is maximized; instead, the optimization problem must be formulated so that one searches for the best path through time for the firm's control variables.

The question of the development of advertising through time for a firm which in this way can build up a stock of customers (i.e., create good will) has been analyzed in an interesting article by John Gould.[2)] Here the firm varies its

---

1) The question of the interval within which a firm can set its price without its sales shrinking to zero is connected with the question of whether there exists at all any "equilibrium price distribution". This matter is treated below.

2) Gould (1970).

advertising over time so that the future revenues of an increased flow of customers is balanced by the immediate investment costs in the form of advertising expenses. The price is assumed to be determined at every instant of time so that instantaneous profit is maximized. The firm thus is assumed to be able to affect future demand only by making itself "known". It is not possible to make itself known for a low price. It is obvious, however, that the price also plays a significant role for a firm's future sales possibilities. This aspect of the problem has been singled out for attention in a pathbreaking article by Edmund Phelps and Sidney Winter, Jr.[1)]

Phelps-Winter start from relatively simple assumptions about the search behavior of consumers in a market for a homogeneous, non-durable commodity in which different firms maintain different prices. The customers of the various firms meet randomly from time to time and exchange information about the prices of firms. The probability of meeting a customer who buys from a certain firm is proportional to the number of customers of that firm. A consumer who in this way acquires knowledge about a firm which maintains a lower price than his present supplier switches firms. The information mechanism which has been sketched here implies that all information is transmitted <u>indirectly</u>, <u>i.e</u>., that households do not have collection of information as an instrument (<u>e.g</u>., they cannot search more intensively if they are customers in a firm which maintains a relatively high price), and that the only possibility of the firms to affect the flow of customers is to maintain a low price. Under these assumptions the net flow of customers to a given firm is a multiplicative function of the number of its customers at the initial time point and a negative function of the firm's price.[2)]

---

1) Phelps and Winter (1970).

2) The flow of customers to a certain firm is proportional to the information about the firm which reaches customers in firms with a higher price. In the same way the flow of customers from the firm is proportional to the information about other firms with lower prices which reaches the firm's customers.

The firm is assumed to behave as if it maximizes the discounted sum of all future profits, given the differential equation which determines the net flow of customers. The solution to the maximization problem (which is obtained via Pontryagin's Maximum Principle) implies an optimal path through time for the stock of customers, from an arbitrary initial stock to the stationary optimum stock (where the transversality conditions are fulfilled). In order that this path be feasible, the firm's price is required to have a certain development over time. While a low price reduces current profits, at the same time it builds up the customer stock, since the net flow depends negatively on the price. Accordingly, if a firm initially has less than the stationary stock of customers, it will in the beginning maintain a low price so as to invest in new customers. As the stock grows, the firm will increase its price. When the stationary stock is reached, the price is stabilized at the higher level. In a corresponding way a firm with more than the stationary optimum number of customers will plan a certain cutting back, which takes place via a high, but successively falling, price.

The Phelps-Winter article raises several interesting questions. First, they indicate a reason for price spreading in a market for a homogenous commodity. If firms are alike in all respects except for their initial stocks of customers, this automatically implies different prices. Firms with a high demand for their product (_i.e._, with many customers) maintain a higher price than do firms with a low demand. However, the price spread shrinks, _ceteris paribus_, since the differences between firms in the number of customers are evened out. Hence this mechanism is only able to explain a _temporary_ price spread; the price distribution later collapses to a single price.

However, it should be observed that the Phelps-Winter analysis cannot be used directly to motivate Arrow's hypothesis concerning price differentials in a perfectly competitive market which is not in equilibrium. While we can conceive that disequilibrium implies, among other things, an uneven distribution of customers between firms and that this leads to different prices, on the other hand the Phelps-

Winter market does not converge to a perfectly competitive equilibrium. This is the case since the firms, even when they all have achieved their stationary optima, and the price distribution has collapsed, still retain a degree of monopoly power. A firm can still raise its price without all of its customers disappearing to the other firms, even though there will take place a certain successive reduction of the stock of customers. This last consideration implies that the firm does not set a monopoly price either (defined so that, given the number of customers, marginal revenue equals marginal cost). The price will instead lie between the static monopoly price and the perfectly competitive price.[1)]

Exactly where the price lies in this interval has an interesting economic explanation. The firm's stock of customers can be regarded analytically as a part of its capital ("good-will" capital). This capital can be built up through temporarily maintaining a low price. The terminal value for the capital stock the firm is aiming for, and how quickly that state is to be achieved, depends on the balance between present and future revenues and costs involved in investments in accumulation of customers -- i.e., on the discount rate. The lower the discount rate, the greater the number of customers at the stationary optimum and the greater the speed with which the firm plans to reach this state. Thus, the lower the rate, the closer is the stationary price to that price which would obtain under perfect competition.

Both Gould's analysis of the firm's intertemporal planning of its supply of information and the Phelps-Winter analysis of price policy build on the assumption that the stock of customers can only be affected successively via a flow equation. The choice of values for the control variables affects the net inflow of customers and thus at length also

---

1) This reasoning is implicit in the Phelps-Winter analysis. For a more detailed discussion and references to a number of articles of direct relevance for Arrow's hypothesis, cf. Rothschild (1973a), sections III and IV. The question is also discussed in chapter V, below.

the stock of customers. The corresponding principle of capital theory is perhaps more naturally applicable to the factor markets. Here it is not only a question of applying control theory to the firm's planning of its investments in physical capital; adjustment costs of different types imply that the firm's personnel policy must be developed as a part of its longterm planning.[1)]

Those costs, which depend on the net flow of employees to a certain firm, may be summarized under the headings of training costs and recruiting costs.[2)] The latter comprises costs of spreading knowledge about the firm among potential job applicants and costs in the form of a high wage which makes the firm more attractive among those job applicants with whom the firm comes into contact.[3)] This latter question, which parallels Phelps-Winter's discussion of the firm's price policy, is treated as a part of the analytical derivation of the Phillips curve by Dale Mortensen.[4)] Mortensen's very interesting analysis is summarized below in the section which deals with the relation between in-

---

1) For a survey of the theory of adjustment costs, cf. Söderström (1974).

2) An interesting implication of the occurrence of internal training costs is that the firm has a negatively sloped supply curve if it is in perfect competition in the commodity and factor markets and if homogeneous labor is the only factor of production. This factor is used partly for current production and partly for instructing new employees. Cf. Söderström (1974).

The firm's intertemporal planning in the case in which there exist costs of both recruitment and training has been treated in an article by Salop (1973). Salop discusses two net flows of labor to the firm. The first of these is the flow of job applicants which depends on, among other things, the firm's relative wage (i.e., the firm's wage in relation to the average in the market) and the number of unemployed workers in relation to the number of unfilled job openings. This flow is reduced through hirings. The second flow is the net inflow of employees. This flow depends positively on the firm's relative wage and training costs. An interesting result of Salop's analysis is that the properties of the model are not changed if one abstracts from the net flow and the stock of job applicants.

3) Costs of an attractive work environment also belong here, for example.

4) Mortensen (1970a).

flation and unemployment. Finally, it may be noted that in the case in which labor is not homogeneous, the firm has the possibility of increasing the inflow of employees through reducing its quality requirements; cf., e.g., Mortensen (1971).

3.5. The existence of price and quality distributions

The behavior of firms and households has been discussed up to now for the case in which there actually exists a price or wage distribution. One way to justify this assumption is to note empirical observations of relatively stable distributions in certain markets.[1] In such observations it is obviously important that the variance is not completely explained by quality variations.[2] Another point of departure is to explain analytically the existence of distributions with a positive variance. This question will now be discussed.

In principle there are two ways to justify the occurrence of a "stable" price or wage distribution with a positive variance. One possibility is that a unique price exists in equilibrium, but that price differentials are a phenomenon connected with the process of adjusting toward equilibrium. (Cf. the discussion in section 2.4.) In this case the economy (market) must continually be subject to disturbances which cause the equilibrium never to be achieved, so that the price or wage differentials persist. It is obvious that the disturbance mechanism must fulfill certain restrictions in order that the distribution be stable.

The second possibility is that the equilibrium solution involves, not a unique price, but a distribution. In this case it is a matter of finding the conditions which must be fulfilled in order for the equilibrium solution to have this property.

What requirements for mutual consistence between the plans

---

1) Cf. Axell (1974), pp. 77-78.

2) David Metcalf has investigated wage differentials and the expected returns of searching in certain markets for university instructors in Britain. In so doing, he has attempted to eliminate that part of the wage differentials which is the consequence of the fact that labor and jobs are not homogeneous. Even after quality variations have been controlled for, there remain relatively large wage differentials. Cf. Metcalf (1973).

of households and firms are implied by the existence of a partial, instantaneous equilibrium in a market with incomplete information? The equilibrium conditions cannot imply that the economic subjects can carry out their plans deterministically. For example, the search activities of households can be seen as a production process in which the result (the number of contacts during a certain time period, the content of firms' offers, etc.) is stochastically determined. A possible definition is thus that the market solution is constituted by a distribution (over prices, qualities of commodities, probabilities of contacts, etc.) the parameters of which are determined through the equilibrium condition that the households and firms expect that precisely these parameter values shall obtain.

This definition assumes that the economic subjects have subjectively certain expectations concerning the parameter values of the market solution. If one instead assumes that the economic subjects' expectations with respect to the parameters of the market solution can be described by a probability distribution over them, the expectations will be continually revised.[1] The equilibrium condition must in this case be specified so that the individual economic subject's expectations concerning the market solution (these determine the equilibrium values of the parameters of the market solution together with those variables which are exogenously given in relation to the market solution) are revised in such a way that the same parameter values for the market solution are repeated period after period.[2]

Let us now take up the question of the circumstances under which the market solution implies price differentials.

---

1) The fact that firms are imperfectly informed about the parameter values of the market solution constitutes a central feature in explanations of the occurrence of price differentials; see p. 68 below.

2) Cf. the discussion on p.31 above concerning equilibrium defined with reference to forces in balance. For further discussion of the concept of equilibrium in connection with markets with stochastic features, cf. Hahn (1973), pp. 25-28.

It can be noted first that the occurrence of costs to make contact with different sellers, and thus of imperfectly informed customers, is not sufficient to explain price differentials as a property of the equilibrium solution in a market for a homogeneous commodity. To begin with, assume that we have a market in which the purchase occurs only once. If the firms have identical cost functions, they will have identical optimization problems, and thus they will all set the same price.[1] If instead it is a question of a daily commodity market, one can certainly explain temporary price differences which can occur because different firms have different numbers of customers. But the distribution converges to a single price in connection with the spreading out of the stock of customers among the firms; *cf.*, the discussion of the Phelps-Winter article above.

If one assumes both that consumers have a limited comprehension of the market and that firms' production functions differ, it is not certain that there exists any equilibrium price distribution. Assume first that the commodity in question is a consumer durable which is only bought one time by every household. Those consumers who plan to buy the commodity and search over the price distribution have in general an acceptance price which is lower than the maximum value of the price distribution. If, more specially, all consumers are alike and thus have a common acceptance price, firms which

---

[1] Obviously it is also required that the firms have the same expectations. A common requirement for the equilibrium price distribution is however that both firms and households have proper expectations concerning the shape of the distribution. In that case the preceding, additional specification is unnecessary. However, one can also conceive that neither the firms nor the households have proper expectations with respect to the shape of the distribution, but that it is stationary anyway. In this case we must conceive of the errors of expectations cancelling out. In this latter case firms can of course set different prices, despite the fact that they have the same production function. *Cf.* Rothschild (1973a), pp. 1288-1289. It should be pointed out, however, that even if the firms are identical in all respects and thus have the same optimization problem, they can nevertheless choose different prices if there exists more than one value of the instrument which maximizes the objective function; *cf.* Axell (1973), p. 4.

maintain a higher price cannot sell anything. If they reduce their prices, the price distribution is shifted, and the common acceptance price falls. The process goes on until the distribution collapses around a single price.[1] A possibility to save the situation is to assume that not only firms but also households are different and that the latter therefore have different optimum solutions for their search problems, i.e., different acceptance prices.[2]

If instead one assumes a market for a nondurable commodity, there is automatically an acceptance-price distribution, since the acceptance price in this case is equal to that price which one pays at every instant for the commodity.[3] If the households are distributed among firms which maintain different prices, there is generated an acceptance-price distribution which is identical to the price distribution.[4] But one cannot reckon with an equilibrium price distribution in this case, either. In the long run consumers, if they search at all, will end up at the firm which maintains the lowest price.[5] It is therefore necessary to assume in addition that there is a certain turnover of consumers.[6] New generations of households

---

1) Telser (1973), p. 43.

2) If there is more than one value of the acceptance price which gives a solution to the maximization problem, then even in the case of identical consumers there can be an acceptance-price distribution. Cf. footnote 1, p. 65.

3) This assumes of course that there do not exist any costs of switching from one seller to another.

4) The price distribution is then defined as the frequency with which households purchase at a certain price. This distribution obviously need not agree with the firms' distribution over different prices.

5) If the households do not search, the firms' price setting problem is transformed to the static monopoly case. In that case there are obviously no difficulties to explaining a stable price distribution. The only requirement is that the individual firms' cost or demand situation differ. However, this case is not of any great interest.

6) Cf. Stigler (1961), p. 220.

are continually added to the stock, which is continually reduced by deaths, among other things. While in this case high price firms continually lose customers who seek out firms which maintain a lower price, the reduction can now be compensated by an inflow of new consumers. It can also be noted that the assumption that the stock of customers turns over is necessary in a market for a one-time purchase, since otherwise all transactions would cease.[1] Finally, the assumption of customer turnover is formally parallel to Charles Holt's analysis of the labor market as a dynamic system.[2]

A conclusion of the preceding discussion is that it is clearly required that the planning problems of both firms and households differ between themselves in order to explain the occurrence of a stable price or wage distribution. Besides those causes which have already been discussed, the differences in price setting and search behavior can also be a consequence of different expectations on the part of different firms and households. It is therefore important to emphasize that the equilibrium price distribution is not defined so that all economic subjects have correct expectations with respect to its shape. We require only that the distribution is stable.

One reason why firms' expectations differ is that it is costly for them to collect information about the shape of the price distribution.[3] The firms can experiment through setting different prices and in this way acquire information about their respective demand curves. If the consumers search randomly over the price distribution (which is the case in a one-time purchase), the firm's sales, given the price, will be stochastically determined.[4] Thus the firm's sales do not

---

1) Donald A. Nichols has studied a market for capital goods in which the inflow of new consumers plays a very significant role for the analysis; <u>cf</u>. Nichols (1970).

2) <u>Cf</u>. Holt (1970). Holt´s labor-market model is presented in abreviated form in the next section.

3) <u>Cf</u>. the preceding discussion of the household´s behavior when it does not have complete knowledge about the parameters of the price distribution.

4) This of course assumes that the number of customers per firm is not too large.

give any complete information about the demand curve for its product. This observation implies instead that the subjective probability distribution which describes the firm's expectations with respect to the parameters of the price distribution will be revised. While the firm can in this case collect more information about the demand relation, it is costly to do so: the price which one has set today may be the best price, given the available information. Under certain conditions, therefore, the firm will cease collecting information before it has obtained complete information about the parameters of the price distribution.[1)] Since firms' expectations will thus differ, they will set different prices.

Even if the economic subjects have complete knowledge about the parameters of the distribution, price or wage differentials can still be explained by stochastic variations in demand. Lucas and Prescott[2)] have analyzed a situation in which the economy is divided into a large number of local submarkets. In each of these there exists perfect competition and equilibrium in each period. Total commodity demand is assumed to be constant for the economy as a whole, but its distribution among different submarkets is subject to autocorrelated stochastic demand variations. This gives rise to price differentials between the local commodity markets and to wage and employment variations in the associated local labor markets.

Those price variations which give the consumers an incentive to search must be explained endogenously. It is perhaps not equally natural to make the same requirement of quality variations and the search activity which they call

---

1) A possible reason for this is that the firms plan with a finite time horizon. Another possibility is that the price is not continually variable. The latter assumption lies behind Michael Rothschild's remarkable application of the theory of the two-armed bandit to the firm's price setting; cf. Rothschild (1974). The reasoning is summarized in the appendix to Rothschild (1973a).

2) Lucas and Prescott (1974).

forth. Even if a part of the heterogeneity in the different commodity and factor markets likely has a non-economic explanation, there nevertheless remains a significant differential which is the result of the reactions of economic subjects to their environment.[1] A part of these "endogenous" variations is explained by search behavior on the part of individuals other than those who have quality properties as instruments. This reasoning is exemplified in Akerlof's investigation of the effects which the assymetry in quality information in the car market has on the composition of supply.[2] Those who own a good used car know its quality and prefer not to sell it, since good and bad used cars have the same price. This state of affairs depends in turn on the difficulties with which buyers evaluate the quality of used cars.[3] Thus supply comes to consist in large part of "lemons". This implies that the market price falls, which further tends to drive the good cars out of the market -- a variant of Gresham's Law.

But it is not only the quality of those commodities which are offered for sale which can be affected by the fact that it is costly for buyers to estimate quality. If the buyers are guided by certain observable outer characteristics when they make their choices, it can be in the interest of sellers to affect them. Michael Spence has discussed the following case.[4] Assume that there are two types of workers: one with high productivity and one with low productivity. Assume further that it is impossible for employers to determine which is the case at the time of employment and that the employees therefore receive the same wage, regardless of the group to which they

---

1) It must be admitted that it is very difficult at present to draw a boundary between economic and non-economic explanations of different events; cf. Gary Becker's investigations of the economics of crime and marriage. One is possibly on the safe side in saying that non-economic explanations refer to those which in one way or another do not take as a point of departure the economization of scarce resources.

2) Akerlof (1970).

3) The costs for the intensive search are so high that the potential buyers abstain from acquiring information about the qualities of the commodity. Directly observable outer characteristics are assumed not to give any information.

4) Spence (1973).

belong.[1)] The highly productive have, however, an incentive to reveal their quality. They can do this through education, which is less costly for them than for those with low productivity, since less time and other resources ("extra instruction") are required for the former to achieve a given grade. These assumptions can lead to different results, depending on how large the differences are in productivity and study costs between those with high and low productivity. A possible solution is that all the highly productive acquire education (and thereby reveal their qualities for the employers), while none of those with low productivity study. If studies do not have any effects on productivity, but instead serve only as a selection instrument, then although they will reveal productivity differences and lead to wages differences, this will involve a cost to which there are no corresponding revenues for society.[2)]

The investigations of Akerlof and Spence raise several interesting questions. In the first place, their analyses have a clear normative aspect: how do the conditions for economic efficiency change if we drop the assumption of perfect market information?[3)]

In the second place, their attempts to explain endogenously quality variations among supplied commodities and services and variations in their observable outer characteristics underlines the importance of studying the interdependence between buyers and sellers in markets characterized by imperfect information. Even in markets which do not function according to the neoclassical model, the equilibrium analysis can make valuable contributions to our knowledge of economic

---

1) This can either depend on the fact that all periods of employment are so short that the observed differences of productivity cannot affect wages in continued employment or that, for some reason, it is not possible during the course of the work to observe productivity differences.

2) This is the case under the assumption that education only reveals absolute -- not comparative -- advantages and that the wage differences which are generated by education do not affect the balance between labor and leisure for individuals belonging to the different productivity groups.

3) Note Hirschleifer's distinction between technological information and market information. The latter concerns information about transaction possibilities. Cf. Hirschleifer (1973).

reality.[1]

Finally, the analysis of endogenously explained price and quality variations gives us a new point of departure for the study of the development of economic processes through time. The interdependence of search behavior on the one hand and the occurrence of price and quality differences on the other is connected with the fact that it is not in general profitable for the economic subject to acquire perfect information about the parameters of the price and quality distribution. This makes possible the occurrence of erroneous expectations concerning the market situation. These erroneous expectations constitute a strategic explanatory factor in the new theory of inflation and unemployment which is presented in the next section.[2]

4. The Market Process as a Costly Coordination Mechanism: The Theory of Inflation and Unemployment

4.1. Introduction

The theory of inflation and unemployment which we had until approximately the end of the 1960's was very unsatisfactory in several respects. In the first place, there was no clear microtheoretic foundation for the macro theory; what behavior on the part of individual subjects could be assumed to lie behind the postulated macroeconomic relationships?

---

1) This is one of the main points in Rothschild's excellent survey article on market organization in the presence of imperfect information; cf. Rothschild (1973a).

2) Note also the Stockholm School's business cycle analyses of the 1930's. An important point of departure for the studies was that the development was driven forward by the gap between actual and expected values of the variables being studied. The Stockholm School's analysis has received renewed attention in the new view of the forces behind the processes of inflation and unemployment which is presented in section 4. For surveys of the contributions of the Stockholm School to economic theory, cf. Ohlin (1937), Lundberg (1953), chapter 9, Landgren (1960), and the debate which Landgren's book called forth in Ekonomisk Tidskrift 1960:3.

The weakness of the microeconomic foundation was perhaps clearest in the case of the theory of inflation.[1] While the theory of demand-pull inflation has a connection to the micro theory in the sense that the rates of increase of prices and wages in the various (aggregated) commodity and factor markets are dependent on the excess demands in the markets, nevertheless the parallel refers to the neoclassical stability analysis in which the process of price increases is also "explained" by the excess demands in the various markets. To the extent that the theory of demand-pull inflation is based on "micro economic theory" in the sense of neoclassical stability analysis, it is subject to the same criticism which was leveled against the latter in section 2: there is no economic theory which justified the postulated adjustment mechanisms.[2]

The theory of cost-push inflation is subject to a similar criticism. To the extent that one means by cost-push inflation price and wage increases which are initiated by cost impulses from other parts of the economy, this problem can be analyzed within the theory of demand-pull inflation. An excess demand in a certain market can evidently occur both because the demand curve is shifted outward or because the supply curve is shifted inward. Often, however, one means that cost-push inflation is caused by monopolistic features of price determination. A common objection to this view is that while monopolistic price determination can explain high prices (and wages), it cannot explain price and wage increases. Perhaps in spite of everything one can justify the usage of the term by noting that it says something essential about the way in which a demand impulse is propagated. The excess demand which starts the inflation process involves, among other things, disequilibrium in those markets which are first affected. This

---

1) For surveys of this inflation theory (or rather, class of inflation theories), cf. Hagger (1964) and Bronfenbrenner and Holzman (1965). Cf. also Harry Johnson's criticism of "traditional" inflation theory in Johnson (1972).

2) I want to emphasize strongly that this argument only concerns the theoretical foundation for models of demand-pull inflation. The older theories of demand-pull inflation may very well give good forecasts.

implies in turn that the degree of monopoly in these markets is increased.[1] Cost-push inflation should thus be more a name for the mechanism which operates during an inflationary process than a description of how the process is started.[2] Finally, cost-push inflation has been used to refer to a situation with price and wages increases which cannot be explained by inflationary gaps in the commodity and factor markets. This aspect is taken up below in connection with the significance of inflationary expectations.

Nor can Keynesian unemployment theory (and the business cycle theory which builds on the multiplier theory) be justified by neoclassical price theory.[3] However, the lack of an explicit microeconomic justification is not so problematic for the unemployment theory as it is for the inflation theory (the theory of demand-pull inflation). This is because one can justify the multiplier theory by taking as a point of departure the behavior of individual subjects under more general conditions than those permitted by neoclassical equilibrium theory.[4] As for the theory of inflation -- interpreted as a relation between excess demand functions and rates of increase of prices -- there exist more fundamental difficulties, which are conditioned by precisely the same problems which were reviewed in section 2.

However, the most serious problem with the theory of inflation and unemployment, at least from the viewpoint of economic policy, is precisely the fact that it is two theories. Inflation and unemployment occur simultaneously in reality but not in the theory. An economic theory is needed

---

1) Cf. the presentation in section 2 of Arrow's theory of price adjustment.

2) This argument is to be found in Arrow (1959), p. 50.

3) In the neoclassical general equilibrium theory the economic system is described by a number of structural equations (excess demand functions). These contain (if we abstract from externalities) only prices as arguments. In other words, the solution to the system of equations consists of a set of equilibrium prices. On the other hand, if we represent the Keynesian theory with a system of equations, these contain both prices and quantities as arguments.

4) This is discussed in more detail in section 5.

which explains the interplay between inflation and unemployment. It is not sufficient that one can justify the simultaneous occurrence of unemployment and cost-push inflation in a recession and of demand-pull inflation and structural and frictional unemployment in a boom.

Phillips' discovery at the end of the 1950's of a long-run, stable empirical relationship between inflation (more precisely, the rate of increase of wages) and unemployment in England initiated at first a discussion of the trade-off problem which the Phillips curve created for economic policy.[1] Which point on the "transformation curve" should one choose?[2] Was there any possibility to shift the curve inward through "technical development", *e.g.*, through measures of labor-market policy?[3] The development during the 1960's involved tests of the Phillips hypothesis for ever more countries; inclusion of more variables in larger econometric models of, in the first hand, the labor market; the beginning of doubts about the stability of the Phillips curve; and, finally, analytical derivations of the Phillips curve. It is this last aspect of the development which is treated in this section.

---

1) Phillips (1958).

2) Samuelson and Solow (1960).

3) This idea is not new, and the problem was discussed long before the concept of the Phillips curve was established. In Sweden there took place an intensive discussion of labor-market policy at the end of the 1940's and the beginning of the 1950's which concerned how labor-market policy measures might be able to achieve full employment without inflation. Some important contributions of Erik Lundberg, Rudolf Meidner, Gösta Rehn, and Krister Wickman are available in English translation in Turvey (1952). *Cf.* also Hansen (1955). The discussion later resulted in the development of a very ambitious labor-market policy in the 1960's. Through moving assistance, retraining at state expense, and localization policy, the Swedish government attempted to channel people from declining to expanding industries and regions. The demand for labor was also affected by the localization policy in an attempt to reduce structural unemployment.

Probably the most promising development work in the area of labor-market policy and theory is now being done in a group led by Charles Holt at the Urban Institute in Washington, D.C.; *cf.* Holt, *et al.* (1973) and Toikka (1974).

The major part of the contributions to the theory of the Phillips curve are to be found in The Microeconomic Foundations of Employment and Inflation Theory. They are characterized by the assumption that firms and households exist in the stochastic environment which was discussed in the preceding section. They therefore do not have the possibility of determining with certainty whether an event is randomly conditioned or whether it is the result of a structural change. Mistakes of various kinds are possible. Erroneous expectations constitute a strategic force behind variations in inflation and unemployment. Furthermore, the inflation theory which is presented is a partial theory in the sense that interest is concentrated on the development in the labor market. The interplay between price and wage increases is described at best through the effect of an exogenously given rate of inflation in the commodity market has on the development of wages. Unemployment consists of frictional unemployment, but the interesting feature is that it varies with the business cycle and that the mechanisms which affect its development are compatible with models which work with an aggregated demand on the one hand, and with more disaggregated models on the other. Finally, an important common feature is that the various analyses treat the labor market as a dynamic system.

4.2. Holt's analysis of the labor market as a dynamic system

An important point of departure for the analytical derivations of the Phillips curve is that one studies the development over time of the number of unemployed, employed, and vacancies through analyzing the flows which link these stocks.[1] Figure 2 gives a schematic survey of the interplay between the various stocks in the labor market.[2]

---

1) Cf. Holt (1970).

2) The figure is taken from Holt (1970).

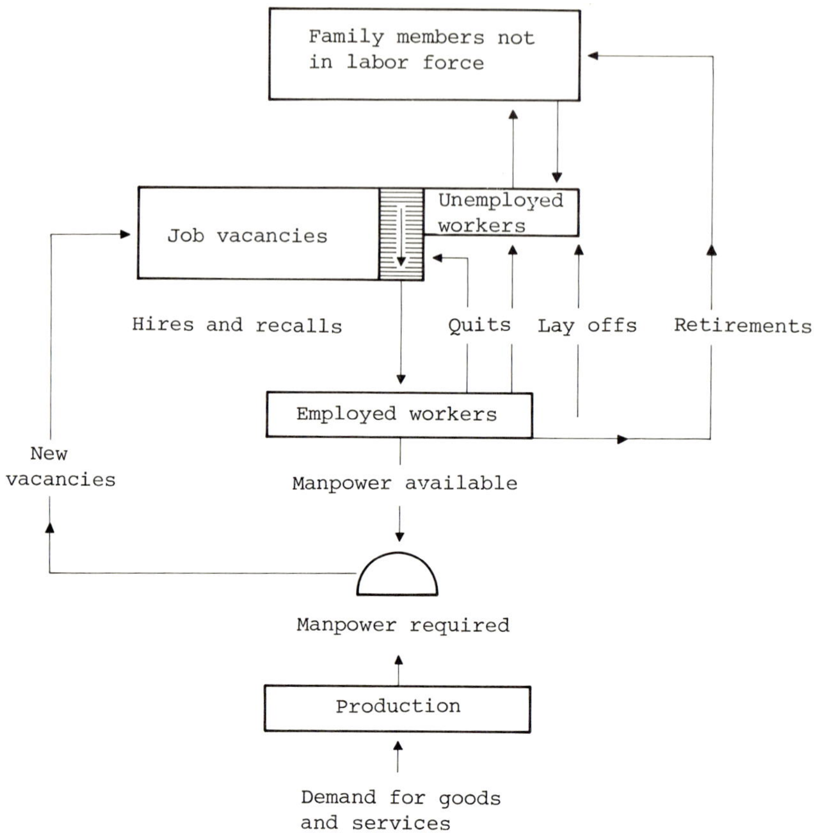

Fig. II:2. Stocks and flows on the labor market.

At the bottom of the figure is marked production of goods and services. Demand for goods implies a derived demand for labor.[1)] To the extent that the number of employees is less than the number firms demand, vacancies are created. These are equal to the difference between the demanded and the available labor force. In the ring between production and employees are noted new vacancies. These arise through the increase of labor demanded due to changed relative factor

---

1) One can either conceive of it applying to an aggregated demand for labor or to a certain type of labor (certain educational level, localization, etc.). In the case in which one studies a part of the labor market, it is obviously interesting to investigate the flows between the various parts of the labor market.

prices[1] or due to increased demand for goods and services. New vacancies can also occur as a result of the oldest employees leaving the firms and being pensioned or some of the employees being fired or resigning. The reason for the latter can either be that those who have become unemployed wish to search for a more attractive job or that they switch directly to another firm. Even with unchanged demand for labor, there are continually created new vacancies for these reasons. A continual inflow of the stock of vacancies takes place.

The stock of vacancies is reduced through recruitment in the form of reemployment of those temporarily laid off and of new hirings. This inflow of employees thus takes place both through the stock of unemployed being reduced and through workers switching from one firm to another. In the latter case the move involves the filling of a vacancy in one place and the automatic creation of another vacancy in another place. Neither the stock of vacancies nor the stock of employees is affected. In the figure is also shown how the stock of unemployed is affected. It increases through resignations and firings, as well as through new generations being added to the labor force. The stock declines through rehirings and new hirings, as well as through certain unemployed persons resigning from the labor force, e.g. in order to switch to household work.

In every part of the labor market there takes place a continual inflow of unemployed persons. These consist of, among others, youths seeking work for the first time, married women returning to the labor market, persons completing temporary work (e.g., construction workers), laid off workers, and persons who for some reason have left their jobs to look for others. It should be observed that it is not only demographic factors which determine the inflow of youths and married women. If the labor-market situation is bad, students may extend their studies, and women with small children may

---

[1] This is the case with perfect competition in the different factor markets. If one imagines another market form instead in which it is costly for buyers and sellers to make contact with each other and in which there does not necessarily exist a unique price in the different markets, the assumption must be formulated somewhat differently.

prefer to continue working at home. In such a case there is, instead of an inflow of unemployed, an increase of hidden unemployment.

A large inflow of new, unemployed workers leads in itself to high unemployment. The inflow is affected partly by the business situation and the general course of business development through personnel reductions and lay-offs. The worse the business situation, the greater the inflow for these reasons. But since other parts of the inflow likely decline during recessions, it is uncertain whether that part of unemployment which depends on the inflow of newly unemployed workers can explain completely the cyclical swings in the numbers of unemployed.

If the number of unemployed increases as a result of an inflow of newly unemployed, it naturally declines when unemployed workers obtain work or for some reason cease to belong to the labor force (e.g., switch to hidden unemployment). Increasing unemployment is thus identical to the excess of the inflow of newly unemployed over the outflow of unemployed. The fewer the persons who cease to be unemployed, the longer the periods of unemployment. We can say therefore that unemployment can increase either as a result of many persons becoming unemployed or of those who are unemployed continuing to be so for a long time. In order for unemployment to remain at a high level there is required an unchanged, high inflow of newly unemployed or continuing long periods of unemployment.

The length of the expected period of unemployment is affected both by the possibilities for the job seeker and the employer to come into contact with each other and the proportion of contacts which can lead to hiring. High minimum requirements on the part of the job seeker together with only a small number of vacancies for which the job seeker is judged by the employer to be suitable naturally increase the length of the search period. This implies that labor markets, with a poorly developed contact network, and in which job seekers' demands and employers' offers do not mesh well with each other, will have long search periods and high frictional unemployment.

A poor adjustment between the demands of different types of job seekers and the supplies of different types of jobs not only implies long periods of unemployment and search for those who wish to switch jobs, but also implies that it takes a long time for firms to fill their vacancies. Thus in these parts of the labor market there can occur side by side many job seekers and many vacant jobs. The analogy with structural unemployment is obvious. While structural unemployment refers to the situation of vacancies in certain industries and regions with job seekers in other parts of the labor market, nevertheless the difference between structural and frictional unemployment is a matter of degree, not of kind.

The hatched area in figure 2 between the stock of vacancies and the stock of unemployed is central for the following reasoning. It is here that the search processes in the labor market take place. It is here that firms with vacancies recruit labor, while unemployed workers search for an acceptable,[1] and employed workers a better,[2] job.

4.3. Holt's derivation of the Phillips curve[3]

If one takes as a point of departure the labor market as a dynamic system, it is natural to represent the development of unemployment through time by a differential equation. The development is thus determined by the net flow to the stock of unemployed. From this point of view the Phillips curve can be represented as one of the structural equations in a larger dynamic system, the differential equation for the number of unemployed. In order for this equation to have the "Phillips property", it is necessary that the rate of increase of wages <u>and</u> unemployment be arguments with negative partial derivatives. The Phillips curve then consists of the locus of combinations of rates of wage increase and unemployment where the time derivative of unemployment is zero.[4] A Phillips curve constructed in this way also produces automatically the Phillips-Lipsey loop: the higher the rate of increase of wages, the faster the <u>decline</u> of unemployment.[5]

In order to derive the negative relation between the rate of increase of wages and the time derivative of unemployment, Holt assumes that the inflow of new unemployed is relatively stable over the business cycle. While the inflow of fired and laid-off workers increases the stock of unemployed during a recession, at the same time there are fewer who voluntarily

---

1) *I.e.*, an offer which exceeds the aspiration level of the unemployed; *cf.* the discussion in section 3.

2) If there exist various sorts of costs of switching, the aspiration level of a worker seeking to switch jobs will, however, be higher than that corresponding to the conditions of his present employment.

3) Holt (1970).

4) The reader can easily verify the argument by refering to the following differential equation: $\dot{u}=f(\dot{w}/w,u)$ in which the time derivative is indicated in the usual way with a dot over the relevant variable. u is the percentage rate of unemployment, and w is the average wage. Stipulate further that $f_1<0$ and $f_2<0$. The Phillips curve is obtained by setting f equal to zero.

5) Changes in the rate of unemployment and the rate of increase of wages tend to take place in a cyclical movement counterclockwise around the Phillips curve; *cf.* Phillips (1958) and Lipsey (1960).

quit their jobs in order, as unemployed, to search for new and better jobs.[1] Furthermore, the inflow of youths and married women attempting to enter the labor market is also reduced. According to Holt, the fluctuations in unemployment are instead a consequence of fluctuations in the periods of unemployment. The next step in the argument is that the periods of unemployment are a negative function of the rate of increase of wages, so that the time derivative of unemployment will fall as the rate of increase of wages accelerates.

The negative relation between the rate of increase of wages and the length of the period of unemployment is a consequence of the decline of the aspiration wages of the unemployed as the period of their unemployment is lengthened.[2] Hirings take place when an unemployed person comes in contact with a firm which offers a wage which exceeds the aspiration

---

1) This assumption has been criticized. As far as Sweden is concerned, it is very unusual for a worker to quit his job before he has obtained other employment. Peter Mattila (1974) has furthermore collected a number of investigations which suggest that it is not common in the US either. However, it should be pointed out that even if the average number of persons who voluntarily quit their jobs in order to look for new ones as unemployed is low, large percentage fluctuations in this flow can suffice as an explanation. It should also be noted that the flow of "voluntarily" unemployed workers also stems from those who are entering the labor market, and this latter flow is of significant scale.

2) There are several explanations for this. The longer one has been unemployed, the lower is the marginal valuation of more leisure time; cf. Kasper (1967), p. 166. Moreover, wealth and liquidity decline as the period of unemployment lengthens. This implies that the "internal rate of return" in the calculation of the value of continued search activity rises, which tends to reduce investment in continued search activity, and the aspiration wage falls. Cf. Kasper (1967) and Holt (1970), pp. 61-63. A further reason why the aspiration wage declines with the length of the period of search is the finite time horizon. The longer one has searched, the closer he has moved to the day he departs from working life (the summer vacation ends or he becomes pensioned), and the shorter the time remaining for amortization of the costs which searching has incurred. This effect should be stronger the shorter the time one has left in the labor force. Cf. Gronau (1971), p. 294, and also the discussion in chapter IV in which it is shown that the aspiration wage is also connected with the results of search activity in the commodity market.

wage. The faster the wage level rises, the more aspiration wages which are passed by (these are distributed over the unemployed according to, among other things, the length of time they have been unemployed), and the faster unemployment falls. The negative relation between unemployment and its time derivative is an example of the negative feedbacks which Holt postulates in his labor-market model. When unemployment increases, search activity in the labor market also increases, and the number of contacts between firms and job seekers increases. In itself this tends to reduce the net inflow to the stock of unemployed.

4.4. Phelps' derivation of the Phillips curve[1)]

In Holt's derivation of the Phillips curve, the rate of increase of wages is assumed to be exogenously given. The behavior of firms is scarcely discussed at all. In contrast, Phelps has concentrated on the behavior of firms. Purely technically this implies that he has derived a differential equation for wages as a function of unemployment and the time derivative of unemployment. The economic content of the Phillips curve is thus altered. It no longer consists of a structural equation which describes the behavior of households, but instead is the equation which, within the scope of the whole dynamic labor-market model, describes the behavior of firms. I shall now present Phelps' argument in somewhat more detail.[2)]

To begin with, Phelps emphasizes that the wage is an important recruitment instrument for firms. In a labor market characterized by imperfect information both on the seller's and buyer's sides, the inflow of job seekers to a firm will be a function of the firm's wage offer in relation to the average market wage. For a given inflow of job seekers, the number of appointments will be a positive function of the size of the wage. The firm has thus a temporary monopsony position which need not imply static monopsony. The

---

1) Phelps (1970). An earlier version of this article is Phelps (1968).

2) For a more detailed survey, cf. Siven (1972).

firm's relative wage, i.e., its wage rate as a proportion of the market average, is a positive function of, among other things, the number of vacancies. These are defined as the number of workers the firm would wish to employ if it could employ as many as it wished at the prevailing market wage, minus the number employed. The number of vacancies can increase either through the real wage falling or through a ceteris paribus decline of the number of employees.

The higher unemployment is, the greater is also the inflow of job seekers to the firm. Now if the number of unemployed increases, the firm can, with constant recruitment, have an unchanged relative wage or also reduce the relative wage while retaining an unchanged inflow of new employees. Phelps assumes that the firm chooses a middle course.

If all firms are alike for the most part, we can say that the relative wage which they wish to maintain on the average is a function of the average vacancies and of unemployment, both expressed as a percentage of the total labor force. But if all firms strive individually to raise their relative wages in relation to the market average, only the average wage will increase. We thus find that the percentage increase in the market wage is a positive function of the number of vacancies and a negative function of the number of unemployed, both expressed as a percentage of the total labor force:

(1) $\dot{w}/w = f(u,v)$, where $f_1 < 0$, $f_2 > 0$.

In order to describe what happens in the labor market, it is necessary to have, in addition to the equation which describes the increase in the average wage, also an equation which describes the change in the number of employees, or alternatively the change in the number of unemployed.[1)] Phelps conceives that the percentage change in the number of employed workers is a positive function of the number of unemployed and the number of vacancies, both as a percentage of the total number of workers. The justification is that if

---

1) If the labor force is given, an increase in employment leads to an equally large decline in unemployment.

the number of vacancies increases, the number of jobs acceptable to the job seekers will increase, so that the probability of an individual job seeker being hired increases.

Since the increase in the number of employed is a positive function of the number of unemployed and the number of vacancies, one can say that the increase in the number of unemployed is a negative function of the number of vacancies and the number of unemployed. This implies in turn that the number of vacancies is a negative function of the number of unemployed and of the change in the number of unemployed:

(2) $v = g(u,\dot{u})$ where $g_1 < 0$ and $g_2 < 0$.

This expression can be substituted for the vacancy argument in the equation for the increase in wages, and the percentage increase in wages is then obtained as a negative function of the number of unemployed and of the change in the number of unemployed as a percentage of the total number of workers:

(3) $\dot{w}/w = h(u,\dot{u})$, where $h_1 < 0$ and $h_2 < 0$.

This is the analytical expression for the Phillips curve: the increase of wages depends on <u>both</u> the unemployment rate and its time derivative. A sharp reduction in unemployment at a given level of unemployment implies that the rate of increase of wages accelerates. In other words, Phelps' model generates not only the usual Phillips curve, but also the oscillations around it.

The above results were derived under the assumption that the firms did not expect other firms to raise their wages. This is obviously an assumption which must be made if an individual firm's increasing its wage is to be an increase in the relative wage. If <u>all</u> firms raise wages by 2%, an individual firm must first raise wages by 2% and then further by that amount which is necessary to achieve a certain increase in the relative wage. This argument leads to the conclusion that the equation which we have written out above only applies if the firms have static expectations vis à vis the market wage. If all firms expect the market wage to rise by a certain percentage, we must add this percentage to the expression in order to obtain the final wage increases:

$$(4) \quad \dot{w}/w = h(u,\dot{u}) + (\dot{w}/w)^e$$

where $(\dot{w}/w)^e$ denotes the expected wage increases. The expression implies that if expected wage increases rise by 2%, the Phillips curve will be shifted upward by the same amount. We thus obtain a long-run vertical Phillips curve which denotes the "natural rate of unemployment".[1] An increased rate of inflation would thus only be able to reduce unemployment until expectations had adjusted to the higher rate of inflation. In the long run the policy conclusion is that one must reduce people's inflationary expectations and simultaneously reduce the "natural" rate of unemployment, and that these problems are independent of one another.

4.5. Derivation of the Phillips curve with a completely dynamic labor-market model as a point of departure

Holt's analysis of the wage change process took into consideration only the supply side, *i.e.* the behavior of workers. Phelps' paper gives a better description of the behavior of firms, but this description is merely based on rather plausible assumptions and lacks a more fundamental basis. The behavior functions are not autonomous since they are not the result of a rigorous analysis based on some optimization assumption. Nor does Phelps link the behavior of firms to that of workers, something which would have been natural had he studied the flow supply of workers confronting individual firms.

Holt's penetrating analysis of the supply side and Phelps' of the demand side are combined in an essay by Dale Mortensen.[2]

---

1) The terminology is due to Milton Friedman; *cf*. Friedman (1968).

2) Mortensen (1970a).

In an analysis similar to Holt's, Mortensen explains unemployment by the search behavior of workers. Contrary to Holt, Mortensen assumes that jobs and workers are homogeneous[1] and that no rationing exists. The number of vacancies, then does not affect the change in unemployment or wage rates. Furthermore, an aspiration level determines whether the unemployed worker goes on searching or accepts an offer of work. If the wage rate of an employed worker falls under that level, he will quit and start searching for another job. A direct transfer from one job to another is effected if an employee is offered better pay by another firm.

Mortensen's treatment of the aspiration level is somewhat different from that of Holt. Holt assumes that the aspiration level is negatively correlated with the duration of unemployment, and since different unemployed workers have experienced different durations of unemployment at any given moment, the flow supply of labor will depend positively on the wage rate offered. Mortensen instead assumes that the aspiration level is affected by the information acquired by workers about the wage distribution and the change of the wage distribution. If different firms have different wage rates and/or the market wage rate has changed over time, different workers will have different expectations on account of the different samples of wages information they have received. Unemployed people are able to sample wage messages

---

1) In a later article, Mortenson (1970b), is analyzed the relation between unemployment and the process of wage inflation in a labor market in which labor is heterogenous but substitutable. Different firms have different wages but also different minimum requirements for job applicants. A hiring takes place if the unemployed worker comes into contact with a firm which can offer a higher wage than the acceptance wage and if the job applicant's productivity exceeds the firm's minimum requirements. Firms' wage offers are, in equilibrium, positively correlated with their requirements for job applicants. However, over the business cycle a negative relation is obtained between firms' minimum requirements and the wage offers. Namely, in a boom firms seek to increase their recruitment possibilities through both raising their wage offers and reducing their minimum requirements. This mechanism also produces a negative relation between (non-expected) wage increases and unemployment.

more intensively than employed ones, and therefore probably have a more compact and exact picture of the wage distribution. In any case, this spread of expectations about the wage distribution over different workers will make the aspiration level different for different workers. Moreover, this means that the higher the wage rate of an individual firm, the fewer of its employees that will quit, and the greater the number of people employed by other firms or unemployed workers that contact the firm to find that the offer exceeds their aspiration levels. The higher the wage rate of an individual firm, the faster the net flow of workers to that firm will be. Mortensen further assumes that the number of workers contacting a certain firm is proportional to the number already employed by that firm. This implies that the proportional change of the number employed by the firm may be written as a positive function of the relative wage rate (the wage rate of the firm as a proportion to the wage rate workers expect to be the market average) and unemployment. The higher the unemployment, the more search activity there will be and the greater the number of applicants contacting the firm per unit of time.

The firm is then assumed to behave as if, subject to the above-mentioned flow equation (and assuming a certain number of workers initially), it maximizes its capital value, *i.e.*, the discounted sum of all future profits.[1] The rate of discount equals the market rate of interest less expected price inflation. This problem could either be solved using the classical calculus of variations or its modern variant, Pontryagin's Maximum Principle. Mortensen has chosen the first method, and the solution can be described in the following way. If the firm maximizes the discounted sum of all future profits, it will choose a best trajectory over time for its wage rate. This trajectory determines the net increase in the number of employees, which in turn determines the development of production over time. Whatever the number of employees initially, the

---

[1] Note the great similarities to the Phelps-Winter analysis, which was reviewed in section 3, above.

optimal trajectory will always reach a stationary state where the number of employees is constant. The location of the stationary point and the exact shape of the optimal trajectory of course depend on exogenous parameters. If the number of employees is initially lower than that of the stationary optimum the firm will set a wage rate higher than the market average in order to attract workers. The greater the discrepancy between the stationary number of employees and the initial one, the higher the relative wage rate will be. But the firm will not adjust immediately. To do so would mean excessively high costs in the form of an extremely high initial wage rate. The firm instead balances current costs against future revenues, the latter being represented by a large stock of employees. The higher the real rate of interest, the less are discounted future revenues, and the slower the adjustment process will be. Also, the firm's relative wage rate will then be lower.

Having derived the behavior functions for the individual workers and firms, Mortensen aggregates the functions. The result may be summarized in the following way:

The change in the unemployment rate, $\underline{\dot{u}}$, depends positively on the flow of new vintages of workers entering the labor market and negatively on the aggregate acceptance rate - the offered wage rate in comparison to the expected average wage rate, which would induce an unemployed worker to accept employment, or which would induce an employee to leave his employment if the wage rate should fall under this level. Furthermore, the acceptance rate depends positively on the differences in the possible intensity of search activity when unemployed as compared with when employed, and negatively on the difference between the actual rate of wage inflation and the expected one. The first conclusion is self-evident. The second needs an explanation. A higher rate of wage inflation than the expected one will make workers confuse a good wage offer on account of getting into contact with a firm on the upper end of the wage distribution for an unexpected shift upwards of the wage distribution.[1] The longer it takes for workers to observe that a shift of the wage distribution has occurred, the more important this difference between actual and expected wage inflation will be.

This lag plays a central role in the analysis. Having observed the average wage rate at time $t-h$, the workers estimate the average wage rate at time t. This is done by adding the expected wage inflation to the average wage rate at time $t-h$. The higher the actual wage inflation is in comparison to the expected one and the longer the observation lag, the more likely the workers are to confuse a shift in the wage distribution and a wandering along the wage distribution. A long observation lag will then increase employment via a lower acceptance rate. Moreover, the larger the spread between the differnt firms' wage offers (a larger variance of the wage distribution), the lower the acceptance rate will be. It appears from the above discussion that the rate of unemployment is determined from the supply side, even if it is affected by the behavior of firms via the wage structure and the change in this structure over time.

Wage inflation depends additively on price inflation and a term which has to do with the wage policy of firms. The higher the number of employees, the lower this latter wage inflation term will be. As pointed out above, the greater the number of workers in a firm, the smaller the inducements that will be required to increase that number through a high relative wage rate. The wage inflation also depends positively on the inverse of the real wage. The lower the real wage, the higher the stationary state employment level of the individual firms will be, and the more workers they will want to acquire by keeping a high relative wage rate. In addition, wage inflation is negatively affected by the level of the market rate of interest. In the model, this has nothing to do with a high interest rate causing a low demand pressure on the goods markets and, consequently, a low derived demand for workers. Rather, it has to do with the intertemporal planning

---

[1] This expectations mechanism constitutes the core of an early (the earliest?) attempt to justify the Phillips curve on the basis of search theory; cf. Alchian (1969).

of the firms. A higher interest rate will mean that a rapid expansion of employment will be expensive. The firms will not then try to maintain a high relative wage rate. Finally, the rate of wage inflation depends negatively on the length of the observation lag discussed above. The longer this lag, the lower the relative wages needed to get a certain increase in the number of employees.

To show that Mortensen's model generates a Phillips curve we will now trace the transition from one rate of inflation to another. Assume that for a long time there has been a rate of inflation completely expected by firms and employees. Price inflation has been equal to wage inflation, and thus the average real wage rate has been constant, as has the rate of unemployment.

Now, let an increased demand for goods and services accelerate price increases. This means that if prices increase relative to the wage rates of the firms, they will wish to expand production and increase the number of their employees. The stationary-state number of employees will then exceed the present employment level, so that firms will increase relative wages to attract more workers. The quicker firms plan to adjust to the higher level of production and, concomitantly, increase the number of their employees, the higher the wage levels of individual firms will have to be in comparison to the expected average wage level. This further implies that the more rapid the decrease of the unemployment rate, the greater the rate of wage inflation will be.

When, after a time, firms have acquired the long-run desired number of employees, wage increases will fall and stabilize at a level appropriate to the lower level of unemployment. The reason for the lower rate of unemployment after the transition to the new, higher stationary level of inflation is that the rate of inflation expected by the workers is still at the original level. The observation lag is also important. The workers are continuously being cheated, believing that they are receiving better relative wage offers than they are actually given. Instead, average wage increases will be faster than expected. Mortensen's model is thus capable of generating both the Phillips curve and the counter-clockwise rotations around it.

However, in the long run there is no trade-off between unemployment and inflation. The reason unemployment is pushed down in the story above is that expectations are consistently wrong. Expectations of inflation are too low, If expectations adjust to the actual rate of inflation, unemployment will increase again to the "natural rate of unemployment".

Mortensen also discusses the factors influencing this "natural rate". It depends positively on the flow of new workers to the market and on the differential efficiency of searching while unemployed as compared to that while employed.

An interesting implication of Mortensen's and Phelps' analysis of the relation between unemployment and the wage inflation process is that the relation between demand-pull and cost-push inflation is illuminated from an entirely new point of view.[1)] From the point of view of the new theory of inflation, changes of demand both reduce unemployment and widen the gap between the actual and expected rates of inflation. This movement along the short-run Phillips curve can be said to be the result of demand-pull inflation. When expectations of inflation are later affected in a positive direction, the aspiration wages of job seekers will rise. They compensate themselves, so to speak, for the higher expected rate of inflation, and firms must raise their wages at a faster rate in order for a given level of employment to be maintained. One can therefore say that the cost element in the new theory of inflation comes in through inflationary expectations. A higher expected rate of inflation implies an upward shift of the short-run Phillips curve. Therefore, for every level of demand, one obtains a higher actual rate of wage increase or, given the actual rate of inflation, a higher level of unemployment than before. The only way to reduce the rate of inflation in the long run is to restrain the "cost element" through reducing inflationary expectations. This can take

1) Neither Phelps nor Mortensen discusses the question of the relation between demand-pull and cost-push inflation explicitly.

place through a long-term restrictive demand policy, with its associated higher unemployment and lower demand-pull inflation. There is a clear connection between the above argument and Arrow's discussion of the relation between demand-pull and cost-push inflation.[1] Arrow emphasizes that the term demand-pull inflation describes foremost the way in which the inflationary process is started, while the term cost-push inflation has to do with the mechanism which generates a continuing inflationary process.

4.6. Some problems with the Phillips-curve analysis

The contributions which were presented in the preceding pages together constitute a large step along the way to an integrated theory of inflation and unemployment. The fact that the macroeconomic theory is based on relevant microeconomic theory implies also that it rests on a significantly more stable foundation than the earlier theory of inflation and unemployment. But there are naturally weaknesses. In part these are connected with the fact that the new theory of inflation and unemployment is still relatively young. For example, it has not reached the level of acceptance which the "older" theory of inflation received through many institutional investigations. One thing which is striking is that the new theory contains so little discussion of the role of labor organizations in the inflationary process.[2] Another example of a "childhood disease" is that the macroeconomic analyses were worked out before the new microeconomic theory achieved any comparable degree of acceptance. None of the three derivations of the Phillips curve which were presented above builds on a rigorous investigation of the behavior of unemployed workers on the basis of preference theory.[3]

---

1) Arrow (1959), p. 50.

2) Holt (1970) contains, however, a discussion of the role of labor unions in the wage inflation process during different phases of the business cycle.

3) Dale Mortensen was the first who carried out this task; cf. Mortensen (1970b).

Perhaps a more serious problem is that the theory presented only covers the labor market. A theory of inflation worth the name should obviously explain the relation between the development of inflation in the commodity and factor markets. While the effect of the inflation rate on wages is discussed in the analyses of Phelps and Mortensen, the rate of inflation in the goods market is assumed exogenously given. A principal objective of the following chapters is precisely to build, on the basis of relevant microeconomic theory, a model of inflation and unemployment which simultaneously explains the development in the goods and labor markets.[1)]

A further problem in the way of using the analyses of the Phillips curve as an explanation of the development of inflation is that the models are real; the market for liabilities is unrepresented, just as is the goods market. Behind long-run equilibrium inflation lie assumptions concerning a continued expansion of nominal demand in the goods and factor markets. Since the real value of financial assets is affect by the inflationary process, and can in turn influence demand in the goods and factor markets, the analysis must be filled out with a discussion of the mechanism which results in an expansion of the nominal holdings of liabilities of households and firms which is parallel to the course of inflation.[2)]

Both Phelps' and Mortensen's models have the property that it is the difference between the actual and expected rate of increase of wages which affects (or is affected by) unemployment. The system is at rest when the actual rate of inflation agrees with the expected rate. This in turn implies that the level of unemployment which is achieved when the actual rate of inflation is equal to the expected is not

---

1) A parallel relationship existed for the "older" theory of inflation, which prior to 1951 only described the development of inflation in the goods market. Bent Hansen´s A Study in the Theory of Inflation constitutes the first theoretical study of the interplay between the course of inflation in different markets.

2) The question of integration between the "new" macroeconomic theory and monetary theory has also been raised by Brunner and Meltzer´s analysis of the role of money as a medium of exchange. There they use the "new" microeconomics to justify the existence of money. Cf. Brunner and Meltzer (1971).

affected by inflation. This unemployment, "the natural rate of unemployment", can be achieved at any rate of inflation. Thus with completely anticipated inflation, the Phillips curve is vertical. The assumption of a long-run vertical Phillips curve has been criticized from various points of departure.

Assume that the expected rate of inflation has agreed with the actual rate for a long time. Later the actual rate increases, for example as a result of expansive fiscal policy. Unemployment falls in accordance with the short-run Phillips curve. But afterwards inflationary expectations are adjusted to the higher actual rate of inflation, and unemployment rises again to the "natural rate of unemployment".[1] Now *temporary* reduction of unemployment can have permanent effects. Groups which have difficulties getting ahead in the labor market can be provided employment through temporary reductions in employers' minimum requirements for those they wish to employ. During this time they accumulate practical experience which, together with the knowledge which the employers obtain about these employees,[2] implies permanent increases in the rate of employment.[3]

This argument has been used to support the view that the long-run Phillips curve also has a negative slope, so that the hypothesis of the "natural rate of unemployment" is not fulfilled in reality. However, the argument is erroneous. Even if temporary increases in employment have permanent effects, this

---

1) This implies that the short-run Phillips curve is shifted parallel and upwards by as much as the expectations of inflation have increased.

2) The argument rests basically on the occurrence of statistical discrimination; *cf*. Phelps (1971), pp. 25-27. The employers do not know the properties of the job applicants, and it is costly for them to increase their information about the job applicants (*i.e.*, the employers' intensive search activity is costly). In the recruitment process rules of thumb are therefore used in selection, such as age, sex, and marriage status. This implies, however, that many job applicants are "unjustly" treated. For given outer observable characteristics, they have higher productivity than the average for the group. But during a period of employment, the employers will automatically get more certain information about their properties, which tends permanently to improve their employment possibilities and conditions.

3) *Cf*. Rees (1970), Gayer and Goldfarb (1972), and Tobin (1972).

does not imply that the long-run Phillips curve has negative slope. Instead, what one has shown is that the parameters which determine the natural rate of unemployment have been changed so that the Phillips curve has been shifted. The natural rate of unemployment thus depends on the historical course of inflation and employment. In order to be able to speak of a negatively sloping long-run Phillips curve, it is required that unemployment in long-run equilibrium varies with the (actual and expected) inflation rate. The central question is whether the level of a completely anticipated rate of inflation affects relative prices and quantities in the long-run equilibrium solution. One possibility which has been discussed relatively extensively in this context is that the cost of holding cash is higher the higher the expected rate of inflation.[1] If for various reasons it is impossible to make money bear interest, the higher actual and expected rate of inflation implies that the real rate of return on cash declines, which will affect the behavior of firms and households in various respects. Furthermore, the higher rate of inflation can be seen as a tax on real cash holdings. For a public sector of a given size, this tax reduces the need for other taxes. In other words, the higher rate of equilibrium inflation implies that the taxation system will be changed. Both of these arguments imply that the parameters of the economic system are being changed and thus that the endogenously determined variables are being affected. In particular, we cannot merely assume that the equilibrium unemployment is unaffected by changes in a completely anticipated rate of inflation.[2]

Inflationary expectations play an important role in the new theory of inflation and unemployment. The difference between the actual and expected rates of increase of wages is the strategic variable in the analysis of the development of unemployment. Erroneous expectations concerning the wage

---

1) Kessel and Alchian (1962), Phelps (1965), and Friedman (1969).

2) Cf. Phelps (1972), pp. 52-57.

distribution affect, through the behavior of job seekers, the time derivative of unemployment. But erroneous expectations are also an important explanatory variable on the part of firms. It is precisely the individual firm's attempt to increase its recruitment by raising its wage rate in relation to the other firms which, in the presence of given inflationary expectations, creates the difference between the actual and expected rate of inflation. An individual firm may raise its relative wage, but that is not possible for the firms as a group.

An immediate problem concerns inflationary expectations with respect to what? The new theory of the Phillips curve is still a partial theory of the labor market. Inflationary expectations thus concern the expected rate of increase of wages. In a fully developed inflation theory which takes account of the interplay between the course of inflation in different markets, it is naturally important to distinguish between expectations of price increases in different markets. For example, what is the significance of the expectations of real wage increases connected with the course of economic growth for the inflationary process?

But even if one restricts the analysis to a single market, e.g., the labor market, the question of inflationary expectations is hardly free of difficulties. In the new theory the inflationary expectations are "single valued". Differences of actual and expected inflation rates imply revisions of the expectations, but these are still single valued. The natural point of departure for a more general analysis is that neither households nor firms have complete information about the parameters of the wage distribution and about the future course of inflation. Instead, expectations with respect to the parameters of the wage distribution may be represented by a multivariate probability distribution.[1] If in particular we assume that the wage distribution is and is expected to be constant over time except for the inflation factor (i.e., all wage rates in the distribution are changed by the inflation

---

1) Cf. Werin (1974)

rate) and furthermore that its parameters are known at the initial point of time, the difficulty of an unknown wage distribution still remains. While the distribution is known at the instant of time when plans are made, if the rate of inflation is unknown so that inflationary expectations are described by a probability distribution, this automatically implies uncertainty with respect to the shape of the future wage distribution. And the future wage distribution is also important for the economic subjects, since their expectations of it affect their intertemporal planning.

The hypothesis of a vertical long-run Phillips curve is based on the premise that inflationary expectations are adjusted to the actual rate of inflation. That is why a permanent increase in the rate of inflation only reduces unemployment temporarily. In this context one usually assumes that households and firms have subjectively certain expectations with respect to the rate of inflation,[1)] that observed discrepancies between actual and expected inflation rates call forth revisions of the inflationary expectations, but that the observation that expectations were erroneous does not effect the subjective certainty concerning the correctness of the inflationary expectations.

A common assumption is that inflationary expectations are a weighted average of all earlier actual rates of inflation, where the weights decline geometrically (exponentially if time is continuous) with the length of the time lag.[2)] This mechanism implies that the change of the inflationary expectations is proportional to the difference between the actual and expected rates of inflation.[3)] John Muth[4)] has shown that this type of

---

1) The wage distribution is also assumed to be known with subjective certainty.

2) Cf. Cagan (1956), pp. 37-41; Phelps (1967), p. 263; Mortensen (1970a), pp. 210-211; Phelps (1972), pp. 43-49; and also the discussion in chapter VI, below.

3) If time varies continuously, one obtains the result that the derivative of inflationary expectations with respect to time is equal to a constant times the difference between the actual and expected rates of inflation. Note the similarity to the capital-stock-adjustment mechanism, which also builds on an assumption of exponentially distributed lags; cf. Allen (1959), pp. 166-168.

4) Muth (1960); cf. also Muth (1961).

expectation is rational in the sense that the expected rate of inflation constitutes the best estimator for the actual rate of inflation if the actual rate is generated by a stochastic process with a serially correlated random term. The weighting mechanism for earlier observations of the rate of inflation is thus obviously connected with how quickly the effect of a random disturbance dissipates over time.

Muth's result implies conditional support for the stipulated expectation mechanism. However, the fundamental question is evidently whether the observations really are generated by a stochastic process of this type.[1] The problem can be illustrated in the following way. Assume that the authorities attempt to reduce unemployment by pursuing an inflationary policy. Unemployment sinks under the natural rate of unemployment, and the actual rate of inflation exceeds the expected. In order for this situation to persist, the actual rate of inflation must accelerate at an even rate, since inflationary expectations are successively adjusted to the higher rate of inflation. However, it is reasonable to assume that firms' and households' expectations will later be affected by the acceleration in the rate of inflation. We can then imagine that the time derivative of the expected acceleration depends proportionally on the difference between the actual and expected acceleration in the rate of inflation. Thus the authorities must continually increase the acceleration in the rate of inflation in order to preserve a given difference between the actual and natural rates of unemployment. Later, however, firms and households learn that the rate of acceleration is increasing, which in turn...[2]

The existence of adaptive expectations of inflation involves an interesting consequence for the dynamic relation between inflation and unemployment. Assume that the short-run Phillips curve describes the difference between actual and expected rates of inflation as a negative function of unemployment. Furthermore, if the time derivative for the expected rate of inflation is a positive function of the

---

[1] This is also emphasized by Muth; cf. Muth (1960), p. 299.

[2] Cf. Gordon and Hynes (1970), pp. 387-389.

difference between the actual and expected rates of inflation, one can show that changes in the level of the actual rate of inflation not only produce parallel shifts of the short-run Phillips curve, but also clockwise oscillations around it.[1] The analytical derivations discussed above implied, among other things, the counterclockwise loop around the curve which has been observed empirically.[2] If we now combine these dynamic systems with another differential equation which describes the development of inflationary expectations over time, we can neither expect that the Phillips curve is stable nor that the short-run dynamic development exactly follows the postulated laws of movement. The introduction of adaptive expectations constitutes as example of the complications which a change in the model specification always involves.

Holt's and Phelps' derivations of the Phillips curve can both be criticized for not paying sufficient attention to the interaction between the behavior of households and firms in the labor market. While both sides are represented in Mortensen's analysis in the sense that the time derivatives of the rate of unemployment and wages are endogenously determined, the wage distribution is nevertheless assumed given. It is changed only through the "scale shifting" which the rate of wage increase involves. In a complete theory both the equilibrium wage distribution and the development of the wage distribution over time should be determined endogenously. It is likely that the form of the wage distribution is changed during a non-anticipated wage-inflation process and that this change of the functional form plays an important role for the course of events. The question is important not least for the reason that households and firms do not have certain knowledge about the parameters of the wage distribution. A disturbance which leads to a non-anticipated inflation will in general affect different parts of the labor market in different ways, which affects the shape of the wage distribution. This implies that the information which one earlier had concerning the functional form becomes obsolete, so that there arise further

---

1) Phelps (1972), pp. 43-49, Grossman (1974b).

2) Phillips (1958).

sources of error in the decision basis, besides those caused by mistaken expectations concerning the initial location of the wage distribution. But this factor also creates a stronger motive for collecting information about the parameters of the wage distribution. However, it should be emphasized that this desire for realism leads to a very great increase in the complexity of the problem. In actual practice it is likely that a good deal more time will be required before anyone even succeeds in solving for the equilibrium wage distribution in a satisfactory way. The assumption of a (relatively) stable wage distribution can also be justified by noting that the distribution's functional form is changed significantly less than its location and that it therefore can be a reasonable approximation to assume that the functional form is constant. The problem, however, is that it is impossible to clarify the adequacy of this argument before one has carried out the general analysis.[1)]

The analysis of the relation between inflation and unemployment which has led to the analytical derivations of the Phillips curve has its strength -- but also its weakness -- in the assumption of equilibrium. The natural rate of unemployment is, like the completely expected rate of increase of wages, an equilibrium phenomenon. Unemployment in the presence of equilibrium expectations is connected with those search processes which continually take place in the labor market and which are extremely dependent on the heterogeneity of jobs and workers in combination with the continual in- and outflows to and from the labor force.[2)] Unemployment is

1) In the following chapters it is assumed that firms and households take the wage and price distributions to be stable. Possible changes in the functional forms of the distributions are not discussed.

2) "Voluntary" unemployment has also been discussed under the headings of speculative unemployment (as a result of the intertemporal distribution of leisure, one chooses to be unemployed if one believes that the real wage is temporarily low), wait-unemployment (if the demand for services varies stochastically, it is advantageous to be able to stand ready for the next assignment; this is the case for lawyers and other independent professionals), queue-unemployment (one waits for employment which one knows for sure will turn up; the situation arises, for example, in connection with temporary layoffs and has great similarities to "wait-unemployment"); cf. Phelps (1972), chapter I.

"voluntary" in the sense that, given the environment of the unemployed workers, they will only accept job offers which meet a certain minimum standard. Unemployment is productive; it constitutes an investment in a better future job for the job seeker. For society at large it constitutes an investment in a better future allocation of the labor force among different jobs.[1)]

The element of "involuntary" unemployment comes into the analysis principally through erroneous expectations on the part of the job seeker. Discrepancies between actual and expected rates of wage increase generate variations in unemployment, since unemployed workers' minimum requirements for accepting job offers are based on erroneous expectations. Disequilibrium, which in the traditional theory is the central force in the inflationary process and the explanation of cyclical and structural unemployment, plays a much less prominent role in the "new" theory: it is manifested through erroneous expectations.

The final verdict can be made less severe, however. In the first place firms' supply of information in the labor market (e.g., through job advertisements) has great significance for the frequency of contact and thus the probability of employment for an individual unemployed worker. The firm's supply of information has a natural place in the new theory, and even if this aspect of its behavior has not played any central role heretofore, it nevertheless shows that the function of firms in the employment process is not limited to setting a wage sufficiently high that the job seekers accept the offer of employment.[2)] In the second place, if one takes note of the heterogeneity of the job seekers and also of the fact that firms stipulate minimum employment requirements which vary over the business cycle, then the step to

---

1) This is one of the main arguments in Alchian (1969).

2) To the degree that the number of vacancies can be regarded as a proxy for firms´ supplies of information in the labor market, this problem is treated in Phelps (1970). In chapter V below is treated not only the firm´s wage policy, but also its information policy.

"involuntary" unemployment is not so great.[1] Despite these modifications, however, something essential is still missing in the new, integrated theory of inflation and unemployment. Involuntary unemployment, rationing, quantity adjustments, and multiplier processes have not, at least heretofore, constituted central elements in the type of macroeconomic theory which has been presented in this section. These phenomena have become much more prominent in the directions of research which are perhaps most associated with the names of Clower, Patinkin, Leijonhufvud, Barro, and Grossman.

5. The Market Process as a Costly Coordination Mechanism: Quantity Adjustments and the Collapse of the Price System as an Information Mechanism

A common feature of the macroeconomic theory which was presented in the preceding section was the attempt to derive macroeconomic relations on the basis of the behavior of individual firms and households. Optimization theory was taken as the point of departure for explaining behavior, but the economic subjects were assumed to optimize in an environment different from the neoclassical. Incomplete comprehension of markets and costs for collecting information led to behavior different from that in perfect markets. The class of macroeconomic theories which are treated in the following pages also explicitly assumes rational behavior of individual firms and households in an environment which differs from the neoclassical, but here the choice instruments are further restricted, not by search and information costs, but by quantity and rationing constraints. However, not only the assumptions but also the objectives of the two types of macroeconomic theory differ; one major (attempted) result of the preceding analysis was the derivation of the Phillips curve, while the

---

1) Cf. the discussion in section 2, above. Changes in firms´ minimum requirements for those they wish to employ play a very important role in Mortensen´s analysis of the Phillips curve in Mortensen (1970b).

objektive is now to give a microtheoretic justification for multiplier processes.

5.1. Microtheoretic foundations for the multiplier and accelerator mechanisms

Keynes' General Theory not only involved the breakthrough for a theory of employment with a high predictive ability; it also created a theoretical gap between micro- and macroeconomic theory. Even if pre-Keynesian macroeconomic theory, the quantity theory, was not adequately integrated with price theory,[1] the Keynesian breakthrough sharpened the problem still further: economic reality was described by two completely separate theories, of which the first achieved coordination of the plans of economic subjects through the price system, and the second through the "quantity system". Leijonhufvud has described the Keynesian system as involving a reversal of the assumptions of adjustment speeds for price and quantity changes.[2]

Naturally, the problem of two separate theoretical systems disturbed economists. A widespread debate concerning the relation between Keynes and "the classics" was started by Hicks.[3] But twenty years went by before the first really fundamental contribution came in the form of Patinkin's discussion of involuntary unemployment.[4]

Patinkin emphasized that the absence of immediate adjustment of the price system in connection with a disturbance

---

1) Cf. Patinkin´s discussion of the classical dichotomy in Patinkin (1965), chapter VIII. Cf. also Lindbeck (1961).

2) Leijonhufvud (1968). In neoclassical theory (specifically, in Marshall´s version) a disturbance leads immediately to a new (momentary) equilibrium through a change of price. The quantity adjustment takes place more slowly, first in the "short run" and to a more pronounced extent in the "long run". In the Keynesian theory quantity adjustments take place faster than price adjustments. In static Keynesian theory it is assumed that the quantity adjustment takes place immediately.

3) Hicks (1937). Garner Ackley´s Macroeconomic Theory marks the end of the "traditional" discussion of the relationship between Keynes and the neoclassicals.

4) Patinkin (1956, 1965).

leads to the result that the economic subject's planning situation is not the same as it is in equilibrium. There are further constraints in addition to the budget constraint, and it is precisely these which constitute the "involuntariness".[1)]

Thus Keynesian theory need not be incompatible with the neoclassical analysis. In the former case one investigates the situation outside of equilibrium, while the latter case restricts itself to the study of equilibrium states. This relationship is illustrated by Patinkin's discussion of how reduced demand in the goods market is transfered through the economic system.[2)] If prices are not immediately adjusted, firms will not be able to sell all of their production. For a given system of prices, they do not maximize profit any longer through determining inputs and outputs so that the marginal productivity of labor is equal to the real wage. Instead, production is cut back until it is equal to sales. Profit is maximized if the firms' demand for labor is adjusted to the lower volume of production. The new feature of this situation is thus that the firms, which even outside of equilibrium are assumed to take the system of prices as given, now adjust their planning to the constraint on sales. This results in a spill-over effect in the labor market. The real wage is thus no longer bound to the marginal product of labor. It is only in equilibrium that this is the necessary consequence of profit maximization by firms in perfect competition. In disequilibrium there arise new constraints for the firms' planning, which in turn affect the optimal solution and thus the values of their instruments.

The next step in the discussion of the relationship between Keynesian and neoclassical theory was taken in

---

1) Cf. Patinkin (1965), pp. 313-314 for an extraordinarily clear discussion of this point. Patinkin emphasizes, among other things, that the involuntariness does not imply that one acts irrationally. Households and firms continue to optimize, but the constraints which they must observe are different in equilibrium and disequilibrium. In the latter case the choice space is reduced by more constraints.

2) Patinkin (1965), chapter XIII.

Clower's analysis of the consumption function.[1] An important point of departure for Clower is that while the arguments in the behavioral equations of economic subjects are only prices in the neoclassical theory, in the Keynesian theory quantities also appear as arguments.[2] Clower then shows that the neoclassical consumption theory is a special case of the Keynesian theory. In the former case households plan with the budget equation as the only constraint, but in the latter case there occur quantitative constraints on factor supplies. These constraints -- the real incomes of households -- affect the optimal solution for the households' planning problem and thus are arguments in the behavioral equations. Changes in consumption can therefore be seen as spill-over effects from the labor market to the goods market.

The existence of quantities as arguments in the behavioral equations implies that transactions actually carried out will affect behavior.[3] This in turn implies that offers to buy and sell do not any longer reflect with certainty the demand and supply relationships which, given the prevailing system of prices, would apply in equilibrium.[4] Price movements thus do not depend any longer on the hypothetical supply and demand

---

1) Clower (1965).

2) One can naturally object that external effects imply that quantities are arguments in the behavioral equations. Peter Bohm has pointed out the formal similarity between external effects (in production) and rationing constraints in the case that the price in a market lies over the equilibrium price so that firms do not have the possibility of selling the quantity which would maximize profit at the prevailing price. *Cf*. Bohm (1964), p. 18.

3) *Cf*. the discussion of the *non-tâtonnement* mechanism in section 2.

4) Given a prevailing general equilibrium, the behavioral equations are often called the *nominal* supply and demand equations. In the presence of disequilibrium in one or more of the submarkets of the system, the behavioral equations are termed the *effective* supply and demand equations. The nominal behavior equations contain (if we abstract from external effects) only prices as endogenously determined arguments. The effective behavioral equations contain quantities in addition to prices as endogenously determined arguments.

relations in equilibrium, but on the effective excess demands which are a result of the optimizing behavior of economic subjects <u>given</u> the rationing constraints; the information which the price system transmits is distorted.

Patinkin's analysis of how an excess supply in the goods market results in an effective demand which is lower than the nominal demand in the labor market and Clower's analysis of how an excess supply in the labor market results in a level of effective demand which is lower than nominal demand in the goods market are both partial disequilibrium analyses. An excess supply in the goods market which spills over in the labor market and results in lower employment will, however, in turn react back on the goods market. The multiplier process constitutes precisely a study of the interdependence between markets in disequilibrium and thus implies a step from partial to general disequilibrium analysis. Barro and Grossman have carried out this generalization of Patinkin's and Clower's analyses.[1] They have thus studied the system's equilibrium solution both for the case of general excess supply and for the case of general excess demand.

The analysis of Barro and Grossman has several interesting implications. In the first place, further emphasis is given to Patinkin's conclusion that involuntary unemployment and general excess supply do not imply incorrect relative prices and in particular an incorrect real wage. The real wage may very well have its general equilibrium value. The important point is that absolute prices (in Patinkin's termonology, monetary prices) are incorrect. In an economy with only one financial asset, cash, excessively high prices will result in a general excess supply.[2] while excessively low prices will result in a general excess demand. Absolute prices which are too high imply an excess demand for real

---

1) Barro and Grossman (1971).

2) This implies that <u>nominal</u> excess supply prevails in the goods and factor markets. This corresponds to a <u>nominal</u> excess demand for real cash balances.

cash balances. If the absolute prices are not immediately adjusted to their new equilibrium, this will result in an excess supply in the goods market when households attempt to cut back their consumption in order to increase their cash balances. This leads in turn to an excess supply in the labor market when firms must cut back their production, and the reduced demand for goods spills over in the labor market.

For a given set of prices, the equilibrium solution becomes a solution in quantities. One seeks those values of production and factor inputs which clear the goods and labor markets with respect to the feedbacks which both spill-over effects represent. If one interprets the concept of equilibrium as forces in balance, the notion of a Keynesian equilibrium does not constitute a terminological departure. At the same time, however, it is clear that this usage emphasizes the relativeness in the equilibrium concept. We can speak of a hierarchy of equilibrium concepts in which the rank depends on the number of constraints which are assumed to be satisfied.[1)] These constraints imply that certain forces are not allowed to operate on the system. Keynesian equilibrium thus implies that a constraint is put on the rates of change of absolute prices. Given this constraint, the system is in equilibrium in the sense that the spill-over effects have assumed their stationary values. There are no tendencies for spill-over effects from the goods market to the labor market, or _vice versa_, to increase or decrease. Furthermore, in the goods market the _effective_ excess demand equals zero. In the labor market there prevails an effective excess supply which corresponds to an effective excess demand for real cash balances.[2)]

---

1) A corresponding hierarchy also holds in the analysis of the long-run planning of households and firms. Thus, for example, in the short run a firm cannot alter its scale, while this is possible in the long run. Cf. Söderström (1974).

2) The question of whether Walras´ Law applies outside of general equilibrium has been discussed by, among others, Clower (1965) and Leijonhufvud (1968). It should be clear that the answer depends on the precise definition of Walras´ Law.

It is the usual multiplier process which has been sketched above. An interesting symmetry which Barro and Grossman point out is that even in the presence of general excess demand there occur quantity constraints, but now from the supply side. If households cannot buy the quantity of goods and services stated by the nominal demand equations, the unsatisfied demand will spill over into the labor market in the form of a lower effective factor supply and into the money market (if there is only one type of financial asset) in the form of an increased demand for real money balances in order to make possible a higher level of consumption later on.[1] The more the unsatisfied demand for consumption goods leads to reduced supply of factors, the lower production will be. This makes the effective excess demand in the goods market increase still more, which in turn spills over into the labor market. We have here an additional example of the multiplier mechanism, though it now operates on the supply side, while the usual multiplier is a demand multiplier. The greater the inclination to increase leisure (instead of increasing saving) when one cannot satisfy the demand for consumption goods at prevailing prices, the larger the supply multiplier will be.[2]

The existence of a multiplier mechanism in the presence of general excess demand means, among other things, that national income is maximized at the point of full employment. In the presence of general excess supply, production is held back as a result of insufficient supply in the factor

---

1) Donald Tucker has expressed this in the following way: "If a consumer finds that he is unable to buy today the new dishwasher he wants, then he is likely to decide to invest the money in a bond instead, in order to earn some interest income until dishwashers are available again. Or he may decide to work fewer hours on his job and take more leisure if he feels that there is no point in earning money which he cannot spend. In either case his offers to buy or sell other commodities are different from what they would have been if he had not encountered the constraint in the goods market. His effective demands are different in magnitude from his unconstrained demands." Tucker (1971), pp. 62-63.

2) The theory of the supply multiplier is developed in more detail in Barro and Grossman (1974).

markets.[1)]

The study of the behavior of households and firms in the presence of constraints created by disequilibrium has not only made possible a preference-theoretic justification for the multiplier, but for the accelerator as well. The common objection to the accelerator theory is that no theory of choice lies behind it. The assumption that output (or the quantity demanded) is exogenously given can obviously find no place in neoclassical theory. However, Grossman has shown that it is sufficient to introduce an assumption that the goods market is not in equilibrium in order that the accelerator theory be consistent with the neoclassical theory for profit maximizing firms.

Grossman has calculated the optimal paths for an individual firm's capital accumulation for both the case in which there is equilibrium in the goods market and the case in which there is excess supply involving a constraint on the firm's sales possibilities. An important restriction is that the actual capital stock in both cases is less than the stationary optimum level. With static expectations -- i.e., expectations of a given constant level of sales -- an increase in the time derivative of sales will have no immediate effect on the firm's investment. However, the effect is built up gradually, and as time tends to infinity, the accelerator relation is obtained. With extrapolative expectations -- i.e., expectations of a given constant percentage rate of increase of sales -- an immediate accelerator effect is obtained which is identical to the asymptotical accelerator in the static expectations case. From this point of view, fast capital adjustment with static expectations has the same implication as extrapolative expectations.

Grossman's result is interesting, but it builds on highly restrictive assumptions. The capital stock is assumed not to wear out, and the theory therefore functions only for the case

---

1) Here there is an interesting parallel to the discussion in the 1940's and 1950's concerning the disorganizational phenomena which are created, among other places, in the labor market as a result of an inflationary gap; cf., e.g. Meidner (1954) and Lindbeck (1968), chapter 3 för surveys of the Swedish debate. The same kind of idea was naturally discussed in a number of other countries.

in which the steady state capital stock is larger than the initial capital stock. This is naturally problematic if one wishes to study the course of investment during a deep recession when firms perhaps plan to reduce the capital stock over time. On the other hand, if one regards a recession as merely an occasional movement around a growth trend, it is naturally not so problematic to abstract from depreciation.

Spill-over effects can be seen as the reaction of rational economic subjects to disquilibrium and its related quantity constraints in certain markets. They give not only a preference-theoretic justification for the multiplier and accelerator, but also throw light on the "Keynesian" controversy concerning the extent to which the rate of interest is determined in the money market (the liquidity-preference theory) or in the bond market (the loanable-funds theory). If one assumes that disequilibrium generates spill-over effects so that the effective excess demands differ from the nominal, and that it is effective excess demands which cause price changes, then one can justify the liquidity-preference theory in the following way. Assume that a nominal excess demand arises in the money market.[1)] If this spills over into the bond market so that an effective excess supply is created there, one can say in a certain sense that it is an excess demand for money which drives up the interest rate. Which theory of interest is valid (or more precisely, how large a

---

1) If we interpret Walras´ Law as a consistency condition for the plans of the economic subjects, i.e. fulfillment of the budget equations, this implies that the sum of all the nominal, aggregated monetary excess demands in all markets is equal to zero. Similarly, the sum over all markets of the monetary effective excess demands is equal to zero. This implies in turn that the excess demand for money automatically corresponds to an identical monetary excess supply in one or more of the other markets in the economy. In this sense we can conceive of the excess demand for money corresponding to an identical excess supply of bonds. However, it is also possible according to Walras´ Law for compensating excess supplies to exist in another part of the economy (e.g., in one of the goods markets), so that disequilibrium in the money market and the other markets implies that the nominal excess demand for bonds differs from the effective excess demand. It is in this last sense that one usually employs the term "spill-over effect".

part of interest rate movements the theories explain) thus depends on what happens outside of equilibrium.[1)]

5.2. The theory of rationing and intertemporal spill-over effects

The preference-theoretic justification for spill-over effects makes it possible to derive them from consumption and production theory. The constraint on sales possibilities which an excess supply in the labor market creates can be thought of as a rationing constraint on the possible number of working hours for a household. The corresponding argument for an inflationary situation can of course be made with respect to an excess demand in the goods market(s), which involves a constraint on the purchasing possibilities of a household. The theory of rationing which was developed during the 1940's and 1950's is precisely a theory which explains how behavior (in the first place that of households) is affected by the existence of rationing constraints on the possibilities of purchase of one or more goods and services.[2)] The essential point is that one can show how behavior in the presence of rationing can be expressed in terms of behavior when rationing does not exist. Even if the theory of rationing was developed to explain the effects of administrative rationing in crisis situations, it is clear that its possibilities of use are not limited to these institutional relationships. The theory of rationing is applicable in all situations in which the economic subjects' possibilities of action are

---

1) These ideas are developed in more detail in Patinkin (1965), pp. 375-381 and Grossman (1971).

The existence of spill-over effects implies, among other things, that the structural equations of the economic system are not the same in equilibrium and disequilibrium. This in turn implies that econometric models should be specified with respect to which markets are in equilibrium, since otherwise the parameter estimates are not necessarily consistent. Cf. Tucker (1971), p. 81 and Fair and Jaffé (1972).

2) The two most important references are Samuelson (1961) and Tobin and Houthakker (1950-51). Tobin (1952) and Ysander (1974) contain excellent surveys of the theory of rationing.

limited by constraints in addition to the budget equation. However, it is important to make clear whether the differences in the apparatus of administrative rationing on the one hand and a more "decentralized" rationing on the other involve further consequences for the planning situation of the individual economic subjects. If they do, then apart from the complications created by rationing constraints, further aspects of the problem must be considered; these are discussed in more detail below.

The results of the theory of rationing can be summarized in the following way. First, there is a (local) tendency for demand to increase for goods which are substitutes and to decrease for goods which are complements for the rationed goods.[1)] However, the question is complicated by the fact that substitution and complementarity among the rationed goods affects the values of the spill-over effects.[2)] Inter-locally -- i.e., when the rationing constraints are strictly binding, and it is therefore a question of nonmarginal comparisons between behavior when certain goods and services are rationed and when they are not -- income effects are also of significance for the values of the spill-over effects.

The existence of binding rationing constraints will not, however, result only in shifts of the demand relations in markets where equilibrium prevails. Even the functional forms will be affected by the fact that the planning of households is now conditioned by binding rationing constraints in certain markets; specifically, both income and substitution effects are so affected.[3)]

Naturally, the altered behavior of firms as a consequence of the fact that certain of its instruments can no longer be varied freely can be expressed in terms of their behavior when

---

1) Tobin and Houthakker (1950-51) contains a derivation of the rationing or spill-over effects when only one good is rationed. The result for the general case with many rationed goods is derived in Siven (1969), pp. 36-41.

2) Cf. Siven (1969), pp. 40-41.

3) This was shown first in Tobin and Houthakker (1950-51).

these conditions do not apply. However, I am unaware of an investigation of this problem. Such an investigation could be very worthwhile, since it would also throw light on the firm's planning in the long and short runs.

The fact that the form of the demand and supply functions is changed as a result of (binding) rationing constraints means of course that the economic system's dynamic movement out of equilibrium will be more complicated than would be the case if notice were taken only of spill-over effects. For example, price changes will have effects other than those which occur when all markets are in equilibrium. There are thus interactions between price and quantity movements above and beyond those which are represented by the spill-over effects. These interactions have hertofore not been studied by anyone.

Besides the changes of the system's behavioral equations which are caused by the fact that individual firms and households react differently to price changes, for example, in equilibrium and disequilibrium, rationing in disequilibrium also raises a host of distributional effects. If the behavioral equations differ between households and between firms, or if the behavioral equations are identical but the parameter values differ between households and between firms, the aggregate supply and demand equations will be affected by the distribution of the rationing tickets.[1] In this context the essential point is not, for example, whether all households receive the same allocation of a good for which there is an excess demand, but rather the extent to which the alloted quantities and the quantities which would be desired in equilibrium differ between different households and firms. The occurrence of distributional effects in connection with disequilibrium caused by rationing underlines the importance of explaining the allotment principles endogenously.

The theory of rationing is a generalization of traditional consumption theory. An advantage of this is that the theory of rationing is built on a stable foundation of preference theory.

---

1) *Cf.* Gould and Henry (1967).

A disadvantage is that the theory of rationing has become altogether too "general". Its conclusions lie on a very abstract level. Now one can naturally object that this in itself is a great advantage and that more definite conclusions are possible as soon as one makes more specific assumptions with respect to the functional relations. For example, one can filter out the intertemporal aspect of the rationing situation through atemporal aggregation. In such a case the household is assumed to consume only one kind of commodity, and an occasional restriction of its consumption possibilities can thus lead to a lower supply of labor or a higher level of saving and thus higher future consumption. Barro and Grossman have carried out such an intertemporal analysis of the planning of households in the presence of excess demand in the goods market.[1] It is shown there that the expected length of the period of rationing is an important factor determining the spill-over effects. The shorter the unsatisfied consumption demand is expected to be, the greater will be its effect on saving (which increases), and the less will be its effect on the supply of labor. Therefore, if rationing is expected to be of short duration, the size of the supply multiplier will be small.

However, a problem with Barro and Grossman's analysis is that they assume fixed prices. It is reasonable to assume that the excess demand in the goods market is filled in by a process of price increases. If consumers also expect that the price level will advance at the same time that the scarcity situation ceases, then one must analyze the combined effects of rationing and price changes.[2] The theory of rationing is relevant for this purpose, since it also forms the basis for a study of the interaction between price and constraint

---

[1] Barro and Grossman (1974).

[2] A similar problem has been discussed in Tucker (1968). He has analyzed the effects of lags in interest rate changes in connection with a credit contraction and discussed the extent to which the initial sharpening of credit rationing (before the level of interest rates has had time to rise) increases or reduces the speed with which credit restrictiveness works.

changes. The theory of rationing really does not only give information as to how the unsatisfied demand spills over into other markets, but also as to how the functional relationships of the behavioral equations are affected. In Barro and Grossman's case this may be illustrated in the following way.

A result in the theory of rationing is that the absolute values of the own substitution effects --i.e., the substitution effect of the $i^{\underline{th}}$ good when its own price is changed -- declines with the number of binding constraints.[1] This implies, if we abstract from the changes in the size of the income effects which can occur as a result of rationing, that the absolute values of the price elasticities decline. This in turn implies that the effects of price increases will be less than would have been the case if the good had not been rationed in an initial period. The unsatisfied demand for consumption goods in the initial phase will thus reduce the price sensitivity of future consumption, which in turn makes necessary larger future price increases in order for an equilibrium to be created.

The intertemporal aspects of the spill-over mechanism are also naturally important in situations with general excess supply. This can be illustrated with Cross and Williamson's critique of Patinkin's analysis of involuntary unemployment.[2] They point out correctly that an excess supply in the goods market and the related reduction of firms' effective demand for labor are not compatible with the assumptions of perfect competition and quantity adjusting firms. Instead, Cross and Williamson assume that the firms' unsatisfied supply of goods leads to inventory increases which are financed by loans.[3] It should be clear that Cross

---

1) Cf. Samuelson´s "generalized Le Chatelier principle" in Samuelson (1961), pp. 36-39 and Siven (1969), pp. 41-43.

2) Cross and Williamson (1962).

3) Cross and Williamson point out that if Patinkin´s "bond-market imperfection" holds -- i.e., if firms cannot borrow an unrestricted quantity at a given rate of interest, but are bound to the amount which they can repay, then one can imagine that it is not possible for the firms to finance inventory accumulation to the necessary extent. In such a case Patinkin´s argument still holds. Cf. Cross and Williamson (1962), p. 79.

and Williams' criticism of Patinkin, that he introduces assumptions which are inconsistent with the assumption of perfect competition, also applies to themselves. While the assumption of non-intended inventory increases implies that firms continue to demand labor in accordance with the nominal demand curves, Cross and Williamson's assumption that inventory accumulation is financed by issues of bonds implies that the firms' effective supply of bonds will be larger than the nominal supply. Cross and Williamson have thus proposed a spill-over mechanism which is alternative to Patinkin's: instead of the unsatisfied goods supply leading to reduced effective demand for labor, they assume that the effective supply of bonds increases.

However, Cross and Williamson's critique of Patinkin draws attention to several interesting intertemporal aspects of spill-over effects. If firms are subject to a binding constraint on sales, and if we assume that the price is given from the outside, then they can in principle take two courses of action. They can either cut back production and reduce the effective demand for factors of production (Patinkin) or maintain the volume of production and let inventories increase (Cross and Williamson). They can also choose a middle course. It is impossible to say exactly what will take place without reference to the firms' intertemporal planning. What the firm chooses to do depends on its expectations of future sales possibilities and prices. If they believe, for example, that the price level will be unchanged and that the sales constraint in the goods market will later cease to apply, they will both cut back production <u>and</u> let inventories increase. The shorter the time the sales constraint is assumed to be binding and the lower the interest rate, the greater will be the spill-over effect in the bond market and the less that in the labor market, which leads to a lower demand multiplier. In actual practice the occurrence of a spill-over effect in the bond market (and the related, reduced spill-over effect in the labor market) will <u>always</u> lead to a lower demand multiplier compared to the traditional analysis. Just as saving constitutes a leakage via the spill-over effect from the labor market to the goods market, inventory accumulation involves a leakage via the spill-over effect from the goods market to the labor market. This leakage also reduces the size of the multiplier.

Now one can naturally maintain that it is not particularly likely that the firms will react to a reduction of demand with an accumulation of inventories. If firms believe that the shift of the demand function in the goods market is permanent, the excess supply will only be able to be reduced by a fall in price. This in turn implies that the expected (real) interest costs for holding inventories will rise.[1] But the point is precisely that the size of the spill-over effect should be judged in an analysis of the firm's intertemporal planning, since one has the possibility of investigating in that way which factors affect its size.

The intertemporal aspect of spill-over effects can also be discussed from the point of view of the reaction of households to an increase in involuntary unemployment. To what extent does a reduction of income lead to reduced consumption or reduced saving? If households expect that the reduction of income is temporary, and if there are no disadvantages associated with reducing financial assets or borrowing, it is likely that it is their permanent income, not the temporarily low income, which affects their consumption. On the other hand, if households' elasticity of expectations is so high that a reduction of income has a stong effect on expectations of income in future periods <u>or</u> if sales of financial assets take place only at unfavorable prices, and loans are expensive, then the marginal propensity to consume will be high and the multiplier large. The effect on expectations and the functioning of liabilities markets are clearly of decisive importance for the way an excess supply or demand

---

[1] Note that even in this case there occur interactions between the quantitative constraints and the effects of the emerging price changes.

will affect the other markets in the economy.[1)]

5.3. The "new" theory of the multiplier, problems and possibilities

In this section I will take up several problems in connection with the "new" theory of the multiplier. The word "problem" can be interpreted in many ways. In this case it is specifically a matter of a number of fundamental problems which heretofore have not received sufficient attention, and which must be taken up for a proper treatment before the new theory can be said to rest on a stable foundation.

The first question concerns whether the new theory of the multiplier is an equilibrium theory or not. If one interprets the concept of equilibrium so that it implies a balance of forces, one can say that the system is in equilibrium when there is no tendency toward changes in the size of the spill-over effects. But this interpretation involves several new problems. In the first place, it is necessary to specify the dynamic model whose stationary solution is identical to the equilibrium model. In the second place, the question arises as to the respects in which the forces are in balance. As was pointed out earlier, one must assume that a number of constraints are laid on the system, and that these constraints prevent certain forces from operating -- e.g., those forces which affect the price system.

---

1) These ideas have been developed in more detail in Leijonhufvud (1973); cf. in particular pp. 37-43. In this context Leijonhufvud advances an interesting hypothesis concerning the sensitivity of the economic system for disturbances. He suggests that there exists a large number of buffers -- e.g., inventories and cash balances -- which absorb disturbances if they are not too great. Thus, in the case of small disturbances, the price mechanism functions according to the neoclassical model. But if the disturbances are sufficiently large, the buffers are no longer adequate. For example, households which become involved in a period of unemployment can only temporarily maintain their consumption at its old level. Later their liquidity dries up as do their possibilities to borrow, and the excess supply in the labor market leads to a spill-over effect in the goods market. There thus exists a "corridor" within which disturbances are absorbed. If the disturbance is too great, it leads instead to a multiplier process in which the original change in supply or demand is enlarged.

In general equilibrium theory, when we say that the system is in equilibrium, we mean that a point in price space has been reached where the force which nominal demand has on the price of each of the submarkets in the economy is balanced by an equally large opposing force in the form of nominal supply. In the new theory of the multiplier, there has been reached instead a point in quantity space where the gap between effective supply and effective demand does not generate any changes in the size of the spill-over effects.

In both cases the term "forces" should be interpreted as offers to buy and sell. That which separates the theories is, in the first place, that the determining factors behind the forces differ. In the case of general equilibrium, the economic subjects are not exposed to any quantity constraints other than the budget constraint, while such is the case in the "Keynesian" analysis. The balance between offers to buy and sell does not constitute any real problem in general equilibrium, but in the new multiplier theory their interpretation is significantly more difficult.

An economic subject who is subject to quantity constraints on his possibilities of buying or selling in certain markets may have the opportunity of turning to several potential "trading partners" in order to ease the rationing constraint(s). In that case one can imagine that unsatisfied demand creates more purchase order than those compatible with the budget equations. In the presence of excess supply selling offers will in a corresponding way give an exaggerated picture of sales and production possibilities. If it is costly to submit these purchase and sales orders,[1] it can be imagined instead that the existence of excess

---

[1] The costs can take different forms. One example is the costs of making contacts which were discussed in the two preceding sections. One can also imagine that there are great disutilities associated with breaking the promises or contracts which are constituted by sales or purchase offers, and that therefore a significant risk is associated with accepting orders which exceed those which one can fulfill.

demand reduces attempts to buy, since potential buyers really do not expect that demand can be satisfied. The corresponding argument for the supply side can be applied in the presence of excess supply. This argument implies that it is not sufficient to distinguish between nominal and effective demand and supply. It is also necessary in disequilibrium to introduce active offers to sell and buy.[1)]

These new concepts have several important implications. The forces which generate price and quantity movements should be tied to active attempts to buy and sell. But these forces do not any longer have a foundation in the traditional supply and demand concepts, since they are not necessarily based on the requirement of consistent planning. For example, in the presence of general excess supply, we can conceive that the sum of the active monetary offers to sell in all markets exceeds demand and that Walras' Law (in Patinkin's terminology) is thus not fulfilled. Besides the fact that effective demand may differ from nominal demand, there clearly exists here a further factor which tends to distort the information which the price system (and quantity system) provides in disequilibrium.

However, active attempts to buy and sell imply a promising possibility to tie together the arguments which have been made in this section with the new theory of inflation and unemployment, which is built on the theory of costly market processes. If one is going to explain the

---

1) This distinction was probably made first in Hansen (1951). Hansen distinguishes between "planned purchases which are expected to be realizable", "purchases which he attempts to carry out", "those purchases which it would be reasonable for him to carry out if he did not need to take any limitations into account". In modern terminology these concepts should correspond most closely to effective demand, active demand, and nominal demand. Cf. Hansen (1951), p. 23. Grossman has recently revived Hansen's distinction between different types of quantities in Grossman (1974).

The distinction between these concepts has been used, for example, in the Swedish debate concerning the effects of rent control. The question has concerned the usefulness of the housing queue as a measure of excess demand in the housing market. Cf. Bentzel et al. (1963).

size ordering of offers to sell and buy out of equilibrium, a discussion is required of the costs and revenues which these cause for the economic subjects. Costs of contact and evaluation -- i.e., the costs of extensive and intensive search -- have been discussed in section 3 above, and even if these costs do not, perhaps, constitute an exhaustive account of all the factors which affect active offers to buy and sell, there exists here in each case a promising parallel.

The next question -- and perhaps the most important -- concerns the role of the price system and price variations in the new theory of the multiplier. Who sets the price? In any given market is there a unique price or a price distribution? Are prices rigid, or do quantity movements rather take place significantly faster than do price changes?

The question of the uniqueness of the price and of who in disequilibrium sets the price are closely connected. If there is a market administrator who determines the price, then there is also a unique price. If instead price determination is decentralized among the individual firms, it is likely that at least in disequilibrium there exists a price distribution with a positive variance. (Cf. the discussion in section 2.)

With one exception -- Leijonhufvud (1968) -- there is nowhere in the literature which has been surveyed in this section any discussion of how prices are determined in the various markets. Since the price is assumed to be unique and exogenously given, this implies implicitly that there exists a market administrator. We can therefore characterize the main part of the models which have been discussed in this section as non-tâtonnement models. The multiplier mechanisms are a result of the spill-over effects which are generated when transactions take place out of general equilibrium. If this is a reasonable characterization of the theory of the multiplier, it implies that the theory suffers from the same criticisms which were leveled against non-tâtonnement models in section 2.

At the beginning of this section I mentioned that the new theory of the multiplier is characterized by, and has its attractiveness in, the fact that it builds on an analysis of the behavior of utility maximizing households and profit maximizing firms outside of equilibrium. The disequilibrium is marked by binding constraints on the possibilities of buying or selling in certain markets. But at the same time, this structure constitutes only a partial preference theoretic foundation, since there is not room for the rational behavior of individual economic subjects vis à vis the price.

Taking as a point of departure Arrow's article from 1959, Gogerty and Winston (1964) have criticized Patinkin's analysis of involuntary unemployment for not taking note of firms' price-determination problem in the presence of excess supply in the goods market. Patinkin argued that the constraint on sales possibilities caused by the excess supply in the goods market implies a spill-over effect in the goods market so that the firm's effective demand for labor becomes lower than the nominal demand. Gogerty and Winston point out instead that there is another mechanism which tends to reduce demand in the labor market. Following Arrow, they note first that perfect competition only can exist in equilibrium. The excess supply in the goods market implies that the demand curves for the individual firms have a negative slope, since they can sell more if they reduce their prices. Thus in disequilibrium firms will, if they continue to behave rationally, act as monopolists and set their prices higher than marginal cost. As far as the factor markets are concerned, this implies that firms' demand for labor is less than the quantity at which the marginal product of labor is equal to the real wage. Thus even in Gogerty and Winston's version there is obtained an inward shift of firms' demand curves for labor, although the motivation is different from Patinkin's.

However, one can criticize Gogerty and Winston for not having followed their analysis through to its logical conclusion. Their argument holds only if the wage is immediately adjusted to its new equilibrium. If this is not the case, we obtain an excess supply in the labor market as well, and in that case firms will behave as monopsonists in the labor market. Since the market situation of any one firm differs in general from that of the others, this implies that there are not only price differentials in the goods market, but wage differentials in the labor market.

Gogerty and Winston's critique of Patinkin concerns his assumption in disequilibrium of a system of prices which is unique and exogenously given from the point of view of the individual economic subjects. This criticism can of course be leveled against the other contributions to the "new" theory of the multiplier. However, an important question is whether decentralized price and wage changes in disequilibrium are compatible with rationing and involuntary unemployment. Disequilibrium for the market as a whole can occur simultaneously as each firm is continually varying prices and wages so that its planned sales are equal to households' demand for its product, and its planned input of labor is equal to employees' supply.[1)]

The essential question is which factors cause price and wage differentials in disequilibrium. One interpretation is that households are imperfectly informed about different firms' prices and wage rates and that this, and the fact that the planning situation of different firms is different, gives different profit-maximizing prices and wages for different firms. However, this interpretation is problematic to the extent that the imperfect information of households implies search costs, and that this in turn is incompatible with the system converging to a perfectly competitive solution. (Cf. the discussion in connection with Arrow's article in section 2, above.) If one drops the requirement that the market fulfill the conditions for perfect competition in equilibrium, this interpretation involves no problems problems of consistency; however, it does exclude, among other things, involuntary unemployment.

The other possibility for price and wage differentials in disequilibrium is that firms are imperfectly informed, but that households have perfect information about which prices and wage rates the various firms maintain. The firms'

---

1) Disequilibrium expresses itself in the fact that imperfectly informed households, dependent on erroneous expectations, search more or less than they otherwise would do.

informational requirements are indeed -- as Arrow emphasizes in his article -- greater in disequilibrium than in equilibrium. In equilibrium it is sufficient for them to know the market price (and the market wage). But in disequilibrium they must know the functional form of the demand curve for their product. This latter depends in turn on the shape of the hypothetical market demand curve, the size of the excess demand, and the prices and other sales conditions which other firms offer. If a firm must plan its production in advance and furthermore does not have the possibility of continually varying its price,[1)] or only receives information about the quantity of sales with a lag, sales will in general differ from production. When this happens, the discrepancy can either be borne by the firm or its customers. Strictly speaking, what happens should be explained endogenously -- as, for example, in the incidence problem -- but I must be content here merely to give some *ad hoc* views.

In a market for storable goods, a difference between production and sales causes inventory changes. To the extent that actual sales differ from the expected, the inventory change is unexpected. In the presence of excess supply inventories increase, and in the presence of excess demand they decline. These unplanned inventory changes affect, of course, the firm's future price policy, which Arrow has discussed rather throughly in his article discussed above. If the good is not storable, or if a service is involved, an

---

1) One can imagine that it is only possible for the firm to change its price within certain intervals. Another, more satisfying possibility is that there are certain costs associated with price changes. In part there are purely administrative costs: new price catalogues must be printed; the personnel must be informed about the new prices, etc. In part the firm's customers can react negatively to the price changes. Indeed, it always takes time to seek out a firm, and the "investment" which this involves should take place under reliable premises. A fixed price is a kind of insurance which the firm gives its customers, and a firm which makes itself known for a shifty price police easily loses customers. Robert Barro has discussed the implications of a fixed cost of changing the price for the policy of the firm in Barro (1972). *Cf.* also Scitovsky (1951), chapter XII.

excess supply will involve a drying up of production or an inability of the firm to obtain employment for its factors of production. In the presence of excess of demand, a rationing situation is automatically created.

A sufficient condition for excess supply in a factor market -- e.g., the labor market -- to lead to rationing is that the firm determines the size of the input of the factor of production and in addition does not have the possibility of immediately changing the wage rate if it should turn out that the supply curve for labor has another form or location than that which the firm reckoned with. Incomplete information (or more precisely, costs for collecting information) together with costs associated with continually varying wages thus lead to rationing. It is this rationing which in turn makes possible wages differentials despite the fact that households are perfectly informed as to what wage rates the individual firms maintain. All workers will not flow into the firm which maintains the highest wage rate, since it cannot possibly employ all job applicants. The corresponding argument can be made with respect to the goods market. This implies also that Arrow's hypothesis concerning a market which is perfectly competitive in equilibrium does not conflict with the existence of price differentials in disequilibrium.

Regardless of whether one assumes that it is households or firms which have imperfect market information, one can expect price differentials in disequilibrium. With imperfectly informed firms we have in addition rationing in the goods markets in the presence of excess demand and in the factor markets in the presence of excess supply. This rationing naturally does not imply that households as a whole, given the price, can buy up to a certain quantity of a given commodity. Rather, the limitation of the possible quantity purchased concerns a certain supplier. If one wishes to buy more, one must turn to another firm and pay a higher price. With decentralized price determination, the household is confronted with a stepwise supply curve, in which the steps denote the purchase possibilities from different firms.[1)]

If instead households are inperfectly informed concerning the market, there does not any longer exist any involuntary rationing, but quite possibly voluntary rationing. Price differentials imply -- in any case in markets for durable goods -- that households apply a decision rule with a reservation price at which they refrain from purchasing until they have come into contact with a firm which maintains a price not exceeding it. In a corresponding way the unemployed will not accept offers of employment in which the wage lies under the acceptance wage, so that a certain "voluntary" unemployment is created. Delays in purchases and extensions of unemployment periods can be created by the fact that households' expectations with respect to the location of the price and wage distributions are erroneous. In this sense one can speak of "involuntarily voluntary" rationing in the goods and labor markets.

Now if it is the degree of "voluntariness" which distinguishes the quantitative constraints which one works with in the new theory of inflation and unemployment from those in the new theory of the multiplier, the question arises as to <u>why</u> the former class of models does not generate multiplier effects. These are obviously characterized by quantity interactions between different markets, not primarily by the fact that the quantity constraints are involuntary. A possible answer to this question is that the new theory of the Phillips curve has heretofore only been developed as a partial theory for the labor market. By generalizing it to a multiple-market theory, one should be able to obtain effects which resemble the multiplier mechanism. An increase in unemployment reduces households' disposable income and thus their demand for consumption goods. This reduces firms' demand for labor, which, through changes in the rate of increase of wages, further increases

---

1) <u>Cf</u>. Assar Lindbeck´s discussion of credit rationing in Lindbeck (1963), pp. 88-90 and 242-245.

unemployment.[1] This hypothesis is an important point of departure for the analysis of the following chapters. In these, an integrated model of inflation and unemployment is built up on the basis of rational behavior of households and firms. This model covers both the labor and goods markets and thus makes possible an investigation of the interplay between these markets during the course of inflation and unemployment.

Despite the fact that the new theory of inflation and unemployment thus has development potential vis à vis the study of quantity interactions between markets in the economy, nevertheless the absence of involuntary unemployment and other forms of rationing is a serious disadvantage. At the same time the new theory of the multiplier is saddled with weaknesses: changes in the system of prices are not explained as a result of behavior of individual economic subjects, nor does the theory give any explanation of the interplay of inflation and unemployment. It is therefore an important objective to develop a more general macroeconomic theory. My prognosis is that this will be one of the most interesting areas of research during the coming decade.

---

1) This type of discussion is to be found in Leijonhufvud (1968). In his attempt to interpret Keynes, Leijonhufvud has, on the basis of modern theory, discussed among other things the forces behind the multiplier process. Leijonhufvud has explained the rise in cyclical unemployment with the same type of argument which lies behind the analytical derivations of the Phillips curve and refers in that context to Arrow (1959) and Alchian (1969). In Leijonhufvud´s argument it is the increase in "voluntary" unemployment which starts the process. When the wage and salary income of households then fall, consumption is also reduced. This latter step builds on Clower´s interpretation of the consumption function in Clower (1965).

CHAPTER III. CONSUMPTION, SUPPLY OF LABOR, AND SEARCH ACTIVITY IN AN INTERTEMPORAL PERSPECTIVE

1. Introduction

In the survey of modern short-run macroeconomics in the previous chapter it was stressed that one can distinguish between two lines of development. The first of these implies an attempt, starting from preference theory, to examine how disequilibrium in some of the markets of the economy may affect developments in the other markets and thus produce the quantitative feedback mechanisms which constitute the basis of the multiplier theory. A problem with this line of development is that it has not been possible to analyze rational, decentralized decisions vis à vis prices. It has therefore not been possible to study the interaction between unemployment and inflation within the limits of this approach.

The second course of development also implies an attempt to derive macroeconomic relationships from preference theory. But here the interest is centered on the connection between inflation and unemployment. A problem with this analysis is that it is limited to only one market, the labor market, although the interaction between price and wage increases is of central importance for inflation theory. This means that it is necessary at least to extend the analysis to include the goods market. This is the main goal for the present and for the following chapters.

The present chapter contains an analysis of the behavior of an employed household in an inflationary milieu. How are consumption, the supply of labor, and the search activity in the goods and labor markets influenced by variations in the rate of price and wage inflation?

1.1. Some important issues

The goal of the present chapter, together with the two following chapters, is to supply the necessary microeconomic foundation for the macroeconomic model of inflation and unemployment in chapter VI. At the same time, there are a number of related issues which are of interest on their own right.

First, the chapter contains an analysis of household search activity in two markets, the goods market and the labor market. Since resources allocated to search in a certain market not only could be used for other activities than search, but could also be used for search in other markets, it is important to study the interactions between search in several markets.[1)]

Second, search in both the goods market and the labor market is repetitive. In the goods market this means that the household is customer of a certain supplier until a better offer (a lower price) is obtained. In many instances, this is a much more realistic situation than the one-time purchase traditionally analyzed in search theory. Even when it comes to capital goods, it is often impossible to analyze the search before purchase as a one-time decision. This is due to the fact that the value of a certain price offer must not only be evaluated with respect to possible lower price offers obtained through more searching, it must also take account of the future search which will be necessary when the good has to be renewed or resold.[2)]

Also, the analysis of search activity in the labor market will receive a repetitive element in this chapter. Earlier studies have mainly centered around the "one time event" which the step into employment constitutes.[3)]

---

1) This problem has been discussed by Stigler (1961) and Gould (1972)

2) Cf. the discussion in chapter II, pp. 49-50.

3) There are exceptions. Cf. Whipple (1973) and Parsons (1973).

However, for a person already employed, a new job merely constitutes a link in a future chain of events. The new job merely changes the starting point for future search activities. This of course must be taken into consideration when planning the search activity. In the same way, the search activity of the unemployed must be planned against the background of future search activity. The value of the first job is conditional upon the jobs which it could lead to in the future. The analysis of the present chapter thus gives information necessary for the discussion in the next chapter of the behavior of the unemployed.

The fact that search may be looked upon as an investment activity is of central importance for the discussion of this and the following chapter. The resources which the household allocates to search are assumed to consist of time which is taken from working time. The more intensively the household searches, the less time there is left over for work, and the smaller are income and instantaneous consumption. On the other hand, the probability of getting into contact with a firm which could offer a lower price than the present supplier, and a higher wage rate than the present employer will increase. Increased search will therefore decrease instantaneous consumption but increase the expected future real wage rate and hence also the future consumption level.

1.2. An overview of the following analysis

In the following, the behavior of an employed household[1)]

---

1) No distinction is made between individuals and households. In cases where the household consists of several members, there is still assumed to exist a stable preference function. Moreover, only one member of the household is working, and it is the time of this person which is divided between work and search. The assumption is of course made for analytical convenience, but it should be stressed that great problems, both in theory and in empirical relevance, are swept under the carpet. One may cite the discussion of group preferences in Arrow (1951) on the one hand and the fact that different members of the household specialize in different time-consuming activities on the other.

will be discussed. This means that the latter part of the life cycle will be treated. The idea is that the new generations entering the labor force will be unemployed during some initial period. When they receive an employment offer surmounting the aspiration wage rate, they will become employed. The first part of the life cycle, the unemployment period, is treated in the next chapter.[1] Persons belonging to the labor force are moreover assumed to be subject to a constant death risk.[2] The death risk implies that the time horizon of the household is stochastic.

The behavior of the employed household, which consists of choices of the amount of consumption, working time, and search on the goods and the labor market, depends (*inter alia*) on the milieu the household is living in. This milieu, the expectations about the milieu, and household preferences will be outlined below. In addition, the character of the planning problem will shortly be touched upon.

---

1) In order of the chapters thus do not correspond to chronology, but to the order of planning. Planning is done "backwards" in time. To be able to analyze the behavior of the unemployed, it is necessary to know the optimal planning after the moment of the first employment, *i.e.*, the planning of the employed worker which is treated in the present chapter. Note that there is an implicit assumption that an employed person will never go back into unemployment. It is possible to analyze that case too (it has been done in a previous version), but for the sake of simplicity it is assumed that the employed worker will only leave his employer for a new job.

2) Of course, this risk could be more broadly interpreted as a risk of leaving the labor force. In this case the relevant part of the life cycle could be divided into an unemployment period (search for the first job), an employment period, and the pensioning period. To simplify, the risk will be strictly interpreted as a death risk. It is assumed to be constant in time (independent of the age of the individual). Furthermore, the death risk could not be influenced by the individual. It is exogeniously given. The assumption of a death risk is made to get a turn-over of the labor force, necessary for the unemployment analysis of the last chapter. The assumption is also of importance for the problem of the existence of stable distributions over relative prices and relative wage rates. *Cf.* the discussion of pp. 66-67.

1.2.1. The milieu of the household

The economy consists of essentially two markets,[1] a homogenous goods market and a homogenous labor market. However, there does not exist a unique market price, nor a unique market wage rate. Instead, the firms are assumed to be distributed over prices and wage rates in such a way that the distributions of relative prices (the prices of the individual firms in comparison to the average price in the market) and relative wage rates (the wage rates of the individual firms in comparison to the average wage rate in the market) are constant.

If the distribution of relative prices and relative wage rates over firms is assumed to be constant over time, this is not the case for monetary prices and wage rates. The household is living in an inflationary milieu, where prices and wage rates are continually increasing. This means that the distribution of firms over monetary prices is successively "blow up" so that all prices increase by the percentage of inflation. But if all prices increase by the same percentage, the distribution over relative prices will be constant. It should be observed that this reasoning does not presuppose that the individual firms keep constant relative prices. But the distribution of firms over relative prices must be constant. The reasoning is exactly analogous with respect to the distribution of firms over relative wage rates. The rate of price inflation may of course differ from the rate of wage inflation.

The above reasoning is illustrated in figure 1 below. At point of time t_0 the firms are distributed over monetary prices according to the first probability density function. The price level increases from t_0 to t_1 by the actual rate of price inflation, g_p. This means that for all frequencies of firms, prices will increase by the same percentage, but the distribution over relative prices is left unchanged by this operation. The average price level on the market is denoted by $\bar{p}$.

---

[1] In addition, there is a loan market. The households are assumed not to be engaged in financial saving or borrowing, however.

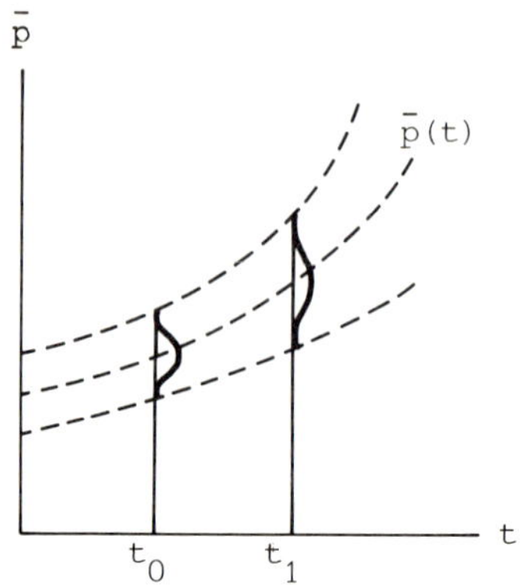

Fig. III:1. The development of the price distribution when the rate of inflation is constant.

1.2.2. The expectations of the household

All economic agents are assumed to have an incomplete overview of the goods market and the labor market. This means that they do not know the actual average price, $\bar{p}(t)$, and the actual average wage rate, $\bar{w}(t)$, at time t. Following Mortensen, they are however assumed to have perfect information concerning the average price level with a lag of h_p time units and the average wage level with a lag of h_w time units.[1)]

The average price level at time t_1 expected by the households is then projected from point of time $t_1 - h_p$ to time t_1 through the expected rate of price inflation, g_p^e.[2)] If the actual rate of price inflation, g_p, is higher

1) Cf. Mortensen (1970).

2) Inflationary expectations are held with subjective certainty. As the household observes that actual rates of price and wage inflation differ from the expected rates, inflationary expectations may be revised. This question will be discussed in chapter VI. Until then, expectations of inflation are assumed to be exogenously given.

than that expected the actual average price level exceeds that expected, $\bar{p}^e$, at time t_1, cf. figure 2.

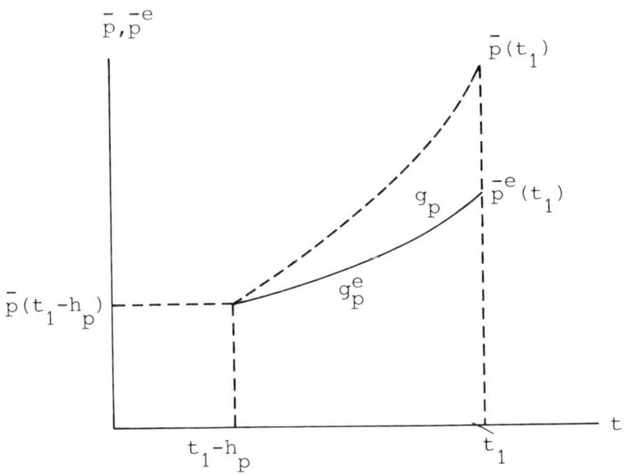

Fig. III:2. The actual and the expected average price level at t_1 when the actual rate of price inflation is greater than the expected rate of price inflation.

The corresponding reasoning holds exactly with respect to the actual and expected rates of wage inflation and the actual and expected average wage rates. The expected rate of price inflation is assumed to be equal to the expected rate of wage inflation, i.e., $g_p^e = g_w^e$. The actual rates of price and wage inflation may of course differ.

It should be noted that the expectations with respect to the rates of price and wage inflation and the average price level and wage rate are held with subjective certainty. Expectations are continually revised as time develops,[1)] but the new expectations are also held with subjective certainty. The expected average price level at a certain point of time has nothing to do with mathematical expectation; instead, it is the price level expected with subjective certainty by households.

It should be noted that the rates of price and wage inflation are to be interpreted strictly as time averages over

---

1) At point of time t_2, where $t_2 > t_1$, the household has the more actual information about the price level at $t_2 - h_p$.

periods of length h_p and h_w, respectively, not as instantaneous rates.

The fact that the household does not know the actual average price level at a certain instant of time further implies that it does not know what relative price it pays. If, for example, the actual average price on the market is higher than the expected average price, the household will believe that it is paying a higher relative price, p^e, than is actually the case. The analogous reasoning holds with respect to the wage rate, w, and the expected relative wage rate, w^e. Expectations about relative prices and relative wage rates are held with subjective certainty.

1.2.3. The planning of the household

The household is assumed to behave as if it tried to maximize the mathematical expectation of the discounted sum of all future utilities. The stochastic elements taken into account in the planning[1)] consist of the stochastically determined horizon and the inability of the household to know exactly when it will get into contact with various firms and what exact price and wage offers will result from these contacts. Time is not divided into periods, but is assumed to vary continuously.[2)]

While the instantaneous utility function contains instantaneous consumption as an argument, leisure time is

---

1) It should be stressed that even if, e.g., actual and expected rates of price inflation differ, this incomplete knowledge is not taken into account in the planning of the household. This is due to the fact that these expectations are held with subjective certainty. When these expectations are revised, the new expectations will equally well be held with subjective certainty.

2) This assumption has been made both for theoretical reasons and for convenience. First, a problem with all period analysis is that it builds on aggregation over time, where events during a certain time period are of equal importance whenever they happen during the time period. Second, although more advanced mathematics has to be used for continuous time analysis, the mathematics will in many respects become more compact and simple. This is especially the case when stochastic processes are involved.

assumed to be exogeniously given and thus does not constitute an element of the analysis.[1)]

The maximization of the utility functional (i.e., the discounted sum of all future utilities) is restricted by a number of constraints. These are both instantaneous and intertemporal.

To start with the instantaneous constraints, the budget and the time budget equations must be fulfilled at each point of time. Since the household is assumed not to operate in the loan market or to own any financial assets (or to have any debts), its disposable labor income must be equal at each point of time to the total used for consumption purchases.[2)] The time-budget constraint implies that the consumer at each point of time allocates the total time available[3)] between labor and search in the goods and the labor markets.

The greater the share of time used for work, the higher instantaneous consumption will be. On the other hand, there will be less time left over for search, which diminishes the frequency of contacts with firms other than the present supplier and present employer. Thus the number of recieved price and wage offers will fall. This diminishes the probability of getting into contact with a firm offering a lower price than the present supplier and a higher wage rate than the present employer.[4)] Higher instantaneous consumption will then, by reducing time left over for search, imply a lower expected future real wage rate and consumption level.

---

1) This assumption is not very satisfactory from an empirical point of view (it is probable that a great amount of the variation of the search activity on the goods market is compensated by variations in leisure time), but it has been necessary in order to keep the analysis within reasonable limits.

2) This assumption has been made to keep the analysis within reasonable bounds. The case of financial saving has been analyzed in a prototype to this chapter, consumption, saving, and optimal information collection, stencil, Stockholm 1971.

3) Since time varies continuously, the time allocated to various activities strictly must be interpreted as proportions.

4) It is assumed that there are no costs associated with the transfer from one supplier to another or from one employer to another.

In addition to the constraints on household choice constituted at each point of time by the budget and the time-budget equations, there are two intertemporal stochastic constraints with respect to possible changes in the price which the household pays and the wage rate which it receives, which are affected by variations in search activity on the two markets.

The reason why it is possible for the household to improve its real wage rate via search is of course that there does not exist any unique market price or market wage rate.

The assumption made earlier that the expected rate of price inflation is equal to the expected rate of wage inflation implies that the household will base its planning on a constant average real wage rate, $\bar{w}^e/\bar{p}^e$.[1] On the other hand, it is possible for the household to affect its own disposable real wage rate, $(1 - s)w^e\bar{w}^e/p^e\bar{p}^e$, through its search activity.[2]

Starting from the situation at an arbitrary point of time (i.e., the relative price which the household believes that it pays, the values of the exogenous variables and so on), the planning problem is to choose the trajectories for the control variables (the supply of labor, the search activity on the goods market and on the labor market, and the consumption level) which maximize the mathematical expectation of the utility functional. In this choice the household has to take into consideration the stochastic elements of the planning.

The first of these is that the horizon is uncertain. It will be shown below that the maximization of the expected value of the utility functional up to a stochastic finite

---

1) Here $\bar{w}^e$ denotes the expected (with subjective certainty) average wage rate, and $\bar{p}^e$ denotes the expected (with subjective certainty) average price on the market.

2) Here s denotes the income tax rate, w^e the expected (with subjective certainty) relative wage rate, and p^e the expected (with subjective certainty) relative price. It should be noted that $p^e\bar{p}^e$ is the (monetary) price which the household actually is paying.

time horizon may be transformed into a deterministic problem with an infinite time horizon.

The second stochastic element has to do with the fact that the household cannot know exactly when it will get into contact with a firm in the goods or the labor markets and what price or wage offer will result from this contact. This influences planning at each point of time and will moreover have consequences for the interpretation of the planning problem.

This stochastic element implies that the planning problem at any point in time involves an optimization over all possible future developments of relative prices and relative wage rates. It is possible to show, however, that subject to certain conditions which are fulfilled in the present case, optimization under risk will imply the same behavior as if the planning problem involved only the mathematical expectations of the time derivatives of the relative price and relative wage rate. The household will thus behave as if it were risk neutral. This in turn implies that the household will behave at each point of time as if it planned its behavior for the whole future, given that the expected relative price and relative wage rate will change continuously according to the mathematical expectations of their time derivatives.

But since the household will merely get into contact now and then with various firms which can offer a lower relative price than the present supplier and a higher relative wage rate than the present employer, these trajectories for the relative price and relative wage rate will not of course be followed continuously. The changes will instead be discrete.

The second reason for surprises in context of the planning problem, which assumes a continuous development of the relative price and the relative wage rate, is that the actual rates of price and wage inflation may differ from the expected rates.

Discrepancies between the relative price and the relative wage rate expected by the household at a certain point of time in comparison to the development predicted when planning at an earlier point of time imply that the behavior of the household will not develop over time in exactly the way it would if the relative price and relative wage rate followed the continuous trajectories which the original planning problem assumed. Deviations from these trajectories imply that the household in each point of time must replan subject to the new conditions, i.e., the new starting values for the expected relative price and the expected relative wage rate.

In connection with the optimization analysis, the behavior equations of the household will be derived. In these equations the initial values of the expected relative price and the expected relative wage rate appear as arguments. The behavior equations are further independent of chronological time.[1] This implies that, irrespective of whether or not the relative price and the relative wage rate develop according to the planning presumptions at an earlier point of time, these equations will describe the behavior of the household at each point of time.

1.3. Plan of the chapter

The chapter is arranged in the following way. In section two the search process in the goods and labor markets is discussed and the mathematical expectation of the time derivative of the relative price and the relative wage rate expected by the household is derived. In the following section the intertemporal planning problem is formulated and the behavior equations of the household derived subject to the condition that the shadow prices of the time derivatives of the relative price and the relative wage rate are constant. Section four contains a phase-diagram analysis. The last section is devoted to deriving the complete behavior equations of the household. These are defined for the case in which the shadow prices mentioned above are endogenously determined.

---

1) Note that the horizon is infinite.

In this way it is taken into account that parameter changes will not only influence the household's choice of action directly (as analyzed in section three) but also indirectly, via changed values of the shadow prices.

2. Information Gathering by the Household

2.1. The goods market

This section contains a discussion of the household's search activity on the commodity and labor markets. We begin with the commodity market. The analysis is concentrated on a single commodity market where a large number of firms sell a homogeneous commodity. The household is indifferent with respect to which firm it buys from but, of course, not to the price it pays. If the household comes into contact with a firm whose price is lower than that of the firm it currently buys from, it will switch suppliers.

Let us assume that at the outset the household buys from firm k. A stochastic mechanism generates price signals from other firms. If any of the prices quoted is lower than firm k's, the household abandons k and switches to the firm with the lower price. The probability that this will occur during a short period of time of length dt is equal to the probability that the household will receive information about the price charged by at least one other firm multiplied by the probability that at least one of these prices is lower than that of the firm k. If instead of discussing the price quoted by some firm, we deal with its price in relation to the average market price -- *i.e.*, the firm's relative price -- then, given that it has received price information, the household will switch suppliers if the relative price quoted, p^e, is less than relative price, p_k^e, which the household pays its current supplier.[1] The absolute prices are obtained when p^e and

[1] Note that the household does not know the true relative price, p, but has subjectively certain expectations about it. If the actual rate of price inflation is equal to the expected rate, the true or actual relative price will coincide with the expected relative price, p^e. Further note that differences between the relative prices of two firms will always, except for a scale factor, coincide with the difference between the actual relative prices.

p_k^e are multiplied by the average market price, $\bar{p}^e$.

It is now assumed that the signals from firms to the household are generated by a Poisson process.[1] This is probably the simplest type of stochastic process. It also has particularly attractive properties from an analytical point of view. Assuming that the number of signals is Poisson distributed, the probability that the household will receive exactly j price messages during the period of length dt is:

(1) $$P_j(dt) = \frac{(\varepsilon dt)^j}{j!} \cdot e^{-\varepsilon dt}$$

The parameter ε, of course, depends on the size of the information flow. The greater the amount of time, τ_{sp}, the household devotes to gathering information about prices and the more the firms advertise their prices, a_p, the greater

(2) $\varepsilon = \varepsilon(\tau_{sp}, a_p)$ where $\varepsilon_1>0$, $\varepsilon_2>0$, $\varepsilon_{11}<0$, $\varepsilon_{22}<0$ and $\varepsilon_{12}>0$.

will be. In other words, it is assumed that there are decreasing returns to the production factors employed in the generation of signals, but that an increase, for instance, in the household's search activity increases the marginal product of the firms' advertising activities.[2]

If the household receives a price message, the probability that the price specified is lower than that which the consumer pays his supplier is equal to the share of the total information flow concerning prices quoted by firms that maintain a lower relative price than p_k^e. This is also the probability that the household, given that it has received one and only one price message, will abandon its supplier. If the frequency of firms that maintain the relative price p^e is designated $f(p^e)$,[3] the

1) Cf. Hadley (1967), chapter 10.

2) The number of price messages is thus generated by a stochastic production function with one internal and one external factor of production. If price information is indirectly transmitted (e.g., via friends), this could be taken into consideration by an additional argument of the function.

3) Note that the frequency function over expected relative prices always coincides with the probability density over actual relative prices. This is due to the fact that expectations are only wrong with respect to the average price on the market, not with respect to other aspects of the price distribution.

average information flow from a firm that maintains the relative price p^e is $a_p(p^e)$, the total number of firms is F, and the total price information from all firms is a_p, where $a_p = F \int_0^{\infty} a_p(\pi)\ f(\pi)\ d\pi$, then this probability is equal to

$$\frac{\int_0^{p_k^e} f(\pi)\ a_p\ (\pi)\ d\pi}{\int_0^{\infty} f(\pi)\ a_p(\pi)\ d\pi} = \int_0^{p_k^e} \hat{f}(\pi)\ d\pi \quad {}^{1)}$$

This probability -- that for a given recieved price message the household will switch to another firm with a lower price -- is equal to hatched area in figure 3:

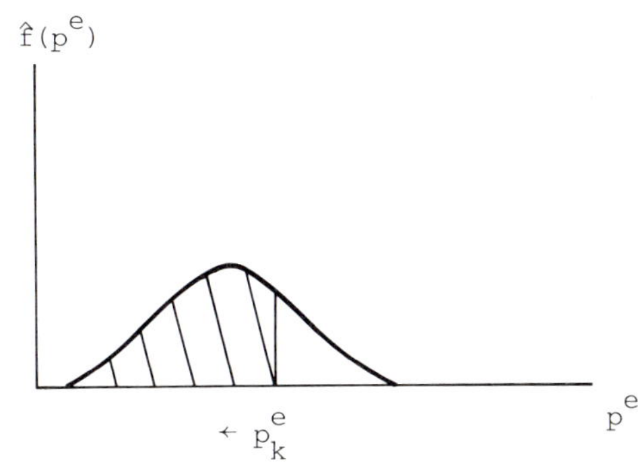

Fig. III:3. The present (expected) relative price and the probability of finding a firm offering a lower price.

In figure 3, p_k^e denotes the (expected) relative price that the household presently pays and the arrow indicates the direction in which it will move when transferring from one firm to another.

The mathematical expectation of the relative price paid at point of time t+dt if the household pays the relative

---

1) It assumed that all firms change their supply of information by the same percentage. This means that $f(p^e)$ is independent of a_p.

price $p^e(t) = p_k^e(t)$ at point of time t will now be derived.

The mathematical expectation of the relative price at time t+dt, $E\{p^e(t+dt)\}$, is equal to the probability that the household will not receive any message during period dt multiplied by $p_k^e(t+dt)$[1] plus the probability that it will receive one and only one message during the period, multiplied by the expected value of the minimum of p_k^e and the price message received during the period $t, t+dt$ (since the household can always continue to buy from firm k if its price is lower than that quoted in the price message) plus the probability that two messages will be received multiplied by the expected value of the minimum of p_k^e and the two price messages received, and so on.

This may be written as:

$$(3) \qquad E\{p^e(t+dt)\} = P_o\left[p_k^e(t+dt)\right] + P_1\left[\int_o^{p_k^e} \pi(t+dt)\ \hat{f}(\pi)\ d\pi + \right.$$

$$\left. + p_k^e(t+dt) \int_{p_k^e}^{\infty} \hat{f}(\pi)\ d\pi\right] + P_2\left[\ldots\right] + \ldots$$

where P_j is the probability of receiving j messages during time period dt.

We may now substitute into equation (3) the probability of recieving j messages, P_j, from equation (1), subtract $p_k^e(t)$, and divide by dt:

---

1) It should be observed that the firms´ relative prices are not necessarily constant. For example, if the number of customers who buy from firm k -- and thus the demand for its product -- increase, the firm will raise its price; cf. Phelps and Winter (1970), pp. 325-331.

$$(4)\quad \frac{E\{p^e(t+dt) - p^e(t)\}}{dt} = \frac{(e^{-\varepsilon dt} - 1)}{dt} p_k^e(t+dt) +$$

$$+ \frac{p_k^e(t+dt) - p_k^e(t)}{dt} + \varepsilon\, e^{-\varepsilon dt}\left[\int_0^{p_k^e} \pi(t+dt)\, \hat{f}(\pi)\, d\pi + \right.$$

$$\left. + p_k^e(t+dt) \int_{p_k^e}^{\infty} \hat{f}(\pi)\, d\pi\right] + \frac{\varepsilon^2 dt}{2!} e^{-\varepsilon dt}\left[\ldots\right] + \ldots\ldots$$

In the limit, the first term on the right hand side is, according to l'Hospital's rule (both the numerator and denominator tend to zero when dt tends to zero) obtained as $-\varepsilon p_k^e$. The second term tends to $\dot{p}_k^e(t)$.

All terms connected with recieving two or more price messages vanish when dt tends towards zero. Thus in the limit, (4) is transformed to

$$(5)\quad E\{\dot{p}^e\} = -\varepsilon p_k^e + \dot{p}_k^e + \varepsilon \cdot \left[\int_0^{p_k^e} \pi \hat{f}(\pi)\, d\pi + p_k^e \int_{p_k^e}^{\infty} \hat{f}(\pi)\, d\pi\right].$$

Furthermore, from the definition of a probability density function, $\int_{p_k^e}^{\infty} \hat{f}(\pi)\, d\pi + \int_0^{p_k^e} \hat{f}(\pi)\, d\pi = 1$. (5) may thus be rewritten as

$$(6)\quad E\{\dot{p}^e\} = \dot{p}_k^e + \varepsilon \int_0^{p_k^e} (\pi - p_k^e)\, \hat{f}(\pi)\, d\pi$$

Equation (6) states that the expected value of the rate of change in the price paid by the household is equal to the time derivative (expected by the household) of the current supplier's price plus the probability that the household will make contact with another firm, multiplied by the difference between the expected value of the price message (given that it is lower than the current supplier's price) and the price the household pays at present.

The higher ε is, *i.e.*, the more frequently price messages are received, the more rapidly the price will decrease. Since ε depends positively on the household's search activity and on firms' advertising activities, then the higher these become, the more rapid the decrease in the average price paid by the consumer will be.

The rate of price decrease also depends on the relative price paid by the household. The higher p_k^e is, the more rapidly the price will decrease on the average:

$$(7) \qquad \frac{\partial E\{\dot{p}^e\}}{\partial p_k^e} = \frac{\partial \dot{p}_k^e}{\partial p_k^e} - \varepsilon \int_0^{p_k^e} \hat{f}(\pi)\, d\pi < 0$$

It should be observed that $\frac{\partial \dot{p}_k^e}{\partial p_k^e}$ is also negative. The higher a firm's relative price, the more rapidly it loses customers to other firms and thus, owing to the decreasing demand for its product, the more quickly the firm will lower its price.

It is also assumed that

$$\frac{\partial^2 \dot{p}_k^e}{\partial p_k^{e2}} > 0$$

i.e., that the household expects the firm whose price is somewhat lower than the market average to raise its price more rapidly than a firm, whose price exceeds the market average by the same amount, lowers its price. This is because a low-price firm advertises more. Thus it gains customers not only because of its low price, but also because of a comparatively larger advertising volume. The household is assumed to expect a firm to possess this price-change function, but in reality there is no guarantee for this. Indeed, customers gained are acquired from other firms.

The assumption about the firm's price-change function implies that the second price derivative of the expected value of the time derivative of the price the household pays can be positive or negative:

$$(8) \qquad \frac{\partial^2 E\{\dot{p}^e\}}{\partial p_k^{e2}} = \frac{\partial^2 \dot{p}_k^e}{\partial p_k^{e2}} - \varepsilon\, f(p_k^e) \gtreqless 0$$

It is assumed that the effects cancel each other so that

$$\frac{\partial^2 E\{\dot{p}^e\}}{\partial p^{e2}} = 0 \quad {}^{1)}$$

2.2. The labor market

In conformity with conditions on the commodity market, an employee is assumed to be able to choose from among a large number of employers, and the places of work are regarded as equivalent. Thus the only reason for changing one's place of work is to obtain higher wages. The factors which affect (the expected value of) the rate of change of wages are assumed to be analogous to those for price changes on the commodity market. Therefore the following presentation can be brief.

At the outset the employee works for a firm which pays the hourly wage $\bar{w}^e w_1^e$, $\bar{w}^e$ is the expected average wage on the labor market, and w_1^e is the firm's expected relative wage. The household constantly receives information about the wage offers of other employers, and the mechanism which generates these messages is assumed to be of the Poisson type. In this case,

---

1) This assumption will greatly simplify the following analysis. It implies that the adjoint variable of the relative price is constant in time, and thus (together with the analogous assumption with respect to the adjoint variable of the relative wage rate) that the utility functional is linear in the phase variables.

the ε-variable, ε_w[1], is a function of the amount of time the household spends gathering information about the wages paid by other employers, τ_{sw}, and of the firms' advertising volume with respect to vacancies, a_w:

(9) $\varepsilon = \varepsilon(\tau_{sw}, a_w)$ where $\varepsilon_1 > 0$, $\varepsilon_2 > 0$, $\varepsilon_{11} < 0$, $\varepsilon_{22} < 0$ and $\varepsilon_{12} > 0$.

The more time the household allocates to search activity on the labor market, and the more information the firms produce about vacancies, the greater the probability that the household recieves a wage message during the short time period dt. The inputs of search time and firm advertising obey the "law" of decreasing returns and the increased input of one factor will increase the marginal productivity of the other.

Given the difference that in this instance the household searches for firms that offer a <u>higher</u> relative wage, the expected value of the rate of increase of the relative wage can be derived analogously to the case of the expected value of the relative price:

---

1) Observe that the form of the function for ε may be different between the goods market and labor markets. To the extent that information about vacancies is indirectly transmitted (via friends and fellow workers) an additional argument will be added to the "production function". An employment exchange (public or private) implies that a new information channel is opened on the labor market. This could also be taken into consideration by an additional argument in (9). If the employment exchange produces a selective sample of suggestions for employment interviews, this will not only increase the probability of an employment offer, but also affect the probabilities of different wage offers.

The own search time is assumed to be the only internal factor of production in the signal-generating production function. More generally, however, one could assume that in addition there will be monetary costs attached to the search activity. A private employment exchange could for example take a certain fee for its services, and this fee could depend on how many resources the exchange allocates to serve the job seeker.

$$(10) \qquad E\{\dot{w}^e\} = \dot{w}_1^e + \varepsilon_w \int_{w_1^e}^{\infty} (v - w_1^e)\, \hat{f}(v)\, dv \quad ^{1)}$$

On the basis of the assumption that the places of work are homogeneous and that therefore, there can be no compensatory wage differences between the various firms, it seems reasonable that high-wage firms reduce their wages and low-wage firms raise them. This is analogous to the discussion of price setting in the sense that a firm which maintains high wages does so in order to increase its recruitment of employees and that a firm gradually lowers wages when the number of employees increases and approaches the stationary optimum. Similarly a firm which maintains low wages plans to reduce the number of employees and will thus raise wages when the number of employees decreases towards the stationary optimum.

The household is further assumed to expect that $\frac{\partial^2 \dot{w}_1^e}{\partial w_1^{e2}} < 0$. This assumption is based on the idea that high-wage firms not only attract new employees by a higher wage rate but in addition advertise more for labor. This means that high-wage firms accumulate employees faster than low-wage firms loose employees and that they therefore decrease their wage rates faster than the low-wage firms increase their wage rates. However, note the objection with respect to the corresponding reasoning as to the rates of price change for firms with different prices.

These assumptions imply that the mathematical expectation of the time derivative of the relative wage rate which the household recieves depends negatively on the relative wage rate:

$$(11) \qquad \frac{\partial E\{\dot{w}^e\}}{\partial w^e} = \frac{\partial \dot{w}_1^e}{\partial w_1^e} - \varepsilon \int_{w_1^e}^{\infty} \hat{f}(v)\, dv < 0$$

while the second-order derivative is undetermined:

---

1) $\hat{f}(w^e)$ is defined analogously to $\hat{f}(p^e)$.

$$(12) \qquad \frac{\partial^2 E\{\dot{w}^e\}}{\partial w^{e2}} = \frac{\partial^2 \dot{w}_1^e}{\partial w_1^{e2}} + \varepsilon \, \hat{f}(w_1^e) \gtreqless 0$$

The household is assumed to expect that the effects cancel so that

$$\frac{\partial^2 E\{\dot{w}^e\}}{\partial w^{e2}} = 0.$$ [1)]

3. Optimal Consumption, Supply of Labor, and Search over Time

The state equations for the price paid by the individual household and the wages it receives were derived in the preceding section. The household can force wages upwards and the price downwards by devoting time to search activity. Of course this will improve the household's future situation, although its present leisure and working time will be reduced. The household can improve its future situation through search activity, but this reduces its possibilities for consumption today. This intertemporal problem of weighing the present against the future will be discussed in this section.

3.1. The utility functional

The household is assumed to plan for a very large number of very short time periods. To simplify, the length of individual time periods tends to zero.[2)] Since instantaneous consumption is the only argument of the utility function, the planning problem consists of choosing a best trajectory in time for consumption so that the utility functional is maximized.

It is further assumed that the instantaneous utilities are additive and that consumption at a certain point of time gives the same utility as consumption at another point of

---

1) Cf. footnote 1, p. 145.

2) Cf. the discussion of the continuous time assumption in section 1.

time, except for a discount factor (the subjective rate of time preference), ρ'. The utility function $u(x)$ is moreover assumed to be twice continuously differentiable with a positive first derivative and a negative second derivative.[1] These assumptions imply that the utility function is cardinally measurable and that the marginal rate of substitution between present and future consumption is independent *inter alia* of consumption at points of time other than the two being compared.

The discounted value of consumption at point of time t is then equal to $e^{-\rho' t} \cdot (u\, x(t))$, where x denotes the consumption level. The total discounted utility of the consumption program from the planning point of time, t=0, to the horizon, t=T, is obtained as:

$$(13) \qquad V\left(\overrightarrow{x(t)}\right) = \int_{0}^{T} e^{-\rho' t}\, u\left(x(t)\right)\, dt$$

where the arrow over $x(t)$ on the left hand side denotes a trajectory to be chosen for x, not a single value.

The horizon is stochastically determined by the time of death. It is assumed that life in itself does not appear as an argument of the utility functional, but is taken into consideration by the fact that the stream of utilities stops at the time of death. This of course is an extreme assumption and could not be defended if the purpose of the analysis were to investigate problems having to do with, for example, health service, hospital care or traffic policy.[2] However, the assumption does not imply anything more than that the risk of death cannot be influenced by the individual. The value of life itself, however it may depend on one's own feeling or on considerations of family, relatives and friends, may be regarded in this connection as a constant which is independent of the behavior of the individual. It is thus not necessary to take this aspect into consideration when formulating the planning problem.

---

[1] A further specification as to the elasticity of the marginal utility with respect to the consumption level will be made below.

[2] *Cf.* Schelling (1968).

Assume that the probability of experiencing an event which causes death is approximately proportional to the length of the time period considered, dt, and that this proportionality holds exactly as dt tends towards zero. Furthermore, assume that two such events could not happen at exactly the same time. Both assumptions are relatively harmless, given the fact that the probability of death cannot be influenced by the individual. If finally the probability is assumed to be independent of chronological time, the number of death-causing events will be generated by a Poisson distribution. The assumption of independence with respect to chronological time simply means that the probability of death is independent of the age of the individual. This assumption is of course unrealistic, but it will considerably simplify the analysis. It should be stressed that the assumption only affects the analysis via the formulation of the planning problem. It is still possible to consider ad hoc the fact that the probability of survival will fall with increasing age.

If the number of fatal events is Poisson distributed, the probability of not experiencing such an event during the time period of length t is equal to $e^{-\delta t}$. The probability of dying during this time period is equal to $1 - e^{-\delta t}$. By definition, the probability of dying at point of time t is equal to the derivative with respect to t of the probability of being dead in the point of time t. This means that the probability of dying at point of time t may be written as $\delta e^{-\delta t}$.

The mathematical expectation of the value of the utility functional may then be calculated by weighting the values of the functional at different horizon time points with their respective probabilities and then summing:

$$\underset{T}{E}\left\{\int_0^T e^{-\rho' t}\, u\big(x(t)\big)\, dt\right\} = \int_0^\infty \delta e^{-\delta T} \int_0^T e^{-\rho'\tau}\, u\big(x(\tau)\big)\, d\tau\, dT$$

The integral may be solved by partial integration and converted to:

(14) $$E\{\int_0^T e^{-\rho' t} u(x(t))\, dt\} = \int_0^\infty e^{-(\delta+\rho')t} u(x(t)) \cdot dt =$$

$$= \int_0^\infty e^{-\rho t} u(x(t))\, dt$$

The mathematical expectation of the value of the utility functional may thus be written as the integral over all instantaneous utilities, weighted by a factor of discount which now depends on not only the subjective rate of time preference, but also the death risk. The integral is taken over an infinite time horizon.

This result is of interest from several points of view. First, in early works in risk theory,[1] it was usual to add a risk factor to the market rate of interest in order to consider the presence of risk. However, it was not clear whether this was permissible, and the procedure was gradually discarded. But in the present case it is evidently permissible to adjust for risk in this way. The procedure is based on the "expected utility hypothesis" and is applicable when risk is present as a stochastically determined time horizon in which the stochastic mechanism is independent of the actions of the individual.

One may further conclude that the presence of death risk automatically causes the individual to behave as if there exists a positive subjective time preference. Even if the "pure" rate of time preference, ρ', is equal to zero, positive time preference will still be revealed by the individual's behavior. The greater the death risk, the higher the "total" subjective rate of time preference, ρ.

Finally, the result is interesting since it shows how a problem principally concerning a finite time horizon may be transformed into a problem with an infinite time horizon. The latter problem is much easier to treat.

The mathematical expectation of the horizon point of time may be calculated as.

$$E\{T\} = \int_0^\infty \delta t\, e^{-\delta t}\, dt = \frac{1}{\delta}$$

---

1) Cf. Schneider (1966), p. 201.

The mathematical expectation of the horizon point of time is thus equal to the inverted value of the parameter of the Poisson distribution. An increased risk of death will, as expected, diminish the mathematical expectation of the remaining life time.

3.2. The choice set

At each point of time, the choice of values for the households' control variables is subject to two constraints, the budget equation and the time-budget equation. The budget equation may be written:

$$(15) \qquad (1-s)\, w^e \bar{w}^e \tau_w - p^e \bar{p}^e x = 0 \quad {}^{1)}$$

i.e., disposable labor income, which is equal to one minus the income tax rate, multiplied by the hourly wage rate and by the working time, should be equal to consumption outlays, the (absolute or monetary) price times the quantity purchas-

---

1) Note that the hourly wage rate is equal to the relative wage rate, w, multiplied by the average wage rate on the market, $\bar{w}$. Moreover, $w\bar{w} = w^e\bar{w}^e$; the actual relative wage rate multiplied with the actual average wage rate on the market is always equal to the expected (with subjective certainty) relative wage rate multiplied by the expected (with subjective certainty) average wage rate on the market. One always knows the hourly wage rate actually paid. The reason why the household may have false expectations as to the average or relative wage rate is that it has an incomplete overview of the labor market and thus does not immediately observe changes in market conditions. In addition, the actual rate of wage inflation may differ from the expected rate. As discussed in section 1, the household is only assumed to have correct information about the average wage level with a lag of h_w time units. The household then makes a projection of the average wage level from that date on to the present point of time with the help of the expected rate of wage inflation, g_w^e. If, for example, the actual rate of wage inflation is higher than the expected rate, the average wage level on the market will be underestimated by the household. This in turn will mean that the relative wage rate is overestimated. This in turn implies that the household believes that wage offers are relatively more attractive than is actually the case. The corresponding argument may be made with respect to the price.

ed.[1]

Secondly, the time budget equation must be fulfilled at each point of time:

$$(16) \qquad 1 - \tau_w - \tau_{sw} - \tau_{sp} = 0$$

i.e., the total available time should be allocated to work and to search on the labor and on the goods market. Since time varies continually, τ_w, τ_{sw} and τ_{sp} should be interpreted as intencities. Furthermore, note that leisure time is not explicitly included in the time budget equation. In the present case it should not be considered as equal to zero, but rather as exogenously given and not constituting any part of the planning problem studied here. Note also that leisure has not been included as an argument of the utility function.

3.3. The change of the choice set over time

The hourly wage and the price in the budget equation (15) are exogenously determined. This means that they are given at each point of time. But the household can influence the rates of change of these two factors by varying its search activity in the labor and goods markets. The mathematical expectation of the rate of change of the relative price is given by equation (6), and the corresponding rate of change of the relative wage rate is given by equation (10). It should be emphasized that these equations only provide information about the average change in the relative price and the relative wage rate. Price and wage changes are stochastic variables and their outcomes can vary considerably around the mathematical expectations. Generally, therefore, the household must formulate alternative plans (strategies) for its future behavior as different changes of the expected

---

[1] Income is thus identical to labor income. The household is assumed to not have any assets or liabilities, and is thus not recieving or paying any interest.

relative price and the expected relative wage rate emerge.[1)]

However, it will be assumed that the mathematical expectations of the rate of increase of the relative price and the relative wage rate serve as a guideline for <u>planning</u>.[2)] When this problem is formulated in terms of dynamic programming, it can be shown[3)] that if (8) and (12) hold[4)], then the solution of the planning problem which is obtained is the same as that based on the general attempt to maximize the mathematical

---

1) If the assumption of subjectively certain expectations is dropped, these alternative plans may also take into consideration the fact that the knowledge of the parameters of the price and the wage distribution is incomplete. The recieved messages then not only influence behavior via a changed price or a changed wage rate, but also change expectations of the characteristics of the distributions, and thus the starting point for future planning.

Technically, the situation could be formulated as a problem within dynamic programming. (For a pedagogical introduction, see Hadley (1964), chapters 10-11.) The problem is to find the optimal policy for steering a stochastic process, where the parameters of the process are not perfectly known and where the information recieved is not necessarily correct; <u>cf</u>. Aoki (1967). The solution of such a problem involves formulation of conditional decision rules. This implies that the best choice at a certain point of time depends not only on the state of the system at that point of time, but also on what has happened before. This is due to the fact that previous events will influence the expectations of the household. Bygones are <u>not</u> bygones. The plans will therefore take the form of strategies, <u>i.e.</u>, rules for choices which give information as to how to behave under all possible alternative future events.

2) The fact that the outcomes of $\dot{w}^e$ and $\dot{p}^e$ can deviate from their mathematical expectations is taken into account through continual revisions of plans.

3) This is done in the appendix to this chapter.

4) It should be noted that (8) and (12) are <u>not</u> identities. If this were the case τ_{sp} and τ_{sw} (and, via the time budget equation, τ_w) would already by determined <u>before</u> the maximization of the utility functional. I am grateful to Tönu Puu for pointing out this problem.

expectation of the utility functional.[1)] Later on, it will be shown that (8) and (12) also imply that the optimal value of (14) is linear with respect to w^e and p^e. The linearity of the utility functional is thus intimately connected with the possibility of working with certainty equivalents.

This result is intuitively appealing. One may draw a parallel with risk theory where it is shown that if the utility function is linear, then the maximum of the mathematical expectation of the utility function is equal to the maximum value or the utility function which is obtained if the stochastic variables attain their mathematical expectations. It should be stressed that the important thing is that the objective function is linear. It is true that the utility function is non-linear, but it is the utility functional, the discounted sum of all future utilities, not the utility function itself -- which represents the preferences.

3.4. The formulation of the optimization problem

The optimization problem may be formulated in the following way. Find trajectories for the control variables-consumption $x(t)$, labor time $\tau_w(t)$, search on the labor market $\tau_{sw}(t)$ and search on the goods market $\tau_{sp}(t)$ -- so as to maximize

---

1) It should be noted that the two sorts of uncertainties, that with respect to the horizon, and that with respect to possible developments of the relative price and the relative wage rate, are independent. What was done in the previous subsection was to show that the mathematical expectation of the utility functional, the date of the horizon being the stochastic variable, could be converted into a deterministic problem with an infinite horizon and an adjusted rate of time preference. Since the death risk is independent of the possibilities of getting into contact with firms offering various relative prices and relative wage rates, the mathematical expectation of the time of the horizon may be taken independently of the other risks. In addition, recall that the date of the horizon is independent of the behavior of the household. The value of the mathematical expectation of the utility functional with respect to the time of the horizon is still a stochastic variable since the risks with respect to different price and wage developments are still present. What is needed, then, is to take the mathematical expectation of the utility functional with respect to different future relative prices and relative wage rates. It is this problem which is now discussed.

the utility functional (14) subject to the constraints that the budget equation (15) and the time budget equation (16) are fulfilled at each point of time and where the phase variables $p^e(t)$ and $w^e(t)$ are determined by the differential equations (6) and (10) and the initial conditions $p^e(0) = p_o^e$ and $w^e(0) = w_o^e$. We assume that the marginal utility $\frac{\partial u}{\partial x}$ and the partial derivatives with respect to the search activity of the production functions generating price and wage messages, $\frac{\partial \varepsilon_p}{\partial \tau_{sp}}$ and $\frac{\partial \varepsilon_w}{\partial \tau_{sw}}$, get so large when the values of the control variables tend towards zero that only inner solutions are obtained.[1]

It should be stressed that this formulation of the problem does not necessarily mean that the household consciously should calculate and choose the best trajectories for the control variables. The interpretation is instead that the household behaves as if it had solved the present infinite dimensional maximization problem. Basically, this does not say anything more than that the household acts according to consistent preferences.

The problem outlined above -- that of choosing optimal trajectories of the action parameters, instead of their optimal values -- is a problem treated by the classical calculus of variations.[2] However, the solution is easier to calculate and the economic significance more clear if one starts from the modern form of the calculus of variations developed by Pontryagin.[3] The following discussion will be based on Arrow's version of Pontryagin's maximum principle.[4]

---

1) The two last conditions are necessary but not sufficient for inner solutions.

2) For a pedagogical treatment which also takes up the problem of maximization subject to constraints, see Forray (1968), chapters 2 and 3.

3) Cf. Pontryagin et. al. (1964).

4) Arrow (1968) and a later version, Arrow and Kurtz (1970). For a very pedagogical derivation of the central theorems of the maximum principle, see Dorfman (1969).

Assume now that there is a program for the control variables $x^x(t)$, $\tau_w^x(t)$, $\tau_{sw}^x(t)$ and $\tau_{sp}^x(t)$, which maximizes (14) and in which the budget equations (15) and (16) and the differential equations (6) and (10) continue to be valid. There are then[1] adjoint variables $\lambda_1(t)$ and $\lambda_2(t)$ and Lagrange multipliers $\mu_1(t)$ and $\mu_2(t)$ such that the instantaneous Hamiltonian

$$(17)\quad H\big(w^e(t),\ p^e(t),\ x(t),\ \tau_w(t),\ \tau_{sw}(t),\ \tau_{sp}(t),\ \lambda_1(t),\ \lambda_2(t),\ \mu_1(t),\ \mu_2(t)\big) = u(x) + \lambda_1\dot{w}^e + \lambda_2\dot{p}^e + \mu_1(1-\tau_w-\tau_{sw}-\tau_{sp}) + \mu_2\Big(\frac{(1-s)w^e\bar{w}^e\tau_w}{\bar{p}^e} - p^e x\Big)$$

is maximized at every point in time t. In addition, if the optimal policy is adhered to, then the adjoint variables $\lambda_1(t)$ and $\lambda_2(t)$ are determined by the differential equations

$$(18)\quad \dot{\lambda}_1 = \rho\lambda_1 - \frac{\partial H^*}{\partial w^e} \quad \text{och} \quad \dot{\lambda}_2 = \rho\lambda_2 - \frac{\partial H^*}{\partial p^e} \text{ [2]}$$

and some transversality conditions which determine the final values of λ_1 and λ_2. These will be discussed later on. Equation (17) is called the instantaneous Hamiltonian because it is not discounted to the planning time $t=0$. This can be done by multiplying (17) by $e^{-\rho t}$. Of course this only affects the scale of the maximum and not its position.

The maximization of (17) implies that the utility of consumption at time t and a weighted sum of the time derivatives of the relative wage rate and the relative price is maximized subject to the budget and the time-budget equations.[3] The maximization of $u(x) + \lambda_1\dot{w}^e + \lambda_2\dot{p}^e$ implies

---

[1] Cf. Arrow (1968), Propositions 4 and 6.

[2] The star indicates that the Hamiltonian is maximized.

[3] The term Hamiltonian is often reserved for the expression $u(x) + \lambda_1\dot{w}^e + \lambda_2\dot{p}^e$. It is clear, however, that the maximization of this sum subject to the budget and the time budget equations is equivalent to the maximization of (17).

that consumption (and indirectly the supply of labor) via the budget equation should be choosen so that the best balance is obtained between present and future utilities. When consumption increases, instantaneous utility will increase. But this implies, given the hourly wage rate, that the supply of labor must increase. And then less time is left over (cf. the time-budget equation) for search in the goods and labor markets.

This in turn implies that the relative wage rate will increase more slowly (fall faster) and the relative price will fall more slowly (increase faster) than before. The future real wage rate of the household will thus be lower, the higher is present consumption. The higher present consumption, the lower is future consumption. There is thus first a problem of balance between present and future consumption.

The effect on the maximum value of the utility functional,

$$\int_t^{\infty} e^{-\rho(\tau-t)} u(x(\tau))\, d\tau,$$

of a variation of the consumption program after the point of time t caused by an increased rate of relative wage increase, $\dot{w}^e$, is accounted for by the marginal present value product of the relative wage rate, λ_1.[1)] The effect on the utility functional of an increased time derivative of the relative wage rate, $\dot{p}^e$, is accounted for by the marginal present value product of the relative price, λ_2. The marginal present value products are calculated in the point of time t. Should they be discounted to the planning point of time, t=0, they must be multiplied by $e^{-\rho t}$. Furthermore, it should be stressed that the marginal present value products are defined for an increase of the relative wage rate and the relative price, not for the rates of increase of the relative wage rate and the relative price.[2)]

---

1) This terminology is quite natural since it stresses the significant parallel to, e.g., the marginal revenue product in production theory. The term present value underlines the fact that it is the effect on a discounted sum which is discussed.

2) Cf. Arrow (1968), p. 88 and Dorfman (1969), p. 820.

3.5. The maximum conditions

In order to simplify the analysis, $\tau_w = 1 - \tau_{sw} - \tau_{sp}$ is substituted into the Hamiltonian. Then the first-order conditions for the Hamiltonian to have an internal maximum can be written:

$$\frac{\partial u}{\partial x} - \mu_2 p^e = 0$$

$$\lambda_1 \frac{\partial \dot{w}^e}{\partial \tau_{sw}} - \mu_2 \frac{(1-s)w^e \bar{w}^e}{\bar{p}^e} = 0$$

(19)

$$\lambda_2 \frac{\partial \dot{p}^e}{\partial \tau_{sp}} - \mu_2 \frac{(1-s)w^e \bar{w}^e}{\bar{p}^e} = 0$$

$$\frac{(1-s)w^e \bar{w}^e}{\bar{p}^e}(1 - \tau_{sw} - \tau_{sp}) - p^e x = 0$$

The first two equations of (19) may be combined to give:

$$\lambda_1 \frac{\partial \dot{w}^e}{\partial \tau_{sw}} = \frac{\partial u}{\partial x} \frac{(1-s)w^e \bar{w}^e}{p^e \bar{p}^e}$$

but the disposable real wage rate of the household, $\frac{(1-s)w^e \bar{w}^e}{p^e \bar{p}^e}$ indicates how much consumption can rise when working time increases. Thus these equations can be rewritten:

$$\lambda_1 \frac{\partial \dot{w}^e}{\partial \tau_{sw}} = \frac{\partial u}{\partial x} \frac{\partial x}{\partial \tau_w}$$

This is a condition for the optimal choice between present and future consumption. The change in the rate of increase in the relative wage rate which occurs if an additional working hour is allocated to search activity on the labor market, multiplied by the marginal present value product of the relative wage rate, λ_1, should be equal to the increase in consumption which could be attained if this hour were used for work instead, multiplied by the utility increase resulting from the rise in consumption.

But the choice does not only concern present and future consumption. There is an additional problem as to how much time should be allocated to search in the goods and labor markets. This is analogous to the problem in growth of choosing not only between consumption and investment, but also allocating the total volume of investment between different investment goods. The second and third equations of (19) may be combined into:

$$\lambda_1 \frac{\partial \dot{w}^e}{\partial \tau_{sw}} = \lambda_2 \frac{\partial \dot{p}^e}{\partial \tau_{sp}}$$

This equation states that if an additional hour were to be allocated to search activity in the labor market, the marginal present value product of the expected relative wage increase which this would bring about is as large as the relative price increase[1)] this same hour would yield if it were used for search activity on the goods market instead, multiplied by the marginal present value product of the price increase, λ_2.

The last equation of (19) is the budget equation. Note that labor time, τ_w, has been substituted for by the time remaining after search in the goods and labor markets according to the time-budget equation.

Equations (19) are necessary but not sufficient conditions for the maximization of the Hamiltonian. In addition, the second-order conditions for maximization of the function must be fulfilled:

---

1) Which actually is a price decrease. Note that both λ_2 and $\frac{\partial \dot{p}^e}{\partial \tau_{sp}}$ are negative.

$$(20)\qquad (dx,\ d\tau_{sw},\ d\tau_{sp},\ d\mu_2)\begin{bmatrix} \frac{\partial^2 H}{\partial x^2} & \cdots & \frac{\partial^2 H}{\partial x \partial \mu_2} \\ \vdots & & \vdots \\ \frac{\partial^2 H}{\partial \mu_2 \partial x} & \cdots & \frac{\partial^2 H}{\partial \mu_2} \end{bmatrix}\begin{bmatrix} dx \\ d\tau_{sw} \\ d\tau_{sp} \\ d\mu_2 \end{bmatrix} < 0$$

for $(1-s)w^e\bar{w}^e(1-\tau_{sw}-\tau_{sp}) - p^e\bar{p}^e x = 0$ and $(dx, d\tau_{sw}, d\tau_{sp}, d\mu_2) \neq 0$.

By investigating the "bordered" principal minors of the matrix above, it is easy to show that the second order conditions are fulfilled.[1]

3.6. Comparative statics: The "incomplete" behavior equations

The next step in the analysis involves investigating how the household's consumption and search activity (and thus, indirectly, its working time) vary with changes in the exogenous variables.

Since λ_1 and λ_2 are regarded as exogenously given at this stage, the complete behavior equations are not obtained. In other words, a change in one of the other exogenous variables will generally affect both λ_1 and λ_2. Thus the behavior obtained would apply <u>if</u> the marginal present value products of relative wages and relative price were constant.[2]

The complete system of behavior equations, which in addition takes account of changes in the two marginal present value products caused by the different parameter changes, will be derived in a later section. This is also the reason for not investigating in this section the effects on the control variables of changes in the (total) subjective time preference,

---

1) Cf. Samuelson (1961), pp. 377-378.

2) The preliminary assumption of exogenous values of the marginal present value products is made for analytical convenience. The economic significance is to study the behavior if the effects on the two shadow prices were compensated for (as in the case of compensated demand curves). It should be emphasized, however, that the incomplete behavior equations are of little interest in themselves, except for their usefulness as a preparation for the later analysis.

ρ, this parameter change will only affect the behavior of the household indirectly, through changed values of the two marginal present value products.

In order to derive the (incomplete) behavior equations, the system (19) is totally differentiated and solved for x, τ_w, τ_{sw} and τ_{sp}. By assuming that the elasticity of the marginal utility (the coefficient of relative risk aversion),

$$R_r = -x \frac{\frac{\partial^2 u}{\partial x^2}}{\frac{\partial u}{\partial x}},$$

is approximately equal to one,[1] the signs of all partial derivatives of the behavior equations will be unambigous and may be written as:[2]

---

1) The argument that the elasticity of the marginal utility (if it is more or less constant) should be equal to one is based on conditions for the utility function to be bounded; see Arrow (1965), pp. 36-37. It can also be shown that a utility function with this property is identical to the utility function exemplified by Bernoulli in the famous St. Petersburg game. If the argument is instead based on the hypothesis of increasing relative risk aversion, then it can be assumed to be approximately equal to one for "normal" consumption levels.

2) Since maximization is done subject to a budget equation, the effect on the behavior of a parameter change may be separated in the usual way into substitution and income effects. Then one may write the following equations:

$$dx = \underset{+}{x_1} dA + \underset{-}{x_2} dB + \underset{-}{x_3} dC + \underset{+}{x_4} dD$$

$$d\tau_{sw} = \underset{-}{\tau_{sw_1}} dA + \underset{+}{\tau_{sw_2}} dB + \underset{-}{\tau_{sw_3}} dC + \underset{+}{\tau_{sw_4}} dD$$

$$d\tau_{sp} = \underset{-}{\tau_{sp_1}} dA + \underset{-}{\tau_{sp_2}} dB + \underset{+}{\tau_{sp_3}} dC + \underset{+}{\tau_{sp_4}} dD$$

where: $dA = -\mu_2 dp^e$

$$dB = \lambda_1 \frac{\partial^2 \dot{w}^e}{\partial w^e \partial \tau_{sw}} dw^e + \lambda_1 \frac{\partial^2 \dot{w}^e}{\partial a_w \partial \tau_{sw}} da_w + \frac{\partial \dot{w}^e}{\partial \tau_{sw}} d\lambda_1$$

$$-\mu_2 \frac{(1-s)\bar{w}^e}{\bar{p}^e} dw^e - \mu_2 w^e d\left[\frac{(1-s)\bar{w}^e}{\bar{p}^e}\right]$$

$$dC = \lambda_2 \frac{\partial^2 \dot{p}^e}{\partial p^e \partial \tau_{sp}} dp^e + \lambda_2 \frac{\partial^2 \dot{p}^e}{\partial a_p \partial \tau_{sp}} da_p + \frac{\partial \dot{p}^e}{\partial \tau_{sp}} d\lambda_2$$

$$-\mu_2 \frac{(1-s)\bar{w}^e}{\bar{p}^e} dw^e - \mu_2 w^e d\left[\frac{(1-s)\bar{w}^e}{\bar{p}^e}\right]$$

(The footnote continues on p. 163)

(21)

$$x = \phi(p^e, w^e, a_w, a_p, \frac{(1-s)\bar{w}^e}{\bar{p}^e}, \lambda_1, \lambda_2)$$
$$\quad - \quad + \quad - \quad - \quad + \quad - \quad +$$

$$\tau_w = \psi(p^e, w^e, a_w, a_p, \frac{(1-s)\bar{w}^e}{\bar{p}^e}, \lambda_1, \lambda_2)$$
$$\quad - \quad + \quad - \quad - \quad o \quad - \quad +$$

$$\tau_{sw} = \chi_w(p^e, w^e, a_w, a_p, \frac{(1-s)\bar{w}^e}{\bar{p}^e}, \lambda_1, \lambda_2)$$
$$\quad - \quad - \quad + \quad - \quad o \quad + \quad +$$

$$\tau_{sp} = \chi_p(p^e, w^e, a_w, a_p, \frac{(1-s)\bar{w}^e}{\bar{p}^e}, \lambda_1, \lambda_2)$$
$$\quad + \quad + \quad - \quad + \quad o \quad - \quad -$$

where the signs of the partial derivatives are indicated under the respective variable in the behavior equations.

(Continuation of footnote 2 from the preceding page)

$$dD = (1 - \tau_{sw} - \tau_{sp})\frac{(1-s)\bar{w}^e}{\bar{p}^e}\,dw^e + (1 - \tau_{sw} - \tau_{sp})w^e d[\frac{(1-s)\bar{w}^e}{\bar{p}^e}]$$
$$-xdp^e$$

and where the signs of the partial derivatives have been indicated under the respective variables in the usual way. The first three arguments of the functions represent substitution effects while the last argument represents the income effect. If for example the relative price, p^e, increases, the effect on consumption may be analyzed with the help of the following Slutsky equation:

$$\frac{\partial x}{\partial p^e} = -\frac{\partial x}{\partial A}\mu_2 + \frac{\partial x}{\partial C}\lambda_2 \frac{\partial^2 \dot{p}^e}{\partial p^e \partial \tau_{sp}} - \frac{\partial x}{\partial D} x < 0$$

Consumption will always fall when p^e increases. The "own" substitution effect (the first term) will always work in that direction. The substitution effect with respect to search activity on the goods market (the second term) as well. If the relative price increases this will namely increase search activity on the goods market. But this implies that there is less time left over for work, which will diminish labor income and thus consumption. The last term represents the income effect. When the relative price increases, this will reduce the disposable real wage of the household. The greater the consumption level to start with, the greater this effect will be. Consumption always decreases when real income falls. Thus, the income effect will also tend to reduce consumption when the relative price increases. It should be noted that the behavior equations written down in this footnote are incomplete. This is because no consideration has been taken of induced changes in λ_1 and λ_2 due to changed parameter values. Finally, observe that the different effects will in some cases be in different directions. However, the assumption that the elasticity of the marginal utility approximately equals one implies that the net effects of all disturbances are of unique signs.

It appears from system (21) that an increase of the relative price, for example, will diminish consumption (and thereby indirectly the supply of labor). Search activity in the goods market will increase, while the search activity in the labor market will diminish. It should be observed that in addition the increased relative price may affect λ_1 and λ_2, and thereby indirectly x, τ_w, τ_{sw} and τ_{sp}. These indirect effects will be considered in the complete behavior equations.

3.7. The transversality conditions

Equations (19) define the household's best policy, given the values of λ_1 and λ_2. However, the marginal present value products of the relative wages and relative price depend on what happens in the future. They are determined only if the best policy is always adhered to. But there is one point in time at which something more definite can be said about these two shadow prices. When the horizon has been reached, relative wages and the relative price should both be non-negative. This implies that the following restrictions (transversality conditions) apply to the shadow prices:

$$\lim_{t\to\infty} \lambda_1(t) \cdot e^{-\rho t} \geq 0, \quad \lim_{t\to\infty} - \lambda_2(t) \cdot e^{-\rho t} \geq 0$$

(22) and

$$\lim_{t\to\infty} e^{-\rho t} \left[\lambda_1(t) w^e(t) - \lambda_2(t) p^e(t)\right] = 0$$

This situation will be reached *inter alia* if w^e and p^e converge towards w^e_∞ and p^e_∞ and the shadow prices towards $\lambda_{1\infty} \geq 0$ and $\lambda_{2\infty} \leq 0$.

If we know the stationary values of λ_1 and λ_2, it is possible to derive "backwards" the initial values $\lambda_1(0)$ and $\lambda_2(0)$ since the changes of the shadow prices, if an optimal policy is followed, are governed by the differential equations (18):

$$\dot{\lambda}_1 = \rho\lambda_1 - \frac{\partial H^*}{\partial w^e} \quad \text{and} \quad \dot{\lambda}_2 = \lambda_2 - \frac{\partial H^*}{\partial p^e}$$

The first of these equations may be rewritten as:

$$\frac{\dot{\lambda}_1}{\lambda_1} + \frac{\partial H^*}{\partial w^e} \cdot \frac{1}{\lambda_1} = \rho$$

If λ_1 is interpreted as the price of the "capital" which is constituted by a high relative wage rate, we may say that this "capital" should be choosen so that a small increase in the relative wage rate (an increase of the "capital") should give a total return equal to the "market rate of interest" -- here equal to the (total) subjective rate of time preference. The total return of this increase in the relative wage rate may be separated into a capital gain part, which consists of the price change on the "capital", and a direct return, consisting of the effect on the Hamiltonian of the change of the "capital".[1] It should be stressed, however, that it is not possible for the household to choose the initial "capital" so that the above optimum condition is fulfilled. It is rather a question of choosing trajectories for the relative wage rate and its marginal present value product so as to fulfill the equation. The second equation may be interpreted analogously.

3.8. A sufficient condition for maximization of the utility functional

If there exists a stationary solution, and if the policy which maximizes the Hamiltonian implies that w^e, p^e, λ_1 and λ_2 converge towards this stationary solution, then there exists a sufficiency condition due to Arrow[2] which says that this policy will maximize the utility functional

---

1) Cf. Dorfman, Samuelson, and Solow (1958), pp. 317-318.

2) See Arrow (1968), proposition 9. For a verification of this condition, cf. Arrow and Kurz (1970), pp. 43-45 and Kamien and Schwartz (1971).

If H^{*}[1] is concave in the phase variables w^e and p^e. Let us investigate whether this condition is fulfilled. First, the following hold:

$$\frac{\partial^2 H^*}{\partial w^{e2}} = \lambda_1 \frac{\partial^2 \dot{w}^e}{\partial w^{e2}} = 0 \quad ; \quad \frac{\partial^2 H^*}{\partial p^{e2}} = \lambda_2 \frac{\partial^2 \dot{p}^e}{\partial p^{e2}} = 0$$

Furthermore,

$$\frac{\partial^2 H^*}{\partial p^e \partial w^e} = \frac{\partial^2 H^*}{\partial w^e \partial p^e} = 0$$

Thus the concavity condition

$$(dw^e,\ dp^e) \begin{bmatrix} \dfrac{\partial^2 H^*}{\partial w^{e2}} & \dfrac{\partial^2 H^*}{\partial p^e \partial w^e} \\ \\ \dfrac{\partial^2 H^*}{\partial w^e \partial p^e} & \dfrac{\partial^2 H^*}{\partial p^{e2}} \end{bmatrix} \begin{bmatrix} dw^e \\ \\ dp^e \end{bmatrix} \leq 0$$

is fulfilled.

4. Phase Diagram Analysis

The policy which maximizes the Hamiltonian, given the values of the phase variables w^e and p^e and the shadow prices λ_1 and λ_2, was derived in the preceding section. Both w^e and p^e have a certain value at the outset. Then, given a policy which maximizes the Hamiltonian, the initial values of the shadow prices will determine the trajectories of the phase variables and the shadow prices. Every choice of initial values for λ_1 and λ_2 leads to a definite path. Thus $\lambda_1(0)$

---

[1] The star indicates that the Hamiltonian is maximized. It is easy to show that the total derivatives of the Hamiltonian, where the effects of compensating changes in the control variables due to changes in the exogenous variables have been taken into consideration, are equal to the direct partial derivatives. This further means that the concavity conditions do not locally restrict the signs and magnitudes of the partial derivatives of the incomplete behavior equations. Nevertheless, since (8) and (12) are not to be interpreted as identities (cf. note 4 on page 154), parameter changes may affect the value of $\partial^2\dot{w}^e/\partial w^{e2}$ and $\partial^2\dot{p}^e/\partial p^{e2}$. For the concavity conditions still to be fulfilled, even when disturbances are not "very small", $\partial^2\dot{w}^e/\partial w^{e2}$ and $\partial^2\dot{p}^e/\partial p^{e2}$ have to be negative. The solution of the planning problem, as presented in the present chapter, will then only be approximate.

and $\lambda_2(0)$ have to be chosen so that the transversality conditions (22) are satisfied. For this purpose a diagrammatic method is used to examine how $\dot{w}^e$, $\dot{p}^e$, $\dot{\lambda}_1$ and $\dot{\lambda}_2$ depend on w^e, p^e, λ_1 and λ_2. The type of diagram employed is a phase diagram, and the curves drawn describe the locus of w^e, p^e, λ_1 and λ_2 where, for example, $\dot{w}^e = 0$. The task is then to investigate what will happen when $\dot{w}^e$ is off of this curve. The analysis is quite similar to that of market equilibrium curves and on the whole serves the same purpose.[1] Where the phase curves intersect, all changes cease, and the point of stationary equilibrium is attained. The transversality conditions are fulfilled at that point. There are, however, important differences between this analysis and that of market equilibrium curves. In the latter case the stability of the model will generally be examined by starting from any point in a small neighborhood of the stationary solution. In analysis of phase diagrams, all points but those lying on a certain curve are inconsistent with convergence. The initial values of λ_1 and λ_2 are then choosen so that the trajectory generated will meet the point of intersection between and phase curves.

It may also be added that points outside the market equilibrium curves are not even characterized by flow equilibrium. The trajectory chosen with the aid of the phase diagram is on the other hand characterized by flow equilibrium in each and every point. Furthermore, the point where the trajectory meets the intersection between the phase curves is even characterized by stock equilibrium in the present analysis. Finally, the behavior of entire markets is analyzed with the help of market equilibrium curves, whereas we only consider the behavior of individual households. With these differences in mind, the parallels between the two methods of analysis can be instructive.

The first phase curve studied is that defining the rate of increase in the relative wage rate. The behavior equations derived from the policy that maximized the Hamiltonian are substituted into (10) to obtain:

---

1) See Patinkin (1965), chapter X.

$$\dot{w}^e = \dot{w}_1^e + \varepsilon_w(\chi_w, a_w) \int_{w_1^e}^{\infty} (v - w_1^e)\, \hat{f}(v)\, dv$$

Differentiation of $\dot{w}^e$ yields

$$(23) \qquad \dot{w}^e = \dot{w}^e(\underset{-}{p^e}, \underset{-}{w^e}, \underset{+}{a_w}, \underset{-}{a_p}, \underset{o}{\frac{(1-s)\bar{w}^e}{\bar{p}^e}}, \underset{+}{\lambda_1}, \underset{+}{\lambda_2})$$

where the signs for the partial derivatives are shown under the appropriate variables. The projection of the phase curve $\dot{w}^e = 0$ onto the (λ_1, w^e)-plane has a positive slope:

$$\left.\frac{\partial \lambda_1}{\partial w^e}\right|_{\dot{w}^e = o} = - \frac{\dfrac{\partial \dot{w}^e}{\partial w^e}}{\dfrac{\partial \dot{w}^e}{\partial \lambda_1}} > 0$$

The time derivative of the marginal present value product of wage increases can be written as:

$$(24) \qquad \dot{\lambda}_1 = \rho \lambda_1 - \frac{\partial H^*}{\partial w^e}$$

This equation will be differentiated with respect to the phase variables, the exogenous variables and the shadow prices.

Thus the time derivative of the marginal revenue product of wage increases can be written as the following function:

$$(25) \qquad \dot{\lambda}_1 = \dot{\lambda}_1(\underset{o}{p^e}, \underset{o}{w^e}, \underset{+}{a_w}, \underset{o}{a_p}, \underset{-}{\frac{(1-s)\bar{w}^e}{\bar{p}^e}}, \underset{+}{\lambda_1}, \underset{o}{\lambda_2}, \underset{+}{\rho})$$ [1)]

where the signs for the partial derivatives are indicated

1) Note that the time derivative of the marginal present value product is homogeneous of zero degree in $(1-s)\bar{w}^e$ and $\bar{p}^e$. This means that a proportional increase of the average wage and price level will not influence the planning of the household.

under the variables. The slope of the projection of the phase curve in the (λ_1, w^e)-plane is obtained as

$$\left.\frac{\partial \lambda_1}{\partial w^e}\right|_{\dot{\lambda}_1 = 0} = - \frac{\dfrac{\partial \dot{\lambda}_1}{\partial w^e}}{\dfrac{\partial \dot{\lambda}_1}{\partial \lambda_1}} = 0$$

In other words, the slope of the phase curve is equal to zero and is closely associated with Arrow's sufficiency conditions because

$$\frac{\partial \dot{\lambda}_1}{\partial w^e} = - \frac{\partial^2 H^*}{\partial w^{e2}} = 0$$

The two phase curves $\dot{\lambda}_1 = 0$ and $\dot{w}^e = 0$ are now collected in a diagram (see figure 4).

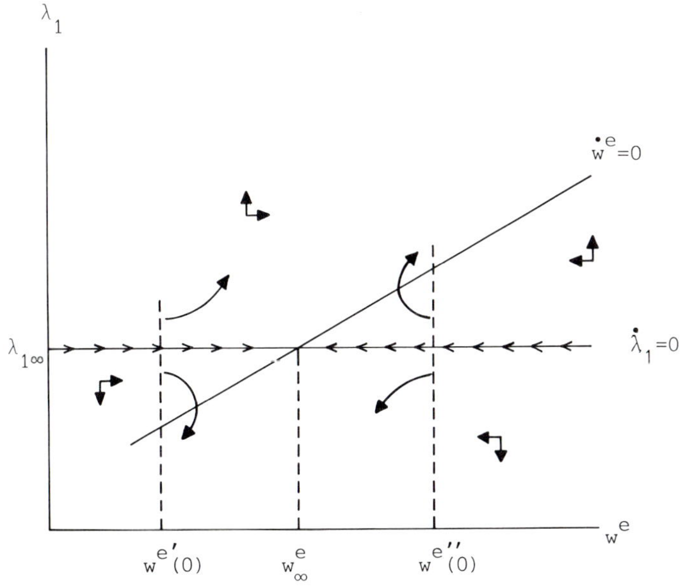

Fig. III:4. The phase diagram in the w^e, λ_1-plane.

The curve $\dot{w}^e = 0$ in Figure 4 indicates the locus of the values of λ_1 and w^e where, all else being constant, relative wages are constant. Wage increases or decreases are obtained by choosing values of w^e and λ_1 which lie off the phase curve. Since $\frac{\partial \dot{w}^e}{\partial w^e}$ is negative, relative wages will rise if they are less than the relative wages where $\dot{w}^e = 0$ and vice versa. This is illustrated in the figure by horizontal arrows. Furthermore, if λ_1 is greater than the value which implies that $\dot{w}^e = 0$, then relative wages will rise since $\frac{\partial \dot{w}^e}{\partial \lambda_1}$ is greater than zero. The situation is reversed for the case where λ_1 is lower than the value located on the phase curve. These forces are also illustrated by the horizontal arrows in the figure. It can be observed in both cases that if wages are not on the phase curve $\dot{w}^e = 0$ at the outset, they tend to change so as to return to this curve.

The vertical arrows in Figure 4 indicate the direction in which the shadow price will move when it is not on the phase curve $\dot{\lambda}_1 = 0$. Since

$$\frac{\partial \dot{\lambda}_1}{\partial \lambda_1} > 0,$$

the distance from the phase curve will increase from points above or below it.

Thus the "arrow angles" in the figure show the forces which affect relative wages and their marginal present value product at points off the phase curves. A stationary position is reached (in this projection) at the point where curves intersect. All movement stops unless some parameter change occurs. How should $\lambda_1(0)$ be chosen in order to reach the path of the stationary solution? Assume that wages at time zero are equal to $w^{e'}(0)$; see Figure 4. It is obvious that $\lambda_1(0)$ should be chosen to equal $\lambda_{1\infty}$. If $\lambda_1(0)$ is higher than $\lambda_{1\infty}$, we will be moved farther and farther from the stationary solution. The same applies if $\lambda_1(0)$ is lower than $\lambda_{1\infty}$. The same analysis holds for any other initial value of relative wages such as $w^{e''}(0)$. The optimal path in the (λ_1, w^e)-

plane is thus shown to be identical with the phase curve $\dot{\lambda}_1 = 0$.[1] This is a very useful result, even if it is not applicable in general. The path coincides with $\dot{\lambda}_1 = 0$ only when $\dot{\lambda}_1 = 0$ is horizontal. In this case

$$\frac{\partial \lambda_1}{\partial w^e} = 0$$

i.e., the slope of the optimal path in the projection is also horizontal. An additional simplifying result should also be noted. Since

$$\frac{\partial \dot{\lambda}_1}{\partial w^e} = \frac{\partial \dot{\lambda}_1}{\partial p^e} = \frac{\partial \dot{\lambda}_1}{\partial \lambda_2} = 0,$$

λ_1 is not affected by the state of the system, i.e., by the current point in the w^e, p^e, λ_1, λ_2 space (the phase space) at which we find ourselves. Of course, this is true only if the optimal path is adhered to, since $\dot{\lambda}_1$ is affected by λ_1. This means that λ_1 can be regarded as constant which will not change unless some exogenous variable changes.

As in the case of relative wages, the policy that maximizes the Hamiltonian can be substituted in the transfer equation for the relative price, (6):

---

1) It should be stressed that w^e and p^e are stochastic variables. As pointed out before, planning is based on the mathematical expectation of $\dot{w}^e$ and $\dot{p}^e$, respectively. The outcome of the changes of the relative wage rate and the relative price may however differ from the mathematical expectation of the changes. This means that the optimal trajectory in the w^e, λ_1-plane may differ from the depicted one. This is partly due to the fact that the relative wage rate does not move continuously in the plane but is subject to jumps. However, λ_1 is constant and equal to its stationary value, which means that the system moves according to the optimal trajectory. The phase curve $\dot{w}^e = 0$ is further subject to stochastic shifts when p^e changes discretely. This is not a problem, since observation of a stochastic change of w^e or p^e will only mean that the initial conditions have been changed. Given the initial values of w^e and p^e, the planning will then again be based on the mathematical expectation of the time derivatives of the two phase variables. The corresponding comments could of course be made further on in connection with the phase diagram in the p^e, λ_2-plane and the w^e, p^e-plane.

$$\dot{p}^e = \dot{p}_k^e + \varepsilon(\chi_p, a_p) \int_o^{p_k^e} (\tau - p_k^e)\ f(\pi)\ d\pi$$

Differentiation of $\dot{p}^e$ yields

$$(26) \qquad \dot{p}^e = \dot{p}^e(\underset{-}{p^e}, \underset{-}{w^e}, \underset{+}{a_w}, \underset{-}{a_p}, \underset{o}{\frac{(1-s)\bar{w}^e}{\bar{p}^e}}, \underset{+}{\lambda_1}, \underset{+}{\lambda_2})$$

where the signs for the partial derivatives are shown below the relevant argument of the function.

The differential equation for the marginal present value product of an increase in prices can be written as:

$$(27) \qquad \dot{\lambda}_2 = \rho\lambda_2 - \frac{\partial H^*}{\partial p^e}$$

The following function for $\dot{\lambda}_2$ is obtained by differentiation of (18):

$$(28) \qquad \dot{\lambda}_2 = \dot{\lambda}_2(\underset{o}{p^e}, \underset{o}{w^e}, \underset{o}{a_w}, \underset{-}{a_p}, \underset{o}{\frac{(1-s)\bar{w}^e}{\bar{p}^e}}, \underset{o}{\lambda_1}, \underset{+}{\lambda_2}, \underset{-}{\rho})$$ [1)]

where the signs under the arguments are those for the respective partial derivatives of the function.

With a phase diagram analysis of $\dot{p}^e$ and $\dot{\lambda}_2$ corresponding to the analysis of $\dot{w}^e$ and $\dot{\lambda}_1$, it can be shown that the optimal path is identical with the phase curve $\dot{\lambda}_2 = 0$ and therefore that

$$\frac{\partial\lambda_2}{\partial p^e} = 0.$$

It should also be noted that since

---

1) Observe that the time derivative of the marginal present value product of the relative price is homogeneous of degree zero in $(1-s)\bar{w}^e$, $\bar{p}^e$.

$$\frac{\partial \dot{\lambda}_2}{\partial w^e} = \frac{\partial \dot{\lambda}_2}{\partial p^e} = \frac{\partial \dot{\lambda}_2}{\partial \lambda_1} = 0$$

not only λ_1, but also λ_2 can be regarded as constant. In other words, they are not affected by the state of the system, although of course they may change if any of the exogenous variables changes. Since λ_1 and λ_2 are constant, the utility functional (14) is linear in w^e and p^e.

The fact that λ_1 and λ_2 are constant in time means that the optimal path in the phase space can be studied in the projection on the (w^e,p^e)-plane alone without any loss of information. Therefore, $\dot{w}^e = 0$ and $\dot{p}^e = 0$ in the (w^e, p^e)-plane will be examined. The slope of $\dot{w}^e = 0$ is

$$\left.\frac{\partial w^e}{\partial p^e}\right|_{\dot{w}^e=o} = - \frac{\dfrac{\partial \dot{w}^e}{\partial p^e}}{\dfrac{\partial \dot{w}^e}{\partial w^e}} < 0$$

since $\frac{\partial \dot{w}^e}{\partial p^e}$ and $\frac{\partial \dot{w}^e}{\partial w^e}$ are both negative. Analogously, the slope of the phase curve $\dot{p}^e = 0$ is also negative ($\frac{\partial \dot{p}^e}{\partial p^e}$ and $\frac{\partial \dot{p}^e}{\partial w^e}$ are negative):

$$\left.\frac{\partial w^e}{\partial p^e}\right|_{\dot{p}^e=o} = - \frac{\dfrac{\partial \dot{p}^e}{\partial p^e}}{\dfrac{\partial \dot{p}^e}{\partial w^e}} < 0$$

Thus both of the phase curves have a negative slope. This implies that different cases have to be studied, depending on which of the curves has the steeper slope. It will suffice for our purposes here to examine the stable case where the phase curve $\dot{p}^e = 0$ has a steeper slope than $\dot{w}^e = 0$.

Thus we obtain the phase diagram shown in Figure 5.

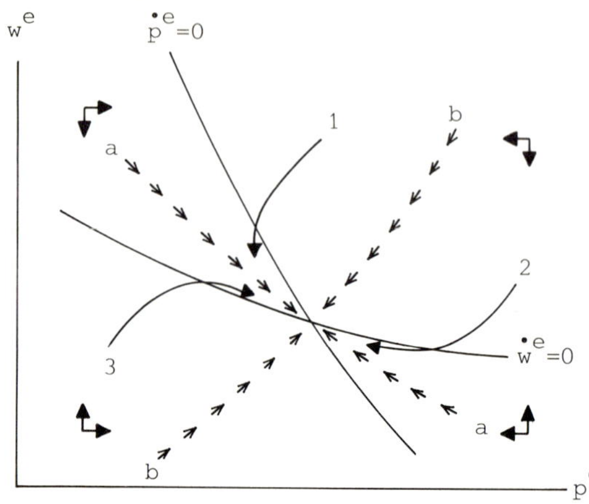

Fig. III:5. The phase diagram in the p^e, w^e-plane.

In this case w^e and p^e will always converge towards (the uniquely determined) stationary solution. There are two "main paths" towards the stationary solution, a - a and b - b. Path a - a is stable in the sense that regardless of the initial position of w^e and p^e, relative wages and the relative price will tend to move towards this main path and then follow it until the stationary solution is reached. The main path a - a can be described as indicating balanced increase or decrease in real wages. If real wages at the outset are higher than stationary real wages (at a point northwest of the intersection of the phase curves) then real wages will decrease because the price rises and wages are reduced. This is brought about by the fact that "net investments" in search activity on the labor and commodity markets are negative. From a state off the main path a-a, at 1 for example, relative wages and the relative price will both decrease at the outset. The household can be regarded as having redistributed the items on the asset side of its fictious balance sheet so that the capital represented by high relative wages decreases while capital in the form of a low relative price increases. However, when the phase curve $\dot{p}^e = 0$ is passed, both types of assets will decrease: relative wages will be lowered while the relative price will rise.

When the initial state is at 2 in Figure 5, relative wages and the relative price will, as in the preceding case, decrease at the outset. When the phase curve $\dot{w}^e = 0$ is passed, relative wages will increase while the relative price will continue to decrease.

The main path a - a is a turnpike. But there is also a knife-edge: the main path b - b. If we find ourselves on the latter, we will follow this path all the way to the stationary solution. But the smallest deviation from b - b at the outset will carry us farther and farther away from this path and towards the main path a - a. If b - b is adhered to, relative wages and the relative price will either decrease or increase monotonically until the stationary solution is reached. This means that the main path b - b is characterized by a redistribution between the two types of capital (high relative wages and low relative price).

Thus far the development of the phase variables and the adjoint variables has been studied under the assumption that the exogenous variables are constant. We conclude this section by investigating how the stationary solution is affected by different parameter changes. The results obtained are also necessary to enable derivation of the complete behavior equations.

Disturbance analysis of the stationary solution is carried out in the usual way by total differentiation of the equation system $\dot{\lambda}_1 = 0$, $\dot{\lambda}_2 = 0$. This yields:

$$\lambda_{1\infty} = \lambda_{1\infty}(\underset{-}{a_w}, \underset{o}{a_p}, \underset{+}{(1-s)\bar{w}^e/\bar{p}^e}, \underset{-}{\rho})$$

(29)

$$\lambda_{2\infty} = \lambda_{2\infty}(\underset{o}{a_w}, \underset{+}{a_p}, \underset{o}{(1-s)\bar{w}^e/\bar{p}^e}, \underset{+}{\rho})$$

5. The Complete Behavior Equations

Section 3 contained a derivation of the behavior equations under the assumption that the adjoint variables λ_1 and λ_2 were exogenously determined. But these marginal present value products usually depend on the values of the exogenous as well as the phase variables. However, the assumption that the adjoint variables do not depend on the state of the system simplifies the analysis considerably. The change in the marginal present value products will then be equal to the change in their stationary values:[1)]

$$\frac{\partial \lambda_i}{\partial \xi} = \frac{\partial \lambda_{i\infty}}{\partial \xi}, \quad i = 1,2$$

Thus, in order to derive the complete behavior equations, it is sufficient to know the incomplete behavior equations (12) and the stationary values with respect to the dependence of the adjoint variables (29) on the exogenous variables.

Equation (29) indicates that only a_w, a_p, $\frac{(1-s)\bar{w}^e}{\bar{p}^e}$ and ρ affect the shadow prices. Thus the other partial derivatives of the complete behavior equations are identical with those in the incomplete equations. Differences can arise only with respect to a_w, a_p, $\frac{(1-s)\bar{w}^e}{\bar{p}^e}$ and ρ. These points will be discussed prior to presentation of the complete behavior equations.

In general, the total effect of an increase in firms' recruitment activities, a_w, on <u>e.g</u>. consumption can be written as

$$\frac{\partial x}{\partial a_w} = \frac{\partial \phi}{\partial a_w} + \frac{\partial \phi}{\partial \lambda_1} \frac{\partial \lambda_1}{\partial a_w} + \frac{\partial \phi}{\partial \lambda_2} \frac{\partial \lambda_2}{\partial a_w}$$

where ϕ is the function sign for the incomplete behavior equation for consumption.

By carrying out a corresponding analysis of the changes in a_p, $(1-s)\bar{w}^e/\bar{p}^e$ and ρ, the signs of the partial derivatives for the complete behavior equations are obtained:

---

1) This line of reasoning presupposes that changes in the exogenous variables do not affect the constancy of the adjoint variables over time. But if a_w and a_p are changed, the slope of $\dot{\lambda}_1 = 0$ and $\dot{\lambda}_2 = 0$ can be affected. These problems are disregarded here.

(30)
$$
\begin{aligned}
x &= x(\underset{-}{p^e}, \underset{+}{w^e}, \underset{?}{a_w}, \underset{?}{a_p}, \underset{+}{\frac{(1-s)\bar{w}^e}{\bar{p}^e}}, \underset{+}{\rho}) \\
\tau_w &= \tau_w(\underset{-}{p^e}, \underset{+}{w^e}, \underset{?}{a_w}, \underset{?}{a_p}, \underset{-}{\frac{(1-s)\bar{w}^e}{\bar{p}^e}}, \underset{+}{\rho}) \\
\tau_{sw} &= \tau_{sw}(\underset{-}{p^e}, \underset{-}{w^e}, \underset{?}{a_w}, \underset{?}{a_p}, \underset{+}{\frac{(1-s)\bar{w}^e}{\bar{p}^e}}, \underset{?}{\rho}) \\
\tau_{sp} &= \tau_{sp}(\underset{+}{p^e}, \underset{+}{w^e}, \underset{?}{a_w}, \underset{?}{a_p}, \underset{-}{\frac{(1-s)\bar{w}^e}{\bar{p}^e}}, \underset{?}{\rho})
\end{aligned}
$$

The effects are as expected and do not require any detailed comments. However, it might be interesting to note that an increase in the flow of information in the commodity and labor markets does not have a unique effect on the control variables. This is because an increase in the information flow in, e.g., the labor market makes it marginally more profitable to search for a better paying job - and this would increase τ_{sw}. On the other hand, even if there is no change in the household's search activity on the labor market, the frequency of signals from the firms increases - with effects in the opposite direction.

The reason why the (total) subjective rate of time preference[1] does not have any unique effects on search activity is the prevalence of cross effects. An increased ρ will reduce the marginal present value product of the relative wage rate, which tends to reduce search activity on the labor market. On the other hand, λ_2 will increase,[2] which tends to increase search on the labor market. The total search activity will however decrease, since the supply of

---

1) Remember that $\rho = \rho' + \delta$; i.e., the "total" subjective rate of time preference equals the sum of the "pure" rate of time preference and the death risk parameter.

2) Note that λ_2 is negative. The increased subjective rate of time preference thus implies that the shadow price of relative price ~~decreases~~ diminishes.

labor and consumption increase. The reason for the uncertainty as to the effects on search activity is that the decreased search activity may be unevenly distributed between the two markets and, in extreme cases, diminish in one of the markets.

It is now time to discuss what effects inflation will have on household behavior. It may first be noted that the relative price, the relative wage rate, and their market averages, are the values expected by the household. They can deviate from the true values. Since the wages and prices observed are always equal to those which were expected -- $w\bar{w} = w^e\bar{w}^e$ and $p\bar{p} = p^e\bar{p}^e$ -- the first two arguments in the behavior equations (30) can be written as

$$(31) \qquad p^e = p \cdot \frac{\bar{p}}{\bar{p}^e} \quad \text{and} \quad w^e = w\,\frac{\bar{w}}{\bar{w}^e},$$

where p^e is the relative price expected by the household, and p is the true relative price.

Since the household continually revises its expectations as to average wages and the average price on the market, the quotient of the true and the expected average price (wages) will be a function of the difference between the actual and expected rates of inflation:[1)]

$$(32) \qquad \frac{\bar{w}}{\bar{w}^e} = e^{h_w(g_w-g_w^e)}\,; \quad \frac{\bar{p}}{\bar{p}^e} = e^{h_p(g_p-g_p^e)}$$

where h_w and h_p are the coefficients which indicate the speed with which expected average wages (price) are adjusted to the actual values, g_w and g_p denote the actual rates of inflation with respect to wages and price, and g_w^e and g_p^e designate the expected rates. By substituting (31) and (32), into (30), the following behavior equations are obtained.

1) Cf. the discussion of section 1.2.1 and 1.2.2 above.

$$
\begin{aligned}
x &= x(\underset{-}{pe^{h_p(g_p-g_p^e)}}, \underset{+}{we^{h_w(g_w-g_w^e)}}, \underset{?}{a_w}, \underset{?}{a_p}, \underset{+}{\frac{(1-s)\bar{w}^e}{\bar{p}^e}}, \underset{+}{\rho}) \\
\tau_w &= \tau_w(\underset{-}{pe^{h_p(g_p-g_p^e)}}, \underset{+}{we^{h_w(g_w-g_w^e)}}, \underset{?}{a_w}, \underset{?}{a_p}, \underset{-}{\frac{(1-s)\bar{w}^e}{\bar{p}^e}}, \underset{+}{\rho}) \\
\tau_{sw} &= \tau_{sw}(\underset{-}{pe^{h_p(g_p-g_p^e)}}, \underset{-}{we^{h_w(g_w-g_w^e)}}, \underset{?}{a_w}, \underset{?}{a_p}, \underset{+}{\frac{(1-s)\bar{w}^e}{\bar{p}^e}}, \underset{?}{\rho}) \\
\tau_{sp} &= \tau_{sp}(\underset{+}{pe^{h_p(g_p-g_p^e)}}, \underset{+}{we^{h_w(g_w-g_w^e)}}, \underset{?}{a_w}, \underset{?}{a_p}, \underset{-}{\frac{(1-s)\bar{w}^e}{\bar{p}^e}}, \underset{?}{\rho})
\end{aligned}
\tag{33}
$$

It appears from the equation system that an increase of the rate of unexpected price inflation will reduce consumption. This effect is consistent with the idea that inflation will generate "forced saving", but it will only happen if actual wage increases are held back, i.e., if there is no parallel increase in the rate of unexpected wage inflation.

The supply of labor also depends negatively on the rate of unexpected price inflation and positively on the rate of unexpected wage inflation. An unexpected increase in the rate of wage inflation in comparison to the rate of price inflation implies that the households believe that they get higher relative wage rates in comparison to the relative prices. This means that an actual increase in the real wage rates of the households in the short run (before expectations are adjusted to changed market conditions) will imply an increased supply of labor. In the long run, when expectations have been adjusted to the actual development of real wage rates, the supply of labor will depend negatively on the real wage rate; note the fifth argument of the second equation of (33).

It also appears from (33) that an increased rate of unexpected price inflation will increase the "price consciousness" of the household; search activity in the goods market will increase. The same effect is obtained if the actual rate of wage inflation increases in comparison to the expected rate. On the other hand, search activity on the labor market will decrease in that case. The increased rate of unexpected wage inflation means that the households believe that they get a higher relative wage rate than is actually the case. This means that they will reallocate their search activity from the labor market (where it is now believed to be less profitable to search very intensively) to the goods market.

Appendix to chapter III

In this chapter, the behavior of the household was derived subject to the assumption that its planning was based on the mathematical expectation of the time derivative of the relative price and the relative wage rate. One may ask how the planning problem would be formulated under more general assumptions. For example, how should one formulate the optimization problem if the household tries to maximize the mathematical expectation of the utility functional

$$\int_0^\infty e^{-\rho t}\, u\{x(t)\}\, dt$$

(and thus behaves according to the von Neumann-Morgenstern conditions)? Under what circumstances will the optimal strategies coincide with the suboptimal strategies derived in this chapter? In the following the general decision problem will be solved with the help of Bellman's programming.[1] It will be shown, that the (optimal value of) the utility functional is linear in the two phase variables p^e and w^e and that the two solutions coincide. The linearity of the utility functional in the (initial values of) the relative price and the relative wage rate implies that

$$\frac{\partial \lambda_1}{\partial w^e} = \frac{\partial \lambda_1}{\partial p^e} = \frac{\partial \lambda_2}{\partial w^e} = \frac{\partial \lambda_2}{\partial p^e} = 0$$

---

1) See Bellman (1957), Bellman and Dreyfus (1962), and Hadley (1964), chapters 10 and 11.

Intuitively, one would also expect that a utility functional, the value of which is linear in the stochastic variables, would give the same maximum solution if the expected values of the stochastic variables are inserted as if the mathematical expectation of the utility functional constitutes the starting point.

To derive the necessary conditions for the maximization of the utility functional, Bellman's principle of optimality will be used. This is the cornerstone in dynamic programming and implics the following: if we start from an additive utility function and want to maximize a weighted sum of the utilities in each point of time, then it is a necessary condition for maximizing the sum from the point of time 0 to the horizon that the sum will be maximized from any arbitrary point of time, t, up to the horizon. The principle of optimality starts from the correct observation that if a sum of say n terms should be maximized, then, independent of the initial value given by the first term, the sum of the additional $n-1$ terms must be maximized. And the maximum of the sum of the n terms is then obtained as the maximized sum of the first term and the remaining $n-1$ terms, where the sum of the latter terms is maximized at each initial value given by the first term.

The necessary conditions for maximizing the mathematical expectation of the utility functional from an arbitrary point of time, t, up to the horizon, will now be derived. Note first that the value of the functional depends on the initial values of the phase variables p^e and w^e and (not written out explicitly), the values of the exogenous variables. The utility functional is thus denoted by:

$$E\{V(w^e(t),\ p^e(t),\ t)\}$$

where E is the mathematical expectation operator. If the utility functional attains its maximum value, this will be denoted by a star. If the value of the utility functional is discounted to the point of time 0, the expression must be multiplied by $e^{-\rho t}$. The utility functional will now be split up into the terms which concern the development during the period from t to t + dt, and the terms which concern the development after t + dt. If the utility functional is maximized from the point of time t + dt and forwards it may be written as:

$$\text{(1)} \quad E\{V(w^e(t),\ p^e(t),\ t)\} = \int_t^{t+dt} e^{-\rho\theta}\, u(x(\theta))\, d\theta \ + $$
$$+\ E\{V^*(w^e(t+dt),\ p^e(t+dt),\ t+dt)\}$$

where the length of the period dt is so short that no changes (stochastic or otherwise) manage to happen. This assumption is fully motivated first when dt tends towards zero.[1] For the utility functional (1) to be maximized, the first term of the right hand side must be maximized subject to the relevant constraints and with consideration of the effect on the value of the utility functional from the point of time t + dt and on. The latter is done by considering the effect the control variables may have on the values of the phase variables at time t + dt. Thus the following expression should be maximized:

$$\max E\{V(w^e(t),\ p^e(t),\ t)\} =$$
$$\text{(2)} \quad = \max \Bigg[\int_t^{t+dt} e^{-\rho\theta}\Big[u(x(\theta)) + \mu_1(1 - \tau_w(\theta) - \tau_{sw}(\theta) - \tau_{sp}(\theta)) + \mu_2 \frac{1-s)w^e(\theta)\bar{w}^e}{\bar{p}^e}\tau_w(\theta) - p^e(\theta)\,x(\theta))\Big]\, d\theta \ +$$
$$+\ E\{V^*(w^e(t+dt),\ p^e(t+dt),\ t+dt)\}\Bigg]$$

---

1) When time varies continually the household will at each instant of time note every change in w^e and p^e and will immediately adjust the values of the control variables to the changed situation. This implies that there does not exist any uncertainty (<u>i.e.</u>, the values of the relative wage rate and the relative price are expected with subjective certainty) for the point of time in which the values of the phase variables are determined. The uncertainty concerns the development after that point of time.

Here it is assumed that the length of the time period dt is so short that the values of the control variables may be constant from t to t + dt. This will of course only be strictly correct when dt tends towards zero. If dt is "small", (2) may be rewritten as:

$$\max E\{V(w^e(t),\ p^e(t),t)\} = \max \Big[\Big(u(x) + \mu_1(1-\tau_w-\tau_{sw}-\tau_{sp}) + \mu_2\Big(\frac{(1-s)w^e\bar{w}^e}{\bar{p}^e}\tau_w - p^e x\Big)\Big) dt + E\{V^*(w^e(t+dt),\ p^e(t+dt),\ t+dt)\} \Big] \tag{3}$$

The expression will form the starting point for the following discussion. Before deriving the necessary conditions for maximizing (3), it is necessary to get a more explicit expression for $E\{V^*(w^e(t+dt),\ p^e(t+dt),\ t+dt)\}$. The expression is an average value of the utility functional as seen from the point of time t + dt. The value depends on the initial values of w^e and p^e, and these are stochastic. The values of $w^e(t+dt)$ and $p^e(t+dt)$ depend on which firms with a lower price than the present supplier, and which firms with a higher wage rate than the present employer, the household happens to get into contact with. To be able to calculate the mathematical expectation of the utility functional, it is necessary to know the probabilities of different relative wage rates and different relative prices at the point of time t + dt.[1)]

---

1) The procedure thus implies that the mathematical expectation of the utility functional is calculated for the point of time t+dt and that the expectations operation is done over all concievable values of $w^e(t+dt)$ and $p^e(t+dt)$. The mathematical expectation has thus been calculated with respect to the uncertainty concerning the period from t to t + dt. In addition, there is naturally uncertainty about the development of the relative wage rate and the relative price after the latter point of time. When $E\{V^*(w^e(t+dt),\ p^e(t+dt),\ t+dt)\}$ is calculated, the arithmetic average of the utility functional over the relative frequences of different relative wage rates and different relative prices in the period t to t + dt is thus obtained. If the expectations symbol is not used, the value of the utility functional, starting from time t + dt, and knowing the values of the (expected) relative wage rate and relative price at that point of time, is implied. However, even this functional is calculated as a mathematical expectation, now for the integral of the discounted sum of all instantaneous utilities for all points of time from t + dt onward. To derive this value explicitly, it is necessary to go "backwards" in time, starting from the horizon.

To show how the different probabilities may be derived, it will suffice to illustrate with two cases. We start with the probability that the relative wage rate is equal to $w_k^e(t + dt)$, i.e., equal to what the present employer will pay. This probability may be calculated as the probability that the household will not recieve any wage message plus the probability that the household will recieve exactly one wage message, but that this message implies a lower relative wage rate than that paid by the present employer, etc. The probability that the relative wage rate is equal to $w_k^e(t + dt)$ at time $t + dt$ may thus be written as:

$$e^{-\varepsilon dt} + \varepsilon dt e^{-\varepsilon dt} \int_0^{w_k^e} \hat{f}(w) + \frac{(\varepsilon dt)^2}{2!} e^{-\varepsilon dt} \left(\int_0^{w_k^e} \hat{f}(w)\, dw \right)^2 + \ldots$$

$$= e^{-\varepsilon dt} \sum_{i=0}^{\infty} \frac{(\varepsilon dt)^i}{i!} \left(\int_0^{w_k^e} \hat{f}(w)\, dw \right)^i = e^{-\varepsilon dt \int_{w_k^e}^{\infty} \hat{f}(w)\, dw}$$

The probability that the household shifts to a firm which offers the relative wage rate $w^e(t)$ at time t and which is higher than that of the present employer $w_k^e(t)$ is analogously obtained as the probability that the household recieves exactly one wage message times the probability that it exactly implies the relative wage rate $w^e(t)$ plus the probability that the household recieves two messages times the probability that one of these implies the relative wage rate $w^e(t)$ and that the other wage offer does not surmount $w^e(t)$, etc. The probability that the relative wage rate is equal to a value of $w^e(t)$ which is higher than $w_k^e(t)$ at time t and thus $w^e(t + dt)$ at time $t + dt$ may therefore be written:

$$\varepsilon dte^{-\varepsilon dt}\,\hat{f}(w^e) + \frac{(\varepsilon dt)^2}{2!}\, e^{-\varepsilon dt}\left[\binom{2}{1}\,\hat{f}(w^e)\int_0^{w^e}\hat{f}(v)\,dv\right] + \dots$$

$$= \hat{f}(w^e)\;\varepsilon dte^{-\varepsilon dt}\sum_{i=0}^{\infty}\frac{(\varepsilon dt)^i}{i!}\left(\int_0^{w^e}\hat{f}(v)\;dv\right)^i =$$

$$\hat{f}(w^e)\;\varepsilon dte^{-\varepsilon dt\int_{w^e}^{\infty}\hat{f}(v)\,dv}$$

The corresponding probabilities for the relative prices paid by the household in the point of time $t + dt$ are easy to calculate.[1)] Starting from the fact that the probabilities of paying a certain relative price at time $t + dt$ and of recieving a certain relative wage rate at that point of time are stochastically independent, the mathematical expectation for the utility functional, starting from the point of time $t + dt$, may be written as:

---

1) The probability that the household pays the relative price $p_k^e(t)$ may be written as

$$e^{-c_p dt\int_0^{p_k^e}\hat{f}(\pi)\,d\pi}$$

and the probability that the household gets into contact with a firm which keeps the relative price $p^e(t) < p_k^e(t)$ is

$$\hat{f}(p^e)\;\varepsilon_p dt\; e^{-\varepsilon_p dt\int_0^{p^e}\hat{f}(\pi)\,d\pi}$$

$$(4)\quad E\{V^*\big(w^e(t+dt),\ p^e(t+dt),\ t+dt\big)\} =$$

$$e^{-\varepsilon_w dt \int_{w_k^e}^{\infty} \hat{f}(w)\,dw \;-\varepsilon_p dt \int_{o}^{p_k^e} \hat{f}(p)\,dp}\; V^*\big(w_k^e(t+dt),\ p_k^e(t+dt),\ t+dt\big)$$

$$+\; e^{-\varepsilon_w dt \int_{w_k^e}^{\infty} \hat{f}(w)\,dw} \int_{o}^{p_k^e} \hat{f}(p)\ \varepsilon_p dt e^{-\varepsilon_p dt \int_{o}^{p} \hat{f}(\pi)\,d\pi}\; V^*\big(w_k^e(t+dt), p(t+dt),$$

$$t+dt\big) \cdot dp \;+\; e^{-\varepsilon_p dt \int_{o}^{p_k^e} \hat{f}(p)\,dp} \int_{w_k^e}^{\infty} \hat{f}(w)\,\varepsilon_w dt e^{-\varepsilon_w dt \int_{w}^{\infty} \hat{f}(v)\,dv}\ \cdot$$

$$\cdot\ V^*\big(w(t+dt),\ p_k^e(t+dt),\ t+dt\big) \cdot dw$$

$$+ \int_{o}^{p_k^e} \int_{w_k^e}^{\infty} \hat{f}(p)\,\varepsilon_p dt e^{-\varepsilon dt \int_{o}^{p} \hat{f}(\pi)\,d\pi}\ \hat{f}(w)\,\varepsilon_w dt e^{-\varepsilon_w dt \int_{w}^{\infty} \hat{f}(v)\,dv}\ \cdot$$

$$\cdot\ V^*\big(w(t+dt),\ p(t+dt),\ t+dt\big)\ dp\ dw$$

(4) represents the mathematical expectation of the utility functional on the right hand side of (3), with specified probabilities for the different outcomes. By substituting (4) into (3), differentiating with respect to the control variables, setting the partial derivatives equal to zero, and letting dt tend towards zero, the following necessary conditions for maximizing the utility functional (3) are obtained:

$$\frac{\partial u}{\partial x} - \mu_2 p^e = 0$$

$$-\mu_1 + \mu_2 \frac{(1\ \sigma)\, w^e \bar{w}^e}{\bar{p}^e} = 0$$

(5)

$$-\mu_1 - \frac{\partial \varepsilon}{\partial \tau_{sw}} \int_{w_k^e}^{\infty} \hat{f}(w) \Big[V^*(w_k^e,\ p_k^e,\ t) - V^*(w,\ p_k^e,\ t)\Big]\, dw = 0$$

$$-\mu_1 - \frac{\partial \varepsilon}{\partial \tau_{sp}} \int_{o}^{p_k^e} \hat{f}(p) \Big[V^*(w_k^e,\ p_k^e,\ t) - V^*(w_k^e,\ p,\ t)\Big]\, dp = 0$$

If in addition (3) is differentiated with respect to μ_1 and μ_2 the two budget equations will be obtained. An important problem is under what circumstances the marginal conditions of (5) coincide with the necessary conditions for maximizing the Hamiltonian as derived in the chapter. It is easy to show that the conditions coincide if the utility functional $V^*(w^e, p^e, t)$ is linear in w^e and p^e. The two last equations of (5) then become:

$$- \mu_1 + \lambda_1 \frac{\partial \acute{E}\{\dot{w}^e\}}{\partial \tau_{sw}} = 0$$

$$- \mu_1 + \lambda_2 \frac{\partial \acute{E}\{\dot{p}^e\}}{\partial \tau_{sp}} = 0$$

where by definition λ_1 is equal to $\frac{\partial V^*}{\partial w^e}$ and λ_2 similarly equal to $\frac{\partial V^*}{\partial p^e}$.

The differential equations for the two adjoint variables λ_1 and λ_2 will now be derived. The problem still is under what circumstances the maximization of the utility functional (1) will give the same results as if the stochastic variations of the relative wage rate and the relative price are abstracted from and, as was the case in the chapter, the mathematical expectation of the two stochastic variables are merely substituted into the utility functional:

If (3) is differentiated with respect to $w_k^e(t)$ and dt tends towards zero, then:

$$\dot{\lambda}_1 = \rho\lambda_1 - \mu_2 \frac{(1-s)\bar{w}^e}{\bar{p}^e} \tau_w - \left(\frac{\partial \dot{w}_k^e}{\partial w_k^e} - \varepsilon_w \int_{w_k^e}^{\infty} \hat{f}(w)\, dw\right) \lambda_1$$

(6a)

$$- \varepsilon_p \int_{o}^{p_k^e} \hat{f}(p) \left(\frac{\partial V^*(w_k^e, p, t)}{\partial w_k^e} - \frac{\partial V^*(w_k^e, p_k^e, t)}{\partial w_k^e}\right) dp$$

(6a) could be rewritten as

$$\dot{\lambda}_1 = \rho \lambda_1 - \frac{\mu_2 (1-s) \bar{w}^e}{\bar{p}^e} \tau_w - \frac{\partial \dot{w}^e}{\partial w^e} \lambda_1$$

$$- \varepsilon_p \int_o^{p_k^e} \hat{f}(p) \left[\lambda_1 (w_k^e, p) - \lambda_1 (w_k^e, p_k^e) \right] dp$$

where $\lambda_1 = \lambda_1 (w_k^e, p_k^e)$

It is important to observe that λ_1 is <u>not</u> a function of w_k^e and p_k^e. The notation merely denotes the value of λ_1, which should be chosen, given w_k^e, p_k^e, for λ_1 to converge towards $\lambda_{1\infty}$ and, consequently, fulfilling the transversality conditions.

Differentiating (6a) with respect to w_k^e and p_k^e, respectively, we get:

$$\frac{\partial \dot{\lambda}_1}{\partial w_k^e} = 0$$

$$\frac{\partial \dot{\lambda}_1}{\partial p_k^e} = 0 - \varepsilon_p \hat{f}(p_k^e) \left[\lambda_1 (w_k^e, p_k^e) - \lambda_1 (w_k^e, p_k^e) \right] = 0$$

Furthermore,

$$\frac{\partial \dot{\lambda}_1}{\partial \lambda_1} = \rho - \frac{\partial \dot{w}^e}{\partial w^e} + \lambda_1 \varepsilon_p \int_o^{p_k^e} \hat{f}(p) dp > 0$$

$$\frac{\partial \dot{\lambda}_1}{\partial \lambda_2} = 0$$

This means that we have to choose $\lambda_1(0) = \lambda_{1\infty}$ for λ_1 to converge towards its stationary solution. It also means that $V^*(w_k^e, p^e, t)$ is linear in w_k^e and p^e, and equation (6a) becomes

$$\dot{\lambda}_1 = \rho \lambda_1 - \frac{\partial H^*}{\partial w^e}$$

which is the differential equation for the determination of the development of λ_1 used in the chapter.

The corresponding result holds for λ_2. But λ_1 and λ_2 are the partial derivatives of the utility functional with respect to the phase variables. The linearity with respect to w_k^e and p_k^e is thus shown.

Thus, it has been shown that the utility functional (1) is linear in the phase variables w^e and p^e, and that the general maximization of the mathematical expectation of the utility functional will lead to the same maximization procedure and thus the same choice of values of the control variables as if the maximum principle of Pontryagin is instead used and no consideration is taken of the fact that $\dot{w}^e$ and $\dot{p}^e$ actually are stochastic.[1)] Since the analysis of the chapter has been based on assumptions implying that

$$\frac{\partial^2 H^*}{\partial w^{e2}} = \frac{\partial^2 H^*}{\partial p^{e2}} = \frac{\partial^2 H^*}{\partial p^e \partial w^e} = 0$$

which means that the adjoint variables must be constant in time, independently of the development of w^e and p^e, this implies that

$$\frac{\partial \lambda_1}{\partial w^e} = \frac{\partial \lambda_1}{\partial p^e} = \frac{\partial \lambda_2}{\partial w^e} = \frac{\partial \lambda_2}{\partial p^e} = 0.$$

But λ_1 is the partial derivative of the utility functional with respect to w^e and λ_2 the partial derivative of the utility functional with respect to p^e. Thus the utility functional is linear in w^e and p^e.

---

1) It should be noted, however, that the relationship between the transversality conditions and Arrow's sufficiency condition for the stochastic case remains to be investigated.

CHAPTER IV. THE BEHAVIOR OF THE UNEMPLOYED

1. Introduction

In this chapter the theory of the unemployed searching for a job[1] will be extended in two directions. The simultaneous search on both the labor <u>and</u> a consolidated goods market is considered. Furthermore, the unemployed are free to vary the time spent on the two search activities. Thus, not only decision rules for the aspiration wage are derived, but also those for the proportion of each unit of time spent searching on the two markets. One conclusion of the analysis is that not only variations in the subjective rate of time preference or in expectations, but also variations in the price paid by the unemployed may result in variations of the aspiration wage.

The present analysis is based on the results of the previous chapter, which discussed the search behavior, consumption and supply of labor by the employed. In order to analyze the behavior of the unemployed, we have to take into consideration their balance between the utility of getting a job and the utility of being able to continue searching on a full time basis by remaining unemployed. This presupposes, however, that we know the value of the utility functional of the employed.

The analysis of this chapter is mainly intended to describe the choice situation of people starting to search for their first job, but also persons who willingly or unwillingly have left their jobs and are looking for a new one are covered.

The choice between continuing to search as unemployed or to accept an employment offer implies a form of indivisibility. In the previous chapter it was assumed that the employed was

---

1) The main references here are McCall (1970), Mortensen (1970b) and Gronau (1971).

free to vary the length of the working time. If this had not been the case, the choice of unemployment could be explained by the constraint on the length of the working time which would make it very difficult to search for a new job as soon as an employment offer had been accepted.[1)]

A second possibility for explaining why the unemployed only accepts employment offers above a certain level is that unemployment in itself might imply certain benefits which disappear at employment. In the present case, the starting point will be that the unemployed recieves a tax-free unemployment allowance. It is true that this implies a lower disposable income than that of the employed. But on the other hand, the unemployed is free to search on a full time basis. The unemployment compensation thus represents the indivisibility in the present case. The higher the unemployment compensation, the higher the minimum requirements of the unemployed for accepting an employment offer.

Now a few comments on some important assumptions.

The unemployment compensation is given as a certain fraction of the average wage level on the market. Analogous to the case of the households and firms, the authorities which pay the unemployment compensation have (due to a statistical lag) only knowledge of the average wage level with a certain lag, h_W. To compensate for the expected inflation, the unemployment compensation is then projected to the current date by the expected rate of wage inflation. If the actual rate of wage inflation is higher than the expected rate, the unemployment compensation will fall in comparison to the actual current average wage level.

There are no costs attached to the transition from one state to another. If this assumption did not hold, persons would be reluctant to change jobs, and would therefore claim

---

1) Cf. Alchian's discussion about differential search costs. Search could be more effectively done on a full-time basis, i.e., as unemployed. Of course, there may be draw-backs of searching for a job as unemployed. It may be a recommendation in itself to be employed when one searches for a job. See Alchian (1970).

some margin between a wage offer and the present wage to change. It is also probable that this behavior would increase aspiration wages, since it would imply a longer stay on the first job.

As to search on the goods market, the consumer is sticking to his present supplier until he gets a better price offer. In the labor market there are two possibilities. An unemployed person can remain constantly in contact with at least one employer (recall) or lose contact with the employer as soon as a wage-offer has been rejected (no recall). The last alternative is assumed.

As in chapter III, the unemployed individual is subject to a constant death risk. This means that the horizon is stochastically determined. As shown in chapter III, the expected value of the utility functional (the stochastic element being the horizon) is equal to the discounted sum of all future utilities, from $t=0$ to infinity. But the discount factor is now equal to $e^{-\rho t}$, where the total subjective rate of time preference, ρ, is equal to the sum of the "pure" rate of time preference, ρ', and the death risk parameter, δ.

The sole argument of the utility function is consumption. Since time spent on searching the goods and the labor markets for a lower price and a high enough wage rate, respectively, is a strategic variable in the present analysis it might have been interesting to include leisure time in the utility function. In this way it would be possible to analyze variations in leisure time as an instrument for reallocation present pleasure (leisure) for future utility (a higher future consumption backed up by a higher real wage rate made possible by greater investments in search for lower prices and a firm offering a high wage rate).[1] To keep the analysis simple, we abstain from this interesting excursion.

---

[1] In the description of the behavior of the employed in chapter III, this type of intertemporal reallocation is effected via increased search activities on the two markets, leading to a future higher real wage rate. The increased search time is taken from present working time, however, which means a lower present income and thus lower instantaneous consumption.

The contents of the chapter are as follows. In section two, the Hamiltonian of the unemployed is derived. This is accomplished by using a dynamic programming formulation. As a by-product of this analysis, the first order maximum conditions of the Hamiltonian and the differential equation of the adjoint variable are derived.

In section three, some comparisons between variables at employment and unemployment are made. The values of the adjoint variable as to increases in the relative price, search activity on the goods and the labor market, and the value of the utility functional are compared. These comparisons are of interest in their own, but also necessary for deriving the complete behavior equations in section four.

Finally, section five contains a derivation of the mathematical expectation of the length of the remaining unemployment period. Furthermore, the effects of different parameter changes on the length of this time period is investigated.

2. Derivation of the Hamiltonian of the Unemployed

2.1. The choice set of the unemployed

Similarly to the case of the employed, the unemployed is assumed to maximize the discounted value of all future utilities, the factor of discount being the (total) subjective rate of time preference.[1] But the constraints are different. The unemployed has no earnings since the working time is equal to zero. His disposable income is instead assumed to be equal to the unemployment compensation, which in this analysis is fixed in relation to the average wage rate on the market.[2] The value of the unemployment compensation

---

1) Since no lending or borrowing is possible, the market rate of interest could not be used in this case.

2) There is thus an index clause, tying the unemployment compensation to the general earnings possibilities among the working population, c.f. Mortensen (1970b).

is thus equal to $z\bar{w}^e$, where $\bar{w}^e$ denotes the expected[1] average wage rate and z is the unemployment compensation in relation to the average wage rate. z is considerably smaller than one. Otherwise the incentives of taking a job would be small, especially since the unemployment compensation is assumed to be taxfree. Furthermore, if we denote the consumption of the unemployed by x'[2], the (monetary) budget equation of the unemployed could be written in the following way:

$$(1) \qquad z\bar{w}^e - p^e\bar{p}^e x' = 0 \;^{3)}$$

The working time for an unemployed is, by definition, equal to zero. The time budget equation could therefore be written as:

$$(2) \qquad 1 - \tau'_{sw} - \tau'_{sp} = 0. \;^{4)}$$

i.e. the total time available is allocated between search on the labor and goods markets, respectively. It should be noted that leisure time is not considered a part of the optimization problem.

The transition from unemployment to employment happens when the unemployed receives a wage offer which is at least equal to the aspiration relative wage rate, $\hat{w}^e$. It should be

---

1) This means that not only the individuals searching for a new job, but also the authorities, perceive changes in the general wage level with a certain lag. This lag is assumed to be equal in the both cases. The unemployment compensation is however adjusted each moment of time according to the expected rate of wage inflation.

2) In order to be able to discriminate between the decision variables of the unemployed and the employed, the former are supplied with a prime.

3) For an employed person, the income is instead equal to the disposable wage rate times the proportion of each time interval allocated to working time, $(1-s)w^e\bar{w}^e\tau_w$, where s denotes the tax rate and τ_w the working time.

4) For an employed person, the time is instead allocated between working and search on the two markets. The time budget could in this case instead be written $1 - \tau_w - \tau_{sw} - \tau_{sp} = 0$.

noted that this formulation is quite general, since $\hat{w}^e$ could be equal to zero, in which case the unemployed always would accept employment in the first firm offering it.

The mathematical expectation of the relative wage rate, given that the unemployed receives a wage offer higher or equal to the aspiration wage rate could be written:

$$(3) \qquad E\{w^e | w^e \geq \hat{w}^e\} = \frac{\int_{\hat{w}^e}^{\infty} v \hat{f}(v)\, dv}{\int_{\hat{w}^e}^{\infty} \hat{f}(v)\, dv}. \quad ^{1)}$$

For short, the mathematical expectation for the relative wage rate, given that it is greater than the aspiration wage, will be denoted by $w^e(\hat{w}^e)$. It is clear that $w^e(\hat{w}^e) > \hat{w}^e$.[2)]

The probability that, during a very short period of length dt, an unemployed will start working, is equal to the probability that he receives at least one wage message and that this surmounts the aspiration wage. If the number of signals is generated by a Poisson process the transition probability can be written:

$$(4) \qquad \text{Prob(employed } (t + dt) \mid \text{unemployed } (t)) =$$

$$= \varepsilon_w dt \int_{\hat{w}^e}^{\infty} \hat{f}(v)\, dv = \alpha_w dt$$

---

1) Relative wage rates are distributed over firms according to the frequency function $f(w)$. The relevant frequency, however, is that describing the probability that the unemployed comes into contact with a firm offering the relative wage rate, given that a wage offer is received. This means that the varying amount of wage information from firms offering different relative wages has to be taken account of. Thus we have to adjust the frequency of firms having the relative wage rate w to the fact that the supply of information varies among firms. Thus $\hat{f}(w)$ means the proportion of the total flow of wage offer information emanating from firms offering the relative wage rate w. For the exact way of making this adjustment, see chapter III.

2) There is an uninteresting special case when $\hat{w}^e$ equals $\max\ w^e$. The inequality then becomes an equality.

where ε_w, the parameter of the Poisson distribution, is a function of the intensity of the labor market search of the unemployed and of the supply of wage information from the firms. Formula (4) is approximately correct but will hold exactly as dt tends towards zero.

2.2. A dynamic programming formulation of the maximization problem

A notation for the value of the utility functional is now introduced. For an unemployed the discounted value of all future utilities is a function of the point of time when the analysis starts, t, the (expected) relative price paid at that moment of time, $p^e(t)$, and certain exogenous variables, (e.g., z, $\bar{w}^e$ or $\bar{p}^e$) not written out explicitly: $V'(p^e(t), t)$. It should be noted that according to the assumption of no recall, the unemployed does not have any relative wage rate to begin with.

The utility functional of an employed person is denoted by V. Its value is a function of the (expected) relative wage rate at the starting point of time, the relative price and the starting point of time itself: $V(w^e(t), p^e(t), t)$. It should be noted that the mathematical expectation for the relative wage rate for a person who has just obtained a job is equal to $w^e(\hat{w}^e)$. If the utility functional is maximized, this will be indicated by a star.

We are now going to derive the optimal policy for the unemployed for the period t, t + dt. In order to do that, we split the utility functional into two parts, one covering the time interval t, t + dt, the other covering the time from t + dt onward.

The discounted sum of utilities for the first period may be written as:

$$\int_t^{t+dt} e^{-\rho\theta}\, u(x'(\theta))\, d\theta$$

where ρ denotes the (total) subjective rate of time preference, u is the symbol for the instantaneous utility function. If the length of the time period, dt, tends towards zero, then the value of the integral will tend towards $u(x'(t))dt$. The value of the utility functional from $t + dt$ on will be equal to $V(w^e(\hat{w}^e), p^e(t+dt), t + dt)$ in case of employment and $V'(p^e(t+dt), t + dt)$ if not. The probabilities of the two possibilities are $\alpha_w dt$ and $1 - \alpha_w dt$, respectively. The mathematical expectation of the value of the utility functional from $t + dt$ onward could thus be written as:

$$\alpha_w dt\ V(w^e(\hat{w}^e), p^e(t+dt), t + dt) + (1 - \alpha_w dt)\ V'(p^e(t+dt), t + dt).$$

In order to maximize the value of the utility functional from t onward, we have to maximize the sum of the values for the period $t, t + dt$ and $t + dt, \infty$, respectively. As to the first period, the maximization should be made subject to the monetary and time budget restraints. In this way the problem of choosing optimal trajectories for the control variables could be reformulated so as to choose the best values of consumption, search intensities on the two markets and the aspiration wage rate for the short period between t and $t + dt$, assuming that the optimal solution is choosen thereafter. The length of the period, dt, is assumed to be short enough for holding the control variables approximately constant. Then the maximization problem may be formulated as

$$(5)\quad V'^*(p^e(t),t) = \max\ \{\Big[u(x'(t)) + \mu'_1(1 - \tau'_{sw} - \tau'_{sp}) + \\ + \mu'_2(\frac{z\bar{w}^e}{\bar{p}^e} - p^e x')\Big]\ dt \\ + \alpha_w dt\ V^*(w^e(\hat{w}^e), p^e(t+dt), t + dt) + \\ + (1 - \alpha_w dt)\ V'^*(p^e(t+dt), t + dt)\}$$

It should be noted that both $p^e(t+dt)$ and $w^e(\hat{w}^e)$ are stochastic variables. Consequently, to follow the expected-utility approach strictly, we should integrate V^* and V'^*, respectively, over the frequency distributions of these variables. Instead, we have substituted the expected values of these variables into the utility functionals. However, if the utility functionals are linear in the phase variables (i.e., the values of the adjoint variables are constant), maximizing (5) will also imply maximization of the more general expression involving the mathematical expectation of the utility functionals.[1] In chapter III it has been shown that V^* is linear in p^e and w^e. Since assumptions made below imply that also V'^* is linear in p^e, the simplification does not lead us into trouble.

2.3. Necessary conditions for a maximum

By differentiating (5) with respect to the control variables, putting the derivatives equal to zero, taking fractions of dt and letting dt tend towards zero, the following necessary conditions for the maximization of (5) are obtained:

$$\frac{\partial u}{\partial x} - \mu'_2 p^e = 0$$

$$- \mu'_1 + \frac{\partial \alpha_w}{\partial \tau'_{sw}} \left[V^* (w^e(\hat{w}^e), p^e(t), t) - V^{*\prime} (p^e(t), t)\right] = 0$$

(6)

$$- \mu'_1 + \lambda'_2 \frac{\partial \dot{p}^e}{\partial \tau'_{sp}} = 0$$

$$\frac{\partial \alpha_w}{\partial \hat{w}^e} \left[V^* (w^e(\hat{w}^e), p^e(t), t) - V^{*\prime} (p^e(t), t)\right] + \alpha_w \lambda_1 \frac{\partial w^e}{\partial \hat{w}^e} = 0$$

If we further differentiate (5) by μ'_1 and μ'_2, respectively, and put these derivatives equal to zero, the monetary and time budget equations are obtained.

Since consumption[2] is determined outside the maximization problem in this case (being equal to the real income of the

---

1) This is easily proved with the same method as used in the appendix of chapter III.

2) The consumption of the unemployed could in each instance of time directly be determined from the monetary budget equation.

unemployed), the first of the equations in (6) is just a definition of the marginal utility of the last dollar spent on consumption, μ_2'. By eliminating μ_1', the second and third equations of (6) could be converted into a condition for optimal allocation of "investments" in search on the two markets, increasing the probabilities of getting into contact with low-price firms and firms offering a wage rate exceeding the aspiration wage rate, respectively.[1] In the last equation (where, by definition λ_1 equals $\frac{\partial V^*}{\partial w^e}$) we could, by re-arrangement and using the result that V^* is linear in w^e,[2] obtain the result that the aspiration wage rate, $\hat{w}^e$, should be chosen so as to imply indifference in terms of the discounted utility of all future consumption between accepting a job at that terms or continue searching for the first job: $V^*(\hat{w}^e, p^e(t), t) = V'^*(p^e(t), t)$.

2.4. The Hamiltonian of the unemployed

Using the necessary conditions (6) for the maximization of the utility functional, the following Hamiltonian[3] could be determined implicitly:

$$(7)\quad H' = u(x') + \mu_1'(1 - \tau_{sw}' - \tau_{sp}') + \mu_2'\left(\frac{z\bar{w}^e}{\bar{p}^e} - p^e x'\right)$$

$$+ \alpha_w\left[V^*(w^e(\hat{w}^e), p^e(t), t) - V'^*(p^e(t), t)\right] + \lambda_2'\dot{p}^e$$

where λ_2' is the partial derivative of V'^* with respect to p^e and $\dot{p}^e$ is the mathematical expectation of the time

---

1) The relevant expression will be presented below.

2) <u>C.f.</u> chapter III.

3) For the case of the employed, the Hamiltonian could be written as

$$H = u(x) + \lambda_1\dot{w}^e + \lambda_2\dot{p}^e + \mu_1(1-\tau_w-\tau_{sw}-\tau_{sp}) + \mu_2\left(\frac{(1-s)w^e\bar{w}^e\tau_w}{\bar{p}^e} - p^e x\right).$$

The interpretation of this expression follows immediately, <u>c.f.</u>, chapter III.

derivative of the relative price paid by the unemployed.[1] The maximization of the Hamiltonian (7) could be interpreted as maximizing the sum of the instantaneous utility of consumption in point of time t, and the transition probability of getting a job times the difference between the optimal values of the utility functionals at the states of employment and unemployment, respectively, and the marginal present value product of the relative price[2] times the time derivative with respect to the relative price. As usual, the maximization of (7) does not necessarily imply that (5) is maximized.

2.5. The differential equation of the phase variable

By differentiating both sides of (5) with respect to $p^e(t)$, dividing by dt, and letting dt tend towards zero the following time derivative with respect to the marginal present value product of the relative price is obtained

---

1) The time derivative of the mathematical expectation of the relative price could be divided into two components. First, the search activity on the goods market will result in the unemployed now and then getting into contact with firms offering a lower price than the present supplier. Secondly, all firms are expected to change their prices. Low price firms attract consumers, and when the demand for their products increase, they will increase their prices. And vice versa for high-price firms; c.f. Phelps & Winter (1971). It is possible to show that

$$\frac{\partial \dot{p}^e}{\partial p^e} = \frac{\partial \dot{p}_k^e}{\partial p_k^e} - \varepsilon_p(\tau'_{sp}, a_p) \int_o^{p^e} \hat{f}(\pi)\, d\pi$$

where the first derivative on the right hand side has to do with the expected rate of price change of firms offering different prices, k denoting the number of the present supplier. For a derivation, c.f. chapter III.

2) This vocabulary is quite natural since λ_2' is the partial derivative of V'^* with respect to the (expected, relative price, and since V'^* is the (optimal) value of the discounted sum of all future utilities.

$$(8) \quad \dot{\lambda}_2' = \rho \lambda_2' + \mu_2' x' + \alpha_w (\lambda_2' - \lambda_2) - \lambda_2' \frac{\partial \dot{p}^e}{\partial p^e}$$

The expression (8) could also be obtained from the Hamiltonian since $\dot{\lambda}_2' = \rho\lambda_2' - \frac{\partial H'}{\partial p^e}$. In (8), the difference between the marginal present value products of the relative price of an unemployed and of an employed multiplied by the probability of becoming employed, is included. The intuitive interpretation of this is that the effect on the utility functional of a certain relative price depends on one's situation, i.e., on whether disposable income is low (at unemployment) or high (at employment). Since the unemployed will become employed with a certain probability, this must be taken into consideration when determining the time rate of change (and thus implicitly the value of) the marginal present value product or the relative price.

3. Some Comparisons between Variable Values at Employment and Unemployment

In this section the marginal present value product of the (expected) relative price, the time used for search in the two markets, and the value of the utility functional will be compared for an employed and an unemployed. This information is not only interesting for its own sake; it will also be necessary in order to derive the behavior equations of the unemployed.

3.1. The marginal present value product of the relative price

We start by comparing the stationary value of the marginal present value product of an unemployed and that of an employed.[1] Using (8) and the analogous expression for the employed (this could either be obtained from chapter III or

---

1) The latter value is not dependent on the assumption of stationary conditions; c.f. chapter III.

from the Hamiltonian for an employed, presented in a footnote above), and putting time derivatives equal to zero we obtain:

$$(9) \qquad \lambda'_{2\infty} - \lambda_2 = \frac{\mu_2 x - \mu'_2 x'}{\rho - \frac{\partial \dot{p}^e}{\partial p^e} + \alpha_w}$$

The denominator is always positive. The numerator has the following signs:

$$(10) \qquad \begin{array}{lll} \mu_2 x - \mu'_2 x' > 0 & \text{if} & R_r(x') < 1 \\ \mu_2 x - \mu'_2 x' = 0 & \text{if} & R_r(x') = 1 \\ \mu_2 x - \mu'_2 x' < 0 & \text{if} & R_r(x') > 1 \end{array}$$

where R_r denotes the coefficient of relative risk aversion or the elasticity of marginal utility. Assuming that R_r is an increasing function of consumption[1] and at the same time equal to one for "normal" values of consumption (i.e., at the consumption level attained at employment),[2] the coefficient of relative risk aversion will be less than one for an unemployed. This further means that, according to (9), the marginal present value product of the relative price is higher for an unemployed than for an employed. Since both $\lambda'_{2\infty}$ and λ_2 are negative, this could be reformulated as the absolute value of the marginal present value product of the relative price being greater for an employed than for an unemployed. The economic explanation of this is that a price decrease is more valuable for an employed than for an unemployed, since the former, depending on his higher income, can increase his consumption by a greater amount, given the relative price decrease. However, it should be stressed that the comparison should be made in utility units, and the statement is then only correct under the assumption that the elasticity of the marginal utility of consumption is an increasing function of consumption.

---

1) C.f. Arrow (1970), pp. 96-98.

2) This was assumed for the case of the employed; c.f. chapter III.

3.2. Search intensities on the goods and labor markets

The next step is to compare the amount of time allocated to search on the two markets of an unemployed and an employed. To be able to compare the two situations, the unemployed is assumed to pay the same relative price as the employed and that the relative wage rate of the latter is equal to his aspiration wage rate. This means that the values of the utility functionals of an unemployed and an employed are the same. To start with, the following necessary conditions for maximizing the Hamiltonian of an employed (11a)[1] and an unemployed (11b)[2] are used:

$$\text{(11a)}\quad \lambda_1 \frac{\partial\varepsilon_w}{\partial\tau_{sw}} \int_{\hat{w}^e}^{\infty} (v-\hat{w}^e)\ \hat{f}(v)\,dv = \lambda_2 \frac{\partial\varepsilon_p}{\partial\tau_{sp}} \int_{o}^{p^e} (\pi-p^e)\ \hat{f}(\pi)\,d\pi^{3)}$$

$$\text{(11b)}\quad \lambda_1 \frac{\partial\varepsilon_w}{\partial\tau'_{sw}} \int_{\hat{w}^e}^{\infty} (v-\hat{w}^e)\ \hat{f}(v)\,dv = \lambda'_{2\infty} \frac{\partial\varepsilon_p}{\partial\tau'_{sp}} \int_{o}^{p^e} (\pi-p^e)\ \hat{f}(\pi)\,d\pi$$

It should be noted that the stationary value of the marginal present value product of the (expected) relative price of the unemployed has been chosen. This further means that the relative price paid by the unemployed is the stationary relative price. By using the time budget equations of an employed and an unemployed (11c),

---

1) This is a condition for the optimal balance between "investments" in searching for a high relative wage rate and a low relative price (c.f. chapter III). Both actions will eventually result in a higher future real wage rate. But the given expected real wage rate should be obtained in the most efficient way. This means that the last unit of time allocated to search on the labor market should give the same revenue (in terms of the utility functional of the employed) as the last unit of time allocated to search on the goods market.

2) This condition for the maximization of the Hamiltonian of the unemployed is derived from the second and third equations of (6). It has the same economic interpretation as (11a).

3) λ_1 and λ_2 are independent of w^e and p^e and thus are equal to their stationary values; c.f. chapter III.

(11c) $\tau_w + \tau_{sw} + \tau_{sp} = \tau'_{sw} + \tau'_{sp}$

through linear approximations of $\frac{\partial \varepsilon_w}{\partial \tau_{sw}}$ and $\frac{\partial \varepsilon_p}{\partial \tau_{sp}}$ around τ_{sw} and τ_{sp}, respectively, in (11b), and by using (11a) and (11c) it is easy to show that

(12) $$\text{sign } (\tau'_{sp} - \tau_{sp}) = - \text{ sign } \{\lambda_1 \frac{\partial^2 \varepsilon}{\partial \tau_{sw}^2} \tau_w \int_{\hat{w}^e}^{\infty} (v-\hat{w}^e) \hat{f}(v) dv - (\lambda'_{2_\infty} - \lambda_2) \frac{\partial \varepsilon}{\partial \tau_{sp}} \int_0^{p^e} (\pi - p^e) \hat{f}(\pi) d\pi\} \gtreqless 0$$

Evidently, search on the goods market could be greater or smaller than that for an employed. There are two effects working in opposite directions. There is first a time-income effect (c.f. (12), in which working time is a factor in the first term), which tends to make search on the goods market more extensive at unemployment than at employment. The greater number of hours allocated to work, the more time there is left over for an unemployed to allocate to search on the two markets. Secondly, there is a time-substitution effect. The second term of (12) contains the difference between the (stationary) values of the marginal present value product of the relative price of an unemployed and an employed, respectively. Since this factor has been shown to be positive (c.f. (9) above), the last term of (12) will imply a lower search on the goods market for an unemployed than an employed. Assuming that the time-income and time-substitution effects cancel out, search on the goods market will, ceteris paribus, be equal for an unemployed and an employed. This means that, in the absence of working time, the time left over for an unemployed will be totally devoted to search on the labor market; c.f. (11c).

Since $\tau'_{sp} = \tau_{sp}$, the second derivative with respect to the relative price of the time derivative of the relative price will be equal for the cases of employment and unemployment:[1)]

1) C.f. footnote 1 on page 200.

$$\frac{\partial^2 \dot{p}^e}{\partial p^{e2}} = \frac{\partial^2 \dot{p}_k^e}{\partial p_k^{e2}} - \varepsilon_p(\tau_{sp}, a_p)\, \hat{f}(p^e) = \frac{\partial^2 \dot{p}_k^e}{\partial p_k^{e2}} - \varepsilon_p(\tau'_{sp}, a_p)\, \hat{f}(p^e) = 0$$ [1)]

Expanding λ_2' around its stationary value, the time derivative of the marginal present value product of the relative price of the unemployed (8) could be written as

$$(13)\quad \dot{\lambda}_2'(t) = \left(\rho + \alpha_W - \frac{\partial \dot{p}^e}{\partial p^e}\right)(\lambda_2'(t) - \lambda_{2\infty}') + \lambda_2' \frac{\partial^2 \dot{p}^e}{\partial p^{e2}}(p^e(t) - p_\infty^e)$$

Since $\rho + \alpha_W - \frac{\partial \dot{p}^e}{\partial p^e} > 0$, and since $\lambda_2' \frac{\partial^2 \dot{p}^e}{\partial p^{e2}} = 0$, $\lambda_2'(t)$ will only converge towards its stationary solution if $\lambda_2'(t) \equiv \lambda_{2\infty}'$, all t. But this convergence is a sufficient condition for the transversality conditions

$$(14)\quad \lim_{t\to\infty} - e^{-\rho t} \lambda_2'(t) \geq 0, \quad \lim_{t\to\infty} - e^{-\rho t} \lambda_2'(t)\, p^e(t) = 0$$

to be fulfilled. And these in turn guarantee that the maximization of the Hamiltonian (7) also implies the maximization of the utility functional. This means that, analogously to the case of the employed, λ_2' will be constant in time, equal to its stationary value. This is a most important result. Not only is the following analysis made easier; it further implies that the utility functional V'^* is linear in p^e. This in turn implies that it is sufficient to apply the mathematical expectation of the price increase, since this procedure will give the same optimum as maximization of the mathematical expectation of the utility functional; i.e., max. $V'(E\{p^e(\vec{t})\}) = \max E\{V'(p^e(\vec{t}))\}$.

3.3. The value of the utility functional

The last information needed in order to derive the behavior equations of the unemployed is an expression for the difference

---

1) C.f. chapter III.

between the values of the utility functionals of an employed and an unemployed, respectively: $V^* - V'^*$. This expression appears as a term in the Hamiltonian (7) and we must know how this term is affected by the different parameter changes in order to differentiate the first order maximum conditions for the maximization of the Hamiltonian. As in the derivation of the Hamiltonian (7), we start from the expression (5). By rearranging terms, dividing by dt, and letting dt tend towards zero we get:

$$(15) \quad \rho V'^*\left(p^e(t),\, t\right) = \max \{u(x') + \mu_1'(1 - \tau_{sw}' - \tau_{sp}') + \mu_2'\left(\frac{z\bar{w}^e}{\bar{p}^e} - p^e x'\right) + \lambda_2'\dot{p}^e + \alpha_w\left(V^*\left(w^e(\hat{w}^e),\, p^e(t),\, t\right) - V'^*\left(p^e(t),\, t\right)\right)\}$$

which means that the value of the utility functional of the unemployed, at optimal behavior, is equal to the value of the Hamiltonian divided by the (total) subjective rate of time preference, ρ. If the value of the Hamiltonian is constant in time, this means that the value of the utility functional is equal to the present value of the Hamiltonian of all future points of time:

$$V'^*\left(p^e(t),\, t\right) = \frac{1}{\rho} H'^*$$

Analogously, it is possible to show that the value of the utility functional of an employed is equal to the maximum value of the Hamiltonian for this case, divided by the (total) subjective rate of time preference:

$$(16) \quad \rho V^*\left(w^e(\hat{w}^e),\, p^e(t),\, t\right) = \max \{u(x) + \mu_1(1 - \tau_w - \tau_{sw} - \tau_{sp}) + \mu_2\left(\frac{(1-s)w^e\bar{w}^e}{\bar{p}^e} - p^e x\right) + \lambda_1\dot{w}^e + \lambda_2\dot{p}^e$$

When investigating how the difference between the utility functionals is affected by different parameter changes, the following results will hold by definition:

$$\frac{\partial(V^* - V'^*)}{\partial w^e} = \lambda_1 > 0, \quad \frac{\partial(V^* - V'^*)}{\partial p^e} = \lambda_2 - \lambda_2' < 0$$

To get the other derivatives, we subtract (15) from (16), multiply by ρ, and differentiate the resulting expression. It should then be observed that a change of an exogenous variable will affect the difference between the utility functionals in two ways. The first is a direct effect, the second an indirect effect via changes of the control variables. However, since the derivatives of the utility functionals are zero with respect to the control variables, the indirect effects could be ignored. Through differentiating we get:

$$(17) \quad V^* - V'^* = F(\underset{+}{w^e}, \underset{-}{p^e}, \underset{-}{a_w}, \underset{+}{a_p}, \underset{+}{\frac{\bar{w}^e}{\bar{p}^e}}, \underset{-}{s}, \underset{-}{z}, \underset{-}{\rho})$$

where the signs of the partial derivatives are indicated under the respective variables. The signs of the derivatives imply that the greater the flow of information about vacancies, the less profitable it is to be employed. The opposite happens if the flow of information increases on the goods market. If the average real wage rate on the market $\frac{\bar{w}^e}{\bar{p}^e}$, increases, it will be more profitable than before to have a job. Increased taxes and unemployment compensation will decrease the incentives to take a job. Finally, the higher the subjective rate of time preference, the more immediate consumption is valued in comparison to future consumption, and the less the inducement to have a job now.

4. The Behavior Equations

The behavior of the unemployed, - i.e., the effects on the optimal values of the control variables of changes in the phase or exogenous variables -- will now be analyzed.

The first step is to derive the incomplete behavior equations. These are defined for the adjoint variables λ_1

and λ_2' being exogenously determined.

In order to derive the incomplete behavior equations, we differentiate the first order conditions (6)[1] for the maximization of the Hamiltonian. This system, however, has a recursive structure. Consumption[2] could be choosen, independently of the values of the other variables. Furthermore, the aspiration wage is independent of the choice of search activities on the two markets (c.f., the last equation of (6)), whereas the latter are influenced by the value choosen of $\hat{w}^e$ (c.f. the second equations of (6)). Accordingly, the incomplete behavior equation of the aspiration wage is derived independently of the other equations of the system (6). Differentiation of the last equation of (6), taking (17) into consideration, will give the following signs of the partial derivatives:

$$(18) \quad \hat{w}^e = \sigma(\underset{+}{p^e}, \underset{+}{a_w}, \underset{-}{a_p}, \underset{-}{\frac{\bar{w}^e}{\bar{p}^e}}, \underset{+}{s}, \underset{+}{z}, \underset{+}{\rho}, \underset{+}{\lambda_1})$$

Next, we investigate the effects on search on the two markets of different parameter shifts. Since according to the time-budget equation, $d\tau_{sp}' = - d\tau_{sw}'$, only the effects on search on the labor market will be considered. When differentiating it should be observed that the aspiration wage is now predetermined and thus is included as an argument of the behavior equation of τ_{sw}'. The aspiration wage rate will then fill the same role as the relative wage rate did in the case of deriving the behavior equations of the employed. Taking (18) into consideration the following partial derivatives of τ_{sw}' are obtained:

---

[1] It should be noted that the two budget equations have to be included in the system (6).

[2] Note that consumption is directly determined from the monetary budget equation.

$$(19) \quad \tau'_{sw} = \chi'_{w}(\underset{-}{p^e}, \underset{?}{a_w}, \underset{?}{a_p}, \underset{+}{\frac{\bar{w}^e}{\bar{p}^e}}, \underset{-}{s}, \underset{-}{z}, \underset{-}{\rho}, \underset{0}{\lambda_1}, \underset{+}{\lambda'_2})$$

the only uncertain derivatives in (19) are those with respect to the supply of information on the goods and labor markets.[1)]

What now is left is to determine the complete behavior equations. These are defined for the adjoint variables λ_1 and λ'_2 not being exogenously determined, but adjusted as a result of the planning problem. A change of an exogenously given variable or a phase variable will generally change the adjoint variables. This means that the effects on the control variables of a change of an exogenous variable will not only be directly determined, via the incomplete behavior equations, but also via changes of the marginal present value products. By taking account of the indirect effects of parameter changes, the adjoint variables will be eliminated as independent arguments of the behavior equations.

As follows from the discussion in chapter III, the marginal present value product of the relative wage rate, λ_1, will have the following partial derivatives with respect to the exogenous variables:

$$(20) \quad \lambda_1 = \lambda_1(\underset{-}{a_w}, \underset{+}{(1-s)\bar{w}^e/\bar{p}^e}, \underset{-}{\rho})$$

Starting from equations (9) and the fact (c.f., chapter III) that

$$\lambda_2 = - \frac{\mu_2 x}{\rho - \frac{\partial \dot{p}^e}{\partial p^e}} ,$$

---

1) If, e.g., a_w increases it will on the margin be more profitable to allocate time to search on the labor market. On the other hand, even if the same amount of time as before is used for search on the labor market, the unemployed will receive an increased amount of wage offers. Thus two effects are working in the opposite directions. When analyzing the impacts on search of various parameter changes, the total effects could be separated into substitution and time-income effects.

it is possible to show that the marginal present value product of the relative price of an unemployed has the following partial derivatives of the exogenous variables:

$$(21) \quad \lambda_2' = \lambda_2'(\underset{-}{a_w}, \underset{+}{a_p}, \underset{+}{\rho}) \quad ^{1)}$$

The larger the flow of information about vacancies, a_w, the more valuable it is to pay a low price (note that λ_2' is negative). The greater the flow of information on the goods market, and the greater the subjective rate of time preference, respectively, the higher λ_2' will be (the smaller the absolute number will be). This could be interpreted in the following way. The greater the flow of information on the goods market, the less valuable it will be to pay a low relative price, since this situation is more easy to attain than before. A high rate of interest (i.e., a high subjective rate of time preference) diminishes the value of the "capital" in form of a low relative price. The phase variables w^e and p^e are not included as arguments of the equations (20) and (21). This is due to the fact that the adjoint variables are constant in time, and thus do not depend on the development of w^e and p^e. If a_w or a_p changes, this will not be certain, since the values of

$$\partial^2 \dot{w}^e / \partial w^{e2} \quad \text{and} \quad \partial^2 \dot{p}^e / \partial p^{e2},$$

respectively, will be affected. We abstract from this complication.

By substituting (20) and (21) into the incomplete behavior equations (18) and (19), by using the monetary and time budget equations, the complete behavior equations can finally be written out:

---

1) The signs of the partial derivatives with respect to a_p and ρ will be undertain, however. If $\rho - \partial \dot{p}^e / \partial p^e \geq 1$ the signs will be the indicated one. The uncertainty is a result of the fact that we have to take effects via λ_2 into consideration.

$$\begin{aligned}
x' &= x'(\underset{-}{p^e}, \underset{0}{a_w}, \underset{0}{a_p}, \underset{+}{\bar{w}^e/\bar{p}^e}, \underset{0}{s}, \underset{+}{z}, \underset{0}{\rho}) \\
\tau'_{sw} &= \tau'_{sw}(\underset{-}{p^e}, \underset{?}{a_w}, \underset{?}{a_p}, \underset{+}{\bar{w}^e/\bar{p}^e}, \underset{-}{s}, \underset{-}{z}, \underset{?}{\rho}) \\
\tau'_{sp} &= \tau'_{sp}(\underset{+}{p^e}, \underset{?}{a_w}, \underset{?}{a_p}, \underset{-}{\bar{w}^e/\bar{p}^e}, \underset{+}{s}, \underset{+}{z}, \underset{?}{\rho}) \\
\hat{w}^e &= \hat{w}^e(\underset{+}{p^e}, \underset{?}{a_w}, \underset{-}{a_p}, \underset{?}{\bar{w}^e/\bar{p}^e}, \underset{+}{s}, \underset{+}{z}, \underset{?}{\rho})
\end{aligned} \tag{22}$$

where consumption is directly determined from the monetary budget equation.

It should be noted that an increase of the (total) subjective rate of time preference no longer has unique effects on the search activities on the two markets. If the total time allocated to search on the two markets could vary, it is probable that an increased rate of time preference would increase the profitability requirements on search and thus decrease search on both markets. Since the total supply of time available for search is fixed in the case of the unemployed, this could not happen. A change of ρ will only affect the allocation of time between the two forms of "investment" in a lower relative price and a higher relative wage rate, respectively.

From the last equation of (22), it is seen that the higher the relative price the unemployed pays, the higher the aspiration wage will be. There is no certainty as to the effect on the aspiration wage of an increased flow of information on the labor market. On the one hand, the aspiration wage will be increased since this will mean a higher expected relative wage rate on the first job,[1)] which now does not require a longer expected unemployment period. On the other hand, the marginal present value product of the relative wage will decrease, the effect of which will be to decrease the aspiration wage (c.f. (20).

---

1) This effect is discussed by Holt (1970), p. 73.

The effect of a change of the average (expected) real wage rate, $\bar{w}^e/\bar{p}^e$, on the aspiration wage will be uncertain. On one hand, the higher average real wage rate will mean that, given the aspiration wage (which is expressed as a fraction of the average wage on the market) will imply a higher expected real wage rate on the first job. This means that the aspiration wage could be decreased but still give a higher real wage rate than before. On the other hand, the higher real wage rate implies that the real value of the unemployment compensation increases, which increases the minimum demands on the relative wage rate for accepting an employment offer.

Finally, the effect on the aspiration wage of an increased subjective rate of (total) time preference is not certain. First, this increased "rate of interest" will mean higher profitability demands on the investment in the form of searching for a job on a full time basis. This will increase the aspiration wage. On the other hand, the increased ρ will mean a higher valuation of present consumption in comparison to future consumption. This implies a lowering of the aspiration wage. The net effect is uncertain.

By substituting $pe^{h_p(g_p - g_p^e)} = p^e$ and $\hat{w}e^{h_w(g_w - g_w^e)} = \hat{w}^e$ into (22), unexpected variations in price- and wage inflation are seen to affect the behavior of the unemployed in the following way. If price inflation unexpectedly increases, consumption will fall. Search on the labor market decreases and search on the goods market increases. The aspiration wage increases. This means that the probability of getting employment will fall if there is an unexpected increase in <u>price</u> inflation.

An increase in unexpected wage inflation will only affect the (actual) aspiration wage level, which falls. This means that an unexpected increase in <u>wage</u> inflation will increase the probability of getting employment.

5. The Expected Length of the Remaining Unemployment Time Period

As pointed out before, a higher level of the aspiration wage will mean a longer expected unemployment time period, *ceteris paribus*. This is what one would expect, since the higher aspiration wage level will mean that a smaller proportion of the recieved wage offers will be accepted. The expected length of the unemployment time period will now be derived, and the effects on it of various parameter changes investigated.

The proportion of the wage offers which fall short of the aspiration wage level is denoted by A:

$$A = \int_{o}^{\hat{w}} \hat{f}(v)\, dv.$$

Given that one is unemployed at time t, the probability of remaining unemployed at time $t + dt$ is then equal to the probability of recieving no wage offer, plus the probability of recieving one wage offer times the probability that this offer will be below the aspiration wage level, plus.....

The probability of remaining unemployed in point of time $t + dt$ may then be written as $P_o + P_1A + P_2A^2 + P_3A^3 + \ldots$ where P_i is generated by a Poisson probability density function with the parameter ε_w. The probability of being employed in point of time $t + dt$ is equal to one minus the probability of remaining unemployed. If this probability is denoted by B, it could be written out as:

$$B = 1 - \sum_{i=o}^{\infty} P_i A^i.$$

The probability of *becoming* employed in point of time $t + dt$ is, by definition, equal to the derivative with respect to dt of the probability of being employed in point of time $t + dt$. By substituting the Poisson probability density function into the expression for B, and differentiating with respect to the length of the time period, dt the following probability of getting employment in point of time $t + dt$ is obtained:

$$\varepsilon_w(1 - A) \sum_{i=1}^{\infty} P_i A^i$$

The mathematical expectation of the point of time of transition from unemployment to employment is obtained by multiplying the expression above by dt and integrating over all values of dt. The mathematical expectation of the point of time when employment occurs may thus be written:

$$(23) \quad E\{t+dt\} = \varepsilon_w(1-A) \int_0^{\infty} \tau \sum_{i=1}^{\infty} P_i A^i \, d\tau = \varepsilon_w(1-A) \int_0^{\infty} \tau e^{\varepsilon_w \tau (A-1)} \, d\tau$$

where the length of the time period, dt, is denoted by τ inside the integration sign. By integrating by parts, it is possible to show that the mathematical expectation of the point of time when employment occurs is equal to:[1)]

$$\left[\varepsilon_w(1-A)\right]^{-1} = \frac{1}{\varepsilon_w \int_{\hat{w}}^{\infty} \hat{f}(v) \, dv}$$

This means that the expected length of the remaining unemployment period, $E\{t_u\}$, is equal to

$$(24) \quad E\{t_u\} = \frac{1}{\varepsilon_w \int_{\hat{w}}^{\infty} \hat{f}(v) \, dv}$$

By differentiating (24) with respect to the parameters and taking (22) into consideration, the following effects

---

1) It should be noted that this mathematical expectation is given objectively, unlike the one expected by the unemployed. This is seen in (24), where the aspiration wage is the actual aspiration wage, $\hat{w}$, not the aspiration wage expected by the unemployed, $\hat{w}^e$. If the actual wage inflation equals the expected one, these aspiration wages will coinside, however.

on the mathematical expectation of the length of the remaining unemployment period are obtained:[1)]

$$(25)\quad E\{t_u\} = G(\underset{+}{pe^{h_p(g_p-g_p^e)}},\ \underset{-}{e^{h_w(g_w-g_w^e)}},\ \underset{-}{a_w},\underset{-}{a_p},\ \underset{-}{\frac{\bar{w}^e}{\bar{p}^e}},\ \underset{+}{s},\ \underset{+}{z},\ \underset{?}{\rho})$$

A high relative price <u>or</u> the actual rate of price inflation surmounting the expected rate, increases the expected length of the remaining unemployment period. This is due to the fact that a higher expected relative price, p^e, decreases search on the labor market and increases the aspiration wage rate.

If actual wage inflation increases in comparison to expected wage inflation, the expected aspiration wage level will be unaffected. But this means that a greater proportion than before of wage offers will exceed the (actual) aspiration wage level. The expected remaining unemployment period falls.

The effect on search and aspiration wages of an increased flow of information on the labor market is uncertain. But in itself, the increased flow of information will decrease the expected length of the remaining unemployment period.

If the flow of information on the goods market, a_p, increases, the aspiration wage level will decrease. This means that the mathematical expectation of the length of the remaining unemployment period will decrease.

An increase in the average real wage rate expected by the participants, $\frac{\bar{w}^e}{\bar{p}^e}$, increases search on the labor market, and thereby, decreases the expected length of the unemployment period.

Increases in tax rates and unemployment compensation will make employment relatively less profitable, thus decreasing search on the labor market and increasing reservation wages. This, of course, increases the expected length of the re-

---

1) Note that $pe^{h_p(g_p-g_p^e)}$ has been substituted for p^e, and $\hat{w}e^{h_w(g_w-g_w^e)}$ for $\hat{w}^e$.

maining unemployment period.

Finally, the effect on the expected remaining unemployment period of an increase in the (total) subjective rate of time preference is impossible to uniquely determine. This depends on the fact that an increased ρ will have two effects on both search and aspiration wages. These effects will be of different signs.

CHAPTER V. THE PRICE, WAGE AND INFORMATION POLICY OF THE FIRM IN AN INTERTEMPORAL PERSPECTIVE

1. Introduction

In this chapter, the price, wage and information policy of the firm will be analyzed, and the results of the two preceding chapters will be utilized. The relation between the chapters is interdependent, however, since the discussion of this chapter will clarify and motivate certain assumptions about households expectations of how firms behave. A further motive for the following analysis is to complete the microeconomic foundation for the macroeconomic model in chapter VI.[1)]

The following discussion constitutes an integration of the discussion of Mortensen concerning the firm's wage policy[2)] and that of Phelps and Winter concerning the firm's price policy,[3)] where the wage-rate and the price, by influencing the net rate of increase of employees and customers, respectively, not only affect instantaneous but also future profits. Moreover, the firm's supply of information in the labor and goods markets will be derived. This means that the chapter contains elements of Phelps' analysis of the relationship between unemployment, vacancies and wage increases[4)] (the number of vacancies of a firm is closely related to its recruiting activities) and Gould's derivation of the optimal intertemporal advertising policy of the firm.[5)] From the point

---

1) However, the macroeconomic model builds on a simplified version of firm behavior in which the firm is not assumed to allocate any recources for information production. This simplified firm model is presented in the last section of the chapter.

2) Mortensen (1970a).

3) Phelps and Winter (1970).

4) Phelps (1970).

5) Gould (1970).

of view of the history of economic doctrines, the discussion of this chapter is related to one of the first economic applications of the calculus of variations -- the optimal price policy of the firm when the demand for its product is not only affected by the instantaneous price, but also the time derivative of the price. The motive for this formulation of the problem was not that the price influenced the possibilities of attracting customers from other firms, but that it could affect the expectations of the customers of the future price of the firm.[1)]

1.1. Some important themes in the analysis

The planning of the firm will be discussed in this chapter. This is done against the background of the analysis of household behavior in the two preceding chapters. In what way will the firm take the incomplete overview of the households of the goods and the labor market into consideration? How will this affect the price and wage setting of the individual firm? Is it profitable for the firm to spread information about its price and wage offers and in this way attract customers and employees? How is the price, wage, and information policy of the firm coordinated? Is it possible to motivate the assumptions about household expectations made in chapter III and IV by the actual behavior of firms? Thus, in a certain sense one may say that the present chapter "closes" the microeconomic analysis.

But the chapter also involves a development of the microeconomic foundation of the unemployment and inflation analysis of chapter VI.[2)] An important question in the two preceding chapters was how household behavior is affected by inflation,

---

1) Cf. the discussion in Allen (1938), pp. 533-536 and the references there given.

2) In building the macroeconomic model in the next chapter, the simplified assumption is made that the firm does not allocate any resources for information production in the goods and the labor markets. This special case is presented in the last section of the present chapter.

or more exactly, the gap between the actual and expected rates of price increases and wage increases. But the development over time of these variables is determined by the price and the wage policy of the individual firms.

This chapter also implies a step towards the macroeconomic analysis in the sense that there is a certain amount of aggregation. The number of consumers is assumed to be much larger than the number of firms. The same holds for the labor force in relation to the number of firms. At each moment of time, the firm has a certain number of customers and employees. Given these, the firm has to vary its relative price, relative wage rate and production volume so that equilibrium between production and consumer goods demand on the one hand, and between the total supply of employees' labor hours and their employment on the other hand, is obtained. In principle, the two equilibrium solutions are continually revised. This is due to the fact that the number of customers and the number of employees change. Moreover, events outside the control sphere of the firm affect the instantaneous equilibrium in the "local" goods and labor markets of the firm. If business conditions change, i.e., if unemployment or the average real wage rate change, this will generally influence the demand for the firm's product and the supply of labor which the firm is confronted with. Of course, the instantaneous equilibrium is also affected by other events outside the control of the individual firm, e.g., changes in fiscal policy.

All disturbances imply compensating changes of the firm's control variables. The aim of these changes is not only to preserve equilibrium in the firm's "own" goods and labor markets. The control variables are also adjusted according to the long run goal of the firm. The firm is assumed to behave as if it maximized the discounted sum of all future profits. This is done subject to the two equilibrium conditions.

Regardless of whether the compensating price and wage rate changes are looked upon as new equilibrium solutions or as new optimum values of the firm's maximization problem, an interesting question is how these variables are affected by various disturbances in the firm's markets. A large portion of this chapter will be devoted to this question.

At each and every moment the number of customers and employees is given for the individual firm. But these two stocks change successively over time. It is not possible for the firm to change these stocks instantaneously, but it is possible to affect their time derivatives. This is done through the price, wage, and information policy of the firm. This implies that the firm has a transient monopoly in the "own" goods market and a transient monopsony in the "own" labor market. Now the question is to what extent this implies monopoly price setting and monopsony wage rate setting. Intuitively, one would expect that the price will be lower than the monopoly price. This is due to the fact that customers successively disappear if the price of the firm is higher than those of the other firms. In the limiting case when the number of customers of the different firms is fixed, one would expect the price to equal the monopoly price. In any case, the fact that the firm has a transient monopoly should lead to a higher price than marginal cost.

Thus, the hypothesis is that the price will be set somewhere between the monopoly price and the marginal cost price. A corresponding argument holds for the wage rate. An important task for the following analysis is to examine whether the hypothesis is correct, and if so, what factors determine the exact positions of the price and wage rate.

The discussion above also implies that the chapter contains a study of a generalized dynamic model of the firm, where the dynamics not only covers the development in the factor market but also in the goods market. Presently, an important path of development within the theory of the firm is the study how the behavior of the firm is influenced by costs of changing inputs of various factors of production.[1] This has not only created the possibility of integrating the neoclassical theory of the firm and the theory of capital, it has also led to more realistic descriptions of firm behavior. These costs of change appear in all markets in which the firm

---

1) Söderström (1974) contains a good survey of this theory.

operates. The fact that one sometimes speaks about the "goodwill value" of firms is a consequence of the fact that it is costly to acquire customers. The assets of a firm do not only consist of physical and financial assets, but also of less tangible assets, e.g., the number of employees and customers and the firm's organization.[1] An important task of the following analysis is to study the interdependence between the two investment processes of accumulating stocks of customers and employees. The analysis of the chapter thus involves an extension of the modern theory of the firm to take account of the interaction between costs of change in the factor and the goods markets. This extension is important if one wishes to study the parallel expansion of the firm in the goods and factor markets. In the following, the more short-run expansion during prosperity will be studied. But it is clear that the corresponding formulation of the problem is important for the study of the long-run growth of the firm.

1.2. Some assumptions for the following analysis

The firm is assumed to behave as if it maximized the discounted sum of all future profits. The cash flow generated by instantaneous profit and interest income is used partly to finance the expansion of the firm, partly to increase financial assets. The discount factor is the market rate of interest, net of taxes. This is exogenously given to the firm by the central bank, which lends and borrows at this rate of interest. There is no credit rationing.

There are no dividends. Labor being the sole factor of production, the cash flow is neither used for finansing in-

---

[1] From one point of view, the organization of the firm may be concieved of as an informational net-work. It is costly to set up an organization. The firm lives in a changing milieu, and this means that the existing organization will grow more and more out of date. On the other hand, it is possible both to adjust the organization to changes in the milieu and, in the long run, to extend the organization. The faster changes of the organization are made, the more resources which are required. The organization of the firm may thus be looked upon as an immaterial stock of capital; cf. Marschak and Radner (1972) and Arrow (1974b).

vestments in fixed capital.

The firm is organized in three divisions, the production, personnel, and marketing divisions. The total supply of labor hours of the employees is allocated among these three divisions, i.e., among goods production, supply of information in the labor market, and supply of information in the goods market.

The maximization of the capital value of the firm is subject to two static and two dynamic restrictions. The static constraints consist of the labor-force balance and the goods balance.

The labor force balance states that the number of employees, multiplied by the average number of labor hours of the employees, must equal the sum of labor hours allocated to goods production and information production in the labor and goods markets. The employees are assumed to be free to choose their time of work. This assumption is the same as that made in chapter III. Of course, the assumption is not wholly realistic, since most jobs have regulated working times. On the other hand, it is often possible in practice for employees to vary their working time rather freely.

The assumption of the labor-force balance continuously being fulfilled implies an assumption about the firm's observation possibilities. The management is assumed to have continuous information about the total supply of labor hours and, on this basis, to allocate the labor force between the three production divisions.[1)] Moreover, by varying the wage rate it is possible for the firm to change the supply of working hours.

The goods balance means that the quantitative demand of the firm's customers at each point of time should be equal to the production of goods. The demand for goods is equal to the number of customers multiplied by the average demand per customer. The average consumption per customer in turn depends inter alia on the price. The production of goods is a function

---

1) This assumption means that the firm model, and consequently the macroeconomic model in the next chapter, basically are equilibrium models. At each point of time there is equilibrium in each and everyone of the individual firms' partial goods and labor markets.

of the number of working hours allocated to goods production. The assumption of the goods balance being continuously fulfilled implies that it is possible to adjust goods production continuously to variations in demand and that the management is fully and instantaneously informed of changes in the demand for its good.

The assumptions made above concerning the labor- and the goods balances imply that the firm, by continuously varying its relative wage rate and price, manages to maintain equilibrium in its "own" labor and goods markets. We are thus working with an equilibrium model with perfect wage and price mobility.

In addition to the two static constraints, the planning of the firm is subject to two dynamic restrictions, namely two differential equations governing the net rate of increase of customers and employees. By varying its price, wage rate, and information policy, it is possible for the firm to affect these two flows. The net flow of customers will increase if the firm lowers its relative price or increases the supply of information in the goods market. The net flow of employees increases if the firm increases its relative wage rate or intensifies the supply of information in the labor market. Moreover, both the net flow of customers and the net flow of employees are affected by events outside the firm's control. This is discussed further below.

All firms and all households have the same expectations. This means that the firm has full knowledge of the distribution of relative prices and relative wage rates. But information about the average wage rate and the average price level is only obtained with a lag, h_p time units in the goods market and h_w time units in the labor market. Expectations about the current wage-rate level and price level are then formed via the (subjectively certain) expected rate of wage increase, g_w^e, and the (subjectively certain) expected rate of price increase, g_p^e.

Expectations of inflation may be wrong; the actual rate of wage increase may differ from that expected. The same is true for the rate of price increase. If the actual rate of wage inflation is higher than that expected, the average wage rate in the market will be higher than that expected by the participants.

The firm determines the price and the wage rate by considering the (expected) relative price and (expected) relative wage rate they will produce. The average (expected) price on the market is given, so that it is the relative price which determines how much customers buy and how large the net rate of increase of the stock of customers will be. The corresponding reasoning holds for the wage rate.

Since the actual rate of price increase may differ from that expected, the average price which the firm expects to maintain may differ from the actual average price level in the market. This in turn implies that the relative price the management of the firm believes itself to charge may differ from its actual relative price. If the actual rate of price inflation is faster than that expected, the expected average price level will be lower than the actual, and all the relative prices which the different firms actually charge will be lower than those expected.

Moreover, if the firms are confronted with an increased demand for goods, they will try to increase their relative prices. To increase their relative prices, they must plan first to increase their prices sufficiently to compensate for the expected rate of price inflation, and then increase them further in order to alter their relative prices. But what is possible for an individual firm is impossible for firms as a whole. The result will be of course that the actual rate of price inflation exceeds the expected one. The individual firm's price and wage rate setting in combination with erroneous expectations in thus of central importance for the inflation mechanism.

1.3. Plan of the chapter

The following discussion is arranged as follows. In section 2 are derived the flow equations of the number of customers and employees of the firm. In the next section the intertemporal choice problem of the firm is presented and the behavior equations derived subject to the marginal present value products-- i.e., the shadow prices of the stocks -- being exogenously given. Section 4 contains a phase diagram analysis. In section 5 the complete behavior equations are derived. The last section is devoted to an analysis of the firm's behavior in the special case in which it does not allocate any resources for information production.

2. Inflow and Outflow of Employees and Customers

In this section the equations for changes in the firm's stocks of employees and customers will be derived. Recruitment of employees is discussed first, and then the determinants of the net flow of customers are discussed.

2.1. Changes in the number of employees

The firm denoted by the number of order j initially has a certain number of employees, L_j. This stock is increased through recruitment of workers from firms paying a lower wage rate and from the unemployed. The stock of employees diminishes when employees get into contact with firms paying a higher wage rate or leave the labor force.[1] (See figure 1.)

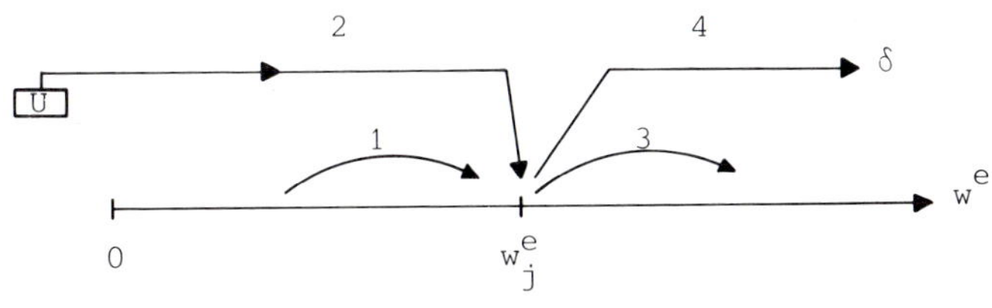

Fig. V:1. Sources of recruitments and diminishments of employees.

[1] The strict assumption of the model recalling the discussion in the preceding chapters, is that workers are subject to a constant death risk. The discussion could of course be extended so as to take into account pensioning and other reasons for leaving the labor force.

In the figure, U denotes the number of unemployed, while δ symbolizes people leaving the labor force. Relative wage rates are marked on the horizontal axis. The inflow of employees to the firm comes partly from firms paying a lower relative wage rate (1) and partly from the stock of unemployed (2). Employees leave the firm to take jobs in firms paying a higher relative wage rate (3) or when leaving the labor force (4).[1)]

The factors determining the inflow of employees will be discussed first. As to recruiting the unemployed, a first condition is that the firm gets into contact with an unemployed worker. If the number of signals is generated by a Poisson process, then the probability that a certain unemployed worker, expecting the relative price p^e, gets into contact during the short time interval dt with the firm will be equal to the portion of the total supply of information emanating from the firm, multiplied by the probability that the unemployed will get into contact with any firm at all.[2)]

$$\frac{a_w^j}{a_w} \varepsilon_w\left(\tau'_{sw}(p^e),\ a_w\right) dt$$

where a_w^j denotes the supply of information in the labor market from firm j. Note that the relative price p^e is that expected by the unemployed worker. Due to discrepancies between the actual and the expected rates of price inflation,

---

1) In an earlier version of this analysis, quits of persons going to look for a new and better job on a full-time basis (i.e., while unemployed) were included. From an empirical point of view this assumption is often criticized, but it does not affect the conclusions qualitatively. Unemployment will be higher, however. In order to simplify the analysis, and in order to stress the fact that variations of unemployment analyzed in this book are of a transient character associated with people entering the labor force, no account is taken of the voluntary flow of employees to the stock of unemployed.

2) This is the same assumption which was made in the two preceding chapters. It is relatively restrictive, since no account is taken of indirect transfer of information. Price information might, e.g., be transferred from one consumer to another; cf. Gould (1970) and Phelps and Winter (1970).

this may not be equal to the actual relative price. Also note that all households and all firms are assumed to have the same expectations. This means that the firm, when calculating the flow of new employees, starts from the same price expectations as determine household behavior.

The flow of formerly unemployed new employees is obtained by weightening the probabilities of different unemployed workers getting into contact with firm j <u>and</u> the probability that the relative wage rate (expected by the firm and by the unemployed worker) of the firm will be equal to or surmount the aspiration wage rate of the unemployed worker:

$$\frac{a_w^j}{a_w} U \int_0^{\Psi(w_j^e)} g(\pi)\, \varepsilon_w\left(\tau'_{sw}(\pi),\, a_w\right) d\pi dt$$

In the expression above, the unemployed are distributed over the relative prices they pay. Since, <u>inter alia</u>, the aspiration wage rate is a positive function of the relative price paid by the unemployed, $\hat{w}^e = \hat{w}^e(p^e)$, there exists an inverse of this function. The inverse function defines the relative price the unemployed worker pays if he has a certain aspiration wage rate: $p^e = \Psi(\hat{w}^e)$. Of course, p^e is a strictly increasing function of $\hat{w}^e$. By integrating over relative prices, from zero to that relative price which means that the relative wage rate of the firm is equal to the corresponding aspiration wage rate, the unemployed who have an aspiration wage level less than or equal to the wage rate of the firm are included. These unemployed workers will accept an employment offer if they get into contact with the firm. The other unemployed who get into contact with the firm will not contribute to the inflow of new employees since their aspiration wage rates are higher than the wage rate offered by the firm. In the formula above, $g(p^e)$ denotes the proportion of the unemployed paying the relative price p^e. The probability densities of unemployed and employed paying different relative prices are demarcated by always writing the latter frequency function multivariately, over relative prices <u>and</u> relative wage rates, $g(p^e, w^e)$. By definition the unemployed are solely distributed over relative prices.

The inflow of employed to the firm's stock of employees comes from firms paying a lower relative wage rate. The probability that a worker employed by an other firm, who pays the relative price p^e and recieves the relative wage rate w^e, makes contact with the firm is equal to the firm's portion of the supply of information on the labor market, multiplied by the probability that during the short time period of length dt, the employed makes contact with any firm:

$$\frac{a_w^j}{a_w} \varepsilon_w\left(\tau_{sw}(p^e, w^e), a_w\right) dt$$

To obtain the inflow of employed to the firm, this probability is integrated over all employed, distributed over relative prices and relative wage rates, where the fact is taken into consideration that only those employed in firms paying a lower wage rate than w_j^e contribute to the flow:

$$\frac{a_w^j}{a_w} L \int_0^{w_j^e} \int_0^{\infty} g(\pi, v)\ \varepsilon_w\left(\tau_{sw}(\pi, v), a_w\right) d\pi dv\ dt$$

Here L denotes the total number of employed in all firms.

Turning to the flows which cause the firm to loose employees, we start with persons who leave the labor force. If the "death-risk" is constant and equal to δdt, then $\delta L_j dt$ persons will leave the firm for this reason.

Furthermore, a part of the employees of the firm get into contact with other firms offering a higher relative wage rate. The probability that any employee of the firm will get into contact with another firm and switch to that firm is equal to the proportion of the flow of information on the labor market coming from firms with a higher relative wage rate than w_j^e, $\int_{w_j^e}^{\infty} \hat{f}(v) dv$, multiplied by the probability that, during the short period of time dt, the employed worker will get into contact with some firm, $\varepsilon_w\left(\tau_{sw}(p^e, w_j^e), a_w\right)dt$. If the employees of firm j are distributed over relative prices according to $g_j(p^e)$,[1] then the loss of employees to other firms during the short time period of length dt will be:

$$L_j \int_{w_j^e}^{\infty} \hat{f}(v)\, dv \int_0^{\infty} g_j(\pi)\, \varepsilon_w\left(\tau_{sw}(\pi, w_j^e), a_w\right) d\pi dt$$

Now we have all information necessary for obtaining the expression for the net flow of employees. This is calculated by taking the inflow from the stock of unemployed and employees in other firms and subtracting quits of employees leaving the labor force and employees leaving the firm for firms paying a higher relative wage rate:

$$\dot{L}_j = \frac{a_w^j}{a_w} U \int_0^{\Psi(w_j^e)} g(\pi)\, \varepsilon_w\left(\tau'_{sw}(\pi), a_w\right) d\pi +$$

$$(1) \quad + \frac{a_w^j}{a_w} L \int_0^{w_j^e} \int_0^{\infty} g(\pi, v)\, \varepsilon_w\left(\tau_{sw}(\pi, v), a_w\right) d\pi dv$$

$$- \delta L_j dt - L_j \int_{w_j^e}^{\infty} \hat{f}(v)\, dv \int_0^{\infty} g_j(\pi)\, \varepsilon_w\left(\tau_{sw}(\pi, w_j^e), a_w\right) d\pi$$

The firm may influence the net flow of employees by varying its control variables. The partial derivative of the net flow of employees with respect to the flow of information on the labor market of firm j is:

$$\frac{\partial \dot{L}_j}{\partial a_w^j} = \frac{L}{a_w} \left[u \int_0^{\Psi(w_j^e)} g_j(\pi)\, \varepsilon_w\left(\tau'_{sw}(\pi), a_w\right) d\pi + \right.$$

(2)

$$\left. + (1-u) \int_0^{w_j^e} \int_0^{\infty} g(\pi, v)\, \varepsilon_w\left(\tau_{sw}(\pi, v), a_w\right) d\pi dv \right] > 0$$

---

1) When speaking about the probability density over relative prices of the employees of a certain firm, it would be natural to write the frequency as a function of relative prices only. Index j then denotes persons employed by firm j.

where u denotes the number of unemployed relative to the labor force; i.e., $u = \frac{U}{U + L}$. If the firm increases the supply of information in the labor market, the net flow of employees will increase. This is due to the fact that the proportion of the total supply of information on the labor market which the firm accounts for will increase and thus the probability that a person searching for a job (whether unemployed or employed by an other firm) gets into contact with firm j. Strictly speaking, if the flow of information from firm j increases there will also be an effect on the total supply of information on the labor market, but since the number of firms is "very large", this effect is negligible.

If the firm increases its relative wage rate w_j^e, the rate of growth of employees will increase (if the number of employees initially is diminishing, this will be counteracted):

$$\frac{\partial \dot{L}_j}{\partial w_j^e} = \frac{a_w^j}{a_w} L \left[u \frac{\partial \Psi}{\partial w^e} g(\Psi) \, \varepsilon_w\left(\tau'_{sw}(\Psi(w_j^e)), a_w\right) + \right.$$

$$\left. + (1-u) \int_0^\infty g(\pi, w_j^e) \, \varepsilon_w\left(\tau_{sw}(\pi, w_j^e), a_w\right) d\pi \right]$$

(3)

$$- L_j \left[- \hat{f}(w_j) \int_0^\infty g_j(\pi) \, \varepsilon_w\left(\tau_{sw}(\pi, w_j^e), a_w\right) d\pi + \right.$$

$$\left. + \int_{w_j^e}^\infty \hat{f}(v) \, dv \int_0^\infty g_j(\pi) \frac{\partial \varepsilon}{\partial \tau_{sw}} \frac{\partial \tau_{sw}}{\partial w_j^e} d\pi \right] > 0$$

The first term in (3) represents the effect on the behavior of the unemployed if the firm increases its relative wage rate. This will mean that the relative wage rate exceeds a greater number of aspiration wage rates than before. This increases the flow of formerly unemployed persons accepting an employment offer made by the firm. Secondly, an increased wage rate means that the wage offer of the firm now exceeds those of a greater number of firms.

If the inflow of new employees increases when the firm increases its relative wage rate, the outflow will decrease. There are now less firms offering a higher wage rate than firm j. Consequently, the risk that a worker employed in firm j will recieve a higher wage offer from another firm is now lower than before. Furthermore, the search activity on the labor market of the employees of firm j will decrease if the relative wage rate increases (recall the discussion in chapter III). This means that the risk that employees of firm j will get into contact with other employers decreases. Consequently, the loss of employees to other firms declines.

The greater the number of employees in a certain firm, the greater the number of employees leaving the firm:

$$(4) \quad \frac{\partial \dot{L}_j}{\partial L_j} = - \left[\delta + \int_{w_j^e}^{\infty} \hat{f}(v)\,dv \int_0^{\infty} g_j(\pi)\ \varepsilon_w\left(\tau_{sw}(\pi,\ w_j^e), a_w\right) d\pi \right] < 0$$

The interpretation of equation (4) is left to the reader.

In the following analysis it is also necessary to know the signs of the second derivatives of $\dot{L}_j$. These are given in table 1:[1)]

Table 1. The signs of the second derivatives of $\dot{L}_j$.

	w_j^e	a_w^j	δ	τ'_{sw}	τ_{sw}	u	L_j
a_w^j	+	o	o	+	+	+	o
w_j^e	-	+	o	+	+	+	+
L_j	+	o	-	o	-	o	o

2.2. Changes in the number of customers of the firm

The inflow of customers to firm j partly stems from other firms having a higher relative price than p_j^e, partly from

1) The signs of $\frac{\partial^2 \dot{L}_j}{\partial u \partial a_w^j}$ and $\frac{\partial^2 \dot{L}_j}{\partial u \partial w_j^e}$ are uncertain, however.

new generations entering the labor force. The firm looses customers when they leave the labor force[1] and when they make contact with other firms maintaining a lower relative price than p_j^e. This is illustrated in figure 2 where β symbolizes new generations and δ customers disappearing from the labor force.[2]

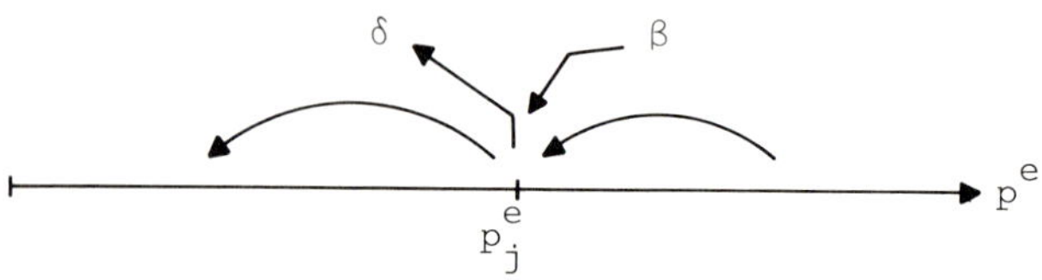

Fig. V:2. Gains and losses of customers.

The inflow of new customers comes first from new generations entering the labor force. At each moment the population is assumed to receive a proportional addition of new individuals. This means that, during the short period of length dt the number of persons entering the population (the labor force) is equal to $\beta K dt$, where β is the factor of growth and $K(= L + U)$ is the labor force, the total number of employed and unemployed workers in the economy. It is assumed that the number of people from new generations entering firm j as customers is proportional to the firm's supply of information in the goods market. The inflow of customers during a short period of length dt to firm j may thus be written:

1) When discussion changes in the number of employees a corresponding assumption was made. Strictly, this means that the customers die. If the pensioning period had been taken into account, withdrawals from the labor force would not automatically mean that the firm looses customers. The same sort of reasoning would apply for temporary retreats from the labor force, due to studies, childcare, and so on.

2) The population (which is equal to the labor force) is assumed to be stationary. This means that $\beta \doteq \delta$.

$$\beta \frac{a_p^j}{a_p} Kdt$$

where a_p^j is the supply of information on the goods market from firm j, while a_p denotes the total supply of information on the goods market, from all firms. It should be noted that this assumption is not completely analogous to that concerning the inflow of new employees. In that case it was assumed that an unemployed worker (possibly newly arrived in the labor force), only with a certain probability would get into contact with a firm. Here we assume that all new persons immediately get into contact with some firm, but later, when they try to get into contact with another supplier offering a lower price, they do so only with a certain probability. This unsymmetric assumption is made to avoid discriminating between unemployed workers who are or are not customers in a firm. In a wider sense, this is a realistic assumption. Furthermore, note that the first contact with a firm will be independent of its relative price. But it is clear that if a newly arrived person gets into contact with a firm demanding a very high relative price, much of his time will be devoted to searching for another supplier offering a lower price.

The second part of the inflow of customers consists of those unemployed who are customers in other firms with relative prices higher than p_j^e. The probability that an unemployed worker during a short time period of length dt, will get into contact with the firm is equal to the probability that the person will get into contact with any firm in the goods market, $\varepsilon_p(\tau'_{sp}(p^e), a_p)dt$, multiplied by the probability that the person, given a contact with any firm, will get into contact with firm j. This latter probability is equal to firm j's proportion of the total supply of information on the goods market, $\frac{a_p^j}{a_p}$. By integrating over all unemployed customers according to their frequency function over relative prices, the inflow of unemployed customers is obtained. It should be observed here that only customers paying a higher relative price than p_j^e will contribute to the inflow. If the probability density of unemployed customers paying the relative price p^e is denoted by $g(p^e)$, the inflow of customers to firm j from this source during a period of length dt will equal:

$$\frac{a_p^j}{a_p} U \int_{p_j^e}^{\infty} g(\pi)\ \varepsilon_p\left(\tau'_{sp}(\pi),\ a_p\right)\ d\pi dt.$$

The third source from which customers flow to firm j is the stock of employed persons paying a higher relative price than p_j^e. Except for the fact that the probabilities of getting into contact with these persons must now be integrated over prices and wage rates, the expression for this stream is analogous to that of unemployed customers:

$$\frac{a_p^j}{a_p} L \int_{p_j^e}^{\infty} \int_{o}^{\infty} g(\pi,v)\ \varepsilon_p\left(\tau_{sp}(\pi,\ v),\ a_p\right)\ d\pi dv\ dt$$

Turning now to the outflow of customers from firm j, the first reason for losing customers is that they die. Since the death risk is equal for all individuals, the number of customers leaving the firm for this reason during a short time period of length dt will equal:

$$\delta K_j dt$$

Furthermore, unemployed and employed customers pass over to other firms offering a lower relative price than p_j^e. If the proportion of unemployed customers in firm j is denoted by u_j, the number of unemployed customers in this firm will be equal to $u_j K_j$. The number of unemployed customers leaving the firm may then be written:

$$u_j K_j \int_{o}^{p_j^e} \hat{f}(\pi)\ \varepsilon_p\left(\tau'_{sp}(p_j^e),\ a_p\right)\ d\pi dt$$

where $\hat{f}(p^e)$ denotes the proportion of the total flow of information on the goods market emanating from firms with the relative price p^e. The number of employed customers leaving the firm may be written correspondingly:

$$(1 - u_j)\, K_j \int_o^{p_j^e} \hat{f}(\pi)\, d\pi \int_o^{\infty} g_j(v)\, \varepsilon_w\big(\tau_{sw}(p_j^e, v), a_p\big)\, dvdt$$

Putting together the expressions for inflows and outflows of customers, the following expression for the time derivative of the number of customers of firm j is obtained:

$$\dot{K}_j = \frac{a_p^j}{a_p} K \Big[\beta + u \int_{p_j^e}^{\infty} g(\pi)\, \varepsilon_p\big(\tau'_{sp}(\pi), a_p\big)\, d\pi +$$

$$+ (1 - u) \int_{p_j^e}^{\infty} \int_o^{\infty} g(\pi, v)\, \varepsilon_p\big(\tau_{sp}(\pi, v), a_p\big)\, d\pi dv\Big] -$$

(5)

$$- K_j \Big[\delta + u_j \int_o^{p_j^e} \hat{f}(\pi)\, \varepsilon_p\big(\tau'_{sp}(p_j^e), a_p\big)\, d\pi +$$

$$+ (1 - u_j) \int_o^{p_j^e} \hat{f}(\pi)\, d\pi \int_o^{\infty} g_j(v)\, \varepsilon_p\big(\tau_{sp}(p_j^e, v), a_p\big)\, dv\Big]$$

By varying its control variables, the firm is able to steer this flow. If the firm increases its supply of information in the goods market, the net flow of customers will increase:

$$\frac{\partial \dot{K}_j}{\partial a_p^j} = \frac{K}{a_p} \Big[\beta + u \int_{p_j^e}^{\infty} g(\pi)\, \varepsilon_p\big(\tau'_{sp}(\pi), a_p\big)\, d\pi +$$

(6)

$$+ (1 - u) \int_{p_j^e}^{\infty} \int_o^{\infty} g(\pi, v)\, \varepsilon_p\big(\tau_{sp}(\pi, v), a_p\big)\, d\pi dv\Big] > 0$$

Similarly to the case of employees, only the inflow of customers will be affected by an increased supply of information on the goods market. The inflow increases since the firm attracts a greater proportion of the new generations entering labor force. Moreover, a greater number of unemployed and employed customers in firms maintaining higher relative prices than p_j^e get into contact with the firm.

If the firm increases its relative price, the net increase of customers will diminish:

$$
\begin{aligned}
\frac{\partial \dot{K}_j}{\partial p_j^e} = K \frac{a_p^j}{a_p} \Big[& - u\, g(p_j^e)\, \varepsilon_p\big(\tau'_{sp}(p_j^e),\, a_p\big) - \\
& - (1-u) \int_0^\infty g(p_j^e,\, v)\, \varepsilon_p\big(\tau_{sp}(p_j^e,\, v),\, a_p\big)\, dv \Big] - \\
& - K_j \Big[u_j\, \hat{f}(p_j^e)\, \varepsilon_p\big(\tau'_{sp}(p_j^e),\, a_p\big) + \\
(7) \quad & + \frac{\partial \varepsilon_p}{\partial \tau'_{sp}} \frac{\partial \tau'_{sp}}{\partial p_j^e}\, u_j \int_0^{p_j^e} \hat{f}(\pi)\, d\pi + \\
& + (1-u_j)\, \hat{f}(p_j^e) \int_0^\infty g_j(v)\, \varepsilon_p\big(\tau_{sp}(p_j^e,\, v),\, a_p\big)\, dv \\
& + (1-u_j) \int_0^{p_j^e} \hat{f}(\pi) \int_0^\infty g_j(v)\, \frac{\partial \varepsilon}{\partial \tau_{sp}} \frac{\partial \tau_{sp}}{\partial p_j^e}\, dv \Big] < 0
\end{aligned}
$$

Since fewer firms with a higher relative price than p_j^e are left after the price increase, the inflow of customers will diminish. The inflow from new generations entering labor force will not be affected, however. The outflow of customers from firm j will increase, both because fewer firms demanding a higher relative price are left after the price increase and because the customers of firm j will increase their search activity on the goods market when the relative price they pay increases.

Similarly to the case of the firm's stock of employees, a greater number of customers will decrease the net flow of customers:

$$\frac{\partial \dot{K}_j}{\partial K_j} = -\left[\delta + u_j \int_0^{p_j^e} \hat{f}(\pi)\, \varepsilon_p\left(\tau'_{sp}(p_j^e),\, a_p\right) d\pi \,+ \right. \tag{8}$$

$$\left. + \,(1 - u_j) \int_0^{p_j^e} \hat{f}(\pi)\, d\pi \int_0^{\infty} g_j(v)\, \varepsilon_p\left(\tau_{sp}(p_j^e,\, v),\, a_p\right) dv \right] < 0$$

For the following analysis, it is necessary to know the signs of the second derivatives of $\dot{K}_j$. These are given in table 2.[1)]

Table 2. The second derivatives of $\dot{K}_j$.

	p_j^e	a_p^j	δ	τ'_{sp}	τ_{sp}	K_j	u	u_j	a_p
a_p^j	-	o	+	+	+	o	o	o	o
p_j^e	-	-	o	-	-	-	o	o	o
K_j	-	o	-	-	-	o	o	o	o

3. The Price, Wage, and Information Policy of the Firm: the Incomplete Behavior Equations

In this section the planning of the firm will be discussed subject to the condition that the marginal present value products of the number of employees and customers, (i.e., the shadow prices of the stock of employees and customers, respectively), are exogenously given. The objective function

1) However, a minor uncertainty is attached to the following cross derivatives:

$\frac{\partial^2 \dot{K}_j}{\partial u \partial a_p^j}$, $\frac{\partial^2 \dot{K}_j}{\partial \tau'_{sp}\, \partial p_j}$, $\frac{\partial^2 \dot{K}_j}{\partial \tau_{sp}\, \partial p_j}$, $\frac{\partial^2 \dot{K}_j}{\partial u \partial p_j}$ and $\frac{\partial^2 \dot{K}_j}{\partial u_j\, \partial p_j}$.

as well as the constraints on the firm's planning problem will be presented. Then (incomplete) behavior equations will be derived through maximization of the Hamiltonian, subject to the relevant constraints. Finally, the section contains a discussion of whether maximization of the Hamiltonian also implies maximization of the objective functional.

3.1. Formulation of the problem

The firm is assumed to behave as if it tried to maximize the discounted sum of all future profits. The factor of discount is equal to the market rate of interest, r. The interest rate is defined net of taxes. The present value may be written:

$$(1 - \sigma) \int_0^{\infty} e^{-rt} \left[p_j^e \bar{p}^e \, \bar{x}_j K_j - w_j^e \bar{w}^e \, \bar{\tau}_{wj} \, L_j \right] dt$$

where the variables inside the bracket are functions of time. σ is the rate of the profit tax, which is assumed to be proportional to profits.[1)] The instantaneous profit inside the brackets is equal to total revenue $p_j^e \bar{p}^e \bar{x}_j K_j$, minus total costs, $w_j^e \bar{w}^e \bar{\tau}_w^j L_j$. $p_j^e \bar{p}^e$ is the price set by the firm at a certain moment. As before, $\bar{p}^e$ is the expected (with subjective certainty) average price level. If the actual rate of price inflation deviates from that expected, the expected average price level will deviate from the actual price level. The product of the actual relative price p_j and the actual price level $\bar{p}$ is always equal to the product of the expected relative price and the expected average price level. $\bar{x}_j$ denotes average consumption per customer and K_j is the number of customers of the firm. The total revenue is thus equal to the price $p_j^e \bar{p}^e$, multiplied by the average consumption per customer $\bar{x}_j$, multiplied by the number of customers K_j.

---

1) To simplify, the tax on profits is assumed to be symmetric -- *i.e.*, the expression also holds for loss periods, when the government pays a certain sum to the firm. This unrealistic (but for, the present purpose, not very important) assumption might be defended by the implicit existence of rules making possible intertemporal offsetting of profits and losses.

Total costs are equal to the wage rate $w_j^e \bar{w}^e$, times the average number of work hours per employee $\bar{\tau}_{wj}$, times the number of employees L_j. Note that there exists only one factor of production and that only costs and revenues of the business are included in the profit concept.

To simplify matters, the expected average price level at the planning moment is placed outside the bracket. Furthermore, by using the assumption that the firm expects a constant future rate of price increase equal to the expected rate of wage increase, the present value of future profits may be written:

$$(9) \qquad (1 - \sigma)\ \bar{p}^e(0) \int_0^{\infty} e^{-(r-g_p^e)} \left[p_j^e \bar{x}_j K_j - w_j^e \frac{\bar{w}^e}{\bar{p}^e} \bar{\tau}_{wj} L_j \right] dt$$

which means that the (expected) real rate of interest, $r-g^e$, now is the factor of discount. By factoring out the average price level at the planning moment, the expression is standardized, so that it is not necessary to study separately the development of the projected average price level and the projected average wage rate.

The average consumption per customer of firm j may be written as the average of the consumption of unemployed and employed customers:

$$(10) \qquad \bar{x}_j = u_j x'(p_j^e) + (1 - u_j) \int_0^{\infty} g_j(v)\ x(p_j^e, v)\ dv$$

It should be noted that the proportion of unemployed customers may vary from firm to firm. The distribution over relative wage rates for the employed customers may also vary. Consumption is the same for all unemployed customers, since they have the same income (the unemployment allowance). On the other hand, depending on the wage rate, consumption varies between employed customers. The employed customers of firm j are distributed over relative wage rates according to $g_j(w^e)$.

In the same way, the average supply of labor per employee of firm j may be written:

$$(11) \qquad \bar{\tau}_w^j = \int_0^\infty g_j(\pi)\ \tau_w(\pi,\ w_j^e)\ d\pi.$$

Supply of labor varies between employees due to the fact that, as customers, they are distributed over firms demanding different relative prices. To the extent that the employees differ in other respects -- *e.g.*, by having different subjective rates of time preference (either depending on differences in the "pure" rate of time preference or on differences in the expected remaining life time; recall the discussion in chapter III) -- this may be taken into account by integrating over these variables also.

3.2. Constraints on the firm's choice set

When maximizing the objective functional (9), the firm has to take certain constraints into consideration. At each point of time there is a certain number of employees, L_j. Labor is the only factor of production, and the total supply of labor hours is allocated between the three production departments. There are three production processes going on, goods production and information production in the goods and labor markets. The following notation is used:

b_q^j = the number of work hours allocated to goods production

b_p^j = the number of work hours allocated to information production in the goods market

b_w^j = the number of work hours allocated to information production in the labor market.

Index q indicates goods production, index p indicates information about the firm's relative price, and w indicates information about the relative wage rate.

The total number of work hours available is equal to the number of employees, multiplied by the average number of work hours per employee: $L_j\bar{\tau}_w^j$. Abstracting from slack, the available number of work hours should be identical to consumption in the three areas of use:

$$(12) \qquad \bar{\tau}^j_w L_j - b^j_q - b^j_p - b^j_w = 0$$

Equation (12) is called the labor force balance of the firm. Note that (12) is an equilibrium condition in the firm's "own" labor market.

At a certain point of time, the firm has no possibility to change the number of available work hours by changing the number of employees. On the other hand, it is possible to increase the number of work hours per employee, by increasing the relative wage rate.

This means that increases in the relative wage rate have two functions. First, it is possible for the firm to increase the net flow of employees. Secondly, increases in production are made possible. Since the time derivative of the number of employees is also affected by the firm's supply of information in the labor market, there is an extra degree of freedom. The net increase in the number of employees and the number of work hours at the firm's disposal do not stand in a one-to-one relationship.

Labor being the only factor of production, the output of goods may be written as a function of the number of work hours allocated to goods production, b^j_q. If the production volume is denoted by q_j, the following function is obtained:

$$(13) \qquad q_j = q_j(b^j_q), \qquad \frac{\partial q_j}{\partial b^j_q} > 0, \; \frac{\partial^2 q_j}{\partial b^{j2}_q} < 0$$

Analogously, the production of price information is a function of the number of work hours allocated to this activity:

$$(14) \qquad a_p^j = a_p^j(b_p^j) \quad \text{where} \quad \frac{\partial a_p^j}{\partial b_p^j} > 0, \quad \frac{\partial^2 a_p^j}{\partial b_p^{j2}} < 0$$

Finally, the production of wage information also functions according to the usual neoclassical conditions with positive marginal productivity and decreasing returns. Production of wage information is a function of the number of work hours allocated to the "personnel department":

$$(15) \qquad a_w^j = a_w^j(b_w^j) \quad \text{where} \quad \frac{\partial a_w^j}{\partial b_w^j} > 0, \quad \frac{\partial^2 a_w^j}{\partial b_w^{j2}} < 0$$

The outputs given by the two last production functions are included as arguments of the equations for the time derivative of the number of customers (5) and the number of employees (1), respectively. The production function (13) gives information about the flow of goods leaving the firm. The assumption is now made that the production volume exactly corresponds to sales:

$$(16) \qquad q(b_q^j) - \bar{x}_j K_j = 0$$

It should be noted that (16) implies an assumption of equilibrium: the firm always varies price and allocation of work hours to goods production so that production always is equal to sales. When sudden changes occur in e.g., the demand of the customers, the firm is assumed to adjust instantaneously its control variables so as to maintain equilibrium in its "own" goods market (and, given the new conditions, to maximize the objective functional).

3.3. The optimization problem

All data needed for formulating the optimization problem are now available. The firm is assumed to behave as if it maximizes its capital value (the discounted value of all future profits):

$$(9)\quad (1-\sigma)\,\bar{p}^{e}(0)\int_{0}^{\infty} e^{-(r-g_{p}^{e})t}\left[p^{e}\bar{x}K - w^{e}\frac{\bar{w}^{e}}{\bar{p}^{e}}\bar{\tau}_{w}L\right]dt$$ [1)]

subject to the constraint that the available number of work hours is fully used:

$$(12)\quad \bar{\tau}_{w}L - b_{q} - b_{p} - b_{w} = 0,$$

that the firm produces as much as is demanded of the good:

$$(16)\quad q(b_{q}) - \bar{x}K = 0,$$

that production functions (13), (14) and (15) apply, that the net increase of employees is determined via differential equation (1) and the initial condition

$$L(0) = L_{0},$$

that the net increase of customers is determined via the differential equation (5) and the initial condition

$$K(0) = K_{0}.$$

Finally, the terminal stocks of employees and customers must be non-negative:

$$(17)\quad \lim_{T\to\infty} L(T) \geq 0,\quad \lim_{T\to\infty} K(T) \geq 0$$

The problem is to find the best trajectories for the control variables -- the relative price $p^{e}(t)$, the relative wage rate $w^{e}(t)$, the number of work hours allocated to goods production $b_{q}(t)$, the number of work hours allocated to supply of information in the goods market $b_{p}(t)$ and the number of work hours allocated to supply of information in the labor market $b_{w}(t)$ -- so that the functional (9) is

---

1) From now on we abstract from the constant $(1-\sigma)\bar{p}^{e}(0)$. This factor will only affect the value of the profit functional, not the location of the maximum. Also, the index j is suppressed.

maximized subject to the constraints noted above. Futhermore, this solution must fulfill the condition that the control variables are non-negative. This is assumed to be the case.

If there exists an optimal trajectory in control space maximizing the value of (9) subject to the constraints noted above, then there exist adjoint variables $\lambda_1(t)$ and $\lambda_2(t)$ and Lagrange multipliers $\mu_1(t)$ and $\mu_2(t)$ so that the extended instantaneous Hamilton-Lagrange function

$$H\left[K(t), L(t), p^e(t), w^e(t), b_q(t), b_p(t), b_w(t), \lambda_1(t), \lambda_2(t), \mu_1(t), \mu_2(t)\right] =$$

$$(18) \quad = \left[p^{e}\bar{x}K - w^e \frac{\bar{w}^e}{\bar{p}^e} \bar{\tau}_w L\right] + \mu_1\left[q(b_q) - \bar{x}K\right] + $$

$$+ \mu_2\left[\bar{\tau}_w L - b_q - b_w - b_p\right] + \lambda_1 \dot{K} + \lambda_2 \dot{L}$$

is maximized at each point of time. The Lagrange multipliers are positive, and the adjoint variables are determined by the differential equations

$$(19) \quad \begin{aligned} \dot{\lambda}_1 &= (r - g^e)\lambda_1 - \frac{\partial H^*}{\partial K} \\ \dot{\lambda}_2 &= (r - g^e)\lambda_2 - \frac{\partial H^*}{\partial L} \end{aligned}$$

where the star denotes that the derivatives are defined for the maximum value of the Hamiltonian. Contrary to the case for the phase variables K and L, the adjoint variables are not determined by initial conditions but by terminal conditions, the transversality conditions

$$(20) \quad \begin{aligned} &\lim_{T\to\infty} e^{-(r-g^e)T} \lambda_1(T) \geq 0, \quad \lim_{T\to\infty} e^{-(r-g^e)T} \lambda_2(T) \geq 0, \\ &\lim_{T\to\infty} e^{-(r-g^e)T} \left[\lambda_1(T)K(T) + \lambda_2(T)L(T)\right] = 0 \end{aligned}$$

If (real disposable) profit at point of time t, $\left[p^{e}\bar{x}K - w^e \frac{\bar{w}^e}{\bar{p}^e} \bar{\tau}_w L\right]$, is denoted by $P(t)$, one may say that maximization of the extended Hamiltonian implies that the expression

$$P(t) + \lambda_1 \dot{K} + \lambda_2 \dot{L}$$

is maximized subject to the labor force balance (12) and the goods balance (16). Real disposable profit $P(t)$ and a weighted sum of the time derivatives of the number of customers and employees at the same point of time are thus maximized subject to (12) and (16). The maximization implies that the control variables should be chosen so that instantaneous profit, $P(t)$, and all future profits should be balanced so that the capital value of the firm is maximized. For example, instantaneous profit increases if labor hours are transferred from information production to goods production, but then the net rate of growth of customers and employees will fall, and this means lower future profits. Thus, there is an optimal balance between present and future profits. The effect on the profit functional

$$\int_t^{\infty} e^{-(r-g^e)(\tau-t)} \left[p^e(\tau)\ \bar{x}\ K(\tau) - w^e(\tau)\ \frac{\bar{w}^e}{\bar{p}^e}\ \bar{\tau}_w\ L(\tau) \right] d\tau$$

of an increase in the number of customers is taken into account by the marginal present value product of the number of customers (the shadow price of customers) λ_1. The effect on the profit functional of an increase in the number of employees is taken into account by the marginal present value of the number of employees (the shadow price of employees) λ_2. The values of the present value products are estimated at time t. If we want to discount them to the planning point of time $(t=0)$, they should be multiplied by $e^{-(r-g^e)t}$. It should be stressed that the marginal present value products are defined for increases in the numbers of customers and employees at time t, not for increases of their time derivatives. Implicitly, the Hamiltonian gives information about how much the profit functional (9) directly and indirectly grows at time t if the optimal policy is chosen thereafter. If the profit functional is maximized, then the Hamiltonian is maximized, but the converse is not necessarily true. To guarantee maximization of the Hamiltonian also implies maximization of the profit functional, additional conditions must be fulfilled. These will be discussed further on.

By differentiating the extended Hamiltonian (18) with respect to the control variables and the lagrange multipliers, and by setting the derivatives equal to zero, the following necessary conditions for maximizing the Hamiltonian are obtained:

$$\frac{\partial H}{\partial p^e} = \left[\bar{x} + p^e \frac{\partial \bar{x}}{\partial p^e}\right] K - \mu_1 \frac{\partial \bar{x}}{\partial p^e} K + \lambda_1 \frac{\partial \dot{K}}{\partial p^e} = 0$$

$$\frac{\partial H}{\partial w^e} = - \frac{\bar{w}^e}{\bar{p}^e} \left[\bar{\tau}_w + w^e \frac{\partial \bar{\tau}_w}{\partial w^e}\right] L + \mu_2 L \frac{\partial \bar{\tau}_w}{\partial w^e} + \lambda_2 \frac{\partial \dot{L}}{\partial w^e} = 0$$

$$\frac{\partial H}{\partial b_q} = \mu_1 \frac{\partial q}{\partial b_q} - \mu_2 = 0$$

$$(21) \quad \frac{\partial H}{\partial b_w} = - \mu_2 + \lambda_2 \frac{\partial \dot{L}}{\partial a_w} \frac{\partial a_w}{\partial b_w} = 0$$

$$\frac{\partial H}{\partial b_p} = - \mu_2 + \lambda_1 \frac{\partial \dot{K}}{\partial a_p} \frac{\partial a_p}{\partial b_p} = 0$$

$$\frac{\partial H}{\partial \mu_1} = q(b_q) - \bar{x}K = 0$$

$$\frac{\partial H}{\partial \mu_2} = \bar{\tau}_w L - b_q - b_w - b_p = 0$$

It might be instructive to investigate the economic implications of the equation system above. The first equation may be rewritten:

$$\mu_1 K = p^e \left[1 + \frac{\bar{x}}{p^e} \frac{\partial p^e}{\partial \bar{x}}\right] K + \lambda_1 \frac{\partial \dot{K}}{\partial p^e} \frac{\partial p^e}{\partial \bar{x}}$$

Here μ_1 is the marginal revenue[1] of selling one unit more of the good. If this is multiplied by the number of customers, the marginal revenue from selling one more unit of the good per customer is obtained. Since the price elasticity is finite, the marginal revenue is lower than the price. This is the usual static result. But there is another term which works in the opposite direction. To be able to increase its sales instantaneously, the firm has to lower its relative price. This will mean a higher net rate of increase of customers which, via the marginal present value product of the number of customers, increases marginal revenue μ_1. This means that the difference between price and marginal revenue is not as great as in the static monopoly case.[2]

The second equation of (21) may be written:

$$\mu_2 L = \frac{\bar{w}^e}{\bar{p}^e} w^e \left[1 + \frac{\bar{\tau}_w}{w^e} \frac{\partial w^e}{\partial \bar{\tau}_w}\right] L - \lambda_2 \frac{\partial \dot{L}}{\partial w^e} \frac{\partial w^e}{\partial \bar{\tau}_w}$$

Here μ_2 denotes the firm's marginal cost[3] of increasing the supply of labor hours by one hour. If μ_2 is multiplied by the number of employees, we get the marginal cost of increasing the number of work hours per employee by one hour on the average. Since the elasticity of supply of labor is not infinite, the marginal cost of increasing the working time by one hour is higher than the hourly wage rate. Alternatively, one may say that the marginal cost is higher than the wage rate, since the latter must be increased in order to increase the supply of labor per employee by one hour, and this higher wage rate also applies to the previous working hours. But since the increased wage rate

---

1) It should be noted that all prices are expressed in real units. This is due to the fact that the (expected) average price level was suppressed in the profit functional and that therefore changes in the level of the capital value of the firm represented by $(1-\sigma)\bar{p}^e$ were abstracted from.

2) Cf. Phelps and Winter (1971), pp. 322-323.

3) Cf. footnote 1, above.

will increase the net rate of flow of the number of employees, the marginal cost of increasing the number of working hours per employee will be less than in the case of static optimization. However, there will always be some degree of monopsony as long as $\lambda_2 > 0$, since the second term of the expression reduces the value of the right hand side.

The interpretation of the third equation of (21) is that the marginal revenue product of increasing the number of working hours in goods production should be equal to the marginal cost of increasing the number of working hours.

The forth equation states that the marginal cost of increasing the supply of labor by one hour should be equal to the marginal revenue of one more hour used for increasing the supply of information on the goods market.

The fifth equation states that the marginal cost of increasing the number of working hours by one should be equal to the marginal revenue of increasing the number of working hours used for information production on the labor market by one.

By combining the fourth and fifth equations, one obtains the result that the last hour allocated to investment purposes should give the same return (expressed as the effect on the profit functional) irrespective of whether it is used for increasing the number of customers or the number of employees. Thus, there should be efficiency in the allocation of recources between the two kinds of "capital accumulation". By comparing the third and fourth equations, one may say that the last labor hour should have the same effect on the profit functional, regardless of whether it is used for current goods production (and thereby increasing instantaneous profit) or used for information production in the goods market (thereby increasing future profits).

Finally the two last equations imply that goods production should be equal to the quantitative demand by the customers of the firm and that the number of working hours supplied by the employees should be distributed exactly between goods production and information production in the goods and labor markets. We may say that these two equations require equilibrium in the firm's "own" goods and labor markets.

The system of equations (21) contains necessary but not sufficient conditions for the maximization of the Hamiltonian. In addition, second order conditions must be fulfilled in order to guarantee a maximum:

$$(22)\quad (dp^e, dw^e, db_q, db_p, db_w, d\mu_1, d\mu_2)\begin{bmatrix} \frac{\partial^2 H}{\partial p^{e2}} & \cdots & \frac{\partial^2 H}{\partial \mu_2 \partial p} \\ \hline \frac{\partial^2 H}{\partial p \partial u_2} & \cdots & \frac{\partial^2 H}{\partial \mu_2^2} \end{bmatrix}\begin{bmatrix} dp^e \\ dw^e \\ db_q \\ db_p \\ db_w \\ d\mu_1 \\ d\mu_2 \end{bmatrix} < 0$$

for $q - \bar{w}K = 0,\ \bar{\tau}_w L - b_q - b_w - b_p = 0,$

$(dp^e,\ dw^e,\ db_q,\ db_p,\ db_w,\ d\mu_1,\ d\mu_2) \neq 0$[1)]

It should be stressed that the discussion above has been devoted to necessary and sufficient conditions for maximizing the Hamiltonian. However, maximization of the Hamiltonian is merely a necessary -- and not a sufficient -- condition for maximizing the profit functional. To guarantee maximization of the profit functional, further conditions are required. These conditions will be discussed further on.

3.4. The incomplete behavior equations

Analogously to the discussion of the previous chapters, the incomplete behavior equations define the behavior of the firm, when the shadow prices of the number of customers, λ_1 and

---

1) This may be shown immediately for the case in which the absolute values of $\frac{\partial^2 H}{\partial b_p \partial p}$ and $\frac{\partial^2 H}{\partial b_w \partial w}$ are "small". By deriving the incomplete behavior equations, the matrix of expression (22) has been inverted, so that the corresponding assumptions have been made about the two partial derivatives.

the number of employees λ_2 are exogenously given. Thus, the optimal change of the control variables will be discussed subject to the condition that the two marginal present value products are determined outside the intertemporal optimization problem. In general, when the exogenous variables or the two phase variables change, the shadow prices also change. The complete behavior equations, which will be presented in section 5 below, give information about the optimal behavior of the firm when the effects on the shadow prices of various disturbances are taken into consideration. Generally, the optimal choice of values of the control variables at each point of time is not only affected by the behavior equations presented in the present section, but also indirectly, through changes in the values of the adjoint variables. Thus the complete behavior equations are not presented in this section. Neither is it possible to examine, for example, the effects on the control variables of a change in the real rate of interest. This is due to the fact that the control variables are only affected indirectly, through changed values of the adjoint variables. By total differentiation of the first-order conditions for maximizing the Hamiltonian. (21), and solving for the variables p^e, w^e, b_q, b_w and b_p, the incomplete behavior equations are obtained:

$$dp^e = \underset{+}{p_1^e}dA + \underset{-}{p_2^e}dB + \underset{-}{p_3^e}dC + \underset{+}{p_4^e}dD + \underset{+}{p_5^e}dE + \underset{-}{p_6^e}dF + \underset{-}{p_7^e}dG$$

$$dw^e = \underset{-}{w_1^e}dA + \underset{+}{w_2^e}dB + \underset{+}{w_3^e}dC + \underset{+}{w_4^e}dD + \underset{+}{w_5^e}dE + \underset{-}{w_6^e}dF + \underset{-}{w_7^e}dG$$

(23) $$db_q = \underset{-}{b_{q_1}}dA + \underset{+}{b_{q_2}}dB + \underset{+}{b_{q_3}}dC + \underset{-}{b_{q_4}}dD + \underset{-}{b_{q_5}}dE + \underset{-}{b_{q_6}}dF + \underset{-}{b_{q_7}}dG$$

$$db_w = \underset{+}{b_{w_1}}dA + \underset{+}{b_{w_2}}dB + \underset{-}{b_{w_3}}dC + \underset{+}{b_{w_4}}dD + \underset{-}{b_{w_5}}dE + \underset{+}{b_{w_6}}dF + \underset{+}{b_{w_7}}dG$$

$$db_p = \underset{+}{b_{p_1}}dA + \underset{+}{b_{p_2}}dB + \underset{-}{b_{p_3}}dC + \underset{-}{b_{p_4}}dD + \underset{+}{b_{p_5}}dE + \underset{+}{b_{p_6}}dF + \underset{+}{b_{p_7}}dG$$

where

$$dA = \lambda_1 \frac{\partial^2 \dot{K}}{\partial \tau_{sp} \partial p^e} d\tau_{sp} + \lambda_1 \frac{\partial^2 \dot{K}}{\partial \tau'_{sp} \partial p^e} d\tau_{sp} + [K \frac{\partial \bar{x}}{\partial u} + K(p^e - \mu_1) \frac{\partial^2 \bar{x}}{\partial u \partial p^e}]du$$

$$+ (\frac{\partial^2 \dot{K}}{\partial u \partial p^e} + \bar{x} + p^e \frac{\partial \bar{x}}{\partial p^e} - \mu_1 \frac{\partial \bar{x}}{\partial p^e})dK + Kd\bar{x} + \frac{\partial \dot{K}}{\partial p^e} d\lambda_1$$

$$dB = \lambda_2 \frac{\partial^2 \dot{L}}{\partial \tau_{sw} \partial w^e} d\tau_{sw} + \lambda_2 \frac{\partial^2 \dot{L}}{\partial \tau'_{sw} \partial w^e} d\tau'_{sw} + \lambda_2 \frac{\partial^2 \dot{L}}{\partial u \partial w^e} du$$

$$+ (\lambda_2 \frac{\partial^2 \dot{L}}{\partial L \partial w^e} - \frac{\bar{w}^e}{\bar{p}^e} (\bar{\tau}_w + w^e \frac{\partial \bar{\tau}_w}{\partial w^e}) + \mu_2 \frac{\partial \bar{\tau}_w}{\partial w^e}) dL - \frac{\bar{w}^e}{\bar{p}^e} L \, d\bar{\tau}_w$$

$$+ \frac{\partial \dot{L}}{\partial w^e} d\lambda_2 - L (\bar{\tau}_w + w^e \frac{\partial \bar{\tau}_w}{\partial w^e}) d(\frac{\bar{w}^e}{\bar{p}^e})$$

$$dC = \mu_2 \frac{\partial^2 q}{\partial g \partial b_q} dg$$

$$dD = \lambda_2 \frac{\partial^2 \dot{L}}{\partial \tau_{sw} \partial a_w} \frac{\partial a_w}{\partial b_w} d\tau_{sw} + \lambda_2 \frac{\partial^2 \dot{L}}{\partial \tau'_{sw} \partial a_w} \frac{\partial a_w}{\partial b_w} d\tau'_{sw}$$

$$+ \lambda_2 \frac{\partial^2 \dot{L}}{\partial u \partial a_w} \frac{\partial a_w}{\partial b_w} d\tau_{sw} + \frac{\partial \dot{L}}{\partial a_w} \frac{\partial a_w}{\partial b_w} d\lambda_2$$

$$dE = \lambda_1 \frac{\partial^2 \dot{K}}{\partial \tau_{sp} \partial a_p} \frac{\partial a_p}{\partial b_p} d\tau_{sp} + \lambda_1 \frac{\partial^2 \dot{K}}{\partial \tau'_{sp} \partial a_p} \frac{\partial a_p}{\partial b_p} d\tau'_{sp}$$

$$+ \frac{\partial \dot{K}}{\partial a_p} \frac{\partial a_p}{\partial b_p} d\lambda_1 + \lambda_1 \frac{\partial^2 \dot{K}}{\partial \delta \partial a_p} \frac{\partial a_p}{\partial b_p} d\delta$$

$$dF = -\bar{x} dK - K d\bar{x} + \frac{\partial q}{\partial g} dg$$

$$dG = \bar{\tau}_w dL + L d\bar{\tau}_w$$

The first five arguments contain "substitution effects", while the next-to-last argument takes the production-volume effect (or the goods-balance effect) of a parameter change into consideration. The last argument takes the labor-force-balance effect into consideration. These two arguments have to do with the two balance constraints, the goods balance and the labor-force balance. The analysis of the effects of parameter changes affecting these two constraints is analogous to the analysis of income effects in consumer theory.

Note that $d\bar{x}$ in its turn is the differential of (10) where, however, dp^e does not appear. The same holds for $d\bar{\tau}_w$ with respect to (11). Here dw^e does not appear. $d\bar{x}$ and $d\bar{\tau}_w$ are thus the differentials of $\bar{x}$ and $\bar{\tau}_w$ with respect to the shift variables which are not controlled by the firm.

It may be of interest to analyze the effects on the control variables of some parameter changes, and to split up these effects into partial effects. If the search activity of the unemployed worker in the labor market, τ'_{sw}, increases, this will have the following effects on the firm's behavior.

$$\frac{\partial p^e}{\partial \tau'_{sw}} = \underset{-}{\frac{\partial p^e}{\partial B}} \lambda_2 \underset{+}{\frac{\partial^2 \dot{L}}{\partial \tau'_{sw} \partial w^e}} + \underset{+}{\frac{\partial p^e}{\partial D}} \lambda_2 \underset{+}{\frac{\partial^2 \dot{L}}{\partial \tau'_{sw} \partial a_w}} \underset{+}{\frac{\partial a_w}{\partial b_w}} \gtreqless 0$$

$$\frac{\partial w^e}{\partial \tau'_{sw}} = \underset{+}{\frac{\partial w^e}{\partial B}} \lambda_2 \underset{+}{\frac{\partial^2 \dot{L}}{\partial \tau'_{sw} \partial w^e}} + \underset{+}{\frac{\partial w^e}{\partial D}} \lambda_2 \underset{+}{\frac{\partial^2 \dot{L}}{\partial \tau'_{sw} \partial a_w}} \underset{+}{\frac{\partial a_w}{\partial b_w}} > 0$$

$$\frac{\partial b_q}{\partial \tau'_{sw}} = \underset{+}{\frac{\partial b_q}{\partial B}} \lambda_2 \underset{+}{\frac{\partial^2 \dot{L}}{\partial \tau'_{sw} \partial w^e}} + \underset{-}{\frac{\partial b_q}{\partial D}} \lambda_2 \underset{+}{\frac{\partial^2 \dot{L}}{\partial \tau'_{sw} \partial a_w}} \underset{+}{\frac{\partial a_w}{\partial b_w}} \gtreqless 0$$

$$\frac{\partial b_w}{\partial \tau'_{sw}} = \underset{+}{\frac{\partial b_w}{\partial B}} \lambda_2 \underset{+}{\frac{\partial^2 \dot{L}}{\partial \tau'_{sw} \partial w^e}} + \underset{+}{\frac{\partial b_w}{\partial D}} \lambda_2 \underset{+}{\frac{\partial^2 \dot{L}}{\partial \tau'_{sw} \partial a_w}} \underset{+}{\frac{\partial a_w}{\partial b_w}} > 0$$

$$\frac{\partial b_p}{\partial \tau'_{sw}} = \underset{+}{\frac{\partial b_p}{\partial B}} \lambda_2 \underset{+}{\frac{\partial^2 \dot{L}}{\partial \tau'_{sw} \partial w^e}} + \underset{-}{\frac{\partial b_p}{\partial D}} \lambda_2 \underset{+}{\frac{\partial^2 \dot{L}}{\partial \tau'_{sw} \partial a_w}} \underset{+}{\frac{\partial a_w}{\partial b_w}} \gtreqless 0$$

The signs under the partial derivatives are taken partly from (23) and partly from table 1. If the search activity of the unemployed households in the labor market increases, neither the goods balance nor the labor-force balance will be affected. The effects on the control variables of this disturbance will thus only be transmitted through "substitution effects". These are the substitution effects between the firm's relative wage rate and its supply of information in the labor market, respectively, and the other control variables. If the search activity of the unemployed in the labor market increases, this will increase the relative wage rate through substitution effects between it and the other control variables.[1] The increased supply of labor hours caused by

[1] Of course, it is impossible for <u>all</u> firms to increase their relative wage rates. If all the firms try to do so, the actual rate of wage inflation will increase relatively to the expected rate. This is the basic mechanism generating inflation as discussed in the next chapter.

the increased relative wage rate is used for increased goods production and an increased supply of information on the goods and the labor market. If the goods production increases the firm must decrease its relative price in order to fulfill the goods balance.

The increased search activity of the unemployed households in the labor market has a further effect on the behavior of the firm. The increase in the net flow of employees caused by an increased flow of information in the labor market will be accentuated. Thus, the firm is motivated to increase the supply of information in the labor market. In order to mobilize an increased number of working hours for this task, the firm increases its relative wage rate. Furthermore, labor hours are reallocated from goods production and information production in the goods market to information production in the labor market. If goods production declines, the firm must increase its relative price in order to fulfill the goods balance.

Since the firm's control variables are affected by the parameter change through two different substitution effects, it is not always possible to determine uniquely the direction of the net effect. However, the effects on the relative wage rate and the supply of information in the labor market are always positive. Furthermore, note that the possible effects through changed values of the shadow prices of the number of customers λ_1 and the number of employees λ_2 have not been examined. These effects will be discussed later on, in connection with the complete behavior equations.

An increase in the rate of unemployment, u, will have analogous effects on the firm's behavior. Thus its behavior will only be affected through substitution effects between its relative wage rate and the number of working hours allocated to information production in the labor market and the other control variables. The signs will be the same as for the case when the search activity of the unemployed increases in the labor market. One should note, however, that demand for the firm's product may be affected. This is due to the fact that the proportion of unemployed customers of the firm will increase. Their income is lower than that of the employed customers, and that means that the demand for the firm's product will decrease. This effect will not be discussed until the next chapter.

An increase in the number of employees of the firm will have the following effects:

$$\frac{\partial p^e}{\partial L} = \underset{-}{\frac{\partial p^e}{\partial B}} \lambda_2 \underset{-}{M} + \underset{-}{\frac{\partial p^e}{\partial G}} \bar{\tau}_w \gtreqless 0$$

$$\frac{\partial w^e}{\partial L} = \underset{+}{\frac{\partial w^e}{\partial B}} \lambda_2 \underset{-}{M} + \underset{-}{\frac{\partial w^e}{\partial G}} \bar{\tau}_w < 0$$

$$\frac{\partial b_q}{\partial L} = \underset{+}{\frac{\partial b_q}{\partial B}} \lambda_2 \underset{-}{M} + \underset{+}{\frac{\partial b_q}{\partial G}} \bar{\tau}_w \gtreqless 0$$

$$\frac{\partial b_w}{\partial L} = \underset{+}{\frac{\partial b_w}{\partial G}} \lambda_2 \underset{-}{M} + \underset{+}{\frac{\partial b_w}{\partial G}} \bar{\tau}_w \gtreqless 0$$

$$\frac{\partial b_p}{\partial L} = \underset{+}{\frac{\partial b_p}{\partial B}} \lambda_2 \underset{-}{M} + \underset{+}{\frac{\partial b_p}{\partial G}} \bar{\tau}_w \gtreqless 0$$

where

$$M = -\frac{1}{L}\frac{\partial \dot{L}}{\partial w^e} + \frac{\partial^2 \dot{L}}{\partial L \partial w^e} < 0$$

The effects of an increased number of employees of the firm are channeled partly through a substitution effect between the firm's relative wage rate and its other control variables and partly through the labor force balance effect. The latter effect is due to the fact that, ceteris paribus, the number of available labor hours will increase when the number of employees increases.

If the number of employees increases, this will decrease the relative wage rate through the substitution effect. The partial effect of this is that the number of labor hours available will decrease. Production of goods and information will therefore be cut back. When goods production declines, the relative price must increase in order for the goods balance to be fulfilled.

The increased number of employees further means that the labor-force balance will be affected directly. The latter effect means that the relative wage rate will be lowered, but not so much as to decrease the available number of labor hours. Thus, the labor-force-balance effect on goods production and on information production will be positive. If a greater number of hours is allocated to goods production, the relative price must be decreased in order to satisfy the goods balance.

The effects on the firm's control variables will thus operate through substitution and labor-force-balance effects. In cases in which these effects are of a different sign, the net effect is uncertain. This will be so for all cases except for the effect on the firm's relative wage rate, which decreases.

The effect of a greater number of customers may be split analogously into a substitution effect between the firm's relative price and the other control variables, and a goods-balance effect:

$$\frac{\partial p^e}{\partial K} = \underset{+}{\frac{\partial p^e}{\partial A}} \lambda_1 \underset{+}{N} - \underset{-}{\frac{\partial p^e}{\partial F}} \bar{x} > 0$$

$$\frac{\partial w^e}{\partial K} = \underset{-}{\frac{\partial w^e}{\partial A}} \lambda_1 \underset{+}{N} - \underset{-}{\frac{\partial w^e}{\partial F}} \bar{x} \gtrless 0$$

$$\frac{\partial b_q}{\partial K} = \underset{-}{\frac{\partial b_q}{\partial A}} \lambda_1 \underset{+}{N} - \underset{-}{\frac{\partial b_q}{\partial F}} \bar{x} \gtrless 0$$

$$\frac{\partial b_w}{\partial K} = \underset{+}{\frac{\partial b_w}{\partial A}} \lambda_1 \underset{+}{N} - \underset{+}{\frac{\partial b_w}{\partial F}} \bar{x} \gtrless 0$$

$$\frac{\partial b_p}{\partial K} = \underset{+}{\frac{\partial b_p}{\partial A}} \lambda_1 \underset{+}{N} - \underset{+}{\frac{\partial b_p}{\partial F}} \bar{x} \gtrless 0$$

where

$$N = -\frac{1}{K} \frac{\partial \dot{K}}{\partial p^e} + \frac{\partial^2 \dot{K}}{\partial K \partial p^e} > 0$$

The substitution effect of an increased number of customers will mean first that the firm's relative price increases and that goods production decreases. The disengaged labor hours will be transmitted to increased information production in the goods and the labor market. The relative wage rate will decline.

However, the increased number of customers means that the demand for the firm's product will increase, *ceteris paribus*. The goods-balance effect means partly an increased relative price, partly that the goods production increases. To increase the total number of labor hours available, the goods-balance effect will imply an increased relative wage rate. The larger number of labor hours available for goods production will not only be supplied through an increased relative wage rate; in addition, information production in the goods and labor markets will be decreased through the goods-balance effect.

The net effect on the firm's control variables will only be certain with respect to the relative price, which increases.[1)]

Finally, it may be of interest to examine the effects on firm behavior of a change of the marginal present value product of the number of customers λ_1:

$$\frac{\partial p^e}{\partial \lambda_1} = \underset{+}{\frac{\partial p^e}{\partial A}} \underset{-}{\frac{\partial \dot{K}}{\partial p^e}} + \underset{+}{\frac{\partial p^e}{\partial E}} \underset{+}{\frac{\partial \dot{K}}{\partial a_p}} \underset{+}{\frac{\partial a_p}{\partial b_p}} \gtreqless 0$$

$$\frac{\partial w^e}{\partial \lambda_1} = \underset{-}{\frac{\partial w^e}{\partial A}} \underset{-}{\frac{\partial \dot{K}}{\partial p^e}} + \underset{+}{\frac{\partial w^e}{\partial E}} \underset{+}{\frac{\partial \dot{K}}{\partial a_p}} \underset{+}{\frac{\partial a_p}{\partial b_p}} > 0$$

$$\frac{\partial b_q}{\partial \lambda_1} = \underset{-}{\frac{\partial b_q}{\partial A}} \underset{-}{\frac{\partial \dot{K}}{\partial p^e}} + \underset{-}{\frac{\partial b_q}{\partial E}} \underset{+}{\frac{\partial \dot{K}}{\partial a_p}} \underset{+}{\frac{\partial a_p}{\partial b_p}} \gtreqless 0$$

$$\frac{\partial b_w}{\partial \lambda_1} = \underset{+}{\frac{\partial b_w}{\partial A}} \underset{-}{\frac{\partial \dot{K}}{\partial p^e}} + \underset{-}{\frac{\partial b_w}{\partial E}} \underset{+}{\frac{\partial \dot{K}}{\partial a_p}} \underset{+}{\frac{\partial a_p}{\partial b_p}} < 0$$

$$\frac{\partial b_p}{\partial \lambda_1} = \underset{+}{\frac{\partial b_p}{\partial A}} \underset{-}{\frac{\partial \dot{K}}{\partial p^e}} + \underset{+}{\frac{\partial b_p}{\partial E}} \underset{+}{\frac{\partial \dot{K}}{\partial a_p}} \underset{+}{\frac{\partial a_p}{\partial b_p}} \gtreqless 0$$

---

1) Note the effect on a profit-maximizing monopoly firm's price of an outward shift of the demand curve for the firm's product.

An increase in the shadow price of customers thus affects the firm's choice of values of the control variables through two substitution effects, the substitution effect between the relative price and the other control variables, and the substitution effect between the number of labor hours allocated to information production in the goods market and the other control variables.

First, the increased marginal present value product of the number of customers will decrease the relative price. This will occur through the "own" substitution effect of the relative price. The net rate of flow of customers thus increases when the shadow price of customers increases. The diminished relative price means that goods production must increase in order to maintain the goods balance. The increased number of work hours allocated to goods production is taken from information production in the labor and goods markets. But the total number of labor hours available is also increased through a higher relative wage rate.

The second substitution effect is between the number of labor hours allocated to information production in the goods market and the other control variables. First, the number of labor hours allocated to the "marketing" department will increase. In that way the net rate of increase in the number of customers will be positively affected. The increased number of labor hours allocated to information production in the goods market is taken partly from goods production and partly from the "personnel" department. Moreover, the total number of labor hours available will increase, since the relative wage rate increases. To satisfy the goods balance, the smaller amount of labor hours allocated to goods production, and consequently, the lower goods production, require a higher relative price to reduce the demand of the firm's customers.

Only two net effects are unambigous: the relative wage rate increases, and the supply of information on the labor market decreases, when the marginal present value product of the number of customers increases.

By working through the parallel analysis for the other parameter changes, the following incomplete behavior equations are obtained:

$$\begin{array}{lcccccccccccccc}
p^e = \phi(& \tau'_{sp}, & \tau_{sp}, & \tau'_{sw}, & \tau_{sw}, & u, & L, & K, & \bar{x}, & \bar{\tau}_w, & \lambda_1, & \lambda_2, & g, & \frac{\bar{w}^e}{\bar{p}^e}, & \delta) \\
 & ? & ? & ? & ? & ? & ? & + & + & ? & ? & ? & - & + & +
\end{array}$$

$$\begin{array}{lcccccccccccccc}
w^e = \psi(& \tau'_{sp}, & \tau_{sp}, & \tau'_{sw}, & \tau_{sw}, & u, & L, & K, & \bar{x}, & \bar{\tau}_w, & \lambda_1, & \lambda_2, & g, & \frac{\bar{w}^e}{\bar{p}^e}, & \delta) \\
 & + & + & + & + & + & - & ? & ? & - & + & + & ? & - & +
\end{array}$$

$$(24) \quad \begin{array}{lcccccccccccccc}
b_q = \chi_q(& \tau'_{sp}, & \tau_{sp}, & \tau'_{sw}, & \tau_{sw}, & u, & L, & K, & \bar{x}, & \bar{\tau}_w, & \lambda_1, & \lambda_2, & g, & \frac{\bar{w}^e}{\bar{p}^e}, & \delta) \\
 & ? & ? & ? & ? & ? & ? & ? & ? & ? & ? & ? & ? & - & -
\end{array}$$

$$\begin{array}{lcccccccccccccc}
b_w = \chi_w(& \tau'_{sp}, & \tau_{sp}, & \tau'_{sw}, & \tau_{sw}, & u, & L, & K, & \bar{x}, & \bar{\tau}_w, & \lambda_1, & \lambda_2, & g, & \frac{\bar{w}^e}{\bar{p}^e}, & \delta) \\
 & - & - & + & + & + & ? & ? & ? & ? & - & + & ? & - & -
\end{array}$$

$$\begin{array}{lcccccccccccccc}
b_p = \chi_p(& \tau'_{sp}, & \tau_{sp}, & \tau'_{sw}, & \tau_{sw}, & u, & L, & K, & \bar{x}, & \bar{\tau}_w, & \lambda_1, & \lambda_2, & g, & \frac{\bar{w}^e}{\bar{p}^e}, & \delta) \\
 & ? & ? & ? & ? & ? & ? & ? & ? & ? & ? & ? & ? & - & +
\end{array}$$

In the order of their appearance, the arguments of the incomplete behavior equations (24) denote the following variables: the search activity in the goods market of the unemployed and the employed, respectively, the search activity in the labor market of the unemployed and the employed, respectively, the rate of unemployment, the number of employees of the firm, the number of customers of the firm, the average consumption of the customers of the firm, the average supply of labor hours of the employees of the firm, the marginal present value product of the number of customers, the marginal present value product of the number of employees, the increase in the average and marginal productivity of labor in goods production, and finally, the average (expected) real wage of the economy.

It should be noted that p^e and w^e are the relative price and the relative wage rate expected by the firm. If the actual rate of price inflation deviates from that expected, the expected relative price will deviate from the actual. The analogous argument holds with respect to the relative wage rate.

In interpreting the arguments of the incomplete behavior equations, it should be emphasized that the arguments which are control variables for the households (e.g., the search activity of the unemployed households in the labor market or the average supply of labor by the employees of the firm) in turn are functions of other variables. Correspondingly, the average supply of labor of the firm's employees is affected by the average real wage rate. A change in the real wage rate thus not only affects the firm's behavior directly, but also indirectly, through changes in the behavior of the households.[1)] On the other hand, the arguments of (24) which are household control variables should not be conceived of as functions of the relative price and the relative wage rate of the firm. This is due to the fact that the firm in its planning already has taken into consideration the effects on household behavior of changes in p^e and w^e.

Finally, it should be stressed once again that the effects of the parameter changes on firm behavior are discussed subject to the preliminary assumption that the shadow prices of the number of customers and employees are exogenously given. Actually, some of the disturbances discussed above will also affect the behavior of the firm through changed values of λ_1 and λ_2, and these effects will be discussed in section 5 below.

3.5. Sufficient conditions for maximization of the profits functional

Maximization of the Hamiltonian is a necessary but not sufficient condition for maximization of the profits functional (9). To guarantee a maximum of the profits functional, further conditions are needed.

Assume first that the phase variables K and L converge to stationary values K_∞ and L_∞ and in addition that the adjoint variables also converge to $\lambda_{1\infty}$ and $\lambda_{2\infty}$. Then the transversality conditions (20) will be fulfilled automatically. In that case there is a sufficiency condition, due to Arrow, which states that the Hamiltonian maximizing policy

---

1) These indirect effects are discussed in the next chapter.

(defined through the incomplete behavior equations) will also maximize the profits functional if H^* is concave in the phase variables K and L. H^* defines the values of the Hamiltonian subject to the condition that the control variables are chosen so as to maximize the Hamiltonian. Arrow's sufficiency condition may be written in the present case:

$$(25) \qquad (dK,\ dL)\begin{pmatrix} \frac{\partial^2 H^*}{\partial K^2} & \frac{\partial^2 H^*}{\partial K \partial L} \\ \frac{\partial^2 H^*}{\partial L \partial K} & \frac{\partial^2 H^*}{\partial L^2} \end{pmatrix}\begin{pmatrix} dK \\ dL \end{pmatrix} \leq 0$$

Now it is true that

$$\frac{\partial^2 H^*}{\partial K^2} = \frac{\partial^2 H}{\partial K^2},\ \frac{\partial^2 H^*}{\partial L^2} = \frac{\partial^2 H}{\partial L^2} \quad \text{and} \quad \frac{\partial^2 H^*}{\partial K \partial L} = \frac{\partial^2 H}{\partial K \partial L}$$

Further,

$$\frac{\partial^2 H}{\partial K^2} = \frac{\partial^2 H}{\partial L^2} = \frac{\partial^2 H}{\partial K \partial L} = 0$$

This means that the sufficiency conditions are satisfied. To examine whether the policy, which maximizes the Hamiltonian also maximizes the firm's capital value, it is sufficient to examine whether the phase variables and the adjoint variables converge to finite stationary values. If so, the transversality conditions will be fulfilled. This condition will be examined in the next section.

4. Phase Diagram Analysis

We have now derived the policy which maximizes the Hamiltonian at each point of time. There are several reasons for placing this maximization in an intertemporal perspective. First, the phase variables K and L are only fixed initially. Thereafter, their development is determined by the values of the control variables chosen by the firm through the differential equations (1) and (5). The changes in the values of the phase variables will in turn influence the future policy and thereby the value of the profits functional.

Second, the policy is also influenced by the values of the adjoint variables λ_1 and λ_2. Their development is determined through differential equation (19). But contrary to the case for the phase variables, the initial values of the adjoint variables are not given <u>a priori</u>. Instead, there is a restriction that the transversality conditions must be fulfilled at the terminal date. The horizon being infinitly far away, the transversality conditions will be fulfilled if the phase variables and the adjoint variables converge to finite stationary values. In that case, the stationary values of λ_1 and λ_2 may be used as end values from which the development of the adjoint variables is derived "backwards". Evidently, it is not enough to know the values of K and L at a certain point of time in order to derive the firm's policy at that point of time. Since the adjoint variables are included as arguments in the (incomplete) behavior equations, it is necessary to know the values of these variables in order to choose the best policy.

The economic reason for determining the values of the marginal present value products backwards is that it is necessary to know the future situation of the firm to know the effect on the profits functional of an increased number of customers or employees at a certain moment of time. It is precisely through the fact that the shadow prices of the number of customers and employees are included in the incomplete behavior equations that the consequences for the firm's future situation of its current behavior are taken into consideration. And due to the fact that λ_1 and λ_2 are determined by the firm's future situation, they are also endogenously determined. Furthermore, when the values of the adjoint variables at each point of time are determined as a result of the intertemporal planning problem, the complete behavior equations may be derived.

In this section the convergence of the system in K, L, λ_1, λ_2-space will be examined. Also, the initial values of the adjoint variables will be determined. These two problems are intimately connected, since generally convergence only occurs for certain values of λ_1 and λ_2, given the values of the phase variables and the exogenous variables. By examining how the initial values of λ_1 and λ_2 necessary for convergence vary when the phase variables and the exogenous variables vary, the information needed for deriving the complete behavior equations in the next section is obtained.

4.1. Stability analysis

We start by examining which initial values of the adjoint variables should be chosen in order to obtain convergence to finite stationary solutions. The differential equations of the two marginal present value products may, starting from (19), be written:

$$(26)\quad \begin{aligned} \dot{\lambda}_1 &= \lambda_1(r - g^e - \frac{\partial \dot{K}}{\partial K}) - (p^e - \mu_1)\,\bar{x} \\ \dot{\lambda}_2 &= \lambda_2(r - g^e - \frac{\partial \dot{L}}{\partial L}) + (w^e \frac{\bar{w}^e}{\bar{p}^e} - \mu_2)\,\bar{\tau}_w \end{aligned}$$

Linear expansion around the stationary solution and use of

$$\frac{\partial^2 \dot{K}}{\partial K^2} = \frac{\partial^2 \dot{K}}{\partial L^2} = \frac{\partial^2 \dot{L}}{\partial L^2} = \frac{\partial^2 \dot{L}}{\partial K^2} = 0$$

give:

$$(27)\quad \begin{pmatrix} \dot{\lambda}_1 \\ \dot{\lambda}_2 \end{pmatrix} = \begin{pmatrix} r - g^e - \frac{\partial \dot{K}}{\partial K} & 0 \\ 0 & r - g^e - \frac{\partial \dot{L}}{\partial L} \end{pmatrix} \begin{pmatrix} \lambda_1(t) - \lambda_{1\infty} \\ \lambda_2(t) - \lambda_{2\infty} \end{pmatrix}$$

Assuming that $r - g^e - \frac{\partial \dot{K}}{\partial K}$ and $r - g^e - \frac{\partial \dot{L}}{\partial L}$ are both positive, convergence will only occur for the case in which the initial values of the phase variables are equal to the stationary values. This result is directly obtained by inspection of (27). Furthermore, since the time derivatives of the adjoint variables are independent of the phase variables K and L, the initial values of λ_1 and λ_2 are independent of the initial values of the phase variables. This result may also be derived by geometrical methods analogous to those used in chapter III, section 4.

The next step is to examine how the number of customers and employees develops over time. Do the phase variables converge towards stationary solutions or will the firm either grow continuously or, finally disappear from the market? It should be noted that it is only for the case of convergence that we may be certain that maximization of the Hamiltonian also implies maximization of the profits functional.

First, the differential equations for the number of customers (5), and the number of employees (1) are approximated around their stationary solution:[1)]

$$(28)\quad \begin{pmatrix} \dot{K} \\ \dot{L} \end{pmatrix} = \begin{pmatrix} \frac{\partial \dot{K}}{\partial K} & \frac{\partial \dot{K}}{\partial L} \\ \frac{\partial \dot{L}}{\partial K} & \frac{\partial \dot{L}}{\partial L} \end{pmatrix} \begin{pmatrix} K(t) - K_\infty \\ L(t) - L_\infty \end{pmatrix}$$

where $\dot{K}$ and $\dot{L}$ are functions of time, the partial derivatives in the matrix approximately constant in a small neighborhood around the stationary solution, and K_∞ and L_∞ denote the stationary values of the phase variables.

The partial derivatives may be calculated as follows:

---

1) These are assumed to exist,to be uniquely determined, and to be positive.

$$\frac{\partial \dot{K}}{\partial K} = \underset{-}{\frac{\partial \dot{K}}{\partial K}} + \underset{-}{\frac{\partial \dot{K}}{\partial p^e}}\,\underset{+}{\frac{\partial \phi}{\partial K}} + \underset{+}{\frac{\partial \dot{K}}{\partial b_p}}\,\underset{?}{\frac{\partial \chi_p}{\partial K}} < 0 \qquad (?)$$

$$\frac{\partial \dot{K}}{\partial L} = \underset{o}{\frac{\partial \dot{K}}{\partial L}} + \underset{-}{\frac{\partial \dot{K}}{\partial p^e}}\,\underset{-}{\frac{\partial \phi}{\partial L}} + \underset{+}{\frac{\partial \dot{K}}{\partial b_p}}\,\underset{?}{\frac{\partial \chi_p}{\partial L}} > 0 \qquad (?)$$

(29)

$$\frac{\partial \dot{L}}{\partial K} = \underset{o}{\frac{\partial \dot{L}}{\partial K}} + \underset{+}{\frac{\partial \dot{L}}{\partial w^e}}\,\underset{?}{\frac{\partial \psi}{\partial K}} + \underset{+}{\frac{\partial \dot{L}}{\partial b_w}}\,\underset{?}{\frac{\partial \chi_w}{\partial K}} \gtreqless 0$$

$$\frac{\partial \dot{L}}{\partial L} = \underset{-}{\frac{\partial \dot{L}}{\partial L}} + \underset{+}{\frac{\partial \dot{L}}{\partial w^e}}\,\underset{-}{\frac{\partial \psi}{\partial L}} + \underset{+}{\frac{\partial \dot{L}}{\partial b_w}}\,\underset{?}{\frac{\partial \chi_w}{\partial L}} < 0 \qquad (?)$$

i.e., the values of the control variables according to the incomplete behavior equations (24) are substituted into the differential equation (1) and (2). Then the differential equations are differentiated with respect to the phase variables. Thus, not only the direct effect on the time derivative of an increased number of customers is taken into consideration. There are also indirect effects, since the optimal values of the firm's control variables (inter alia the relative price and the supply of information on the goods market) are affected and therefore affect indirectly the net flow of the number of customers of the firm.

The solution of the linear homogeneous system of differential equations of the first order (29) may be written:[1)]

$$(30) \qquad \begin{pmatrix} K(t) - K_\infty \\ \\ L(t) - L_\infty \end{pmatrix} = e_1 \begin{pmatrix} h_{11} \\ \\ h_{12} \end{pmatrix} e^{\beta_1 t} + c_2 \begin{pmatrix} h_{21} \\ \\ h_{22} \end{pmatrix} e^{\beta_2 t}$$

---

1) Cf. Pontryagin (1962), chapter 2, for an excellent introduction to the solution of linear differential equations with constant coefficients.

where c_1 and c_2 are (generally complex) constants determined by the initial values of the phase variables $K(0)$ and $L(0)$, β_1 and β_2 are the eigenvalues of the matrix in expression (28). $\begin{pmatrix} h_{11} \\ h_{12} \end{pmatrix}$ and $\begin{pmatrix} h_{21} \\ h_{22} \end{pmatrix}$ are the eigenvectors of the same matrix.

By definition, the eigenvalues β_1 and β_2 are obtained by solving the equation

$$\begin{vmatrix} \frac{\partial \dot{K}}{\partial K} - \beta_i & \frac{\partial \dot{K}}{\partial L} \\ \frac{\partial \dot{L}}{\partial K} & \frac{\partial \dot{L}}{\partial L} - \beta_i \end{vmatrix} = 0$$

<u>i.e.</u>,

$$(31) \quad \beta_{1,2} = \frac{1}{2}\left(\frac{\partial \dot{K}}{\partial K} + \frac{\partial \dot{L}}{\partial L}\right) \pm \frac{1}{2}\sqrt{\left(\frac{\partial \dot{K}}{\partial K} + \frac{\partial \dot{L}}{\partial L}\right)^2 + 4\left(\frac{\partial \dot{K}}{\partial L}\frac{\partial \dot{L}}{\partial K} - \frac{\partial \dot{K}}{\partial K}\frac{\partial \dot{L}}{\partial L}\right)}$$

Now, assume that $\frac{\partial \dot{K}}{\partial K} < 0$, $\frac{\partial \dot{K}}{\partial L} > 0$ and $\frac{\partial \dot{L}}{\partial L} < 0$; recall equation (29). The sign of $\frac{\partial \dot{L}}{\partial K}$ is uncertain, however. It is thus necessary to study different cases, depending on the sign of the last derivative. If $\frac{\partial \dot{L}}{\partial L} \geq 0$, the roots β_1 and β_2 are always real. Furthermore, $\beta_2 < 0$ and $\beta_2 < \beta_1$. For β_1 the following signs obtain:

$$\beta_1 = 0 \quad \text{if} \quad \frac{\partial \dot{K}}{\partial K}\frac{\partial \dot{L}}{\partial L} = \frac{\partial \dot{K}}{\partial L}\frac{\partial \dot{L}}{\partial K}$$

$$\beta_1 < 0 \quad \text{if} \quad \frac{\partial \dot{K}}{\partial K}\frac{\partial \dot{L}}{\partial L} > \frac{\partial \dot{K}}{\partial L}\frac{\partial \dot{L}}{\partial K}$$

$$\beta_1 > 0 \quad \text{if} \quad \frac{\partial \dot{K}}{\partial K}\frac{\partial \dot{L}}{\partial L} < \frac{\partial \dot{K}}{\partial L}\frac{\partial \dot{L}}{\partial K}$$

The condition of stability is that both eigenvalues should be negative, so that the phase variables always converge to their stationary solutions, independent of their initial values; note equation (30). The geometrical import of this is that the phase curve $\dot{K} = 0$ should have a steeper slope than the phase curve $\dot{L} = 0$:

$$-\frac{\frac{\partial \dot{K}}{\partial K}}{\frac{\partial \dot{K}}{\partial L}} > -\frac{\frac{\partial \dot{L}}{\partial K}}{\frac{\partial \dot{L}}{\partial L}} \quad \text{i.e., if} \quad \left.\frac{\partial L}{\partial K}\right|_{\dot{K}=0} > \left.\frac{\partial L}{\partial K}\right|_{\dot{L}=0}$$ [1]

The slopes of the principal trajectories in the K,L-plane may be obtained by calculating the eigenvectors. The eigenvectors are the solutions of the system of equations (32):

$$(32) \quad \begin{pmatrix} \frac{\partial \dot{K}}{\partial K} - \beta_i & \frac{\partial \dot{K}}{\partial L} \\ \frac{\partial \dot{L}}{\partial K} & \frac{\partial \dot{L}}{\partial L} - \beta_i \end{pmatrix} \begin{pmatrix} h_{i1} \\ h_{i2} \end{pmatrix} = \begin{pmatrix} 0 \\ 0 \end{pmatrix} \quad i=1,2$$

By substituting the values of the eigenvalues into the equation system, it is easy to show that the principal trajectory associated with β_1 has a negative slope and that the principal trajectory connected with β_2 has a positive slope. The results are summarized in figure 3. Since the absolute value of the eigenvalue β_2 is greater than that of β_1, the principal trajectory a-a will dominate and function as a "turnpike", while the principal trajectory b-b associated with eigenvalue β_2 is unstable, a "knife-edge".

The fact that the dominating principal trajectory has a positive slope means that the expansion or contraction of the firm will be balanced; i.e., the number of customers and employees will increase or decrease in a parallel fashion.

Assume alternatively that $\frac{\partial \dot{L}}{\partial K} \leq 0$. Starting from (31), three cases are possible.

---

1) Observe that $\frac{\partial \dot{L}}{\partial K} \frac{\partial \dot{L}}{\partial L} > \frac{\partial \dot{K}}{\partial L} \frac{\partial \dot{L}}{\partial K}$ implies that $\frac{\partial \dot{K}}{\partial K} \Big/ \frac{\partial \dot{K}}{\partial L} < \frac{\partial \dot{L}}{\partial K} \Big/ \frac{\partial \dot{K}}{\partial L}$, since $\frac{\partial \dot{K}}{\partial K} < 0$ and $\frac{\partial \dot{L}}{\partial L} < 0$

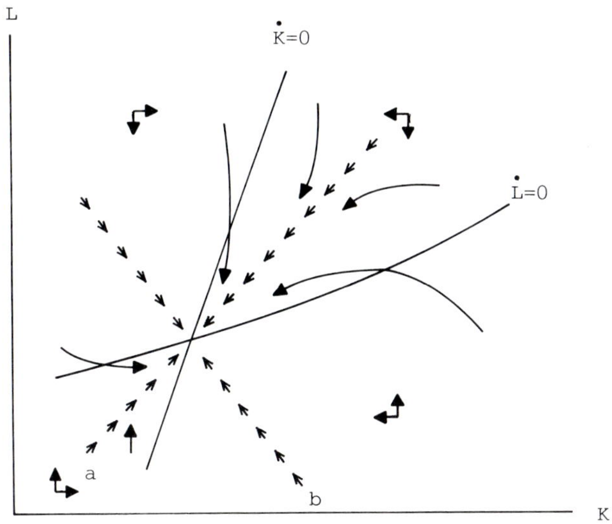

Fig. V:3. The phase diagram in the K, L-plane, convergence without oscillations.

Case I $\beta_2 < \beta_1$ if $\left(\frac{\partial \dot{K}}{\partial K} - \frac{\partial \dot{L}}{\partial L}\right)^2 + 4\,\frac{\partial \dot{K}}{\partial L}\;\frac{\partial \dot{L}}{\partial K} > 0$

This case is for all practical purposes identical to the stable case above.

Case II $\beta_2 = \beta_1 < 0$ if $\left(\frac{\partial \dot{K}}{\partial K} - \frac{\partial \dot{L}}{\partial L}\right)^2 + 4\,\frac{\partial \dot{K}}{\partial L}\;\frac{\partial \dot{L}}{\partial K} = 0$

This case is stable since the eigenvalues are negative. But since the eigenvalues are equal, the solution of the differential equation may not be written in the form (30), but will instead have the following general form:

$$\begin{pmatrix} K(t) - K_\infty \\ L(t) - L_\infty \end{pmatrix} = c_1 \begin{pmatrix} h_{11} \\ h_{12} \end{pmatrix} e^{\beta_1 t} + c_2\, t \begin{pmatrix} h_{21} \\ h_{22} \end{pmatrix} e^{\beta_2 t} \tag{33}$$

The phase variables will therefore approach their stationary values subject to a certain alternation between the two principal trajectories. If K and L are initially situated somewhere outside the two principal trajectories, the phase variables will first approach the first principal trajectory and then, as time passes, will move away from that trajectory and towards the second principal trajectory which will be followed approximately towards the stationary solution. Note the form of the solution (33).

Finally, we have:

Case III $\left(\frac{\partial \dot{K}}{\partial K} - \frac{\partial \dot{L}}{\partial L}\right)^2 + 4\,\frac{\partial \dot{K}}{\partial L}\,\frac{\partial \dot{L}}{\partial K} < 0$

Substitution into (31) gives two conjugate complex eigenvalues with a negative real part, which means that the system is stable and that the stationary solution is approached via oscillations. The geometrical form of this case is illustrated in figure 4.

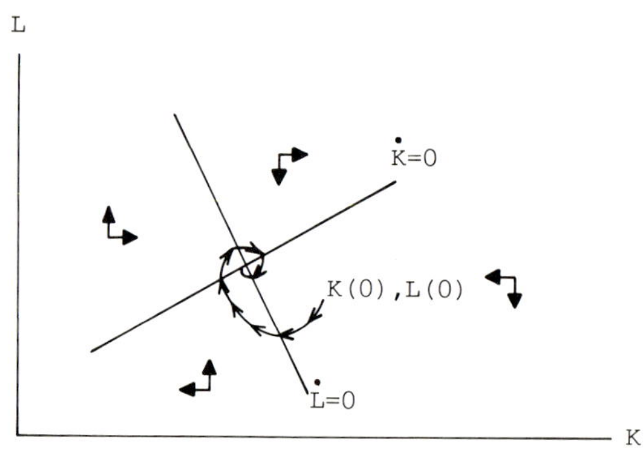

Fig. V:4. The phase diagram in the K, L-plane, convergence with clockwise oscillations.

We need not comment on figure 4 in any detail. The forces acting in the different parts of the diagram have been indicated in the usual way by arrow-hooks. The system is stable and convergence will occur by clockwise oscillations in the K,L-plane.

4.2. Determination of the values of the adjoint variables and comparative statics

In the discussion in section 3 of factors affecting the firm's behavior, it was not possible to derive the complete behavior equations. This was due to the fact that the adjoint variables were assumed to be exogenously given. Generally, however, these variables, representing the marginal valuations of the number of customers and employees will be affected by different parameter changes. To obtain the complete behavior equations, it is thus necessary to derive information about the indirect affects of different parameter changes through changed values of the marginal present value products. In addition, knowledge of the values of the adjoint variables is necessary for obtaining estimates of the firm's monopoly power in the goods market and its monopsony power in the labor market.

Since the two adjoint variables are functions independent of time (and are not dependent on the development of the number of customers and employees), it is enough to examine their stationary solutions. By setting the time derivatives of the adjoint variables in the expression (26) equal to zero, the following stationary solutions are obtained:

$$\lambda_{1\infty} = \frac{(p^e - \mu_1)\ \bar{x}}{r - g^e - \frac{\partial \dot{K}}{\partial K}}$$

(34)

$$\lambda_{2\infty} = - \frac{(w^e \frac{\bar{w}^e}{\bar{p}^e} - \mu_2)\ \bar{\tau}_w}{r - g^e - \frac{\partial \dot{L}}{\partial L}}$$

Both values are positive. The marginal present value product of the number of customers depends inter alia on the monopoly power of the firm, i.e., on the difference between the price and marginal cost, $p^e - \mu_1$.[1] The stronger the

---

[1] Note that all prices are expressed in real terms, since the average price level is set equal to unity.

monopoly position of the firm, the greater the effect on the firm's capital value of an increase of the number of customers. The monopoly power and the marginal present value product must be determined simultaneously, however. By substituting (34) into (21), the following expression for the monopoly power of the firm is obtained:

$$(35) \qquad p^e - \mu_1 = - \frac{\bar{x}\ K}{\frac{\partial \bar{x}}{\partial p^e} K + \frac{\bar{x}}{Q} \frac{\partial \dot{K}}{\partial p^e}} > 0$$

where $\quad Q = r - g^e - \frac{\partial \dot{K}}{\partial K} > 0$

The price of the firm will thus be higher than the marginal cost, but lower than the static monopoly price.[1)] In the long run, a high relative price means that the firm will loose customers. In static monopoly, the net flow of customers will not be affected by the relative price of the firm; $\frac{\partial \dot{K}}{\partial p^e} = 0$. In that case, the difference between the price and the marginal cost will be higher than for the present case, in which the monopoly power is <u>transient</u>. We further note that, according to (35), the difference between price and marginal cost depends positively on the real rate of interest, $r - g^e$. The economic interpretation of this is that the higher the real rate of interest, the less future profits will add to the capital value of the firm, and the less advantageous it will be to invest in many future customers by having a low relative price.

By substituting (35) into (34), the following expression for the marginal present value product of the number of customers is obtained:

$$\lambda_{1\infty} = - \frac{\bar{x}\ K}{\frac{\partial \bar{x}}{\partial p^e} \frac{K}{\bar{x}} Q + \frac{\partial \dot{K}}{\partial p^e}} > 0$$

---

1) <u>Cf</u>. Phelps and Winter (1970), p. 323.

It appears from this expression that the shadow price of the number of customers depends positively on the total demand, $\bar{x}K$; negatively on the term $\frac{\partial \bar{x}}{\partial p^e} \frac{K}{\bar{x}} Q$ which is positively correlated with the value of the demand elasticity, and thus with the degree of static monopoly; and finally, negatively on the term $\frac{\partial \dot{K}}{\partial p^e}$, which could be said to be a measure of the degree of transient monopoly.

Analogously, the marginal present value product of the number of employees depends positively on the firm's monopsony power, i.e., the difference between the real wage rate and the marginal productivity of labor, $w^e \frac{\bar{w}^e}{\bar{p}^e} - \mu_2$. But the monopsony power and the marginal present value product of the number of employees must also be determined simultaneously. By inserting (34) into (21), the following expression for the monopsony power is obtained:

$$w^e \frac{\bar{w}^e}{\bar{p}^e} - \mu_2 = - \frac{\frac{\bar{w}^e}{\bar{p}^e} L}{L \frac{\partial \bar{\tau}_w}{\partial w^e} + \frac{\bar{\tau}_w}{Q} \frac{\partial \dot{L}}{\partial w^e}} < 0 \tag{36}$$

Thus, the real wage rate which the firm pays is lower than the marginal productivity of labor, but the difference between the marginal productivity and the real wage rate is smaller than for the case of static monopsony. By inserting (36) into (34) an expression for the shadow price of the number of customers may be obtained which does not presuppose knowledge of the monpsony power.

By differentiating (34) the following results concerning the dependence of the values of the adjoint variables on the exogenous variables are obtained:

$$\begin{aligned} \lambda_{1\infty} &= \lambda_{1\infty}(\underset{-}{\tau'_{sp}}, \underset{-}{\tau_{sp}}, \underset{+}{\bar{x}}, \underset{-}{\delta}, \underset{-}{r - g^e}) \\ \lambda_{2\infty} &= \lambda_{2\infty}(\underset{-}{\tau_{sw}}, \underset{+}{\bar{\tau}_w}, \underset{+}{g}, \underset{-}{\frac{\bar{w}^e}{\bar{p}^e}}, \underset{-}{\delta}, \underset{-}{r - g^e}) \end{aligned} \tag{37}$$

As usual, the symbols under the function arguments denote the signs of the partial derivatives.

The system (37) serves a double role. First, information is provided as to the direction in which the adjoint variables should be changed in order to obtain convergence of the system. As noted earlier, these changes of the adjoint variables are necessary, but not sufficient, for convergence. Second, equations (37) provide information necessary for deriving the complete behavior equations in the next section.

What is the economic significance of the signs of the partial derivatives in (37)? If the average consumption per customer, $\bar{x}$, increases, the value of an additional customer will increase. A higher real rate of interest means that the effect of an additional customer on the profits functional (9) decreases. This is analogous to the fact that the capitalized value of a revenue stream or the value of a bond will fall when the rate of discount increases.

If the death rate parameter, δ, increases, the possibilities of maintaining the stock of customers will deteriorate. This means that the value of a large number of customers will fall. The analogous reasoning holds for an increase in household search activity in the goods market. If the average real wage rate of the economy, $\frac{\bar{w}^e}{\bar{p}^e}$, increases, the value of an additional employee λ_2 will fall. If the average supply of labor per employee increases, it will be more advantageous, of course, to have a greater number of employees. An increased real rate of interest implies a fall of the marginal present value product of the number of employees. The argumentation is the same as that concerning the marginal present value product of the number of customers. If household search activity increases in the labor market, it will be more difficult than before to retain the employees. The same will happen if the death rate parameter increases. In both cases the shadow price of the number of employees will fall.

5. The Complete Behavior Equations

Having derived the effects on the values of the adjoint variables of different disturbances, it is now possible to derive the complete behavior equations. Of course, it is only for cases where the adjoint variables are affected by the disturbances that the behavior of the firm will differ from that stated in connection with the discussion of the incomplete behavior equations.

To show how, starting from (23) and (37), one may derive the complete behavior equations, it will suffice to examine the effect on the relative price of the firm of an increased real rate of interest. The real rate of interest is not an argument of the incomplete behavior equations. This is due to the fact that the firm's behavior is only affected indirectly by this disturbance, through changes in the marginal present value products. An increased real rate of interest will have the following effects on the firm's (expected) relative price:

$$\frac{\partial p^e}{\partial r-g^e} = \underset{+}{\frac{\partial p^e}{\partial A}}\,\underset{-}{\frac{\partial \dot{K}}{\partial p^e}}\,\underset{-}{\frac{\partial \lambda_1}{\partial r-g^e}} + \underset{-}{\frac{\partial p^e}{\partial B}}\,\underset{+}{\frac{\partial \dot{L}}{\partial w^e}}\,\underset{-}{\frac{\partial \lambda_2}{\partial r-g^e}} + \underset{+}{\frac{\partial p^e}{\partial D}}\,\underset{+}{\frac{\partial \dot{L}}{\partial a_w}}\,\underset{+}{\frac{\partial a_w}{\partial b_w}}\,\underset{-}{\frac{\partial \lambda_2}{\partial r-g^e}} +$$

$$+ \underset{+}{\frac{\partial p^e}{\partial E}}\,\underset{+}{\frac{\partial \dot{K}}{\partial a_p}}\,\underset{+}{\frac{\partial a_p}{\partial b_p}}\,\underset{-}{\frac{\partial \lambda_1}{\partial r-g^e}} \gtreqless 0$$

It appears from this expression that the effects on the firm's relative price of changed values of the marginal present value products are only propagated through substitution effects, not through the goods balance or the labor force balance effect.

The effect on the (expected) relative price of a changed real rate of interest may be analyzed in the following way. An increased real rate of interest means that the marginal present value products of the number of customers and employees will fall. This is due to the fact that the shadow prices may be looked upon as capitalized values, and when the rate of interest increases, these capitalized values will fall. The first partial effect of the increased real rate of interest is transmitted through the "own" substitution effect of the relative price. An increased real rate of interest will mean that it is more "expensive" than before to keep a large number of customers by having a low relative price. The relative price will thus increase for this reason.

The second partial effect is transmitted through the substitution effect between the relative price and the relative wage rate. When the rate of interest increases, the marginal present value product of the number of employees will fall. It will be more expensive than before to keep a high number of employees, which is achieved by a high relative wage rate. Thus the relative wage rate will fall, which means in turn that the number of working hours available to the firm will fall. This implies a fall in the number of labor hours allocated to goods production. In order to adjust the demand of the customers to the fall in goods production, the relative price of the firm will increase.

The third partial effect of the increased real rate of interest of the firm's relative price operates through the substitution effect between the relative price and the number of labor hours allocated to information production in the labor market (the personnel department). The decrease of the marginal present value product of the number of employees means that fewer labor hours are allocated to the personnel department (for investment in a greater number of employees). In accordance with the labor force balance, the labor hours left over will be reallocated to goods production. In order to obtain demand for the increased level of goods production, the relative price must decrease.

The fourth and last partial effect on the relative price operates through the substitution effect between the relative price and the number of labor hours allocated to supply of information in the goods market (the marketing department). Since the increase of the real rate of interest means a lower marginal present value product of the number of customers, investments in a large number of customers will fall. Thus the number of labor hours allocated to the marketing department falls. The labor hours thus freed will instead be used for goods production, which reguires a lower relative price in order that sales may keep track with the increased level of goods production.

The first two partial effects on the relative price will be positive, while the last two effects will tend to lower the relative price. The net effect is thus ambigous.

By making a corresponding study of the effects on the control variables of all parameter changes, the complete behavior equations are obtained:

$$
\begin{array}{lcccccccccccc}
p^e = p^e(& \tau'_{sp}, & \tau_{sp}, & \tau'_{sw}, & \tau_{sw}, & u, & L, & K, & \bar{x}, & g, & \frac{\bar{w}^e}{\bar{p}^e}, & \delta, & r-g^e) \\
 & ? & ? & ? & ? & ? & ? & + & ? & ? & ? & ? & ? \\
 & & & & & & & & & & & & \\
w^e = w^e(& \tau'_{sp}, & \tau_{sp}, & \tau'_{sw}, & \tau_{sw}, & u, & L, & K, & \bar{x}, & g, & \frac{\bar{w}^e}{\bar{p}^e}, & \delta, & r-g^e) \\
 & ? & ? & + & ? & + & - & ? & ? & ? & - & - & - \\
 & & & & & & & & & & & & \\
b_q = b_q(& \tau'_{sp}, & \tau_{sp}, & \tau'_{sw}, & \tau_{sw}, & u, & L, & K, & \bar{x}, & g, & \frac{\bar{w}^e}{\bar{p}^e}, & \delta, & r-g^e) \\
 & ? & ? & ? & ? & ? & ? & ? & ? & ? & ? & ? & ? \\
 & & & & & & & & & & & & \\
b_w = b_w(& \tau'_{sp}, & \tau_{sp}, & \tau'_{sw}, & \tau_{sw}, & u, & L, & K, & \bar{x}, & g, & \frac{\bar{w}^e}{\bar{p}^e}, & \delta, & r-g^e) \\
 & ? & ? & + & ? & + & ? & ? & ? & ? & - & ? & ? \\
 & & & & & & & & & & & & \\
b_p = b_p(& \tau'_{sp}, & \tau_{sp}, & \tau'_{sw}, & \tau_{sw}, & u, & L, & K, & \bar{x}, & g, & \frac{\bar{w}^e}{\bar{p}^e}, & \delta, & r-g^e) \\
 & ? & ? & ? & ? & ? & ? & ? & ? & ? & ? & ? & ?
\end{array}
\tag{38}
$$

The information given by the complete behavior equations is mainly negative, in that it is impossible in most cases to determine the sign of the total effect of a parameter change on the values of the control variables. Only in ten out of sixty cases has it been possible to determine unambigously the signs. To get more information it is necessary to specify in more detail the functions involved.

Negative information may also be of value, however. In the present case one can draw the conclusion that the model produces a relatively rich "flora" of results as to the behavior of the firm. A great number of changes of the values of the control variables are possible, given a certain disturbance. The previous analysis shows why, à priori, it is difficult to draw unambigous conclusions as to the behavior of the firm in different situations. Similarly to the case of consumption theory, which does not give any unambigous results as to the direction of the effects of price or income changes, the analysis of firm behavior should mainly be looked upon as an instrument for investigating which factors should be taken into account when examing the behavior of the firm.

The reason for the ambiguity of most results is of course that the firm model is rather complicated. In the next section a simpler firm model will be examined, in which the only control variables are the relative price and the relative wage rate. The labor hours allocated to information production on the goods and the labor market are put identically equal to zero.

It is true that the symmetry between household and firm behavior will disappear; in contrast to searching households, there are no longer any firms actively spreading information about their relative prices or relative wage rates. On the other hand, the simplified firm model still takes into consideration important aspects of firm behavior in markets with imperfect information. The firm must still consider that a high relative price will decrease the net flow of customers and that a low relative wage rate will decrease the net flow of employees. It appears that the simplifying assumptions will produce a greater number of unambigous results, which will form part of the microtheoretic basis of the macro analysis in the next chapter.

6. Firm Behavior in the Case where Information is not Actively Produced in the Goods and Labor Markets

In the following, a special case of the firm model discussed in the previous sections will be presented. In this special case the number of labor hours allocated to information production in the goods market (the marketing department) and in the labor market (the personnel department) is identically equal to zero.[1] The question is to what extent the results from the previous sections are modified by the more specialized assumptions and, specifically, whether it is possible to derive unambigious results as to the firm's choice of values of its control variables when various disturbances occur. Together with the results from the analysis of household behavior in the previous chapters, this special case of the more general firm model will form the microeconomic basis of the inflation and unemployment analysis of the next chapter.

Since the analysis of the simplified firm model to a large extent coincides with that of the general case, the following discussion will be rather concise. To make comparisons easier, the equations will have the same numbers as those to which they correspond in the previous sections, but they will be denoted by primes.

6.1. Maximizing the Hamiltonian

If the number of labor hours allocated to the market and the personnel department is identically equal to zero, the Hamiltonian (18) becomes:

$$(18')\qquad H\big(K(t),\ L(t),\ p^e(t),\ w^e(t),\ \lambda_1(t),\ \lambda_2(t),\ \mu_1(t)\big) =$$

$$= (1-\sigma)\ \bar{p}^e(0)\left[p^e\bar{x}K - w^e\frac{\bar{w}^e}{\bar{p}^e}\ \bar{\tau}_w\ L\right] + \mu_1\big(q(\bar{\tau}_w L) - \bar{x}K\big) + \lambda_1\dot{K} + \lambda_2\dot{L}$$

---

[1] In this case there is also assumed to exist a certain flow of information from the firm to the goods market, a^j_p, and to the labor market, a^j_w. But the flow of information is exogenously given.

We note that only one restriction is left, the goods balance. It is not necessary any more to take the labor force balance explicitly into consideration, since the total number of labor hours will automatically be allocated to goods production. Consequently, it appears from (18') that goods production is a function of the total number of labor hours available. The firm now has only the relative price and the relative wage rate remaining as (independent) control variables.

For simplicity the constant $(1-\sigma)\bar{p}^e(0)$ will be supressed. This will only affect the magnitude, not the location, of the maximum. If this is done, the first order conditions for maximizing the Hamiltonian (18') may be written:

$$(\bar{x} - p^e \frac{\partial \bar{x}}{\partial p^e}) K - \mu_1 \frac{\partial \bar{x}}{\partial p^e} K + \lambda_1 \frac{\partial \dot{K}}{\partial p^e} = 0$$

$$(21') \quad - \frac{\bar{w}^e}{\bar{p}^e} (\bar{\tau}_w + w^e \frac{\partial \bar{\tau}_w}{\partial w^e}) L + \mu_1 \frac{\partial q}{\partial b_q} L \frac{\partial \bar{\tau}_w}{\partial w^e} + \lambda_2 \frac{\partial \dot{L}}{\partial w^e} = 0$$

$$q(\bar{\tau}_w L) - \bar{x}K = 0$$

These marginal conditions are identical to the first, second and sixth equations of the first-order conditions for maximizing the more general Hamiltonian (18), and their interpretation is analogous. It is very easy to show that the second-order conditions for maximizing the Hamiltonian (18') are fulfilled. By using the results of section 2 concerning the cross derivatives of the flow equations of the number of customers and employees, it is possible to differentiate the system of equations (21') totally, solve for p^e and w^e, and in that to obtain the behavior equations:

$$dp^e = \underset{+}{\frac{\partial p^e}{\partial A}} dA + \underset{-}{\frac{\partial p^e}{\partial B}} dB + \underset{-}{\frac{\partial p^e}{\partial C}} dC$$

$$(23') \quad dw^e = \underset{-}{\frac{\partial w^e}{\partial A}} dA + \underset{+}{\frac{\partial w^e}{\partial B}} dB + \underset{-}{\frac{\partial w^e}{\partial C}} dC$$

where

$$dA = \lambda_1 \frac{\partial^2 \dot{K}}{\partial \tau_{sp} \partial p^e} d\tau_{sp} + \lambda_1 \frac{\partial^2 \dot{K}}{\partial \tau'_{sp} \partial p^e} d\tau'_{sp}$$

$$+ \left[K\frac{\partial \bar{x}}{\partial u} + K(p^e - \mu_1) \frac{\partial^2 \bar{x}}{\partial u \partial p^e}\right] du$$

$$+ \left(\frac{\partial^2 \dot{K}}{\partial K \partial p^e} + \bar{x} + p^e \frac{\partial \bar{x}}{\partial p^e} - \mu_1 \frac{\partial \bar{x}}{\partial p^e}\right) dK + K d\bar{x} + \frac{\partial \dot{K}}{\partial p^e} d\lambda_1$$

$$dB = \lambda_2 \frac{\partial^2 \dot{L}}{\partial \tau_{sw} \partial w^e} d\tau_{sw} + \lambda_2 \frac{\partial^2 \dot{L}}{\partial \tau'_{sw} \partial w^e} d\tau'_{sw} + \lambda_2 \frac{\partial^2 \dot{L}}{\partial u \partial w^e} du$$

$$+ \left(\lambda_2 \frac{\partial^2 \dot{L}}{\partial L \partial w^e} - \frac{\bar{w}^e}{\bar{p}^e} \left(\tau_w + w^e \frac{\partial \bar{\tau}_w}{\partial w^e}\right) + \mu_2 \frac{\partial \bar{\tau}_w}{\partial w^e}\right) dL$$

$$- \frac{\bar{w}^e}{\bar{p}^e} L d\bar{\tau}_w + \frac{\partial \dot{L}}{\partial w^e} d\lambda_2 - L\left(\bar{\tau}_w + w^e \frac{\partial \bar{\tau}_w}{\partial w^e}\right) d\left(\frac{\bar{w}^e}{\bar{p}^e}\right)$$

$$dC = \frac{\partial q}{\partial L} dL - \bar{x} dK - K d\bar{x} + \frac{\partial q}{\partial \bar{\tau}_w} d\bar{\tau}_w + \frac{\partial q}{\partial g} dg$$

The effects of a given parameter change will be propagated through the two "substitution" effects "A" and "B", and through the goods balance effect, "C". In the following, the propagation mechanism will be discussed verbally. The reader is however adivsed to study equations (23') parallel to the text. Note that the same comments to the interpretation of $d\bar{x}$ and $d\bar{\tau}_w$ made in conjunction to equations (23) also apply here.

If the search activity on the goods market of the unemployed households τ'_{sp} increases, the net flow of customers will increase, given a certain decrease of the relative price of the firm. Through the "own" substitution effect of the relative price, $\frac{\partial A}{\partial p^e}$, the relative price will decrease. But if p^e decreases, the demand for the firm's product will increase. In order for goods production to be equal to demand, production must increase. This is done by increasing the number of labor hours, which, given the number of employees, requires a higher relative wage rate. Note the substitution effect between the relative price and the relative wage rate, $\frac{\partial w^e}{\partial A}$. Increased search activity in the goods market by the employed households may be analyzed analogously.

If the search activity of the unemployed households in the labor market τ'_{sw} increases, a given increase of the firm's relative wage rate will increase the net flow of employees to a greater extent than before. The relative wage rate will increase through its "own" substitution effect. But then, given the number of employees, the available number of labor hours will increase, and so will production. To fulfill the goods balance, the demand for the firm's product must increase, and this is effected by a decreased relative price. Formally, this occurs through the substitution effect between the relative wage rate and the relative price $\frac{\partial p^e}{\partial B}$. The analogous argument holds for an increase of the search activity on the labor market by the employed households. An increased rate of unemployment, u, means that search activity in the labor market will increase, due to the fact that the unemployed, on the average, search more intensively then the employed. This increase in turn, be analyzed analogously to the previous parameter change.

If the number of employees of the firm, L, increases, the relative wage rate will decrease through its "own" substitution effect. This is because an increased number of employees will give the firm an incentive to either decrease the speed by which new employees are aquired or, if the number of employees is already greater than the stationary optimum, to decrease the number of employees faster than before. In addition, the increase of the number of employees will have a goods-balance effect on the relative wage rate. The increased number of employees means that a greater number of labor hours is available. To counteract increases in the supply of labor, and thus in production, the relative wage rate declines.

In the same way, the increased number of employees implies a substitution effect and a goods-balance effect on the relative price. The substitution effect implies a higher relative price, since the substitution effect on the relative wage rate caused by the greater number of employees must be offset by a higher relative price for the goods-balance to be satisfied. Moreover, the increased number of employees will have a goods-balance effect (via $\frac{\partial p^e}{\partial C}$) on the relative price, which decreases. Thus the two effects on the relative price are of different directions, and the net effect is uncertain.

If the number of customers, K, increases, this will first have a substitution effect increasing the relative price, since the firm, as a result of its intertemporal planning for a certain optimal stationary number of customers, will plan to decrease the growth rate of the number of customers. *Ceteris paribus*, the increased number of customers will mean an increased demand for the firm's product. The associated goods-balance effect implies a higher relative price. Analogously, the net effect on the relative wage rate of the increased number of customers may be separated into a substitution effect and a goods-balance effect. The substitution effect tends to decrease the relative wage rate, whereas the goods-balance effect tends to increase the relative wage rate, so that the net effect is uncertain.

If the average demand per customer, $\bar{x}$, increases, this will tend to increase the relative price through the "own" substitution effect. The increased demand will also have a goods-balance effect on the relative price, operating in the same direction. The effect on the relative wage rate through the substitution effect between the relative price and the relative wage rate will be negative (a higher relative price means, due to the goods balance, that the relative wage rate must decrease). On the other hand, the increased demand for the firm's product will have a positive goods-balance effect on the relative wage rate, so that the net effect is uncertain.

An increase in the average supply of labor per employee causes the relative wage rate to fall through a substitution effect, and the goods-balance effect is in the same direction. The relative price will be increased by the substitution effect, but the goods-balance effect works in the opposite direction. The net effect is uncertain.

An increase in the marginal present value product of the number of customers λ_1 implies that the firm (through the "own" substitution effect) will try to increase the net flow of customers by decreasing its relative price. To fulfill the goods balance, the relative wage rate must increase.

If the marginal present value of the number of employees λ_2 increases, the firm will try to increase the net flow of employees. Through the "own" substitution effect, the relative wage rate increases. Since this means a greater supply of labor hours, the relative price must decrease in order for the increased production to be sold.

An increase of the average and marginal productivity of labor, g, will have the following effects on the relative wage rate. Through the substitution effect, the increased marginal productivity will increase demand for labor hours, and thus also the relative wage rate. Given the number of labor hours, the increased average productivity increases goods production. According to the goods balance effect, this will decrease the relative wage rate. The net effect is thus uncertain. Both the substitution and the goods-balance effects tend to decrease the relative price.

An increase of the average real wage rate of the economy, $\frac{\bar{w}^e}{\bar{p}^e}$, decreases the relative wage rate through the "own" substitution effect. At the same time, the relative price will increase. It should be noted that the increase of the real wage rate, ceteris paribus, will mean a higher wage rate, $w^e\bar{w}^e$, for the employees of the firm. Therefore, it is not certain that the decrease of the relative wage rate also means a decreased wage rate.

The results of the comparative statics are summed up in the following incomplete behavior equations:

$$
\begin{array}{l}
p^e = \phi(\tau'_{sp}, \tau_{sp}, \tau'_{sw}, \tau_{sw}, u, L, K, \bar{x}, \bar{\tau}_w, \lambda_1, \lambda_2, g, \frac{\bar{w}^e}{\bar{p}^e}) \\
\qquad\quad - \quad - \quad - \quad - \quad - \quad ? \quad + \quad + \quad ? \quad - \quad - \quad - \quad + \\
\\
w^e = \psi(\tau'_{sp}, \tau_{sp}, \tau'_{sw}, \tau_{sw}, u, L, K, \bar{x}, \bar{\tau}_w, \lambda_1, \lambda_2, g, \frac{\bar{w}^e}{\bar{p}^e}) \\
\qquad\quad + \quad + \quad + \quad + \quad + \quad - \quad ? \quad ? \quad - \quad + \quad + \quad ? \quad -
\end{array}
\qquad (24')
$$

6.2. Phase diagram analysis

The maximization of the Hamiltonian does not guarantee the maximization of the profits functional, which requires that additional conditions be fulfilled. The transversality conditions and the convergence of the state and adjoint variables to a stationary solution satisfying the transversality conditions will now be examined.

In the present case, the transversality conditions coincide with those of the general case. The same is true for the differential equations of the adjoint variables. This means, first, that the two marginal present value products are constant over time (so that their values are equal to their stationary solutions), and second, that their values are affected in the same direction -- as in the more general case -- when various disturbances occur. The disturbance analyzis summarized in (37) is thus also valid for the special case.

If the stability analysis for the adjoint variables thus coincides with that for the more general case, such is not the case for the phase variables K and L. When analyzing the differential equations for the number of customers and the number of employees, this will be done for a small environment around the stationary solution. How then are the time derivatives of the phase variables affected by the point of the phase space from which the development starts? This question may be investigated by analyzing the direct and indirect (through changed values of the control variables) effects on the differential equations of changes in the values of the phase variables:

$$(29') \qquad \begin{aligned}
\frac{\partial \dot{K}}{\partial K} &= \underset{-}{\frac{\partial \dot{K}}{\partial K}} + \underset{-}{\frac{\partial \dot{K}}{\partial p^e}}\,\underset{+}{\frac{\partial \phi}{\partial K}} < 0 \\
\frac{\partial \dot{K}}{\partial L} &= \underset{-}{\frac{\partial \dot{K}}{\partial p^e}}\,\underset{?}{\frac{\partial \phi}{\partial L}} \gtrless 0 \\
\frac{\partial \dot{L}}{\partial K} &= \underset{+}{\frac{\partial \dot{L}}{\partial w^e}}\,\underset{?}{\frac{\partial \psi}{\partial K}} \gtrless 0 \\
\frac{\partial \dot{L}}{\partial L} &= \underset{-}{\frac{\partial \dot{L}}{\partial L}} + \underset{+}{\frac{\partial \dot{L}}{\partial w^e}}\,\underset{-}{\frac{\partial \psi}{\partial L}} < 0
\end{aligned}$$

In spite of the fact that the signs of the cross derivatives $\frac{\partial \phi}{\partial L}$ and $\frac{\partial \psi}{\partial K}$ are uncertain, it is still possible to say something about the stability properties of the system.

It is possible to show that $\frac{\partial \dot{K}}{\partial K}\frac{\partial \dot{L}}{\partial L} > \frac{\partial \dot{K}}{\partial L}\frac{\partial \dot{L}}{\partial K}$.[1] This means that the system is stable; note equation (31). Depending on the signs of the two cross derivatives, convergence may be either monotonic or oscillatory.

6.3. The complete behavior equations

Starting from (23'), (37), and the fact that the adjoint variables should be constant in time (this is a necessary condition for convergence, and thus for fulfilling the transversality conditions), the following complete behavior equations are obtained:

$$\text{(38')}\quad \begin{aligned} p^e &= p^e(\underset{?}{\tau'_{sp}}, \underset{?}{\tau_{sp}}, \underset{-}{\tau'_{sw}}, \underset{?}{\tau_{sw}}, \underset{-}{u}, \underset{?}{L}, \underset{+}{K}, \underset{+}{\bar{x}}, \underset{?}{\bar{\tau}_w}, \underset{-}{g}, \underset{+}{\frac{\bar{w}^e}{\bar{p}^e}}, \underset{+}{\delta}, \underset{+}{r-g^e}) \\ w^e &= w^e(\underset{?}{\tau'_{sp}}, \underset{?}{\tau_{sp}}, \underset{+}{\tau'_{sw}}, \underset{?}{\tau_{sw}}, \underset{+}{u}, \underset{-}{L}, \underset{?}{K}, \underset{?}{\bar{x}}, \underset{-}{\bar{\tau}_w}, \underset{?}{g}, \underset{-}{\frac{\bar{w}^e}{\bar{p}^e}}, \underset{-}{\delta}, \underset{-}{r-g^e}) \end{aligned}$$

The reason why it is not always possible any more to determine uniquely the signs of the effects on the control variables of household search activity may be explained in the following way. If the search activity of the unemployed households in the goods market increases, this will primarily increase the net flow of new customers, given a certain price decrease. This tends to decrease the relative price (and, through the goods balance, to increase the relative wage rate). At the same time, the fact that it is now easier to attract new customers (and less easy to retain the old ones) will mean that the marginal present value product of the number of customers will fall. This tends to increase the relative price and thus, through the goods balance, to decrease the relative wage rate. Both of these effects are propagated through the "own" substitution effect of the relative price and the substitution effect

---

1) Starting from total differentiation of (21´), this may be done by direct comparison of the magnitudes of the partial derivatives.

between the relative price and the relative wage rate, but they have different signs.

It also appears from (38') that the effects of increased search activity in the labor market by unemployed households is still unambigous. This is due to the fact that the marginal present value product of the number of employees is not affected by this event.

There are two new arguments included in the complete behavior equations, the parameter δ representing the probability that customers and employees will disappear due to deaths and similar events and the real rate of interest, $r - g^e$. The reason why these variables were not included as arguments of the incomplete behavior equations is that their effects on firm behavior are only propagated through changed values of the shadow prices.

The behavior equations (38') give a much more adequate starting point for developing a macroeconomic model than the corresponding complete behavior equations of the more general firm model. In the latter case, a rather great proportion of the net effects on the firm's control variables of different disturbances were impossible to determine without making more specific assumptions. The special case of the more general model discussed in this section implies <u>one</u> possible way of making these more specific assumptions.

The system of equations (38') constitutes an important link between the microeconomic analysis and the macroeconomic analysis of the inflation and unemployment problem of the next chapter. The firm's control variables are the expected relative price and the expected relative wage rate. Similarly to the case of the households, the firm is assumed to have incomplete information about the prevailing price and wage level. However, the firm is assumed to know the true price level with a lag of h_p time units, and the true wage level with a lag of h_w time units. The firm's expectations about the current price and wage level are then projected through the expected rate of inflation, which is assumed to be the same for the price and the wage level. Firms and households thus have the same expectations about the average price and the average wage level.

If, due to an increased demand for goods, the firms try to increase production, they will try to increase their relative wage rates. If an individual firm increases its relative wage rate, this will mean an increased net flow of employees and an increase in the supply of labor of its employees. However, if all firms try to increase their relative wage rates, the relative positions of the individual firms will be approximately unaffected. Instead, the actual rate of wage inflation will increase in comparison to the expected rate. The analogous line of reasoning holds for the relative prices. This is the basic inflation mechanism investigated in the next chapter.

CHAPTER VI. INFLATION AND UNEMPLOYMENT

1. Introduction

In the present chapter the behavior equations derived in the previous chapters will be aggregated into a dynamic model of inflation and unemployment.

1.1. Some assumptions and delimitations

The "reality" described by the following macro model may be characterized as follows.

The model describes a closed stationary economy without public investment or consumption. Through taxes, transfers, and monetary policy the economy is influenced by the government, however. Essentially, the economy consists of a goods market and a labor market. There is also a loan market, but it affects the development of the economy only through the real rate of interest, which is determined by the Central Bank.

A great number of firms and households trade with each other. The individual firms are wage and price setters. There are no coalitions between the households or between the firms. Thus, there do not exist any unions or collective agreements. The firms are assumed to vary their prices and wage rates continually so as to maintain equilibrium constantly in their "own" goods and labor markets. In this sense the economy is in equilibrium all the time. There is thus no rationing or involuntary unemployment. Still, there may be disequilibrium in the sense that the expectations of the economic agents about the rate of price and wage inflation may be erroneous. Erroneous expectations affect in turn the aspiration of the unemployed and thereby the development of unemployment.

Unemployment is frictional. It has to do with the fact that it takes a certain time for people newly entered into the labor market to find a job opening which fulfills their minimum requirements. Thus only a part of the total flow into unemployment is explained by the model. No account is taken of persons unemployed because of lost jobs. This means that what one usually regards as the most important aspect of unemployment from a social point of view is not included in the model. From this point of view, unemployment in the model may be said to be voluntary, but it should be stressed that variations in the supply of information about vacancies together with faulty expectations may generate variations in unemployment which can hardly be said to be voluntary.

After this summary of the economy described by the model, let me make some more detailed comments concerning its assumptions and delimitations.

A very large number of firms and households transact in the markets of the economy. Even if there are monopolistic elements in pricing and monopsonistic elements in wage setting -- recall the discussion in the previous chapter -- it is not possible to explain endogenously the factors of price and wage setting usually associated with cost inflation. In addition, there do not exist any labor unions or other associations which by collective action could influence pricing or wage setting. It should be observed, however, that it is possible to take collective agreements into consideration by studying the effects of an exogenously given increase in the average wage level.

The possibilities for the government to influence the economy through fiscal policy are limited to variations in unemployment compensation and the tax rate. According to the discussion of chapter IV, unemployment compensation is attached to the average wage rate through an index clause. Due to statistical lags, the authorities who pay unemployment compensation only know the actual wage level with a certain lag, h_w. To maintain the real value of unemployment compensation, the nominal compensation is adjusted according to the expected rate of wage inflation. It is assumed that these expectations are the same for the authorities as for the firms and the households. This further means that neither tax revenues nor unemployment compensation payments are government control variables. This in turn means that fiscal policy may be divided into discretionary and automatic fiscal policy.

While the disposable incomes of the households are affected by unemployment compensation and income tax payments, the disposable profits of firms are affected by the (proportional) profits tax. In addition to costs and revenues of the business, there are interest costs and interest revenues, which may also be taxed. In that case the real rate of interest is defined net of the firm's tax liability.

In accordance with the discussion of the previous chapters, the households are assumed not to be involved in any financial saving. The firms may save financially, since profits from the business and the net disposable interest revenues must be invested, but they invest neither in capital goods nor stocks.

There are the following financial flows. First, the government pays unemployment compensation to the unemployed households, and at the same time receives tax revenues from the employed households. Second, the government receives tax payments from the firms. The firms having a financial surplus after taxes lend to deficit firms. To the extent that the business sector as a whole has a surplus, this is borrowed by the Central Bank.

If the model thus generates financial flows between the household, the business, and the public sector, one still may not say that the security market plays any active part in the model, since financial assets are not included as arguments of the behavior equations of the firms and of the households. However, there is a financial rudiment in the analysis in the form of the effects on firm behavior of variations in the (disposable) real rate of interest.[1)]

The next question is whether the inflation-unemployment model is an equilibrium model. The answer is a conditional affirmative: actually, the analysis hinges on a hierarchy of equilibrium models.

1) The construction of the model thus implies that an increase in the rate of inflation will not be counteracted by effects on the real value of financial assets. Nor will there be any possible destabilizing speculative effects on the demand for non-interest bearing assets (money) when inflationary expectations increase.

The fact that the macroeconomic model is based on an aggregation of the behavior equations of the individual firms and households indicates that the analysis is based on certain equilibrium assumptions. Firstly, it is assumed that the individual households, given their individual suppliers may vary their consumption demands freely within the limits of the budget equation. For the employed households this implies a simultaneous variation of their supply of labor hours.

A decisive criterion for determining whether the household operates in an equilibrium milieu is whether its planning is "voluntary" (cf. Patinkin's discussion referred to in chapter II). The question is thus: do the households need to take into consideration restrictions other than the budget equation? Of course, the fact that both employed and unemployed households have to take account of the time-budget equation is of no importance in this connection. The question is rather if they are forced to take into consideration any additional quantitative restrictions which have to do with the market not being in equilibrium. This is not the case for the employed households.

For the unemployed households, the question is rather more complicated. We may say that in their planning they have to consider that their working time is identically equal to zero and that this restriction is binding up to the point of time when they get into contact with a firm offering a wage rate which is at least as high as the aspiration wage rate. The point of time when this extra restriction is eliminated may be influenced indirectly by the household. By decreasing the aspiration wage rate or intensifying search activity in the labor market, it is possible for the unemployed worker to decrease the mathematical expectation of the length of the remaining unemployment time period. But the control is not complete. If, for example, the firms decrease their supply of information on the labor market, this will increase the length of the average remaining unemployment period, *ceteris paribus*. Further, the point of time when unemployment disappears is stochastically determined. The conclusion is thus that it is a matter of definition whether the unemployed are planning subject to equilibrium conditions or not.

Turning to the planning of the firms, the requirement that they vary continually their relative prices and relative wage rates so as to fulfill their goods balances (and labor-force balances) implies an equilibrium assumption, specifically that there exists at all times equilibrium in all of the individual firm's "own" goods and labor markets.

However, the equilibrium solutions for the relative prices and relative wage rates of the individual firms inter alia depend on the pricing and wage setting of all the other firms. This is due to the fact that a part of the customers of a certain firm are employees of other firms and all the employees are customers of other firms.

If the other firms try to change their relative wage rates (which implies that the gap between the actual and the expected rate of wage inflation changes), this will affect the demand in the individual firm's "own" goods market and, consequently the values of its control variables, inter alia its relative price. When all the individual firms try to change their relative prices, this will affect the supply of labor hours which confronts a firm. Thus, changes in the expected relative prices of the individual firms will feed back through changes in the gap between actual and expected price inflation on the wage setting of the individual firms, and thus on the gap between actual and expected wage increases.

We may say that at each point of time the problem is to find the vector of relative prices and relative wage rates which, together with the actual rate of price inflation and wage inflation, gives a simultaneous equilibrium on all the individual firms' goods and labor markets. However, we abstract from possible necessary variations of relative prices and relative wage rates and concentrate on variations in the gaps between actual and expected rates of price and wage inflation.

The equilibrium model, in which the rates of (unexpected) price and wage increases are endogenously determined, but in which the distributions of relative prices and relative wage rates are exogenous, only generates an instantaneous equilibrium. The equilibrium solution depends on the values of the real wage rate, the rate of unemployment and the expected rate of inflation. The development over time of these variables is determined by differential equations in which the solutions of the instantaneous equilibrium model (the gap between the actual and the expected rates of price inflation, and the gap between the actual and expected rates of wage inflation) appear as arguments.

This in turn means that it is possible to distinguish between the instantaneous equilibrium solution of the static model and long-run equilibrium situations in which one or more of the time derivatives of the differential equations are equal to zero.

The different phases of the macroeconomic analysis may be characterized as a hierarchy of equilibrium situations. In temporary equilibrium only the (unexpected) rates of inflation are endogenously determined. The next step (quasi-equilibrium) is that, in addition, the real wage rate and the rate of unemployment are endogenously determined as equilibrium solutions. The most complete equilibrium concept in this analysis entails as well the endogenous determination of the expected rate of inflation.[1]

1.2. Some themes of the analysis

The analytical derivation of the Phillips curve by Holt, Phelps, and Mortensen[2] have formed an important starting point for the following analysis of the inflation process and the development of unemployment over time. These derivations constituted an important step forward since, for the first time, the simultaneous study of inflation and unemployment on the basis of an analysis of the behavior of "rational" firms and households was made possible. One problem with these investigations, however, was that only the development of the labor market was analyzed. Thus the possibility of studying

---

1) Actually, there is an interesting problem as to the uniqueness of the stationary solution of the expected rate of inflation. Hence what we shall do is to investigate the properties of situations where the actual and expected rates of price and wage inflation are equal.

2) Cf. Holt (1970), Phelps (1970), and Mortensen (1970a).

the interactions between the processes of price and wage increases was not exploited.

From this point of view, it is natural to ask how the interactions between the developments in the goods and labor markets function if the theory of inflation and unemployment which is based on search theory is generalized. One may also inquire whether the conclusions about the relation between inflation and unemployment still hold in a multimarket analysis. It is evident that it is then no longer possible to speak about a unique relation between inflation and unemployment, a Phillips curve. Now the connection between price increases, wage increases, and unemployment -- a Phillips surface -- must be analyzed. Does the Phillips surface have the same general properties as the Phillips curve? Does the Phillips surface imply a negative relation between "inflation" and unemployment? What are the properties of the dynamic movement around the Phillips surface? Does the model generate negative "loops" around the Phillips surface?

In addition, questions of a less concrete and more fundamental nature appear. Is it possible, for example, to conceive of the Phillips curve as a special case of a more general phenomenon, to be denoted in the following as the Phillips surface? How is the Phillips surface to be interpreted? Is it a strutural equation, or is it rather a question of a correspondence which may be derived indirectly from the endogenous movement of the economic system?

An important result of the analyses of Phelps and Mortensen was the long-run independence between inflation and unemployment: if inflation is completely expected, unemployment will be independent of the rate of inflation. The rate of inflation may assume any value, provided only that it is completely expected. The long-run equilibrium values of the rate of unemployment (termed by Milton Friedman "the natural rate of unemployment"[1], and by Edmund Phelps more neutrally "the equilibrium unemployment ratio"[2] is completely independent

---

1) Friedman (1968).

2) Phelps (1967).

of variations in aggregate demand and can only be affected through changes in the structure of the labor market. The question now is whether the hypothesis about a "natural" rate of unemployment also holds for multimarket models. If the natural rate of unemployment also exists for an inflation model with a goods market and a labor market, how is the value of the natural rate affected by various parameter changes? Do there exist other "natural" rates in addition to the natural rate of unemployment?

This question, of course, is only one example of a more general class of questions: how many of the results of a single-market analysis hold when the model is extended to cover several markets? Are there any new results? The answer has a great deal to do with the strategic assumptions which the analysis is based on.

But not only comparisons with the results of the "new" theory of inflation and unemployment are of interest. Also similarities between the new theory and the "traditional" inflation theory merit attention. Is it still possible to classify the inflation mechanisms into "cost" and "demand" components? In chapter II it was argued that the nearest analogy to cost-push inflation was the expected rate of inflation of the new micro-based inflation theory. However, the term "cost-push inflation" is rather wague. It may be regarded as common heading for all factors which can generate a price- and wage-increase process without a "general" excess demand. One may then ask whether it is possible to study the effects of "autonomous" cost increases -- e.g., those caused by collective agreements -- within the framework of the "new" inflation models. Further, what are the possibilities of labor organizations influencing the real wage rate through repeated non-market conforming wage increases? And in that case what are the long run effects on unemployment and the rate of inflation?

One may also ask to what extent variations in aggregate demand for goods influences the rate of inflation. Is it possible to speak about demand-pull inflation in connection with the "new" theory? What are the possibilities in that case for the government to influence aggregate demand and thus the rate of inflation?

The points of comparison above between the "new" and the "traditional" inflation theory are all such that they may be illuminated without difficulty in context of Phelps' and Mortensen's models of the labor market.[1] For comparisons with certain of the results of "traditional" inflation theory it is necessary, however, to start from a model which explicitly treats both the goods market and the labor market. One such example is Bent Hansen's "quasi-equilibrium", a situation in which the rates of price increase and wage increase balance so that the real wage rate is constant.[2] In Hansen's model this results from the fact that the excess demands in the goods market and the labor market both depend on the value of the real wage rate. Given the values of the excess demands in the labor and goods markets, the rate of wage increase and the rate of price increase depend on the values of the wage-increase coefficient and the price-increase coefficient, respectively. If the sensitivity of the rate of price inflation to the excess demand for goods decreases, the real wage rate will increase in Hansen's model. One may ask whether there is correspondence to that phenomenon in the "new" type of inflation models, and whether it is possible to find any reasonable economic interpretation of the possible lags which influence the quasi-equilibrium value of the real wage rate.

1.3. Plan of the chapter

The chapter is arranged as follows. In section 2 the structural equations of the instantaneous equilibrium model are derived. The gaps between the actual and the expected rates of price inflation and wage inflation, the total demand for goods, and the aggregate supply of labor are obtained by aggregation of the behavior equations of the individual households and firms.

---

1) Phelps (1970) and Mortensen (1970a).

2) Hansen (1951).

The two rates of inflation depend inter alia on the rate of unemployment and the real wage rate.

In section 3 the differential equations for the expected real wage rate, the rate of unemployment, and the expected rate of inflation are derived.

Section 4 is devoted to a study of the inflation process and the development of unemployment over time. Here the expected rate of inflation is assumed to be exogenously given. The dynamic system thus consists of the differential equations for the expected real wage rate and the rate of unemployment. The development of these variables implies that the endogenous variables of the instantaneous equilibrium model -- inter alia the gap between the actual and the expected rates of price and wage inflation -- change from one point of time to another. First when the real wage rate and the rate of unemployment have reached their stationary solutions will the endogenous variables of the instantaneous equilibrium model be constant over time.

In this section the stability properties of the system of differential equations and the nature of their convergence is first examined. There follows a discussion of how the stationary values of the real wage rate and the rate of unemployment (the "quasi-equilibrium" values of these variables) are influenced by various disturbances. The section ends with a discussion of the properties, stability, and fundamental significance of the Phillips surface, and the possibilities of shifting this surface "inward".

In section 5 the assumption of an exogenously given expected rate of inflation is dropped. From this starting point the existence and properties of the "natural" rate of unemployment, the stability of the inflation process, and the conditions of long-run stabilization policy are discussed.

The last section contains a number of remarks and retrospects in which the "realism" of the model, possible alternative approaches, and similarities to other inflation and unemployment models are discussed.

2. Aggregation of the Behavior Equations of the Households and the Firms: the Instantaneous Equilibrium Model

The discussion of this section forms a link between the three previous chapters, in which the behavior of the individual firms and households was described, and the dynamic macroeconomic model which is to follow further on. A number of the behavior equations of the individual economic agents will be aggregated. To be able to use this information in the dynamic model, the structural equations will be solved to obtain reduced-form equations. This means that the endogenous variables of the instantaneous equilibrium model are solved for in functions which at each point of time depend only on the exogenous variables and the three phase variables (the expected real wage rate, the rate of unemployment, and the expected rate of inflation).

2.1. Aggregation of the behavior equations

We start by deriving the rates of price and wage increase. As discussed in the previous chapter, the basic inflation mechanism consists of the fact that the firms try to vary their relative prices and relative wage rates so as to maximize their capital values, together with the fact that their information about the price level and the wage level is incomplete.

If all firms try to increase their relative prices (*e.g.*, on account of an increased goods demand), it will not be possible for them to do so. Instead, the gap between the actual and expected rate of price inflation will increase. First, the firms increase their prices as to keep their relative position in line with the expected rate of inflation. On top of that they change their prices so as to obtain a certain change of their relative prices. But what is possible for a single firm is impossible for the firms as a group. Attempts to increase the relative prices will result in a nonexpected increase in the actual rate of inflation and, thus in the actual price level. The analogous reasoning holds for the firms' wage determination.

In the previous chapter information was given concerning the factors which determine the expected relative price of the individual firm, p_j^e. This may always be written as the actual relative price, multiplied by the ratio between the actual average price in the market and the expected average price in the market.[1)] According to the assumptions previously made, both firms and households have incomplete information about the average price on the market. With a lag of length h_p they have correct information about the actual average price, however. They extrapolate this information forward to the current point of time. Since the actual rate of price inflation may be higher or lower than that expected, the actual current average price may also be higher or lower than that expected. If, moreover, the actual average price exceeds that expected, the firm's expected relative price will be higher than the actual relative price.

More formally, the expected relative price of firm j may be written:

$$p_j^e = p_j \frac{\bar{p}}{\bar{p}^e} = p_j \, e^{h_p(g_p - g_p^e)}$$

where p_j is the actual relative price, $\bar{p}$ the actual average current price level, $\bar{p}^e$ the expected current price level, g_p the actual rate of price inflation, and g_p^e the expected rate of price inflation. As before, the expected rate of price inflation is assumed to be equal to the expected rate of wage inflation. Starting from the expression for the firm's expected relative price, using the complete behavior equation for the firm's (expected) relative price (V-38'), and taking into account the fact that the average value of the relative prices is equal to one, the following expression for the difference between the actual and the expected rate of price inflation is obtained:

---

1) It is always true that $p^e \bar{p}^e = p\bar{p}$.

$$(1)\quad e^{h_p(g_p-g_p^e)} = \int_{\Omega} p^e(\bar{\tau}_{sw},\ u,\ L_j,\ K_j,\ \bar{x}_j,\ \bar{\tau}_w^j,\ g,\ \frac{\bar{w}^e}{\bar{p}^e},\ \delta,\ r-g^e)\, f(\omega)\, d\omega$$

$$\qquad - \quad - \quad ? \quad + \quad + \quad ? \quad - \quad + \quad + \quad +$$

By taking logarithms of both sides of (1), the gap between the two rates of price inflation is directly obtained. Analogously, the expression for the difference between the actual and the expected rates of wage inflation is obtained as:

$$(2)\quad e^{h_w(g_w-g_w^e)} = \int_{\Omega} w^e(\tau'_{sw},\ u, L_j, K_j, \bar{x}_j, \bar{\tau}_w, g, \frac{\bar{w}^e}{\bar{p}^e}, \delta, r-g^e)\, f(\omega)\, d\omega$$ [1]

$$\qquad + \quad + \quad - \quad ? \quad ? \quad - \quad ? \quad - \quad - \quad -$$

In equations (1) and (2) we integrate over the firms of the economy. The firms differ with respect to the number of employees and customers, the fraction of unemployed customers, the distribution of customers over relative wage rates and the distribution of employees over relative prices. There are also other possible differences, such as different production functions. The integration over firms is done by integration over the characteristics which differ between firms. The vector of integration, ω, therefore contains the variables which differ between the firms, while the function $f(\omega)$ denotes the relative frequency of firms with certain characteristica.[2] The integration is done over the set Ω.

---

[1] In equations (1) and (2), three arguments have been dropped in comparison to the complete behavior equations (V-38´), namely the search activity in the goods and labor markets of the employed households and the search activity in the goods market of the unemployed households. The reason for this is that the partial derivatives with respect to these variables may have either a positive or negative sign, so that it is assumed that the signs are equal to zero.

[2] In cases where it is not possible to describe the differences between the price distributions over employees and the wage distributions over customers of the individual firms in a parameter form, integration must be done over an infinite-dimensional vector space. It is assumed, however, that the differences between the distribution functions may be described as a parameter variation.

The distribution $f(\omega)$ is intimately connected with the relative price and wage distribution over firms. It is because of differences between the planning situation that the optimal values of the control variables -- <u>inter alia</u> the relative prices and the relative wage rates -- differ between the firms. For the distributions over firms of the relative price and the relative wage rate to be stable, these differences in the planning situation must be permanent. This further implies that there must be other differences between firms than the number of customers and employees. The firms may for instance have different production functions. This may be taken into account by one or several shift variables which vary between firms. The shift variables are included as arguments of the vector ω.

Three of the arguments of (1) and (2) are household control variables: the (average) search activity in the labor market of the unemployed households $\bar{\tau}'_{sw}$, the average consumption of the customers of firm j, $\bar{x}_j$, and the average supply of labor hours of the employees of firm j, $\bar{\tau}^j_w$. These variables are defined in the following system of equations:

$$\bar{\tau}'_{sw} = \int_0^\infty \tau'_{sw}\left(\pi \underset{-}{\frac{\bar{p}}{\bar{p}^e}}, \underset{+}{\frac{\bar{w}^e}{\bar{p}^e}}, \underset{-}{s}, \underset{-}{z}\right) g(\pi)\, d\pi$$

$$\bar{x}_j = u_j\, x'\left(\underset{+}{\frac{\bar{w}^e}{\bar{p}^e}}, \underset{+}{z}\right) + (1 - u_j) \int_0^\infty x\left(v\, \underset{+}{\frac{\bar{w}}{\bar{w}^e}}, \underset{+}{\frac{(1-s)\bar{w}^e}{\bar{p}^e}}, \underset{+}{\rho}\right) g_j(v)\, dv \tag{3}$$

$$\bar{\tau}^j_w = \int_0^\infty \tau_w\left(\pi\, \underset{-}{\frac{\bar{p}}{\bar{p}^e}}, \underset{-}{\frac{(1-s)\bar{w}^e}{\bar{p}^e}}, \underset{+}{\rho}\right) g_j(\pi)\, d\pi$$

The first equation defines the average search activity in the labor market per unemployed worker. This average is constructed from the sum of the search activities of the unemployed, given that they pay a certain relative price, weighted with the relative frequency of unemployed households paying this relative price. It should be noted that it is the expected relative price, p^e, which is included as an argument of the behavior equations of the individual households.

The last two equations of (3) have their counterparts in (V-10) and (V-11). The only difference is that a greater number of arguments of the behavior equations of the individual households have been written out explicitly, as in (III-30).

A still more important observation is that the relative wage rate of firm j is not included as an argument in the labor supply function of its employees and that the relative price of firm j is not included as an argument of the goods-demand function of its customers. This is due to the fact that the firm, when choosing the optimal values of its control variables, has already taken into consideration the effects on the supply of labor hours by its employees of its relative wage rate and the effects on the demand for goods by its customers of its relative price. These variables have thus been "maximized out". It should be stressed, however, that it is possible to abstract from these arguments only when consumption and supply of labor are included as arguments of the behavior equations of the firms. If, for example, we want to calculate aggregate consumption of all the households of the economy, then the relative prices paid by the individual households should be included as arguments of the demand equations for consumption goods.

By integrating equations (1) and (2), the following expressions for the difference between the actual and expected rates of price inflation and wage inflation are obtained:[1)]

---

1) Note that (4) may be rewritten as $g_p - g_p^e = \frac{1}{h_p} \ln \tilde{\tilde{p}}^e$ and $g_w - g_w^e = \frac{1}{h_w} \ln \tilde{\tilde{w}}^e$. Also, the expected rate of price inflation was assumed to be equal to the expected rate of wage inflation, so that $g_p^e = g_w^e = g^e$.

$$e^{h_p(g_p-g_p^e)} = \approx{p}^e\Big(\underset{-}{\bar{\tau}'_{sw}},\ \underset{-}{u},\ \underset{o}{(1-u)K},\ \underset{+}{\bar{x}},\ \underset{o}{\bar{\tau}_w},\ \underset{-}{g},\ \underset{+}{\frac{\bar{w}^e}{\bar{p}^e}},\ \underset{+}{\delta},\ \underset{+}{r-g^e}\Big)$$

(4)

$$e^{h_w(g_w-g_w^e)} = \approx{w}^e\Big(\underset{+}{\bar{\tau}'_{sw}},\ \underset{+}{u},\ \underset{-}{(1-u)K},\ \underset{o}{\bar{x}},\ \underset{-}{\bar{\tau}_w},\ \underset{o}{g},\ \underset{-}{\frac{\bar{w}^e}{\bar{p}^e}},\ \underset{-}{\delta},\ \underset{-}{r-g^e}\Big)$$

Equations (4) are defined for a given distribution $f(\omega)$. This means that the <u>distributional</u> effects of different disturbances are abstracted from. It should be observed that this abstraction is closely related to the assumption of constant distributions of relative prices and relative wage rates over firms. The effects of the approximation will be over- or underestimated values of the partial derivatives of (4). The signs will generally not be affected, however.

A comparison between equations (1) and (2) on the one hand, and equation system (4) on the other, shows that one of the arguments, namely the number of customers of the individual firms, has been dropped. This is due to the fact that the number of customers is constant for the economy as a whole. The number of employees may vary, however, since the number of unemployed may vary. Instead of the number of employed in all firms, L, the total number of employed customers, $(1-u)K$, has been substituted into (4). In the framework of the present model, these variables are equal. Furthermore, the partial derivatives of uncertain sign are assumed to be equal to zero.

Integrating equations (3), the following expressions are obtained for the average search activity in the labor market of the unemployed households, the average consumption per household, and the average supply of labor per household:

$$\bar{\tau}'_{sw} = \tilde{\tilde{\tau}}'_{sw}\Big(\underset{-}{\frac{\bar{p}}{\bar{p}^e}},\ \underset{+}{\frac{\bar{w}^e}{\bar{p}^e}},\ \underset{-}{s},\ \underset{-}{z}\Big)$$

$$\text{(5)}\qquad \bar{x} = u x'\Big(\underset{+}{\frac{\bar{w}^e}{\bar{p}^e}},\ \underset{+}{z}\Big) + (1-u)\,\tilde{\tilde{x}}\Big(\underset{+}{\frac{\bar{w}}{\bar{w}^e}},\ \underset{+}{\frac{(1-s)\bar{w}^e}{\bar{p}^e}},\ \underset{+}{\rho}\Big)$$

$$\bar{\tau}_w = \tilde{\tilde{\tau}}_w\Big(\underset{-}{\frac{\bar{p}}{\bar{p}^e}},\ \underset{-}{\frac{(1-s)\bar{w}^e}{\bar{p}^e}},\ \underset{-}{\rho}\Big)$$

where $\dfrac{\bar{p}}{\bar{p}^e} = e^{h_p(g_p - g_p^e)}$ and $\dfrac{\bar{w}}{\bar{w}^e} = e^{h_w(g_w - g_w^e)}$.

The expected real wage rate is further exogenously given in the instantaneous equilibrium model:

$$\text{(6)}\qquad \frac{\bar{w}^e(t)}{\bar{p}^e(t)} = \frac{\bar{w}(t-h_w)}{\bar{p}(t-h_p)}\, e^{h_w g_w^e - h_p g_p^e}$$

2.2. The instantaneous equilibrium values of the nonexpected rates of price and wage inflation

Among other things the analysis above resulted in structural equations for the nonexpected rates of price and wage inflation. This was achieved through a direct aggregation of the expected relative prices and expected relative wage rates of the individual firms. No account was taken of the interaction between the pricing and wage determination of the individual firms.

As noted in the introduction to this chapter, the pricing process of the present macroeconomic model may be regarded as a general equilibrium phenomenon, where the relative prices, the relative wage rates, and the unexpected rates of price and wage inflation at each point of time attain those values which imply equilibrium in each and every one of the "own" goods and labor markets of the individual firms. Abstracting from variations in relative prices and relative wage rates, the problem is to find the rates of unexpected price inflation and unexpected wage inflation which clear the markets.

It is not possible to use the equations of (4) directly in order, for example, to find the effect of a change in the real rate of interest, $r-g^e$, on the difference between the actual and expected rates of price inflation. This is due to the fact that the system (4)-(5) is interdependent. Increases of the unexpected rate of price inflation mean, for example, that the customers of all the firms think that they are paying a high relative price. This will affect their supply of labor, which influences the wage determination of the individual firms. If the firms try to change their relative wage rates, this will affect the disposable income of the employed customers, and consequently their goods demand. This change in goods demand then feeds back on relative prices and consequently on the rate of unexpected price inflation.

The mechanism outlined above may be compared to "traditional" inflation models. In Bent Hansen's model of open inflation[1)], price inflation and wage inflation are independently determined at each point of time. The two rates of inflation are functions only of the excess demands on the two markets, which in turn are functions of the real wage rate. In Hansen's model the interdependence between the rate of price inflation and the rate of wage inflation is not instantaneous, as in the present model, but will be affected successively by changes in the real wage rate. It will be shown later on that this interdependence through changes of the real wage rate appears also in the present analysis.

To obtain the expression for the difference between the actual and the expected rates of price and wage inflation, (5) is substituted into (4). The equations are then differentiated with respect to the rates of unexpected price and wage inflation, and an arbitrary exogenous variable or phase variable:

---

1) Hansen (1951), chapter VII.

$$d\left(\frac{\bar{p}}{\bar{p}^e}\right) = \underset{-}{\frac{\partial \overset{\approx}{p}^e}{\partial \bar{\tau}'_{sw}}} \; \underset{-}{\frac{\partial \overset{\approx}{\tau}'_{sw}}{\partial \left(\frac{\bar{p}}{\bar{p}^e}\right)}} \; d\left(\frac{\bar{p}}{\bar{p}^e}\right) + (1-u) \cdot$$

$$(7) \qquad \cdot \underset{+}{\frac{\partial \overset{\approx}{p}^e}{\partial \bar{x}}} \; \underset{+}{\frac{\partial \overset{\approx}{x}}{\partial \left(\frac{\bar{w}}{\bar{w}^e}\right)}} \; d\left(\frac{\bar{w}}{\bar{w}^e}\right) + \frac{\partial \overset{\approx}{p}^e}{\partial \xi} \, d\xi$$

$$d\left(\frac{\bar{w}}{\bar{w}^e}\right) = \underset{+}{\frac{\partial \overset{\approx}{w}^e}{\partial \bar{\tau}'_{sw}}} \; \underset{-}{\frac{\partial \overset{\approx}{\tau}'_{sw}}{\partial \left(\frac{\bar{p}}{\bar{p}^e}\right)}} \; d\left(\frac{\bar{p}}{\bar{p}^e}\right) + \underset{-}{\frac{\partial \overset{\approx}{w}^e}{\partial \bar{\tau}_w}} \; \underset{-}{\frac{\partial \overset{\approx}{\tau}_w}{\partial \left(\frac{\bar{p}}{\bar{p}^e}\right)}} \; d\left(\frac{\bar{p}}{\bar{p}^e}\right) + \frac{\partial \overset{\approx}{w}^e}{\partial \xi} \, d\xi$$

where $\frac{\bar{p}}{\bar{p}^e} = e^{h_p(g_p - g_p^e)}$, $\frac{\bar{w}}{\bar{w}^e} = e^{h_w(g_w - g_w^e)}$

The economic significance of the system of equations (7) is the following. If any of the exogenously determined variables or phase variables (the expected real wage rate, the rate of unemployment or the expected rate of inflation) changes, this will trigger a series of direct and indirect effects on the rates of unexpected price and wage inflation. The system of equations (7) thus reflects the simultaneity in, and the interactions between, the behavior of firms and households. It should be stressed that these interactions are defined for <u>given</u> values of the three phase variables. In the long run, we must take into consideration the further interdependences, represented by changed values of the phase variables.

The endogenous variables of the system (7) are the rates of unexpected price and wage inflation. Given the expected rate of inflation, the equilibrium rates of price and wage increase are then searched for. These equilibrium values should be determined as a result of the instantaneous interaction between pricing and wage setting of the individual firms on the one hand, and household search activity in the labor market, supply of labor, and consumption demand on the other.

price inflation and unexpected wage inflation are both positive, it is required that the total effects on these rates, when indirect effects have been taken into consideration, should not both be of the opposite sign. What this essentially means is that the indirect effects should be of a rather small order, and should not dominate the direct effects.[1)]

Starting from the assumption that the direct effects on the rates of unexpected price and wage inflation dominate, (7) may be solved to obtain:

$$(8)\quad \begin{pmatrix} d\left(\frac{\bar{p}}{\bar{p}^e}\right) \\ \\ d\left(\frac{\bar{w}}{\bar{w}^e}\right) \end{pmatrix} = \frac{1}{D} \begin{pmatrix} 1 & (1-u)\frac{\partial \tilde{\tilde{p}}^e}{\partial \bar{x}} \frac{\partial \tilde{\tilde{x}}}{\partial \left(\frac{\bar{w}}{\bar{w}^e}\right)} \\ \\ \frac{\partial \tilde{\tilde{w}}}{\partial \bar{\tau}'_{sw}} \frac{\partial \tilde{\tilde{\tau}}'_{sw}}{\partial \left(\frac{\bar{p}}{\bar{p}^e}\right)} + \frac{\partial \tilde{\tilde{w}}^e}{\partial \bar{\tau}_w} \frac{\partial \tilde{\tilde{\tau}}_w}{\partial \left(\frac{\bar{p}}{\bar{p}^e}\right)} & 1 - \frac{\partial \tilde{\tilde{p}}^e}{\partial \bar{\tau}'_{sw}} \frac{\partial \tilde{\tilde{\tau}}_{sw}}{\partial \left(\frac{\bar{p}}{\bar{p}^e}\right)} \end{pmatrix} \begin{pmatrix} \frac{\partial \tilde{\tilde{p}}^e}{\partial \xi} \\ \\ \frac{\partial \tilde{\tilde{w}}^e}{\partial \xi} \end{pmatrix}$$

where, by assumption,

$$D = 1 - \frac{\partial \tilde{\tilde{p}}^e}{\partial \bar{\tau}'_{sw}} \frac{\partial \tilde{\tilde{\tau}}'_{sw}}{\partial \left(\frac{\bar{p}}{p^e}\right)} - (1-u) \frac{\partial \tilde{\tilde{p}}^e}{\partial \bar{x}} \frac{\partial \tilde{\tilde{x}}}{\partial \left(\frac{\bar{w}}{\bar{w}^e}\right)} \left(\frac{\partial \tilde{\tilde{w}}^e}{\partial \bar{\tau}'_{sw}} \frac{\partial \tilde{\tilde{\tau}}'_{sw}}{\partial \left(\frac{\bar{p}}{\bar{p}^e}\right)} + \frac{\partial \tilde{\tilde{w}}^e}{\partial \bar{\tau}_w} \frac{\partial \tilde{\tilde{\tau}}_w}{\partial \left(\frac{\bar{p}}{\bar{p}^e}\right)} \right) > 0$$

and

$$1 - \frac{\tilde{\tilde{p}}^e}{\partial \bar{\tau}_{sw}} \frac{\partial \tilde{\tilde{\tau}}'_{sw}}{\partial \left(\frac{\bar{p}}{\bar{p}^e}\right)} > 0$$

The next step is to determine how the equilibrium values of the rates of unexpected price inflation and wage inflation are affected by various disturbances. Using (4) and (5) to

---

1) A possible stabilizing mechanism is due to the fact that the demand for goods by the unemployed households will fall during a parallel increase in the unexpected rates of price and wage inflation and increase during a parallel decrease in the unexpected rates of price and wage inflation.

$$d\left(\frac{\bar{p}}{\bar{p}^e}\right) = \underset{-}{\frac{\partial \tilde{\tilde{p}}^e}{\partial \bar{\tau}'_{sw}}}\ \underset{-}{\frac{\partial \tilde{\tilde{\tau}}'_{sw}}{\partial\left(\frac{\bar{p}}{\bar{p}^e}\right)}}\ d\left(\frac{\bar{p}}{\bar{p}^e}\right) + (1-u)\ \cdot$$

$$(7) \qquad \cdot\ \underset{+}{\frac{\partial \tilde{\tilde{p}}^e}{\partial \bar{x}}}\ \underset{+}{\frac{\partial \tilde{\tilde{x}}}{\partial\left(\frac{\bar{w}}{\bar{w}^e}\right)}}\ d\left(\frac{\bar{w}}{\bar{w}^e}\right) + \frac{\partial \tilde{\tilde{p}}^e}{\partial \xi}\, d\xi$$

$$d\left(\frac{\bar{w}}{\bar{w}^e}\right) = \underset{+}{\frac{\partial \tilde{\tilde{w}}^e}{\partial \bar{\tau}'_{sw}}}\ \underset{-}{\frac{\partial \tilde{\tilde{\tau}}'_{sw}}{\partial\left(\frac{\bar{p}}{\bar{p}^e}\right)}}\ d\left(\frac{\bar{p}}{\bar{p}^e}\right) + \underset{-}{\frac{\partial \tilde{\tilde{w}}^e}{\partial \bar{\tau}_w}}\ \underset{-}{\frac{\partial \tilde{\tilde{\tau}}_w}{\partial\left(\frac{\bar{p}}{\bar{p}^e}\right)}}\ d\left(\frac{\bar{p}}{\bar{p}^e}\right) + \frac{\partial \tilde{\tilde{w}}^e}{\partial \xi}\, d\xi$$

where $\frac{\bar{p}}{\bar{p}^e} = e^{h_p(g_p - g_p^e)}$, $\frac{\bar{w}}{\bar{w}^e} = e^{h_w(g_w - g_w^e)}$

The economic significance of the system of equations (7) is the following. If any of the exogenously determined variables or phase variables (the expected real wage rate, the rate of unemployment or the expected rate of inflation) changes, this will trigger a series of direct and indirect effects on the rates of unexpected price and wage inflation. The system of equations (7) thus reflects the simultaneity in, and the interactions between, the behavior of firms and households. It should be stressed that these interactions are defined for <u>given</u> values of the three phase variables. In the long run, we must take into consideration the further interdependences, represented by changed values of the phase variables.

The endogenous variables of the system (7) are the rates of unexpected price and wage inflation. Given the expected rate of inflation, the equilibrium rates of price and wage increase are then searched for. These equilibrium values should be determined as a result of the instantaneous interaction between pricing and wage setting of the individual firms on the one hand, and household search activity in the labor market, supply of labor, and consumption demand on the other.

A disturbance will first have a direct effect on the price and wage setting of the firms. The direct effects are represented by the last term of the equations of the system (7). Now assume that the unexpected rate of inflation increases in both markets. With this assumption, the economic significance of the first equation of (7) will be examined.

An increase of the actual rate of price inflation relative to the expected rate means that the households believe that they are paying higher relative prices. This first implies that the search activity in the labor market of the unemployed households decreases (instead, they search more intensively in the goods market). But a decrease in τ'_{sw} means that the firms try to decrease their relative wage rates, since it is not as profitable as before to hold a high relative wage rate in order to attract a greater number of employees. If the relative wage rate decreases, however, the labor hours supplied by the employees of the individual firms will also decline. To fullfil the goods balance each firm must increase its relative price. But it is impossible for all firms to increase their relative prices; instead, the actual rate of price inflation will increase. Thus, the original increase in the rate of price inflation will be reinforced by this indirect effect.

The first equation of (7) contains an additional term representing an indirect effect on the unexpected rate of price inflation. The increased gap between the actual and the expected rates of wage increase means that the employees believe that they have a higher relative wage rate than is actually the case. This means that their consumption demand increases, which tends to increase the (expected) relative prices of the individual firms, and thus the rate of unexpected price inflation. This effect is stronger the smaller the amount of unemployment. This means that the effect on the rate of price inflation of an increased rate of wage inflation, according to the model, is strongest in periods of high employment.

The last term of the right hand side of the second equation of the system (7) represents the direct effect on the unexpected rate of wage inflation of the disturbance. The other terms represent indirect effects. The increased rate of unexpected price inflation will affect negatively the search activity in the labor market of the unemployed households. The firms will then decrease their (expected) relative wage rates. Thus the actual rate of wage inflation decreases relatively to that expected. Secondly, the initial increase of the rate of unexpected price inflation further implies a decreased supply of labor. This will influence positively the (expected) relative wage rates of the individual firms.

To sum up, the process of wage and price increases depicted in (7) contains the usual cross effects between wages and prices. If the rate of wage inflation increases, consumption demand of the employed households will increase and thus also the rate of price inflation. An increase in the rate of price inflation will decrease the supply of labor by the employed households, which will in turn increase the rate of wage inflation. It should be noted that whereas increased wage rates increase consumer demand and thus prices, increased prices decrease the supply of labor and thus do not work through an increased demand for labor. In addition to these cross effects, there are effects through changes in the amount of search activity in the labor market by the unemployed households.

In "ordinary" inflation models, e.g., Hansen's model of open inflation, there is a stability problem involved in convergence of the inflation process. Will the excess demands in the goods and labor markets be successively eliminated when the price level and the wage level increase, thus putting a stop to further price and wage increases? One possible stabilizing mechanism in this case works through the real balance effect.

In the present model one may not speak about a stability problem in the strict sence of the word, since the rates of unexpected price inflation and wage inflation are simultaneously determined. It is rather a question of the existence of a meaningful instantaneous equilibrium solution to (7). More specifically, if the direct effects on the rates of unexpected price inflation and unexpected wage inflation are both positive, it is required that the total effects on these rates, when indirect effects have been taken into consideration, should not both be of the opposite sign. What this essentially means is that the indirect effects should be of a rather small order, and should not dominate the direct effects.[1]

Starting from the assumption that the direct effects on the rates of unexpected price and wage inflation dominate, (7) may be solved to obtain:

$$(8)\quad \begin{pmatrix} d(\frac{\bar{p}}{\bar{p}^e}) \\ \\ d(\frac{\bar{w}}{\bar{w}^e}) \end{pmatrix} = \frac{1}{D} \begin{pmatrix} 1 & (1-u)\frac{\partial \tilde{\tilde{p}}^e}{\partial \bar{x}} \frac{\partial \tilde{\tilde{x}}}{\partial (\frac{\bar{w}}{\bar{w}^e})} \\ \\ \frac{\partial \tilde{\tilde{w}}}{\partial \bar{\tau}'_{sw}} \frac{\partial \tilde{\tilde{\tau}}'_{sw}}{\partial (\frac{\bar{p}}{\bar{p}^e})} + \frac{\partial \tilde{\tilde{w}}^e}{\partial \bar{\tau}_w} \frac{\partial \tilde{\tilde{\tau}}_w}{\partial (\frac{\bar{p}}{\bar{p}^e})} & 1 - \frac{\partial \tilde{\tilde{p}}^e}{\partial \bar{\tau}'_{sw}} \frac{\partial \tilde{\tilde{\tau}}_{sw}}{\partial (\frac{\bar{p}}{\bar{p}^e})} \end{pmatrix} \begin{pmatrix} \frac{\partial \tilde{\tilde{p}}^e}{\partial \xi} \\ \\ \frac{\partial \tilde{\tilde{w}}^e}{\partial \xi} \end{pmatrix}$$

where, by assumption,

$$D = 1 - \frac{\partial \tilde{\tilde{p}}^e}{\partial \bar{\tau}'_{sw}} \frac{\partial \tilde{\tilde{\tau}}'_{sw}}{\partial (\frac{\bar{p}}{\bar{p}^e})} - (1-u) \frac{\partial \tilde{\tilde{p}}^e}{\partial \bar{x}} \frac{\partial \tilde{\tilde{x}}}{\partial (\frac{\bar{w}}{\bar{w}^e})} \left(\frac{\partial \tilde{\tilde{w}}^e}{\partial \bar{\tau}'_{sw}} \frac{\partial \tilde{\tilde{\tau}}'_{sw}}{\partial (\frac{\bar{p}}{\bar{p}^e})} + \frac{\partial \tilde{\tilde{w}}^e}{\partial \bar{\tau}_w} \frac{\partial \tilde{\tilde{\tau}}_w}{\partial (\frac{\bar{p}}{\bar{p}^e})} \right) > 0$$

and

$$1 - \frac{\tilde{\tilde{p}}^e}{\partial \bar{\tau}_{sw}} \frac{\partial \tilde{\tilde{\tau}}'_{sw}}{\partial (\frac{\bar{p}}{\bar{p}^e})} > 0$$

The next step is to determine how the equilibrium values of the rates of unexpected price inflation and wage inflation are affected by various disturbances. Using (4) and (5) to

---

[1] A possible stabilizing mechanism is due to the fact that the demand for goods by the unemployed households will fall during a parallel increase in the unexpected rates of price and wage inflation and increase during a parallel decrease in the unexpected rates of price and wage inflation.

calculate $\frac{\partial \tilde{\tilde{p}}^e}{\partial \xi}$ and $\frac{\partial \tilde{\tilde{w}}^e}{\partial \xi}$, the following results are obtained from (8):

(9)

$$e^{h_p(g_p - g_p^e)} = \tilde{p}^e(\underset{-}{s},\ \underset{+}{z},\ \underset{-}{u},\ \underset{+}{\rho' + \delta},\ \underset{-}{g},\ \underset{+}{\frac{\bar{w}^e}{\bar{p}^e}},\ \underset{+}{\delta},\ \underset{+}{r - g^e})^{1)}$$

$$e^{h_w(g_w - g_w^e)} = \tilde{w}^e(\underset{-}{s},\ \underset{-}{z},\ \underset{+}{u},\ \underset{-}{\rho' + \delta},\ \underset{o}{g},\ \underset{o}{\frac{\bar{w}^e}{\bar{p}^e}},\ \underset{-}{\delta},\ \underset{-}{r - g^e})$$

The signs of the partial derivatives in (9) are calculated on the assumption that the cross effects between the rate of unexpected price inflation on one hand and the rate of unexpected wage inflation on the other, are not too strong (<u>i.e.</u>, the non-diagonal elements of the matrix in (8) are small in comparison to the diagonal ones). Otherwise, cases where the partial derivatives of the two rates of unexpected inflation are of different sign with respect to the same parameter, the sign of the total effect on the rate of unexpected price inflation <u>or</u> the rate of unexpected wage inflation might change. In the following analysis the direct effects are assumed to dominate, however.[2)]

---

1) Note that (9) may be rewritten:
$g_p - g_p^e = \frac{1}{h_p} \ln \tilde{p}^e$ and $g_w - g_w^e = \frac{1}{h_w} \ln \tilde{w}^e$.

2) The cross effect from the rate of unexpected price inflation to the rate of unexpected wage inflation might be of either sign. It is natural to assume that it is positive, however, since it may be presumed that the positive effect, via a decreased supply of labor, is stronger than the negative effect, a reduced amount of search activity in the labor market.

The partial derivative of the unexpected rate of price inflation with respect to the income tax rate, $\frac{\partial \tilde{p}^e}{\partial s}$, might also have the opposite sign. A tax increase implies that the search activity in the labor market of the unemployed households decreases. This implies that the firms try to decrease their relative wage rates and increase their relative prices. On the other hand, the tax increase means that consumer demand

(the footnote cont. on next page)

The system (9) represents instantaneous equilibrium values of the rates of unexpected price and wage inflation, expressed in a reduced form. This means that the indirect effects, through interactions of the pricing and wage setting process on the one hand, and between firm and household behavior on the other, have been taken into consideration in determining the effects on the two inflation rates of different disturbances.

Comparing equations (9) with corresponding equations in simpler models, in which only the development in the labor market is considered -- e.g., the model of Mortensen (1970) -- the following may be said. In inflation and unemployment models covering only the labor market, the simultaneity between the price inflation and the wage inflation process is not taken into consideration. Thus equation (8) has no counterpart. However, price inflation may be introduced through an exogenously given term, as in Mortensen (1970a) equation (65).

(cont. footnote 2) p. 309

decreases. This tends to decrease relative prices, and thus also the rate of unexpected price inflation. This second effect is assumed to dominate.

Furthermore, the effects of changes in the expected real wage rate, $\frac{\partial \tilde{p}^e}{\partial (\frac{\bar{w}^e}{\bar{p}^e})}$ and $\frac{\partial \tilde{w}^e}{\partial (\frac{\bar{w}^e}{\bar{p}^e})}$, are uncertain. If the expected real wage rate increases, this will directly induce the firms to increase their (expected) prices, as in (4). On the other hand, the increased expected real wage rate will induce unemployed households to increase their search activity in the labor market. At the same time, the increased real incomes will induce all households to increase their consumption. The first effect will induce firms to decrease their relative prices, whereas the effect through consumer demand works in the opposite direction. The net effect is assumed to be positive.

The increase of the expected real wage rate will directly induce firms to try to decrease their relative wage rates. Furthermore, there are indirect effects through unemployed households´ search activity in the labor market and the supply of labor, both tending to increase relative wage rates. It is assumed that the direct effect and the indirect effects through changed household behavior, cancel and that consequently the rate of unexpected wage inflation is not affected by a change in the expected real wage rate.

2.3. The instananeous equilibrium values of labor supply, search activity of unemployed households in the labor market, and aspiration wages

It is now possible to derive the equilibrium values of the other endogenous variables. The discussion will be restricted, however, to the reduced-form equations for the average supply of labor per household, the average search activity in the labor market of unemployed households, and the aspiration wage rate. The first of these variables is of central importance since it is closely related to the level of activity of the economy. The two latter variables are necessary to know in order to derive the differential equation for the rate of unemployment.

By definition, the average supply of labor per household is equal to the employment ratio times the average supply of labor hours per employee:

$$(10)\quad \tau_W = (1-u) \int_0^\infty \int_0^\infty \tau_W\Big(\underset{-}{\pi \tilde{p}^e},\ \underset{+}{v \tilde{w}^e},\ \underset{-}{(1-s) \frac{\bar{w}^e}{\bar{p}^e}},\ \underset{+}{\rho' + \delta}\Big)\, g(\pi, v)\, d\pi dv$$

The average supply of labor hours per employee is obtained by weighting the supply of labor for each combination of a certain relative price and a certain relative wage rate by the relative frequency of employed households paying that relative price and recieving that relative wage rate. It should be noted that equation (10), contrary to the case of equation (3), contains the relative wage rate as an argument. However, the starting point for equation (3) was that the supply of labor by the household should be included as an argument of the firm's behavior equations, and in that case the relative wage rate had been "maximized out", since these equations describe how the behavior of the firm is affected by different disturbances, given that the firm takes into consideration how variations in its relative wage rate influences the supply of labor of its employees.

By substituting (9) into (10), the following reduced-form equation for the average supply of labor per household is obtained:

$$(11) \qquad \tau_w = (1-u)\ \hat{\tau}_w(\underset{?}{s},\ \underset{-}{z},\ \underset{+}{u},\ \underset{?}{\rho' + \delta},\ \underset{+}{g},\ \underset{-}{\frac{\bar{w}^e}{\bar{p}^e}},\ \underset{-}{\delta},\ \underset{-}{r-g^e})$$

The average supply of labor per household is a proxy for total goods production, since labor is the only factor of production in this model. If the average supply of labor increases, this will generally imply increased goods production. There is a margin of uncertainty, however, since the marginal productivity of labor may vary between firms.

An increase of the income-tax rate implies, through (9), a decline in the unexpected rates of price inflation and wage inflation. The households then believe that they pay a lower relative price and receive a lower relative wage rate than before. The first effect tends to increase labor supply, whereas the second effect works in the opposite direction. The increased income-tax rate further implies that the disposable average real wage falls, which tends to increase the supply of labor. The net effect is thus uncertain, but there is a presumption that the supply of labor,and consequently aggregate production, will increase when the tax rate increases.

This possibility does not fit very well with Keynesian theory. However, it should be stressed, that the discussion is limited to the instantaneous equilibrium model, in which the rate of unemployment is exogenously given. Later on it will be shown that an increased income-tax rate will increase unemployment.

If unemployment compensation, z, increases, the rate of price inflation increases, and the rate of wage inflation decreases, as indicated by (9). This in turn means that the total supply of labor hours will fall.

How is the average supply of labor per household affected by an increase in the rate of unemployment? The decreased employment of course will have a direct negative effect on the total amount of labor hours, and hence on production. At the same time, however, the increased rate of unemployment will increase the number of labor hours per employee, due to the fact that the increased rate of unemployment will decrease the rate of unexpected price inflation and increase the rate of unexpected wage inflation. The households then believe that their relative prices have fallen and that their relative wage rates have increased and both of these effects tend to increase the supply of labor per employee. In conclusion, without further specification it is impossible to determine the net effect on production of an increase in unemployment. Nevertheless, production will fall when unemployment increases greatly. In the limiting case when the rate of unemployment tends towards unity, the total number of labor hours will tend towards zero.

Finally, a comment is in order concerning the effect of the real rate of interest on the supply of labor. An increase in the real rate of interest implies an increase in the costs for the individual firms of investing in a greater number of customers and employees through a lower relative price and a higher relative wage rate. The firms will then try to increase their relative prices and decrease their relative wage rates. The rate of unexpected price inflation will thus increase, while the rate of unexpected wage inflation will decrease. The households will react by decreasing their consumption demand and supply of labor. Consequently, aggregate goods production will fall.

It remains to derive a reduced form for the search activity of the unemployed households in the labor market and for the acceptance wage rate. These variables are not as interesting in themselves as the average supply of labor per household. On the other hand, it is necessary to know their values in order to be able to study the development of unemployment.

Search activity in the labor market by an arbitrary unemployed worker may be written as the following function of the expected relative price, the expected real wage rate, the income-tax rate, and the unemployment compensation:

(12) $$\tau'_{sw} = \tau'_{sw}(\underset{-}{p\,\tilde{p}^e}, \underset{+}{\frac{\bar{w}^e}{\bar{p}^e}}, \underset{-}{s}, \underset{-}{z})$$

By substituting (9) into (12), the following reduced-form equation is obtained:

(13) $$\tau'_{sw} = \tau'_{sw}(\underset{-}{p}, \underset{?}{s}, \underset{-}{z}, \underset{+}{u}, \underset{-}{\rho' + \delta}, \underset{+}{g}, \underset{?}{\frac{\bar{w}^e}{\bar{p}^e}}, \underset{-}{\delta}, \underset{-}{r-g^e})$$

The reason for the uncertainty concerning the signs of the partial derivatives with respect to the income-tax rate and the expected real wage rate is that the direct effect on the search activity and the indirect effect, through changed equilibrium values of the rate of unexpected price inflation, are of different signs.

The <u>actual</u> aspiration wage rate of an arbitrary unemployed household may be written:[1)]

(14) $$\hat{w} = \frac{1}{\tilde{w}^e}\,\hat{w}^e(\underset{+}{p\,\tilde{p}^e}, \underset{+}{s}, \underset{+}{z})$$

Substituting (9) into (14), the following reduced-form equation is obtained for the aspiration wage rate of an arbitrary unemployed worker:[2)]

---

1) It should be noted that the expected acceptance wage rate is equal to the actual, multiplied by a function of the rate of unexpected wage inflation:

$$\hat{w}^e = \hat{w}\,\tilde{w}^e = \hat{w}\,e^{h_w(g_w - g_w^e)}$$

2) The partial derivative with respect to the income-tax rate is uncertain. The direct effect is positive: if the income tax rate increases, it will be less advantageous than before to accept an employment offer, which means that the wage demands of the unemployed increase. However, the increased income-tax rate implies that consumption of the employed households will decrease at the same time as their supply of labor will increase. The firms are then induced to try to decrease their relative prices and relative wage rates, which decreases the rates of unexpected price inflation and wage inflation. The decrease in the rate of unexpected price inflation tends to decrease the actual aspiration wage rates, whereas the decrease of the rate of unexpected wage inflation has the opposite effect. These two indirect effects are assumed to approximately cancel. The net effect (which is identical to the direct effect) will then be positive.

$$(15) \qquad \hat{w} = \hat{w}(\underset{+}{p},\ \underset{+}{s},\ \underset{+}{z},\ \underset{-}{u},\ \underset{+}{\rho' + \delta},\ \underset{-}{g},\ \underset{+}{\frac{\bar{w}^e}{\bar{p}^e}},\ \underset{+}{\delta},\ \underset{+}{r-g^e})$$

3. The Dynamic Model of Inflation and Unemployment

In this section the differential equations for the expected real wage rate, the rate of unemployment, and the expected rate of inflation will be derived. These variables are included as arguments of the equations of the instantaneous equilibrium model. Thus, if we know the development over time of these variables, it is possible to describe, for example, the development of the rates of unexpected price and wage inflation. On the other hand, it is necessary to know the properties of the instantaneous equilibrium model in order to determine how the time derivatives of the phase variables are affected by various disturbances. For example, the time derivative of the expected real wage rate is approximately determined by the difference between the actual rate of wage inflation and the actual rate of price inflation. The rates of inflation are in turn determined by equation (9) of the instantaneous equilibrium model.

3.1. The development of the expected real wage rate

By differentiating both sides of equation (6) with respect to time, the following equation is obtained:

$$(16) \qquad \dot{\left(\frac{\bar{w}^e}{\bar{p}^e}\right)} = \frac{\bar{w}^e(t)}{\bar{p}^e(t)} \left(\frac{\dot{\bar{w}}(t - h_w)}{\bar{w}(t - h_w)} - \frac{\dot{\bar{p}}(t - h_p)}{\bar{p}(t - h_p)} \right)$$

The time derivative of the expected real wage rate at time t may thus be expressed as the expected real wage rate at the same point of time, multiplied by the difference between the relative rate of wage increase (calculated at time $t - h_w$) and the relative rate of price increase (calculated at time $t - h_p$). Equation (16) is thus a mixed difference-differential equation.

It is important to note that the actual rates of price and wage increase discussed in the previous section, are not identical to the corresponding variables of (16). This is due to the fact that $g_p(t)$ strictly should be interpreted as the average rate of price increase, from point of time $t - h_p$ to t, while $g_w(t)$ should be interpreted as the average rate of wage increase, from point of time $t - h_w$ to t. The instantaneous rate of wage increase, $\dot{\bar{w}}(t - h_w)/\bar{w}(t - h_w)$, will be approximated by the average, g_w, and the instantaneous rate of price increase, $\dot{\bar{p}}(t - h_p)/\bar{p}(t - h_p)$, by g_p. By using $g_w = g_w^e + \frac{1}{h_w} \ln \tilde{w}^e$ and $g_p = g_p^e + \frac{1}{h_p} \ln \tilde{p}^e$ and recalling that the expected rates of price and wage inflation are assumed to be equal, (16) may be rewritten:

$$(17) \qquad \dot{\left(\frac{\bar{w}^e}{\bar{p}^e}\right)} = \frac{\bar{w}^e}{\bar{p}^e}\left(\frac{1}{h_w} \ln \tilde{w}^e - \frac{1}{h_p} \ln \tilde{p}^e\right)$$

By using (9), the following signs of the partial derivatives with respect to the exogenous variables and the phase variables are obtained:

$$(18) \qquad \dot{\left(\frac{\bar{w}^e}{\bar{p}^e}\right)} = \dot{\left(\frac{\bar{w}^e}{\bar{p}^e}\right)}(\underset{?}{s}, \underset{-}{z}, \underset{+}{u}, \underset{-}{\rho' + \delta}, \underset{+}{g}, \underset{-}{\frac{\bar{w}^e}{\bar{p}^e}}, \underset{-}{\delta}, \underset{-}{r - g^e}, \underset{-}{h_w}, \underset{+}{h_p})$$

Equation (18) is defined for a small neighborhood around the stationary value of the expected real wage rate. The reason for the uncertainty as to the partial derivative with respect to the income-tax rate is that both the actual rate of price inflation and wage inflation will decline when the tax rate increases, as in (9).

3.2. The development of unemployment

The next differential equation describes the development of unemployment over time. This development will be determined by the net between the inflow of new unemployed and the outflow when unemployed get a job or leave the labor force.

The inflow of unemployed comes from the new vintages entering the labor force. This flow is proportional to the labor force and equal to $\beta(L + U)dt$.

The flow from the stock of unemployed consists first of persons leaving the labor force. This flow is proportional to the number of unemployed and equals $\delta U dt$. Here $\delta = \beta$, since we have assumed that the labor force is constant, and since the "death risk" by assumption is independent on whether the person is employed or unemployed.

Second, the flow from the stock of unemployed consists also of persons getting jobs. Here the probabilities that various unemployed workers get into contact with a firm and that the wage offer surmounts the aspiration wages should be weighted. The total flow may be calculated as:

$$U \int_0^{\infty} \int_{\hat{w}}^{\infty} \hat{f}(v)\, g(\pi)\, \varepsilon_w(\tau'_{sw}, a_w)\, d\pi dv\, dt$$

If the partial flows are summed and divided by the number of persons in the labor force, the following expression for the time derivative of the rate of unemployment is obtained:

$$(19) \qquad \dot{u} = (1-u)\delta - u \int_0^{\infty} \int_{\hat{w}}^{\infty} \hat{f}(v)\, g(\pi)\, \varepsilon_w(\tau'_{sw}, a_w)\, d\pi dv$$

The next step is to investigate how the time derivative of the rate of unemployment is affected by various disturbances. Using (13) and (15), one obtains:

$$(20) \qquad \dot{u} = \dot{u}(\underset{+}{s},\ \underset{+}{z},\ \underset{-}{u},\ \underset{+}{\rho' + \delta},\ \underset{-}{g},\ \underset{+}{\frac{\bar{w}^e}{\bar{p}^e}},\ \underset{+}{\delta},\ \underset{+}{r - g^e},\ \underset{-}{\alpha_w})$$

Equation (20) gives information about the direction in which the time derivative of the rate of unemployment will change when various disturbances occur. The disturbances may influence the time derivative in part directly and in part indirectly, through changed values of the actual acceptance wage rate and of the search activity of the unemployed households on the labor market.

The actual acceptance wage rate, $\hat{w}$, is defined as a certain proportion of the average wage level on the market. If the acceptance wage increases, a smaller proportion of the employment offers which the unemployed worker receives will lead to employments. The time derivative of unemployment will thus increase. An increase of unemployed workers' search activity in the labor market implies that the probability of an arbitrary unemployed worker getting into contact with a firm with vacancies will increase and this will reduce the growth of unemployment.

If the income-tax rate increases, the acceptance wage rates increase (note (15)), so that a smaller proportion of the wage offers received by the unemployed will lead to employment. The increased tax rate makes it less profitable than before to become employed and thus also leads to less search activity in the labor market by the unemployed, as in (13). Increased acceptance wages and decreased search activity in the labor market will both contribute to an increasing unemployment rate.

If unemployment compensation increases, acceptance wages will increase, while search activity in the labor market by the unemployed households decreases. This implies that the time derivative of the rate of unemployment will increase.

An increase of unemployment will be counteracted automatically by a decrease in the time derivative of the rate of unemployment. A greater number of unemployed will disappear from the labor force, and a greater number will become employed, as indicated in (19). These two effects are of a "mechanical" kind, and are independent of the behavior of firms and households. In addition, according to (9), the increased rate of unemployment will increase the rate of unexpected wage inflation and decrease the rate of unexpected price inflation. Aspiration wage rates will then fall at the same time as unemployed households' search activity in the labor market is intensified. These effects will also operate in the direction of decreasing unemployment.

An increase of the total subjective time preference of the households implies (inter alia through increases in consumer demand and labor supply) an increased rate of unexpected price inflation and a decreased rate of unexpected wage inflation. The actual acceptance wage rates will thereby increase, while the search activity of the unemployed in the labor market diminishes. The time derivative of the rate of unemployment will increase.[1)]

Increases in the average and marginal productivity of labor have the following effects. The rate of unexpected price inflation declines, the actual acceptance wage rates thus fall, and unemployed households' search activity in the labor market increases. Consequently, the time derivative of the rate of unemployment falls.

An increase of the expected real wage rate means increasing actual aspiration wage rates, so that unemployment tends to increase.

An increased turnover rate of customers and employees (measured by δ) implies that the individual firms try to increase their relative prices and decrease their relative wage rates. The rate of unexpected price inflation will thus increase, and the rate of unexpected wage inflation will decrease. This means higher acceptance wages and less search activity in the labor market, so that time derivative of unemployment increases.

An increase of the real rate of interest will induce firms to try to increase their relative prices and decrease their relative wage rates. The effects on the time derivative of the rate of unemployment will thus be positive.

If finally the supply of information in the labor market increases, the frequency of contacts between the unemployed

---

1) It should be noted that an increase of the rate of time preference implies a lower planned "saving" by the employed household. This lower "saving" takes the form of less search activity in the goods and labor markets, a greater number of working hours, and a higher present consumption. Contrary to the Keynesian analysis, a higher demand for consumer goods implies increasing unemployment figures.

and firms will increase. Ceteris paribus this means less unemployment. It should be stressed, however, that the increased supply of information must be exogenously explained, since, according to the simplified firm model, the firms are assumed not to be able to vary their supply of information through changes in the number of labor hours allocated to the "personnel" department. Also, the increased supply of information will generally influence household behavior, which may have further effects on the time derivative of the rate of unemployment through changes in aspiration wages and search activities.

3.3. Changes in inflationary expectations

The last differential equation to be discussed determines the development of inflationary expectations over time. Since the expected rate of price inflation is assumed to be equal to the expected rate of wage inflation, only one differential equation is necessary for describing those expectations. It is natural to assume that changes in inflationary expectations depend both on actual price inflation and actual wage inflation. Perhaps the simplest assumption is that of linear convexity. We further assume that the time derivative of the expected rate of inflation is a function of the gap between actual and expected rates of inflation:

$$(21) \quad \dot{g}^e = a[\alpha g_w + (1 - \alpha)\, g_p - g^e] \quad \text{where} \quad a \geq 0,\ 0 \leq \alpha \leq 1$$

The assumption that the time derivative of the expected rate of inflation is proportional to the gap between the actual and the expected rates of inflation implies that the expected rate of inflation at a certain point of time is a function of the actual rates of inflation at all previous points of time, with the older actual rates of inflation having progressively less influence on expectations.[1)]

The differential equation (21) represents the same type of expectation assumptions as those discussed in chapter II,

---

1) Cf. Allen (1960), pp. 24-25.

pp. 94 - 97. Hence the postulated expectations mechanism is subject to the same sort of critisism as was made in chapter II.

Since most of the discussion has been in terms of the rates of unexpected price inflation and wage inflation, it may be convenient to rewrite (21):

$$(22)\quad \dot{g}^e = a[\alpha(g_w - g_w^e) + (1-\alpha)(g_p - g_p^e)] \text{ where } g_w^e = g_p^e = g^e.$$

3.4. The development of the public debt

The public debt is of no importance for the present macro analysis, since it does not appear as an argument of any behavior equations. Financial developments only influence the inflation-unemployment process through the exogenously given real rate of interest. The differential equation of the public debt will therefore be stated without further comment:

$$(23)\quad \dot{S} = rS + (1-\sigma)\,\bar{w}K[zu - (1-u)s\int_0^\infty\int_0^\infty v\tau_w g(\pi, v)\, d\pi dv]$$

4. The Inflation Process and the Development of Unemployment when Expectations of Inflation are Exogenously Given

In this section the inflation process will be studied subject to the assumption that inflationary expectations are exogenously given. This assumption is well motivated if inflationary expectations change rather slowly or if we want to study the development of inflation in the short run. It should be pointed out, however, that even if inflationary expectations change slowly, the adjustment process will be affected.[1] A second possibility of motivating exogenously given inflationary expectations is that one wants to study a hypothetical

1) See the discussion in chapter II, pp.97-98.

process in which such expectations are stationary. Stationarity obtains, for example, if the differential equation (21) holds and the constant a, is equal to zero.

This section first discusses of the convergence properties of the dynamic model consisting of the differential equations for the expected real wage rate and the rate of unemployment. By way of illustration the dynamic process initiated by a general proportional wage increase caused by a collective agreement is analyzed. Then the comparative statics analysis is developed: how will the stationary solutions of the expected and actual real wage rates and the rate of unemployment be affected by various disturbances? The section is completed by a discussion of the properties, stability and significance of the Phillips surface.

4.1. Stability analysis of the development of the real wage rate and the rate of unemployment

In the instantaneous equilibrium model of section 2, it was described how the rates of unexpected price inflation and wage inflation were influenced by inter alia the real wage rate and the rate of unemployment. The corresponding analysis was also made with respect to unemployed households' search activity in the labor market and acceptance wages. The equilibrium values of the endogenous values of the instantanous equilibrium model in turn will influence the development of the real wage rate and the rate of unemployment, so that there exists a moving equilibrium of the rates of unexpected price inflation and wage inflation. The stationary solutions of these variables will be reached when the real wage rate and the rate of unemployment reach their stationary values, the quasi-equilibrium solution.[1]

The differential equation for the expected real wage rate, (17) and the rate of unemployment, (19), constitute the start-

---

[1] When not only the expected real wage rate and the rate of unemployment have reached their stationary values, but also the expected rate of inflation, full equilibrium is attained.

ing point for the following analysis. Equations (18) and (20) describe how the values of the two time derivatives are influenced by different disturbances. This system contains the effects of changes in the exogenous variables on the endogenous variables of the instantaneous equilibrium model and consequently on the time derivatives of the real wage rate and the rate of unemployment.

We start by analyzing the two phase curves determined by $\dot{\left(\frac{\bar{w}^e}{\bar{p}^e}\right)} = 0$ and $\dot{u} = 0$. Both phase curves have positive slopes:

$$\left.\frac{du}{d\left(\frac{\bar{w}^e}{\bar{p}^e}\right)}\right|_{\dot{\left(\frac{\bar{w}^e}{\bar{p}^e}\right)} = 0} = -\frac{\partial \dot{\left(\frac{\bar{w}^e}{\bar{p}^e}\right)}}{\partial \left(\frac{\bar{w}^e}{\bar{p}^e}\right)} \Bigg/ \frac{\partial \dot{\left(\frac{\bar{w}^e}{\bar{p}^e}\right)}}{\partial u} > 0$$

$$\left.\frac{du}{d\left(\frac{\bar{w}^e}{\bar{p}^e}\right)}\right|_{\dot{u} = 0} = -\frac{\partial \dot{u}}{\partial \left(\frac{\bar{w}^e}{\bar{p}^e}\right)} \Bigg/ \frac{\partial \dot{u}}{\partial u} > 0$$

It is not possible to draw any unique conclusions as to the relative slopes of the curves. However, one may approach this question indirectly, by studying the slope of $\dot{u} = 0$ in the limit, when u tends to both zero and one. When the rate of unemployment tends to zero, its time derivative will tend to a positive number:

$$\lim_{u \to 0} \dot{u} = \beta > 0$$

When the rate of unemployment tends to one, its time derivative will tend to a negative number:[1)]

---

1) Depending on the value of the expected real wage rate, the time derivative with respect to the unemployment ratio may equal zero when the relative rate of unemployment tends to unity. This will happen if a high enough expected real wage rate implies an acceptance wage which is equal to the maximum value of the distribution over relative wage rates.

$$\lim_{u \to 1} \dot{u} = - u \int_{0}^{\infty} \int_{\hat{w}}^{\infty} \hat{f}(v)\, g(\pi)\, \varepsilon_{w}(\tau'_{sw}, a_{w})\, d\pi dv < 0$$

Which means that the phase curve $\dot{u} = 0$ can not coincide with the two limits $u = 0$ and $u = 1$. Unfortunately, it is not possible to derive any corresponding information concerning the time derivative of the expected real wage rate.

The available information about the two phase curves is summed up in figure 1. As usual, the arrows indicate the forces acting off the two phase curves.

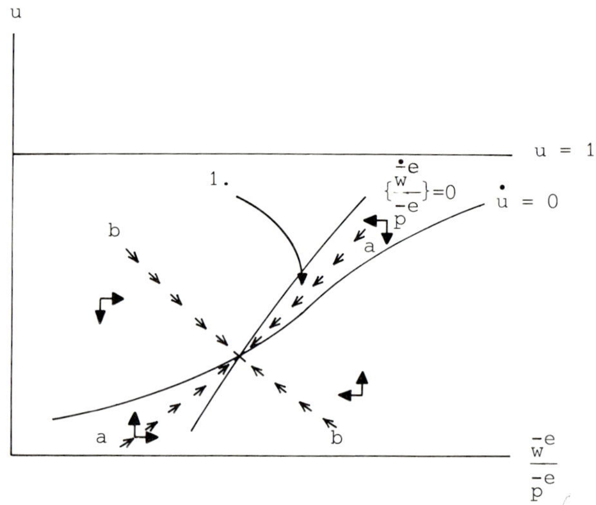

Fig. VI:1. The dynamics of the (expected) real wage rate and the rate of unemployment.

In figure 1, the phase curve $\dot{u} = 0$ has been depicted with a more level slope than that of $(\frac{\dot{\bar{w}}^e}{\bar{p}^e}) = 0$, which implies stability. This is not necessary, of course,[1] but the assymptotic properties of the first curve make it probable in any case that there exists some point of intersection between the two curves which has this property, although there may exist several points of intersection. However, in

---

1) In the case where the rate of unexpected price inflation is exogenously determined and where simpler assumptions are made with respect to the behavior of the unemployed, it is possible to show that the system is stable. Cf. Mortensen (1970), pp. 208-209.

the following discussion it will be assumed that there exists only one point of intersection.

The two main trajectories, a-a and b-b, are depicted in the figure. The first of these trajectories, which has a positive slope, is stable and functions as a "turnpike", while the second trajectory is unstable. Only in cases in which the two phase variables are initially on the trajectory b-b will the expected real wage rate and the rate of unemployment follow that trajectory towards the stationary solution. Otherwise, the phase variables will approach a-a and then follow that trajectory towards the stationary solution.

If initially the economy is in point 1 in figure 1 -- i.e., if the initial expected real wage rate coincides with its stationary value -- while the rate of unemployment is higher than is compatible with stationary conditions, the expected real wage rate will increase initially. When the phase curve for the expected real wage rate has been passed, it will decrease again towards its stationary value. On the other hand, the rate of unemployment will decrease continually towards its stationary value.

It is interesting to note that the stable main trajectory a-a implies that the (expected) real wage rate will increase as the rate of unemployment increases. Recently, Herschel Grossman has criticized this result of the "new" theory of inflation and unemployment on empirical grounds.[1] Unfortunately, however, Grossman depicts the relation between the real wage rate and the rate of unemployment in the "new" theory as a statical result based on an assumption about a given connection between the real wage rate and the marginal

---

1) Grossman refers to Kuh (1966) and Bodkin (1969). It should be pointed out that other investigations support the Keynesian hypothesis; cf. Pen (1971), p. 217.

productivity of labor.[1)]

The stability analysis may also be used to investigate the effects of autonomous cost increases. In spite of the fact that labor unions and collective bargaining do not constitute any element of the present analysis, it is still possible to analyze the effects of these phenomena ad hoc.

Assume therefore that the firms are free to set their wage rates and that the development in the labor market is determined by the factors which have been discussed above. Now and then the average wage level is pushed upwards, however. This may be the outcome of a collective bargain which stipulates that all firms have to increase their wage rates with the same percentage, equal for all firms. This increase of wage rates will leave the distribution over relative wage rates unaffected, at the same time that all firms and households know the exact amount of the wage increase. Consequently, not only will the actual wage level increase according to the agreed percentage, but the expected real wage rate will also increase by the same percentage.

Starting from an initial quasi-equilibrium, the result of the collective agreement will be a one-time increase in the actual and expected real wage rate. The increase of the expected real wage rate implies a higher rate of price increase [note (9)], while the rate of wage increase (wage

---

1) Grossman's survey of the theory of the Phillips curve based on search theory is valuable since it is the first (published) attempt to discuss the possibilities of a simultaneous analysis of the process of price inflation and wage inflation. Unfortunately, there is no mention in his article of the fact that the firms try to reach a certain relative position in comparison to their competitors when they fix their prices and wage rates. This means that it is impossible to follow Grossman's procedure of discussing the pricing and wage setting of the firms in terms of static monopoly theory. Moreover, according to the "new" theory, not only households but also firms have erroneous expectations about the current price and wage level. Cf. Mortensen (1970a).

drift) initially is unchanged. This in turn implies that the rate of unemployment will start to increase, since the acceptance wages of the unemployed will increase when the rate of unexpected price inflation increases. The process is illustrated in figure 2:

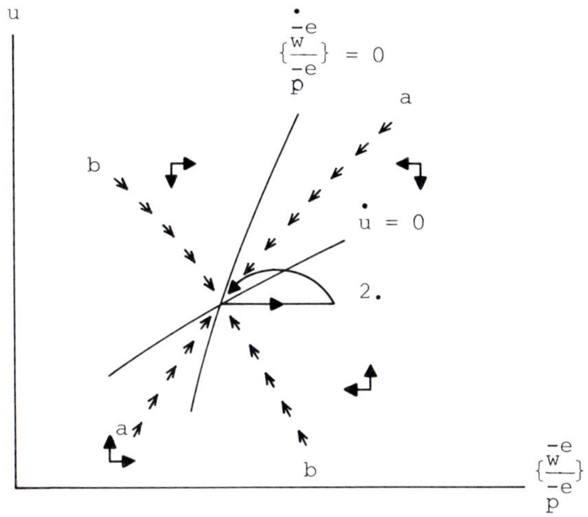

Fig. VI:2. The dynamic effects on the (expected) real wage rate and the rate of unemployment of collective bargaining.

In figure 2, the quasi-equilibrium is denoted by point 1. Here the time derivatives of the rate of unemployment and the actual and expected real wage rates are equal to zero. As a result of the collective agreements, the expected real wage rate will increase from point 1 to point 2. From this point, the expected real wage rate will successively fall back to its original position. Initially, the rate of unemployment will increase. When the phase curve for the relative rate of unemployment is passed, $\dot{u}$ is equal to zero. After that point the rate of unemployment will fall back to its stationary value. Intermittent increases in wage rates due to collective agreement may thus start a cyclical process in which the real wage rate is at its peak at the beginning of the recession (when the rate of unemployment starts to increase).

If instead the average wage rate is continually pushed upwards by collective measures, it has the same effect as if the phase curve for the real wage rate in figure 2 were shifted to the right. This in turn means that the stronger the "cost component" in wage setting, the higher the quasi-equilibrium real wage rate will be, but in addition the rate of unemployment will also be higher. Starting from (9) we note further that the unexpected rate of price inflation will increase. Since both the new quasi-equilibrium and the old one imply that the unexpected rates of price and wage inflation are equal, the rates of price inflation and wage inflation will increase by the same percentage.

4.2. Quasi-equilibrium and comparative statics

The stationary solutions for the real wage rate[1] and the rate of unemployment do not constitute a complete equilibrium, since a stationary real wage rate may coincide with faulty expectations of the rates of price and wage inflation. What is required for quasi-equilibrium is merely that the two rates of unexpected inflation balance. It may therefore be convenient to define a quasi-equilibrium as a situation in which the rate of unemployment is constant and the rates of unexpected price and wage inflation balance, so that the real wage rate is constant. Quasi-equilibrium is thus compatible with disequilibrium in the goods and labor markets in the sense that firms and households have faulty expectations with respect to the average price and wage levels and therefore act in a manner different from the way they would with correct information. Quasi-equilibrium in this sense is analogous to Bent Hansen's notion of equasi-equilibrium. It should be emphasized, however, that the common conception is applied to quite different kinds of inflation models.

By total differentiation of equations (18) and (20), the following expression for the effects on the quasi-equilibrium values of different disturbances is obtained:

---

1) Observe that the stationary solutions of the actual and expected real wage rate coincide; note equations (16) and (17).

$$(24) \quad \begin{pmatrix} d\left(\frac{\bar{w}^e}{\bar{p}^e}\right) \\ \\ du \end{pmatrix} = -\frac{1}{D}\begin{pmatrix} \frac{\partial \dot{u}}{\partial u} & -\frac{\partial \overset{\bullet}{\left(\frac{\bar{w}^e}{\bar{p}^e}\right)}}{\partial u} \\ \\ -\frac{\partial \dot{u}}{\partial \left(\frac{\bar{w}^e}{\bar{p}^e}\right)} & \frac{\partial \overset{\bullet}{\left(\frac{\bar{w}^e}{\bar{p}^e}\right)}}{\partial \left(\frac{\bar{w}^e}{\bar{p}^e}\right)} \end{pmatrix} \begin{pmatrix} \frac{\partial \overset{\bullet}{\left(\frac{\bar{w}^e}{\bar{p}^e}\right)}}{\partial \xi} \\ \\ \frac{\partial \dot{u}}{\partial \xi} \end{pmatrix} d\xi$$

$$\text{where} \quad D = \underset{-}{\frac{\partial \overset{\bullet}{\left(\frac{\bar{w}^e}{\bar{p}^e}\right)}}{\partial \left(\frac{\bar{w}^e}{\bar{p}^e}\right)}} \; \underset{-}{\frac{\partial \dot{u}}{\partial u}} - \underset{+}{\frac{\partial \overset{\bullet}{\left(\frac{\bar{w}^e}{\bar{p}^e}\right)}}{\partial u}} \; \underset{+}{\frac{\partial \dot{u}}{\partial \left(\frac{\bar{w}^e}{\bar{p}^e}\right)}} > 0$$

The sign of the determinant D is given subject to the assumption that the slope of the phase curve of the expected real wage rate is steeper than that of the rate of unemployment, i.e., that the quasi-equilibrium is stable. ξ is an arbitrary shift variable. By substitution of the exogenous variables in (24), the following comparative-static results are obtained:

$$(25) \quad \begin{aligned} \frac{\bar{w}^e}{\bar{p}^e} &= \frac{\bar{w}^e}{\bar{p}^e}(\underset{+}{s}, \underset{?}{z}, \underset{?}{\rho' + \delta}, \underset{?}{g}, \underset{?}{\delta}, \underset{?}{r-g^e}, \underset{-}{h_w}, \underset{+}{h_p}, \underset{-}{a_w}) \\ u &= u(\underset{+}{s}, \underset{?}{z}, \underset{?}{\rho' + \delta}, \underset{?}{g}, \underset{?}{\delta}, \underset{?}{r-g^e}, \underset{-}{h_w}, \underset{+}{h_p}, \underset{-}{a_w}) \end{aligned}$$

As seen from (25), a relatively large number of the effects of various disturbances on the quasi-equilibrium values of the expected real wage rate and the rate of unemployment are uncertain. It may therefore be of some interest to examine more closely the effects of some of the disturbances. We start with the effects of an increase in the income-tax rate.

According to equation (9) the effects of an increased income-tax rate on the rates of unexpected price inflation and wage inflation are negative. Assuming that the two rates of inflation increase by the same amount, the expected real wage rate initially will be unaffected by this disturbance, which means that the phase curve for the real wage rate does not shift when the tax rate changes. According to equation (15), acceptance wages will increase when the income-tax rate increases. This means that the rate of unemployment will start to increase, since a smaller proportion than before of the contacts between unemployed and firms will lead to employment. Geometrically, the phase curve will shift upwards. The effects of the increased income-tax rate are summarized in figure 3:

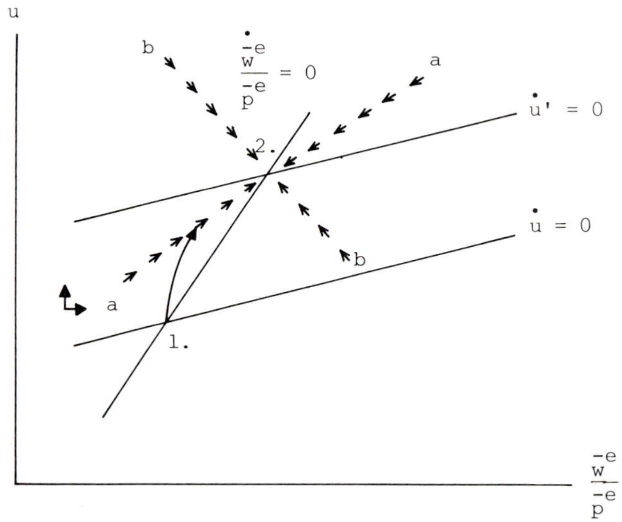

Fig. VI:3. The dynamic effects of an increased income-tax rate on the (expected) real wage rate and the rate of unemployment.

In figure 3, the effect of the disturbance is a shift upwards of the phase curve for the rate of unemployment, $\dot{u}$, which shifts upwards to $\dot{u}'$. The original quasi-equilibrium is indicated by point 1. When the disturbance occurs, and the phase curve for the rate of unemployment shifts upwards, the rate of unemployment and the real wage rate will approach the main trajectory a-a on their way towards the new quasi equilibrium position 2. Initially, the expected real wage rate will not change, but as the rate of unemployment increases, the real wage rate will increase successively. When the new quasi-equilibrium has been reached, the real wage rate and the rate of unemployment become constant once again.

It is impossible to draw any clear conclusion as to the effects on the two rates of inflation when the new quasi-equilibrium has been reached. According to equations (9), the direct effect of the tax increase is to decrease the rates of unexpected inflation. The increased rate of unemployment will work in the same direction with respect to price increases, but it is counteracted by the increased real wage rate, which tends to increase the rate of unexpected price inflation. Turning to the total effect on the rate of unexpected wage inflation, the direct effect of the tax increase is negative, whereas the effect through the increased rate of unemployment is positive. However, if the direct effect dominates, the rates of inflation will decrease.

What will happen to the level of activity in the economy when the income-tax rate increases? Starting from (11), we note that the direct effect is uncertain, and we assume that it is equal to zero. The increased real wage rate implies that the average supply of labor will decrease, which means that total goods production will decrease for this reason. The increased rate of unemployment means first that the number of employees will decrease, which in itself means a lower goods production. But the increased rate of unemployment will indirectly increase the supply of labor per employee. As a result of these effects, the net effect on total goods production is uncertain, but it is likely that it will be negative. Also compare the case when the rate of unemployment increases very much; then it is certain that the total number of labor hours, and thus goods production, will decrease.

The next disturbance to be analyzed is an increase in unemployment compensation or more precisely, the ratio of the expected average wage rate of the market which the unemployment compensation is based on. From (9) it appears that this will lead to an increase in the rate of unexpected price inflation and a decrease in the rate of unexpected wage inflation. This in turn means that the real wage rate shifts inwards.

At the same time that this happens, the search activity in the labor market of the unemployed households will decrease due to (13), and the aspiration wages will increase due to (15). Thus the rate of unemployment will start to increase and the phase curve for the rate of unemployment will shift upwards, as in figure 4.

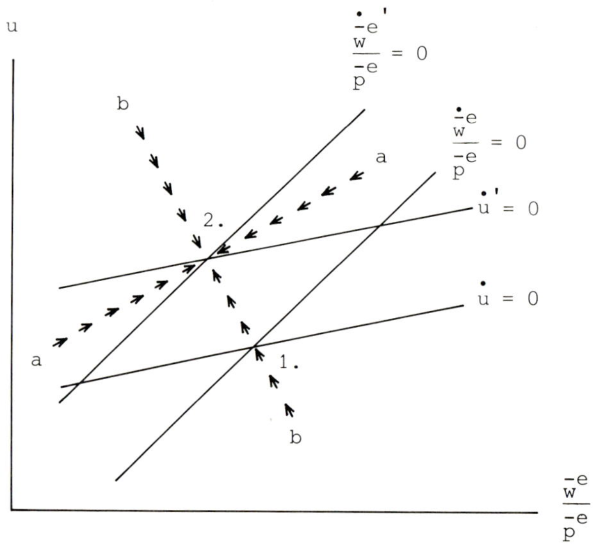

Fig. VI:4. The dynamic effects of an increase in unemployment compensation.

Figure 4 has been drawn so that the original quasi-equilibrium (point 1) happens to be situated on the unstable main trajectory b-b to the new quasi-equilibrium, which implies that this trajectory will be followed during the convergence towards the new equilibrium at point 2. If the original equilibrium had been situated somewhere off the main trajectory b-b, the trajectory of convergence would instead have implied a deviation away from b-b and a convergence towards the new equilibrium through a successive approach to the stable trajectory a-a.

The comparative-static results depend on the relative shifts of the two phase curves. The more the phase curve for the relative rate of unemployment shifts, the greater the tendency for unemployment <u>and</u> the real wage rate to increase. The more the phase curve for the expected real wage rate shifts, the greater the tendency for the real wage rate <u>and</u> the rate of unemployment to decrease. If the immediate dynamic tendencies dominate, unemployment will increase and the real wage rate will fall.

What are the effects of the increased unemployment compensation on the aggregate production volume? Starting from the assumption that the immediate dynamic tendencies dominate (so that the quasi-equilibrium value of the real wage rate decreases and the rate of unemployment increases), it appears from (11) that the direct effect on the total number of labor hours per household, and thus on aggregate goods production, will be negative. The indirect effects are uncertain. The decreased real wage rate implies an increased supply of labor. The increased rate of unemployment will directly decrease the number of labor hours per household, but the average supply of labor per employee will increase. To conclude, the effect on "GNP" of increased unemployment compensation is uncertain; it is possible, however, that aggregate production <u>falls</u>.

This result is contrary to what one would expect from the "traditional" orientation. To explain the difference, it is necessary to clarify the basic differences between the models. In the present case, effects on total production are not generated through changes in aggregate demand with a fixed price system. Instead, the supply of labor of the employed, and thus goods production, are influenced by variations in the rates of unexpected price inflation and wage inflation. Moreover, it is important to stress the important role the acceptance wage rate plays in determining the development of unemployment. If unemployment compensation increases, it will be less profitable than before to accept an employment offer.

The minimum requirements for accepting an offer will thus increase, which means that the number of new hirings will fall. In Keynesian theory it is instead the difficulty of obtaining a job which varies. An increase of unemployment compensation will increase disposable incomes and thus aggregate demand for goods. The firms then wish to increase their goods production, the derived demand for labor will increase, and unemployment will decline.

An important conclusion which may be drawn is that the "new" type of inflation and unemployment theory does not generate any multiplier processes in the traditional sense. On the contrary, the direction of the effects may be contrary to that expected from Keynesian theory. Basically, this has to do with the fact that the present model is an equilibrium model in the sense that there does not exist any rationing in the goods or labor markets.[1)] Disequilibrium instead manifests itself in rates of price and wage inflation which are different from those expected by firms and households.

An increase of the households' total subjective time preference will have the same immediate effect on the real wage rate and the rate of unemployment as if the unemployment compensation increases. The phase curve of the expected real wage rate will shift inwards and the phase curve of the rate of unemployment will shift upwards. This implies that the effects on the stationary values of the real wage rate and the rate of unemployment will be the same in principle as in the previous case. Correspondingly, the new quasi-equilibrium will depend on the relative shifts of the two phase curves. Exactly the same reasoning may be made with respect to increases in the "death probability" and the real rate of interest.

If instead the average and marginal productivity of labor increases, the immediate dynamic tendencies are that the real wage rate increases and that the rate of unemploy-

---

1) In a sense unemployment means that there exists rationing in the labor market. On the other hand, the employed workers are free to vary their supply of labor hours. For multiplier processes to emerge, there has to be quantity restrictions on at least two markets, the labor market and the goods market.

ment falls. The ultimate effect on the quasi-equilibrium is uncertain, since it depends on the relative shifts of the phase curves. "Normally" one would expect the stationary real wage rate to increase and the rate of unemployment to fall.

The next two disturbances are interesting, since they make possible comparisons with Bent Hansen's discussion of the value of the real wage rate at quasi-equilibrium.

If the observation lag in the labor market, h_w, is extended, the rate of unexpected wage inflation will decrease, given the expected relative wage rates.[1] Compare equation (9). Since it is precisely the expected relative wage rates which influence the behavior of the households and firms, this disturbance will merely result in a lower rate of actual wage inflation. This in turn implies that the real wage rate will start to fall. Thus the phase curve of the expected real wage rate will shift inwards, as in figure 5.

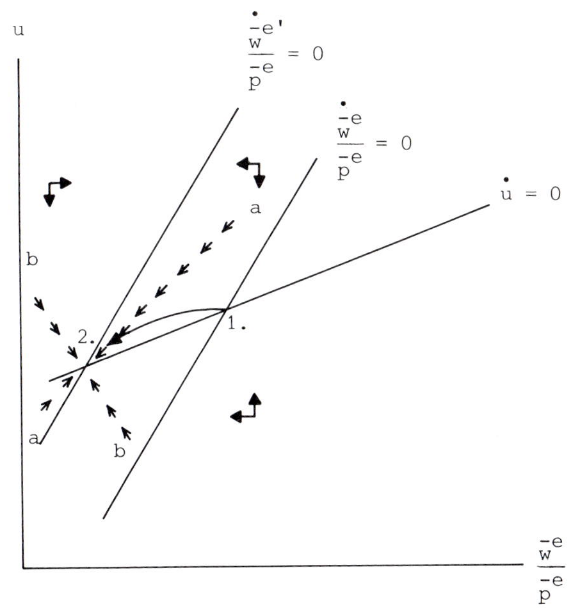

Fig. VI:5. The dynamic effects of an increased observation lag in the labor market.

[1] One possible reason for the extended observation lag may be increased labor market frictions. If this is the case, the frequency of contacts between job seekers and firms will fall and thus directly influence the rate of unemployment in a positive direction.

The real wage rate and the rate of unemployment follow the trajectory from the original quasi-equilibrium (point 1), to the new quasi equilibrium (point 2). Initially, the rate of unemployment is constant (the starting point is on the phase curve $\dot{u} = 0$), while the real wage rate falls. After a while the rate of unemployment will also start to fall at the same time as the trajectory of adjustment will coincide more and more with the main trajectory a-a. The final result will be that both the real wage rate and the rate of unemployment will fall as a consequence of the longer observation lag in the labor market. In the new quasi-equilibrium the rates of price inflation and wage inflation will be lower than before; note (9).

A longer observation lag in the labor market could be compared to a lower rate of wage increase, given the excess demand for labor, in Hansen's analysis. This will also decrease the quasi-equilibrium value of the real wage rate. However, the economic significance of a lower rate of wage increase, given the excess demand for labor, is unclear.

If instead the observation lag in the goods market is extended, the real wage rate increases initially, while the rate of unemployment does not change. The final result will be both a higher rate of unemployment and a higher real wage rate. Also in this case the parallel to Hansen's analysis is evident: given the excess demand for goods the rate of price increase diminishes.

The last disturbance to be analyzed is an increase of the supply of information in the labor market, a_w.[1] It should be observed that since the macro analysis builds on the simplified firm model, this disturbance must be explained exogenously. One possibility is that the government institutes a labor exchange, or, if one already exists, increases its resources.

The increased supply of information in the labor market implies that the probability of contacts between firms and

---

[1] It should be noted that the increased supply of information in the labor market may be associated with a decrease of the information lag in the same market. In that case, the rate of unexpected wage inflation and the time derivative of the expected real wage rate will be influenced directly by the disturbance.

households increases on the labor market. If neither firm nor household behavior is directly influenced by this, the disturbance will primarily imply a falling rate of unemployment. The phase curve for the rate of unemployment will shift downwards, while the phase curve for the expected real wage rate is unaffected, as in figure 6.

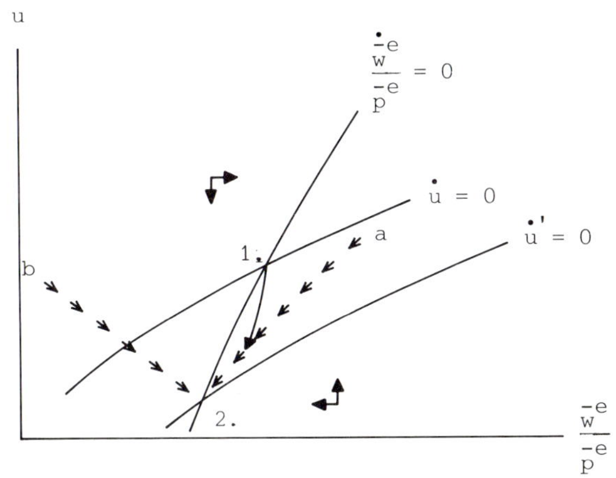

Fig. VI:6. The dynamic effects of an increase of the supply of information in the labor market.

From figure 6 it appears that unemployment will fall initially, while the real wage rate is unaffected. After a while, when employment has increased, the real wage rate will start falling. The adjustment trajectory will successively close in on the main trajectory a-a. The final quasi-equilibrium implies a lower rate of unemployment, but at the same time lower actual and expected real wage rates.

At quasi-equilibrium, the actual rate of price inflation is equal to the actual rate of wage inflation. If we know the quasi-equilibrium values of the real wage rate and the rate of unemployment, it is possible to substitute them into equations (9), and in that way examine how the two unexpected rates of inflation are influenced by various disturbances. For example, it appears from (9) that the direct effect of an increased income-tax rate is to decrease the rates of price and wage inflation. However, in the new quasi-equilibrium this disturbance has led to a higher real wage rate and a higher rate of unemployment. The effects on the two rates of inflation which are transmitted via the changed values of the phase variables are uncertain (recall the discussion on page 331).

The corresponding reasoning may be made with respect to the other disturbances. It thus appears that only for an increase in the length of the observation lag on the labor market and for the supply of information on the labor market are the effects on the two rates of inflation uniquely determined. In both cases the rates of inflation will decrease.

If we further assume that the immediate dynamic tendencies caused by different disturbances remain when the new quasi-equilibrium has been reached, the effects of an increase in the income-tax rate, the average and marginal productivity of labor, and the observation lag on the goods market, are determined. Also in these cases the actual and unexpected rates of price and wage inflation will fall.

What conclusion should be drawn from the difficulties of uniquely determining the effects of different disturbances on the rates of price and wage inflation? Perhaps the most immediate observation is that the quasi-equilibrium model contains negative feedback mechanisms which tend to counteract the instantaneous effects on the rates of unexpected price inflation and wage inflation. These mechanisms work through changed values of the expected real wage rate and the rate of unemployment.

4.3. The Phillips surface

The discovery that the "new" microeconomics had macro implications, more specifically that it was possible to derive analytically a relationship between the rate of wage inflation and the rate of unemployment, contributed a great deal to the interest in the new theory. In the derivations of the Phillips curve referred to in chapter II, the starting point was a partial analysis of the labor market. In the following, the possibilities of deriving a relationship of the Phillips type from a simultaneous analysis of the labor and goods markets will be discussed.

The analytical derivations of the Phillips curve by Holt, Phelps, and Mortensen all constituted a derivation of one of the structural equations of the economy. In the case of Holt and Mortensen one could speak of a dynamic supply curve for labor, where the supply is in terms of not the number of labor hours but the number of employees, and where increases in the rate of unexpected wage inflation tempt marginal unemployed workers to accept employment offers. In the case of Phelps' analysis, the Phillips curve is derived from an aggregated wage determination function, where variations in the number of vacancies and the number of unemployed workers influence the expected relative wage rates of the individual firms in such a way that the postulated negative relationships between the relative rate of unemployment and its time derivative and the unexpected rate of wage inflation are generated.

The Phillips curve does not constitute a complete description of the labor market, however. If it is derived from the supply side, it must be completed with a description of the wage determination process and firms' demand for labor. Dale Mortensen was the first to take this important step.

In Mortensen's analysis the Phillips curve is simply described by the differential equation for the development of unemployment over time.[1)] If its time derivative is put equal to zero, different points on the Phillips curve are generated when the rate of wage inflation varies. If instead the time derivative is different from zero, the dynamic loops around the Phillips curve are generated.

In the present two-market analysis, the relation between inflation and unemployment may be analyzed in the same way. The Phillips relationship is thus represented by the differential equation for the rate of unemployment.

---

1) Cf. Mortensen (1970a),equation (77).

$$(19)\quad \dot{u} = (1-u)\,\delta - u \int_{0}^{\infty}\int_{\hat{w}}^{\infty} \hat{f}(v)\, g(\pi)\, \varepsilon_w(\tau'_{sw}, a_w)\, d\pi dv$$

where

$$(12)\quad \tau'_{sw} = \underset{\quad\;\, - \qquad + \quad\; - \;\; -}{\tau'_{sw}\left(p\tilde{p}^e, \frac{\bar{w}^e}{\bar{p}^e}, s, z\right)}$$

$$(14)\quad \hat{w} = \frac{1}{\tilde{w}^e}\, \underset{\qquad + \qquad\; + \;\; +}{\hat{w}^e(p\tilde{p}^e, s, z)}$$

$$\tilde{p}^e = e^{h_p(g_p - g_p^e)}$$

$$\tilde{w}^e = e^{h_w(g_w - g_w^e)}$$

It should be noted that the rates of unexpected price inflation and wage inflation are exogenously given in the "model" describing the Phillips relationship. If (19) is differentiated with respect to these two variables and with respect to the rate of unemployment, the following equation is obtained:

$$(26)\quad \dot{u} = \underset{\;\;\; - \qquad\;\; + \qquad\qquad -}{\dot{u}(u, g_p - g_p^e, g_w - g_w^e)}$$

The first partial derivative of (26) implies that the higher the rate of unemployment, the faster unemployment will fall. This is the negative feedback between the rate of unemployment and its time derivative postulated by Holt. The second partial derivative implies that the higher the rate of unexpected price inflation, the faster the rate of unemployment will increase,which implies a clockwise loop around the Phillips curve in the price-increase, unemployment plane. The last partial derivative implies that the higher the rate of unexpected wage inflation, the faster the rate of unemployment will fall. The geometrical image of this is the counterclockwise loop in the wage-increase, unemployment plane.

By putting the time derivative for the rate of unemployment in (26) equal to zero, we get a positive relationship between the rate of unemployment and the rate of unexpected price inflation and a negative relationship between the rate of unemployment and the unexpected rate of wage inflation:

$$(27) \quad u = u(\underset{+}{g_p - g_p^e}, \underset{-}{g_w - g_w^e})$$

Equation (27) describes the Phillips surface, the relationship between the rate of unemployment and the unexpected rates of price and wage inflation. The Phillips curve is a special case of this more general concept. Its geometrical image is the projection of the Phillips surface on the unemployment, rate-of-wage-inflation plane. The significance of the Phillips surface is that it is impossible outside quasi-equilibrium to speak of a unique relationship between inflation and unemployment. An increased rate of inflation may equally well be associated with a falling or increasing rate of unemployment. What happens depends on the development of the unexpected rate of price inflation in comparison to the unexpected rate of wage inflation. Nor is a stable Phillips curve to be expected. Generally, the Phillips curve as a projection on the unemployment, unexpected rate-of-wage-inflation plane would shift when the rate of price inflation changes. A further argument against a stable Phillips curve -- expressing the rate of unemployment as a function of the <u>actual</u> rate of wage inflation -- is that shifts in inflationary expectations generally will shift the Phillips curve by the same amount.

Equations (26) and (27) are depicted geometrically in figure 7. Figure 7a contains the projection of the Phillips surface on the unemployment, actual-rate-of-price-inflation plane, while figure 7b contains the projection on the unemployment, actual-rate-of-wage-inflation plane (the usual Phillips curve).

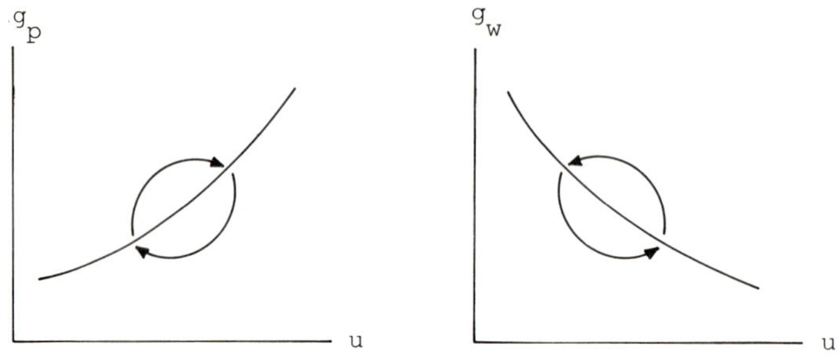

Fig. VI:7a. The dynamic movement around the projection of the Phillips surface on the unemployment, price inflation-plane.

Fig. VI:7b. The dynamic movement around the projection of the Phillips surface on the unemployment, wage inflation-plane.

In figures 7a and 7b the postulated dynamic movements around the Phillips curves have been depicted. Note that an increase in the expected rate of inflation will shift the two Phillips curves upwards by the same amount.

There remains an important question to answer. What empirical relationship does the theory predict? The Phillips surface is only one of the structural equations of the dynamic macroeconomic model. To close the model, information is also needed concerning the determinants of the unexpected rates of price and wage inflation. It should be stressed, however, that the additional information is only necessary for explaining the dynamic movement in time of the rate of unemployment and the unexpected rates of price and wage inflation. Equations (19), (12), (14), and the relationships between the expected relative prices, relative wage rates, and the unexpected rates of price and wage inflation will be fulfilled at all times. This implies that if we know the two rates of unexpected inflation at a certain point of time, (19) will indicate how much unemployment will increase. On the other hand, the Phillips relationship does not give any information about the development of the rates of inflation. Expressed in another way, the Phillips surface supplies information about the time derivative of the rate of unemployment, given the rates of unexpected price and wage inflation. But it only gives partial information about which point on (or around) the Phillips surface will be reached in the next moment. For that a complete dynamic model of the type which was developed in sections 3 and 4.1-4.2 is needed.

This reasoning further implies a positive correlation between the rate of price inflation and the rate of unemployment. Moreover, a negative association between the rate of wage inflation and the rate of unemployment is predicted. These relationships hold at given inflationary expectations and given the values of the other exogenous variables. On the other hand, the theory does not immediately imply that the dynamic motion around the Phillips surface should follow a certain trajectory. Given the rate of unemployment and the unexpected rates of wage and price inflation, we can be sure of the direction of change of the rate of unemployment. But differential equations for the two rates of inflation are also needed in order to fully trace the development of the system.[1)]

Finally it should be stressed that the Phillips surface is defined for given parameter values. If the economy is subject to disturbances which in turn generate dynamic adjustment processes, the scatter of points which is obtained will only have the postulated property if the differential equation for the rate of unemployment is left unaffected. On the other hand, if the parameters which affect the differential equation (19) are changed, the dynamic adjustment generally will not be described by (26) and (27). This is due to the fact that the Phillips surface should be interpreted as the geometrical image of one of the structural equations of the system.

---

1) Since the rates of unexpected price inflation and wage inflation are functions of the rate of unemployment and the expected real wage rate, it is necessary in practice to know the differential equation for the expected real wage rate. To the extent that inflationary expectations are affected by the actual rates of price and wage inflation, it is also necessary to know the differential equation for the expected rate of inflation.

5. The Expected Rate of Inflation and the Long Run Possibilities of Stabilization Policy

Up to this point, inflationary expectations have been assumed exogenously given. Thus it was not necessary to take into consideration that changes in the actual rates of price and wage inflation may influence inflationary expectations and hence the future inflationary development.[1)]

There are several motives for introducing the expected rate of inflation as an endogenous element in the analysis. First, it is reasonable to assume that inflationary expectations really are affected by experiences of inflation, and that changed inflationary expectations play an important role in the planning of households and firms.

Second, the expected rate of inflation is one possible explanation of cost inflation. If by cost inflation is meant the rate of inflation which appears when the economy is in a state of generalized general equilibrium[2)] (inter alia implying a certain amount of "natural" unemployment), there is no rational neoclassical explanation of cost inflation.[3)] However, if the economic agents adjust their price setting and other planning to an expected rate of inflation, and that rate is actually realized, cost inflation is compatible with general equilibrium. The nominal rate of interest then must be completely adjusted to inflation so that the real rate of interest is constant.

The conditions for a long-run equilibrium are that the rates of unexpected price and wage inflation should both be equal to zero and that the rate of unemployment should be constant over time. If these conditions are fulfilled, there

---

1) It should be noted that the quasi-equilibrium does not imply that the actual rates of price and wage inflation are equal to the expected rates. It only implies that the gaps between actual and expected rates of inflation are equal in all markets.

2) In a model where financial markets are essential, increased monetary prices must be backed up by a monetary expansion.

3) Cost inflation as the outcome of an oligopolistic game between labor and employer organizations and, possibly, the government, is then excluded.

is in addition quasi-equilibrium, but the converse of course does not hold.

Starting from equations (9), (12), (14), and (19), the conditions for a long run equilibrium may be written in the following way:[1)]

$$
\begin{aligned}
1 &= \tilde{p}^e(\underset{-}{s},\ \underset{+}{z},\ \underset{-}{u},\ \underset{+}{\rho' + \delta},\ \underset{-}{g},\ \underset{+}{\tfrac{\bar{w}}{p}},\ \underset{+}{\delta},\ \underset{+}{r - g^e}) \\
1 &= \tilde{w}^e(\underset{-}{s},\ \underset{-}{z},\ \underset{+}{u},\ \underset{-}{\rho' + \delta},\ \underset{o}{g},\ \underset{o}{\tfrac{\bar{w}}{p}},\ \underset{-}{\delta},\ \underset{-}{r - g^e}) \\
\tau'_{sw} &= \tau'_{sw}(\underset{-}{p},\ \underset{+}{\tfrac{\bar{w}}{p}},\ \underset{-}{s},\ \underset{-}{z}) \\
\hat{w} &= \hat{w}(\underset{+}{p},\ \underset{+}{s},\ \underset{+}{z}) \\
0 &= (1-u)\,\delta - u \int_0^\infty \int_{\hat{w}}^\infty \hat{f}(v)\, g(\pi)\, \varepsilon_w(\tau'_{sw}, a_w)\, d\pi\, dv
\end{aligned}
\tag{28}
$$

The system of equations (28) contains three equilibrium conditions. The two first equations stipulate that the unexpected rates of price and wage inflation should equal zero.[2)] The last equation implies that the time derivative of the rate of unemployment should be equal to zero.

It immediately appears that if there exists a solution to the system (28), then the same solution exists for each expected rate of inflation, g^e. The only variable affected by the level of a completely predicted inflation process is the nominal rate of interest, r. The nominal rate of interest must therefore be adjusted so that the real rate of interest remains unaffected.

---

1) Note that when the unexpected rates of price and wage inflation are put identically equal to zero, there is no longer any need for a simultaneous solution for these inflation rates.

2) The time derivative of the expected rate of inflation is then equal to zero; note (22).

The neutrality of the long-run equilibrium with respect to changes in the expected rate of inflation may be illustrated in the following way. Assume that the government wishes to decrease the rate of inflation and that the economy to start with is in a long-run equilibrium. By decreasing the actual rates of price and wage inflation, it is possible for the government to decrease successively the inflationary expectations of the households and the firms, as in equation (22).[1)] This may be done through suitable changes in the income-tax rate, the unemployment compensation, and the real rate of interest so that the rates of price and wage increase are decreased in a parallel fashion at the same time as the rate of unemployment is unchanged. After a while, when the inflationary expectations have been pressed down to the extent that was planned, the control variables of the government should revert to their original values. This is due to the fact that this constellation of parameters is compatible with a long-run equilibrium.

Given that the government (central bank) varies the real rate of interest so that the conditions for a long run equilibrium are fulfilled, the system of equations (28) determines the values of three endogenous variables: the rate of unemployment, the real wage rate, and the real rate of interest. The values of these variables are independent of the rate of inflation as long as it is fully expected. We may thus speak of the natural rate of unemployment, the natural real wage rate, and the natural real rate of interest in the sense that these values of the variables solve the equilibrium model, independent of the amount of inflation. Of course, the

---

1) In the case that a fully expected inflation is valued negatively (e.g. on account of implying less monetary efficiency) there may exist an optimal rate of a fully expected inflation. The higher the social rate of time discount, the higher the optimum rate of inflation will be. If the actual rate of inflation deviates from the long run optimum, there will be an optimal trajectory towards the stationary optimum. The theory of optimal intertemporal inflation -- unemployment policy has been developed by Edmund Phelps, cf. Phelps (1967) and (1972).

values of the "natural" rates depend on the exogenous variables.

By total differentiation of the system (28) it is possible to obtain the effects of different disturbances on the "natural" rate of unemployment, real wage rate, and real rate of interest. Subject to the assumption that the effect on the search activity on the labor market of the unemployed households is negligible, the following comparative-static results are obtained:

$$u^* = u^*(\underset{+}{s},\ \underset{+}{z},\ \underset{o}{\rho' + \delta},\ \underset{o}{g},\ \underset{+}{\delta},\ \underset{-}{a_w})$$

$$(29)\qquad \frac{\bar{w}^*}{\bar{p}} = \frac{\bar{w}^*}{\bar{p}}(\underset{?}{s},\ \underset{?}{z},\ \underset{?}{\rho' + \delta},\ \underset{+}{g},\ \underset{?}{\delta},\ \underset{?}{a_w})$$

$$(r-g^e)^* = (r-g^e)^*(\underset{+}{s},\ \underset{+}{z},\ \underset{+}{\rho' + \delta},\ \underset{o}{g},\ \underset{+}{\delta},\ \underset{-}{a_w})$$

A higher income-tax rate means that the "natural" rate of unemployment will increase. The same will happen if the unemployment compensation increases. The first effect is compatible with "ordinary" theory, the second is not. The reason for the increase of the long-run equilibrium rate of unemployment when the unemployment compensation increases is of course that the relative advantages for the unemployed to continue searching or accept an employment offer are changed. The positive effect on the "natural" rate of unemployment of an increased turn-over of the labor force is one of the standard results of the "new" inflation-unemployment theory.[1] The long-run equilibrium rate of unemployment will decrease further if the supply of information on the labor market increases (e.g. on account of the introduction of a public labor exchange). However, this result is contingent on the behavior of the firms and households being unaffected by the disturbance.

---

1) Cf. Mortensen (1970a), p. 203.

We note that all effects on the long-run equilibrium real wage rate are uncertain except the effect of an increase in the average and marginal productivity of labor. The direction of this effect is as expected.

It is interesting to note that if the (total) subjective time preference of the households increases, the "natural" real interest rate will also increase. This is despite the fact that households do not save financially and thus do not directly influence supply and demand for funds. Furthermore, disturbances which imply increased depreciation of the "capital" of the firms in the form of a great number of employees (and customers) imply a higher long-run equilibrium real rate of interest. Compare the effect of an increased rate of turnover of the number of employees (and increase of δ). If instead the supply of information on the labor market, a_W, increases, it will be easier than before to compensate for depreciations in the form of lost employees, and the real rate of interest will fall.

6. Problems and Development Possibilities

The analysis of the present chapter, as well as that of the previous chapters, focuses on a central question: what happens if it is costly for buyers and sellers to get into contact with each other? These contact costs not only constitute a necessary condition (but not sufficient; recall the discussion of chapter II, section 3.5) for the existence of a price distribution with a positive variance on a homogeneous goods market and a wage distribution with positive variance on a homogeneous labor market. Moreover, the contact costs are connected with the lack of overview of the market which makes faulty expectations of the average price and wage level possible. These faulty expectations in turn are of central importance for the inflation process. Frictions in the labor market in combination with the fact that the unemployed only accept employment offers which surmount certain minimum levels imply that changes in the demand for labor will only later lead to changes in the rate of unemployment.

The theory of inflation and unemployment is based on largely the same set of assumptions which were the starting point for the analytical derivations of the Phillips curve referred to in chapter II, section 4. The kinship to Mortensen's contribution is especially close. The most important change is that the area of investigation has been widened from a partial study of the labor market to an explicit consideration of the interdependence between the price and the wage increase processes, both endogenously explained.

It is important to emphasize that the present investigation does not aim at giving an empirically "good" description of the inflation process and its interdependence with the development of unemployment over time. It is rather a question of a further examination of the theoretical implications of the behavior of rational economic agents in a generalized neoclassical milieu.

At the same time it is clear that the mechanisms discussed in this and the previous chapters constitute <u>one</u> important component of a "real" macro dynamic process. Even so, the specialized assumptions imply that many other important aspects have been neglected. Wether this is a drawback or not depends on the question. If, as in the present case, one wants to analyze the macroeconomic implications of incomplete market information, the limitations are clearly permitted. If on the other hand, one wants to construct a realistic integrated theory of unemployment and inflation, the aspects which have been analyzed may not be said to constitute a reasonable approximation to the central propagation forces in real processes. The analysis then must be extended in different directions.

In the following, some remarks will be made concerning the extensions of the model which are necessary if one wishes to apply the analysis to concrete problems. To some extent this discussion will form a catalogue of aspects which have been taken into consideration by "traditional" inflation theory, but which have been neglected in the preceding discussion. Finally, an aspect will be taken up which is of special importance if one wants to construct a realistic integrated theory of unemployment and inflation and thus essential to consider in the future development of the economic theory in this area.

The inflation-unemployment model presented in this chapter describes the economic process in two markets, an aggregated goods market and an aggregated labor market. While the financial flows between the private and the public sector certainly constitute a mirror image of what happens in these two markets, financial developments do not influence the economic process in any interesting way.

Aggregation over different goods markets and over different labor markets has several consequences. First, it is not possible to discuss the structural phenomena which play such an important role in actual inflation processes. Neither is it possible to include structural unemployment as an element of the analysis. In chapter II it was stressed that the difference between frictional unemployment (which is the kind of unemployment which has been studied in the previous analysis) and structural unemployment is more a matter of degree than of kind. In spite of this, the aggregation implies that the possibility of studying the often vary difficult and time consuming adjustment processes caused by demand shifts between different markets is eliminated.

Another problem caused by aggregation is the impossibility of studying the propagation of inflationary impulses through the market system. An original inflationary impulse often only affects some of the markets of the economy. After that, it may be a long lasting process before the disturbance has produced its effects on the whole system. Further, the markets which are immediately affected by the disturbance may not always constitute the starting point of the process of price increases. The sluggish response of prices to demand variations observed on many markets for manufacturing goods implies that demand increases for these goods will first imply increases in the derived demand for goods in previous production stages. Since prices for raw materials are very sensitive with respect to demand changes, these prices will start to increase. Price increases are then propagated "upwards" through the production system and will finally reach the markets which were originally affected by the demand increases. Since pricing in these markets in any case is sensitive to cost increases, the price increases will occur, but with a substantial lag.[1)]

The assumption of a homogeneous goods market implies by definition that it is not possible to study the connection between product differentiation and price increases on the one hand, and household search activity over price and quality distributions on the other hand. It is probable that the firms consider variations of products and product development as one of the main possibilities of influencing market shares, especially in the long run.[2)] Furthermore, the intensity of product development may be influenced by the state of aggregate goods demand and thus be negatively correlated with the rate of inflation.[3)]

The assumption of a homogeneous labor market in which all employees and all jobs have the same characteristics implies both that job searchers merely search over a wage distribution and that employers are indifferent as to what person they employ. The latter consequence may be the most problematical. Even when classified as the same type of labor, different persons differ in their productivity and usefulness for different tasks. Moreover, the firm has different information about the productivity of different persons. For instance, the information about the employees will be relatively good, and this means that the firm ceteris paribus prefers the persons already employed to those searching for a job. Moreover, the preference for the already employed will increase since productivity generally will increase with the length of the employment period.

---

1) Cf. Ball (1964), chapter VI and Cagan (1974).

2) Cf. Meyerson (1972).

3) Kornai´s reasoning (freely interpreted) implies that in cases of low demand for their products, the firms do not try to ameliorate their situation by decreasing their relative prices in the first hand. Instead they try to improve the characteristics of their products or to develop new products in order to secure a good and stable market. Cf. Kornai (1971), chapter 21.

Due to imperfect knowledge about the characteristics of the job searchers, the firms will often use external characteristics which could give some indirect information about their future productivity.[1] This fact in combination with the preference for already employed persons leads to various rationing phenomena in the labor market. As a consequence of the assumptions made, it has not been possible to take these important aspects into consideration.

The fact that the financial markets are not included in the analysis in any essential way means that it has not been possible to investigate how variations in the real value of the assets and debts of the economic agents initiate or break an inflation process. One may ask, for instance, whether some version of the quantity theory of money is compatible with the present inflation-unemployment model. The inclusion of financial assets in the analysis would also make possible a study of the welfare implications of variations in the expected rate of inflation.[2]

The representation of the financial markets in the model as a perfectly functioning loan market within the business sector and between the business and the public sector implies several problems. Due to the risks coupled to credit giving, the credit market constitutes an example of markets where it is not very legitimate to assume a unique market price and the absence of rationing. Quantitative restrictions which vary through the business cycle are of great importance at the same time as they fundamentally influence firm behavior in other markets.

The macroeconomic model essentially describes a stationary economy. Changes in productivity are possible, but they do not constitute an integrated part of the process. Thus, it is not possible to study consequences for wage determination and

---

1) Recall the discussion in chapter II, section 3.

2) This question has been discussed under the heading of "the optimal quantity of money". Cf. for instance Alchian and Kessel (1962), Phelps (1965), Phelps (1972), chapter 6, Friedman (1969), Feige and Parkin (1971), and Johnson (1972b).

the inflation process which differences in the growth rate of productivity between different sectors of the economy may have.[1)]

The abstraction from coalitions means that especially the wage setting process has not been handled adequatly. It is true that the effect on the macroeconomic process of uniform wage increases was discussed in section 4.1. But this of course is only a rudiment of a satisfying treatment of collective bargaining. In addition to the fact that employees as a whole are not only interested in wage rates, bargaining is often more closely related to the wage structure than the wage level.

Finally, the assumption of a closed economy and the abstraction from public consumtion and investment naturally imply difficulties for using the model as a starting point for an analysis of actual business cycles and inflation processes.

The limitations of the analysis do not only imply drawbacks, however; the discussion above also gives examples of possible extensions of the analysis in various directions. On the other hand, there remains a problem of a more fundamental theoretical nature.

One of the basic problems in economic analysis is to integrate flexible-price and fixed-price analysis. Both price and quantity adjustments reflect important and realistic aspects of actual economic processes. The "new" multiplier theory represents an attempt to explain what happens if the economic agents must plan subject to rationing and other quantity restrictions when prices fail to clear the markets. The "new" theory of inflation and unemployment, of which the present analysis is a representative, attempts to integrate quantity and price adjustment in the sense that the adjustment processes both produce variations in the rate of unemployment and in the price system.

Both modes of analysis have serious shortcomings, however. As argued in chapter II, the "new" multiplier theory

---

1) These problems are treated in Edgren, Faxén, and Odhner (1973).

has not succeded in integrating endogenous price changes into the analysis, while the "new" theory of inflation and unemployment is essentially an equilibrium theory in which unemployment is a frictional phenomenon and in which unemployment due to rationing is eliminated by assumption.

From this point of view, the basic problem with the macroeconomic model of this chapter is the equilibrium assumption. One possible solution is to extend the amount of friction in the model to include uncertainty of the firms with respect to the demand for their products and the supply of labor which they are confronted with. This uncertainty was the starting point for Arrow's analysis of price adjustment. It was one explanation for price differences between the firms. And it might, together with costs of changing prices, produce rationing phenomena; recall the discussion in chapter II, section 5.3.

BIBLIOGRAPHY[1]

Ackley, Gardner, Macroeconomic Theory (Macmillan & Co Ltd.), New York 1961.

Akerlof, George A., "The Market for 'Lemons': Quality Uncertainty and the Market Mechanism", Quarterly Journal of Economics, August 1970.

Alchian, Armen A., "Information Costs, Pricing, and Resource Unemployment", Western Economic Journal, June 1969; also reprinted in Edmund S. Phelps (ed.), Microeconomic Foundations of Employment and Inflation Theory, (W.W. Norton & Co. Inc.), New York 1970.

Alchian, Armen A. and Reuben A. Kessel, "Effects of Inflation", Journal of Political Economy, December 1962.

Allen, R.G.D., Mathematical Analysis for Economists (Macmillan & Co Ltd.), London 1938.

--- , Mathematical Economics (Macmillan & Co Ltd.), London 1959.

Aoki, Masanao, Optimization of Stochastic Systems (Academic Press), New York 1967.

Arrow, Kenneth J., Social Choice and Individual Values (John Wiley & Sons Inc.), New York 1951.

--- , "Toward a Theory of Price Adjustment", in Abramovitz, Moses (ed.), The Allocation of Economic Resources (Stanford University Press), Stanford 1959.

--- , Aspects of the Theory of Risk Bearing (Yrjö Jahnsson Lectures), Helsinki 1965.

--- , Applications of Control Theory to Economic Growth, AMS, Mathematics of the Decision Sciences (American Mathematical Society), Providence 1968.

--- , Essays in the Theory of Risk-Bearing (North-Holland Publishing Company), Amsterdam 1970.

--- , "Limited Knowledge and Economic Analysis", American Economic Review, March 1974.

--- , The Limits of Organization (W.W. Norton and Company Inc.), New York 1974b.

---

1) The bibliography is arranged in alphabetical order by the name of author. Entries for each author are presented in chronological order. When there are several entries for the same author for a given year, these are denoted by "a", "b", "c", etc. after the year of publication.

Arrow, Kenneth J. and Frank H. Hahn, General Competitive Analysis (Holden-Day Inc.), San Francisco 1971.

Arrow, Kenneth J. and Mordecai Kurz, Public Investment, The Rate of Return and Optimal Fiscal Policy (The Johns Hopkins Press), London 1970.

Axell, Bo, "Comment on Fisher, F.M., 'Stability and Competitive Equilibrium in Two Models of Search and Individual Price Adjustment'", stencil, Stockholm 1973.

--- , "Price Dispersion and Information: An Adaptive Sequential Search Model", Swedish Journal of Economics, March 1974.

Ball, R.J., Inflation and the Theory of Money (Allen and Unwin), London 1964.

Barro, Robert J., "A Theory of Monopolistic Price Adjustment", Review of Economic Studies, January 1972.

Barro, Robert J. and Herschel I. Grossman, "A General Disequilibrium Model of Income and Employment", American Economic Review, March 1971.

--- , "Suppressed Inflation and the Supply Multiplier", Review of Economic Studies, January 1974.

Bellman, Richard, Dynamic Programming (Princeton University Press), Princeton 1957.

Bellman, Richard and S. Dreyfus, Applied Dynamic Programming (Princeton University Press), Princeton 1962.

Bentzel, Ragnar, Assar Lindbeck, and Ingemar Ståhl, Bostadsbristen (The housing shortage) (Almqvist & Wiksell), Uppsala 1963.

Bodkin, R.G., "Real Wages and Cyclical Variations in Employment", Canadian Journal of Economics, August 1964.

Bohm, Peter, External Effects in Production (Almqvist & Wiksell), Uppsala 1964.

Borch, Karl Hendrik, The Economics of Uncertainty (Princeton University Press), Princeton 1968.

Bronfenbrenner, Martin and Franklin D. Holzman, "A Survey of Inflation Theory", in Surveys of Economic Theory, vol. I (American Economic Association), New York 1965.

Brunner, Karl and Allan H. Meltzer, "The Uses of Money: Money in the Theory of an Exchange Economy", American Economic Review, December 1971.

Cagan, Phillip, "The Monetary Dynamics of Hyperinflation", in Milton Friedman (ed.), Studies in the Quantity Theory of Money (The University of Chicago Press), Chicago 1965.

--- , The Hydra-Headed Monster, The Problem of Inflation in the United States (American Enterprise Institute for Public Policy Research), Washington 1974.

Clower, Robert, "The Keynesian Counterrevolution: A Theoretical Appraisal", in F.H. Hahn and F.P.R. Brechling (eds.), The Theory of Interest Rates (Macmillan & Co Ltd.), London 1965.

Cross, John G. and John Williamson, "Patinkin on Unemployment Disequilibrium", Journal of Political Economy, February 1962.

Demsetz, Harold, "The Exchange and Enforcement of Property Rights", Journal of Law and Economics, October 1964.

Dorfman, Robert, "An Economic Interpretation of Optimal Control Theory", American Economic Review, December 1969.

Dorfman, Robert, Paul A. Samuelson and Robert M. Solow, Linear Programming and Economic Analysis (McGraw-Hill Book Company Inc.), New York 1958.

Edgren, Gösta, Karl-Olof Faxén and Clas-Erik Odhner, Wage Formation and the Economy (Allen and Unwin), London 1973.

Fair, Ray C. and Dwight M. Jaffée, "Methods of Estimation for Markets in Disequilibrium", Econometrica, May 1972.

Feige, Edgar L. and Michael Parkin, "The Optimal Quantity of Money, Bonds, Commodity Inventories, and Capital", American Economic Review, June 1971.

Friedman, Milton, "The Role of Monetary Policy", American Economic Review, March 1968.

--- , The Optimum Quantity of Money (Aldine Publishing Company), Chicago 1969.

Forray, Marvin J., Variational Calculus in Science and Engeneering (McGraw-Hill Book Company), London 1968.

Gayer, Paul and Robert S. Goldfarb, "Job Search, the Duration of Unemployment and the Phillips Curve: Comment", American Economic Review, September 1972.

Gogerty, D. Calvin and Gordon C. Winston, "Patinkin, Perfect Competition, and Unemployment Disequilibria", Review of Economic Studies, April 1964.

Gordon, Donald F. and Allan Hynes, "On the Theory of Price Dynamics", in Edmund S. Phelps (ed.), Microeconomic Foundations of Employment and Inflation Theory (W.W. Norton & Co. Inc.), New York 1970.

Gould, John P., "Diffusion Processes and Optimal Advertising Policy", in Edmund S. Phelps (ed.), Microeconomic Foundations of Employment and Inflation Theory (W.W. Norton & Co Inc.), New York 1970.

--- , "Information and Consumer Behavior: Theory of Optimal Sequential Searching Policies", Stencil, Chicago 1972.

Gould, J.P. and S.G.B. Henry, "The Effects of Price Control on a Related Market", Economica, February 1967.

Gronau, Reuben, "Information and Frictional Unemployment", American Economic Review, June 1971.

Grossman, Herschel I., "Money, Interest, and Prices in Market Disequilibrium", Journal of Political Economy, September-October 1971.

--- , "Aggregate Demand, Job Search, and Employment", Journal of Political Economy, November/ December 1973.

--- , "The Nature of Quantities in Market Disequilibrium", American Economic Review, June 1974a.

--- , "The Cyclical Pattern of Unemployment and Wage Inflation", Economica, November 1974b.

Haavelmo, Trygve, "Hva kan statiske Likevektsmodeller fortelle oss?" (What Can Static Equilibrium Models Tell Us?) in Festskrift till Fredrik Zeuten, Supplement to Vol. 96 of Nationalökonomisk Tidskrift, Copenhagen 1958.

Hadley, G., Nonlinear and Dynamic Programming (Addison-Wesley Publishing Company Inc.), London 1964.

--- , Introduction to Probability and Statistical Decision Theory (Holden-Day Inc.), London 1967.

Hagger, A.J., The Theory of Inflation: A Review (Melbourne University Press), London 1964.

Hahn, F.H., "Some Adjustment Problems", Econometrica, January 1970.

--- , "On Some Problems of Proving the Existence of an Equilibrium in a Monetary Economy", in F.H. Hahn and F.P.R. Brechling (eds.), The Theory of Interest Rates (Macmillan & Co Ltd.), London 1965.

Herin, Jan, "Comment on 'Price Dispersion and Information: An Adaptive Sequential Search Model'", Swedish Journal of Economics, March 1974.

Hansen, Bent, A Study in the Theory of Inflation (Allen and Unwin), London 1951.

--- , Finanspolitikens ekonomiska teori (The Economic Theory of Fiscal Policy), Stockholm 1955.

--- , Lectures in Economic Theory, Part I (Studentlitteratur), Lund 1967.

von Hayek, F.A., "The Use of Knowledge in Society", American Economic Review, 1945.

Hicks, John R., "Mr. Keynes and the 'Classics': A Suggested Interpretation", Econometrica,1937; reprinted in W. Fellner and B. Haley (eds.), Readings in the Theory of Income Distribution (Allen and Unwin), London 1950.

--- , Value and Capital (Oxford University Press), Oxford 1962; reprint of the second edition of 1946.

--- , Capital and Growth (Oxford University Press), Oxford 1965.

Hirshleifer, Jack, "Where Are we in the Theory of Information?", American Economic Review, May 1973.

Holt, Charles C., "Job Search, Phillips' Wage Relation, and Union Influence: Theory and Evidence", in Edmund S. Phelps (ed.) Microeconomic Foundations of Employment and Inflation Theory (W.W. Norton & Co Inc.), New York 1970.

Holt, Charles, Duncan MacRae, Stuart Schweitzer, and Ralph Smith, Manpower Policies to Reduce Inflation and Unemployment (The Urban Institute), Washington 1973.

Iwai, Katsuhito, "The Firm in Uncertain Markets and Its Price, Wage and Employment Adjustments", Review of Economic Studies, April 1974.

Jaffée, William, "Walras' Theory of Tâtonnement: A Critique of Recent Interpretations", Journal of Political Economy, February 1967.

Johnson, Harry G., Inflation and the Monetarist Controversy (North Holland Publishing Company), Amsterdam 1972.

--- , Further Essays in Monetary Economics (Allen and Unwin), Oxford 1972b.

Kamien, Morton and Nancy L. Schwartz, "Sufficient Conditions in Optimal Control Theory", Journal of Economic Theory, 1971.

Kasper, Hirschel, "The Asking Price of Labor and the Duration of Unemployment", Review of Economics and Statistics, May 1967.

Kessel, Reuben A. and Armen A. Alchian, "The Effects of Inflation", Journal of Political Economy, December 1962.

Koopmans, Tjalling C., Three Essays on the State of Economic Science (McGraw-Hill Book Company), New York 1957.

Kornai, János, Anti-Equilibrium (North Holland Publishing Company), Amsterdam 1971.

Kuh, E.,"Unemployment, Production Functions, and Effective Demand", Journal of Political Economy, June 1966.

Lancaster, Kelvin, Consumer Demand: A New Approach (Columbia University Press), New York 1971.

Landgren, Karl-Gustav, Den "nya ekonomien" i Sverige (The "New Economics" in Sweden) (Almqvist & Wiksell), Uppsala 1960.

Leijonhufvud, Axel, On Keynesian Economics and the Economics of Keynes (Oxford University Press), London 1968.

--- , Keynes and the Classics (The Institute of Economic Affairs), London 1971.

--- , "Effective Demand Failures", Swedish Journal of Economics, March 1973.

Lindbeck, Assar, A Study in Monetary Analysis (Almqvist & Wiksell), Stockholm 1963.

--- , Svensk ekonomisk politik (Swedish Economic Policy) (Aldus), Stockholm 1968.

Lipsey, R.G., "The Relation between Unemployment and the Rate of Change of Money Wage Rates in the United Kingdom, 1862-1957: A Further Analysis", Economica, February 1960.

Lucas, Robert E. and Edward C. Prescott, "Equilibrium, Search and Unemployment", Journal of Economic Theory, February 1974.

Lundberg, Erik, Konjunkturer och ekonomisk politik (Business Cycles and Economic Policy) (Studieförbundet Näringsliv och samhälle), Stockholm 1953.

Marschak, Jacob and Roy Radner, Economic Theory of Teams (Yale University Press), London 1972.

Mattila, J. Peter, "Job Quitting and Frictional Unemployment, American Economic Review, March 1974.

McCall, John J., "The Economics of Information and Optimal Stopping Rules", Journal of Business, January 1965.

--- , "The Economics of Information and Job Search", Quarterly Journal of Economics, February 1970.

Meidner, Rudolf, Svensk arbetsmarknad vid full sysselsättning (The Swedish Labor Market at Full Employment) (Konjunkturinstitutet), Stockholm 1954.

Metcalf, David, "Pay Dispersion, Information, and Returns to Search in a Professional Labour Market", Review of Economic Studies, October 1973.

Meyerson, Per-Martin, Företagen och innovationerna (Firms and Innovations), stencil, Stockholm 1973.

Mortensen, Dale T., "A Theory of Wage and Employment Dynamics", in Edmund S. Phelps (ed.), Microeconomic Foundations of Employment and Inflation Theory (W.W. Norton & Co Inc.), New York 1970a.

--- , "Job Search, the Duration of Unemployment and the Phillips Curve", American Economic Review, December 1970b.

Murphy, Roy E., Jr., Adaptive Processes in Economic Systems (Academic Press), New York 1965.

Musgrave, Richard A., The Theory of Public Finance (McGraw-Hill Book Company), New York 1959.

Muth, John F., "Optimal Properties of Exponentially Weighted Forecasts", Journal of the American Statistical Association, June 1960.

--- , "Rational Expectations and the Theory of Price Movements", Econometrica, July 1961.

Negishi, Takashi, "The Stability of a Competitive Economy: A Survey Article", Econometrica, October 1962.

--- , "Market Clearing Processes in a Monetary Economy", in F.H. Hahn and F.P.R. Breckling (eds.), The Theory of Interest Rates (Macmillan & Co Ltd), London 1965.

Nelson, Phillip, "Information and Consumer Behavior", Journal of Political Economy, March-April 1970.

Nerlove, Marc, "Lags in Economic Behavior", Econometrica, March 1972.

Nichols, Donald A., "Market Clearing for Heterogeneous Goods", in Edmund S. Phelps (ed.), Microeconomic Foundations of Employment and Inflation Theory (W.W. Norton & Co Inc.), New York 1970.

Ohlin, Bertil, "Some Notes on the Stockholm Theory of Savings and Investment", Economic Journal, March-June 1937; reprinted in Readings in Business Cycle Theory (Allen and Unwin), London 1950.

Parsons, Donald O., "Quit Rates over Time: A Search and Information Approach", American Economic Review, June 1973.

Patinkin, Don, Money, Interest, and Prices (Harper & Row), New York 1965.

Pen, J., Income Distribution (Allan Lane, Pinguin Press), London 1971.

Phelps, Edmund S., "Anticipated Inflation and Economic Welfare", Journal of Political Economy, January 1965.

--- , "Phillips Curves, Expectations of Inflation, and Optimal Unemployment over Time", Economica, August 1967.

--- , "Money-Wage Dynamics and Labor-Market Equilibrium", in Edmund S. Phelps (ed.), Microeconomic Foundations of Employment and Inflation Theory, (W.W. Norton & Co Inc.), New York 1970.

--- , Inflation Policy and Unemployment Theory: The Cost-Benefit Approach to Monetary Planning (Macmillan & Co Ltd.), London 1972.

--- , "Inflation in the Theory of Public Finance", Swedish Journal of Economics, March 1973.

Phelps, Edmund S. and Sidney G. Winter, Jr., "Optimal Price Policy under Atomistic Competition", in Edmund S. Phelps (ed.), Microeconomic Foundations of Employment and Inflation Theory (W.W. Norton & Co Inc.), New York 1970.

Phillips, A.W., "The Relation between Unemployment and the Rate of Change of Money Wage Rates in the United Kingdom, 1861-1957", Economica, November 1958.

Pontryagin, L.S., Ordinary Differential Equations (Pergamon Press), London 1962.

Pontryagin, L.S., V.G. Bol'tnskii, R.S. Gamkrelidze and E.F. Mischenko, The Mathematical Theory of Optimal Processes (Pergamon Press Ltd.), Oxford 1964.

Radner, Roy, "Aspiration,Bounded Rationality, and Control", lecture at the meeting of the Econometric Society, Oslo 1973.

Raiffa, Howard, Decision Analysis (Addison-Wesley), Reading 1968.

Raiffa, Howard and Robert Schlaifer, Applied Statistical Decision Analysis (The M.I.T. Press), Cambridge 1961.

Reder, M.W., "The Theory of Frictional Unemployment", Economica, February 1969.

Rees, Albert, "Information Networks in the Labor Markets", American Economic Review, May 1966.

--- , "The Phillips Curve as a Menu for Policy Choice", Economica, August 1970.

Rothschild, Michael, "Models of Market Organization with Imperfect Information: A Survey", Journal of Political Economy, November-December 1973a.

--- , "Searching for the Lowest Price when the Distribution of Prices is Unknown", stencil, 1973b.

--- , "A Two-Armed Bandit Theory of Market Pricing", Journal of Economic Theory, October 1974.

Salop, S.C., "Wage Differentials in a Dynamic Theory of the Firm", Journal of Economic Theory, August 1973.

Samuelson, Paul A., Foundations of Economic Analysis (Harvard University Press), Cambridge 1961; reprint of the edition of 1947.

Samuelson, Paul A. and Robert M. Solow, "Analytical Aspects of Anti-Inflation Policy", American Economic Review, May 1960.

Savage, L.J., The Foundations of Statistics (John Wiley & Sons Inc.), New York 1954.

Schelling, T.C., "The Life You Save may be Your Own", in S.B. Chase (ed.), Problems in Public Expenditure Analysis (The Brookings Institution), Washington 1968.

Schneider, Erich, Pricing and Equilibrium (Allen & Unwin), London 1966.

Scitowsky, Tibor, Welfare and Competition (Richard D. Irwin Inc.), Chicago 1951.

Siven, Claes-Henric, "Studier i hushållets beteende vid jämviktsbrist" (Studies in the Behavior of the Household in Disequilibrium), stencil, Stockholm 1969.

--- , "Microeconomic Foundations of Employment and Inflation Theory: A Survey", Swedish Journal of Economics, September 1972.

--- , "Review of Phelps: Inflation Policy and Unemployment Theory", Swedish Journal of Economics, September 1974.

Spence, Michael, "Job Market Signalling", Quarterly Journal of Economics, August 1973.

--- , "Competitive and Optimal Responses to Signals: An Analysis of Efficiency and Distribution", Journal of Economic Theory, March 1974.

Stigler, George J., "The Economics of Information", Journal of Political Economy, June 1961.

--- , "Information in the Labor Market", Journal of Political Economy, October 1962.

Söderström, Hans T., "The Dynamics of Production under Costs of Adjustment: A Survey", stencil, Stockholm 1974.

Telser, Lester C., "Searching for the Lowest Price", American Economic Review, May 1973.

Thalberg, Bjørn, "Om bruken av 'korrespondensprinsippet'", (On the Uses of the 'Correspondence Principle'), Statsøkonomisk Tidskrift, March 1968.

Tobin, James, "A Survey of the Theory of Rationing", Econometrica, October 1952.

--- , "Inflation and Unemployment", American Economic Review, March 1972.

Tobin, James and H.S. Houthakker, "The Effects of Rationing on Demand Elasticities", Review of Economic Studies, 1950-51.

Toikka, Richard S., "The Economics of Information: Labor Market Aspects", Swedish Journal of Economics, March 1974.

Tucker, Donald P., "Macroeconomic Models and the Demand for Money under Market Disequilibrium", Journal of Money, Credit, and Banking, February 1971.

Turvey, Ralph (ed.), Wages Policy under Full Employment (William Hodge and Company Ltd.), London 1952.

Walras, Leon, Elements of Pure Economics (Allen & Unwin), London 1954; translation of the French edition of 1926.

Weiss, Yoram, "Learning by Doing and Occupational Specialization", Journal of Economic Theory, 1971.

Werin, Lars, "Comment on 'Information, Money and the Macroeconomics of Inflation'", Swedish Journal of Economics, March 1974.

Whipple, David, "A Generalized Theory of Job Search", Journal of Political Economy, September-October 1973.

Ysander, Bengt-Christer, "Ransoneringskonstens ABC" (The ABC's of the art of rationing), Ekonomisk Debatt, nr 1 1974.

INDEX OF NAMES

INDEX OF SUBJECTS